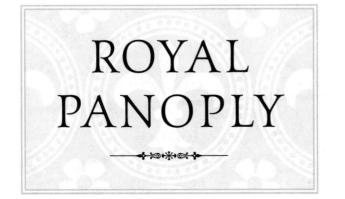

ROYAL PANOPLY

ROYAL PANOPLY

❦❖❖❖❦

BRIEF LIVES OF
THE ENGLISH MONARCHS

CAROLLY ERICKSON

ST. MARTIN'S PRESS

New York

www.stmartins.com

Library of Congress Cataloging-in-Publication Data

Erickson, Carolly, 1943–
    Royal panoply : brief lives of the English monarchs / Carolly Erickson.—1st St. Martin's Press ed.
        p. cm.
    ISBN-13: 978-0-312-31643-3
    ISBN-10: 0-312-31643-7
    1. Great Britain—Kings and rulers—Biography. 2. Queens—Great Britain—Biography. I. Title.

DA28.1.E68 2006
941.009'9—dc22
[B]

                                                                    2006040544

First published, in somewhat different form, by History Book Club,
1271 Avenue of the Americas, New York, N.Y. 10020.

First St. Martin's Press Edition: May 2006

10   9   8   7   6   5   4   3   2   1

*To Maria, Ariana
and Alec Bliss-Pryor
from their loving
Aunt Carolly*

CONTENTS

FOREWORD

A panoply is a splendid and striking array, sometimes an array of knightly arms, sometimes an array of banners or trophies, costumes or works of art. In the following pages I have assembled a royal panoply, an array of monarchical lives, some splendid, a few wretched, all striking in their variety, their vicissitudes, their predictable or improbable fates.

My emphasis is not just on the reigns of the forty-odd rulers here arrayed but on their entire lives, birth to death. These are portraits of individuals, brief biographies rather than mere accounts of what occurred while those individuals occupied the throne. These are kings and queens in love, rulers who trembled in fear at their coronations, monarchs who mourned the loss of children and who rejoiced in living long enough to see their grandchildren and even, in the case of Queen Victoria, great-grandchildren.

Unearthing the details of royal lives is difficult, particularly in the case of those rulers who lived before 1600; much of the familiar day-to-day character of their experience, and their reaction to it, has been lost, and in any case a wide abyss of cultural and psychological distance separates us from those who lived many hundreds of years ago.

But the poignant human reality behind majesty is never entirely out of reach: King Richard II dying of voluntary starvation, after his abdication, in a lonely castle dungeon; Henry Bolingbroke, the future King Henry IV, in exile, banished from his home, his inheritance seized, facing an uncertain future; Queen Mary I shedding tears into her missal as she waited in vain for her beloved husband Philip to come back to her and return her love. And the aging, irascible George II, as much despised by his subjects as he despised them, suddenly becoming a hero after leading a coalition army to overwhelming victory against the French at Dettingen. "Now, boys, for the honor of England," the old king cried as he rode into battle, waving his sword, the French artillery fire thick as hail about him, "for the honor of England, fire, and behave bravely, and the French will soon run!"

Moments of triumph, moments of despair, moments of high drama— and, as in all lives, long stretches of the quotidian. Of such were all royal lives made, and we lose much if we neglect the uncrowded years of a monarch's life in favor of the highly illuminated, and much better documented, eras of turmoil and memorable events. In particular, we lose much in not investigating royal childhoods, which were so often formative. Would Henry VII have been a very different sort of man if he had not been born to a thirteen-year-old mother, and had not spent his own first thirteen years as a prisoner? Would Queen Elizabeth II have been less affected by the unhappy marriages of her own children had she not enjoyed an exceptionally happy and loved childhood herself?

And what of the torturous childhood of the future Edward VII, when as Prince of Wales he screamed and raged, bit his tutors and his brother, and broke furniture in his frustration? The despair of his parents, his sexual waywardness helping to send his morally upstanding father Prince Albert to an early grave, the young Prince Edward was never to outlive these wrenching griefs.

As *Royal Panoply* goes to press, I am ever mindful of those telling incidents for which—alas!—there was no room in these limited pages. The future George IV who as Prince of Wales entertained his drunken companions by mimicking the ravings of his desperately ill father George III. King William IV's off-putting habit of spitting, often and copiously, in public. The warrior Henry V with his massive culverin which was called "The King's Daughter." The night in James II's reign when, during a fearsome gale, the head of Oliver Cromwell blew down off its pole outside Westminster Hall—a gruesome omen, some said, of danger to the realm.

I am reminded too, in closing, of the kings who never were, those promising royal sons who died before they could reign, leaving the throne to less able younger brothers: James I's charismatic, athletic son Henry, on whose death the future ill-fated Charles I became Prince of Wales. Edward, good-humored elder brother of the phlegmatic future George III, who was full of dancing and gallantry. And Catherine of Aragon's one weak little son, called the New Years' Prince, whose birth was greeted with such universal joy and who lived only a few days. Had he lived, King Henry VIII would not have needed to divorce Queen Catherine and England's religious changes might have come about much later, if at all.

But speculation about what might have been, however enjoyable, is at best a parlor game while the realities of royal lives beckon as touchstones to the authentic past, in all its multi-layered complexity. I hope that this panoply of brief biographies will serve to welcome my readers into that rich array of splendors that is the history of the English kings and queens.

—Carolly Erickson
Kailua, Hawaii
January 15, 2003

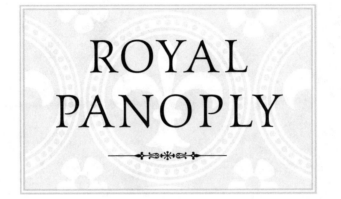

ROYAL
PANOPLY

WILLIAM I

(1066–1087)

❖❖❖

"HE WAS A VERY STERN AND VIOLENT MAN,
SO THAT NO ONE DARED TO DO ANYTHING CONTRARY
TO HIS WILL."

—ANGLO-SAXON CHRONICLE

It was a miracle that William survived his childhood. Born in 1028, the natural son of Robert, Duke of Normandy, young William was left fatherless at age seven when Robert died while on pilgrimage to the Holy Land.

Eleventh-century Normandy was a savagely turbulent society, in which aggressive and unruly landowners struggled endlessly for preeminence, under the overlordship of the duke. At the best of times, these feuding magnates were held in check by the greater power of a strong overlord, as well as by the force of custom and feudal law; at the worst of times, there was little or nothing to restrain their instinct to combat one another in treacherous, frequently brutal warfare.

Before he left for his pilgrimage, Robert had made young William heir to the duchy—and heir to its political turmoil. Protected by his uncle Walter, his mother's brother, who slept in William's room and was his bodyguard, the child duke spent many watchful nights alert for the sound of hoofbeats, listening for marauders and would-be kidnappers intent on capturing and controlling him so that the lands and wealth of Normandy could become theirs.

Year after year, with the Norman countryside in near anarchy, Walter continued to keep the young duke safe, snatching him up when danger threatened and taking him out of the castle and into a nearby village, to some anonymous peasant hut, where they could stay hidden. Meanwhile the great magnates fought among themselves, each one a petty warlord in his castle stronghold, from which he went out from time to time to attack his enemies.

By the time he grew out of childhood, William must have been wary in the extreme, habituated to violence for it was occurring all around him. He lived in the midst of private wars, accustomed to hearing news of assassinations and casual murders. Of his five official guardians, one was murdered while out riding, another poisoned, two others, including William's tutor, assassinated after being violently attacked in William's own bedchamber.

Amid this vortex of mayhem, William grew to young manhood, and at the age of fifteen or sixteen, established his independent court at Valognes. Toughened by his years of exposure to merciless bloodshed and calculated injury, William was becoming a formidable fighter himself, physically strong, skilled with the sword and bow, an expert rider and possessed of uncommon courage and strength of purpose.

He needed no mentor to teach him the tactics of warfare; he had learned them by observation. He knew that territory was captured, and control over it consolidated, by castle-building. That allies had to be won by gifts and benefits conferred, and enemies intimidated by the burning of villages and fields and much pitiless slaughter. To rule, one had to be skilled in making war. And to wage war successfully required a hardened toughness of mind; there was no room for clemency or forgiveness, only a ruthless determination to spread fear.

Though still in his teens, William was already formidable. A rival arose, Guy of Burgundy, and a group of rebel magnates formed around Guy. Their intent was to capture and kill William at Valognes, and to make Guy Duke of Normandy. Somehow, William was warned of what was to happen—or perhaps his heightened instincts were aroused. In any case, he managed to escape his captors, and to ride as fast as he could to Falaise (his birthplace) where his mother's family lived. Still pursued, he made his way to the court of Henry, King of France, his overlord, and begged for protection. Early in 1047 King Henry, William and their fighting men met the rebel magnates at Val-ès-Dunes, a wide plain, and defeated them in a hard-fought, hand-to-hand battle.

The reputation William gained in that battle, a reputation for bravery, ferocity and supreme skill with lance and sword, made his name respected. He killed at least one great warrior, a man much older than himself, on the field of Val-ès-Dunes, and although the victory was in fact won by King Henry and his men, it was William who gained the all-important renown, and about whom songs began to be sung and stories to grow.

"Great was the mass of fugitives, and fierce the pursuit," wrote the chronicler Wace of the rebels' flight. "Horses were to be seen running over the plain, and the field of battle was covered with knights running haphazard for their lives." Bodies were heaped in mounds, corpses clogged the river, filling it so completely that mill wheels could not turn.

William's repute was growing, but in order to maintain the authority he had gained, he had to subdue the entire duchy, castle by castle, town by town. For the next thirteen years, from the age of nineteen to thirty-two, the duke devoted himself to the bloody work of reconquering the lands with which his father had invested him.

He invaded towns, burning them and seizing everything of value, then killing the defenders and installing his men in newly built castles to guard them. He besieged castles held by rebel lords and stormed them, in scenes of great slaughter. He seized defiant landholders and had them blinded and castrated as punishment for their disloyalty. His calculated ruthlessness was successful: convinced that they could not escape the duke's wrath, towns surrendered and asked for William's protection, and magnates swore loyalty to him, offering their wives and children as hostages, pledges of their good faith.

In his thirties, Duke William ruled over Normandy with an iron hand, keeping order among the ever restless feudatories, presiding over his ducal council, dispensing justice, holding the everpresent threat of anarchy at bay. Though he could no longer count on the support of the French king—King Henry had in fact turned against William and become his enemy—he gained the alliance of Baldwin V, Count of Flanders, who became his father-in-law. William married Baldwin's daughter Matilda, with whom he had nine children, four sons and five daughters.

A larger arena of opportunity offered itself when William's distant cousin Edward the Confessor named William his heir. Edward, a Norman by culture and with many Norman courtiers, had been crowned king of England in 1042, and had no children; though others claimed the succession, William believed it to be his by right, because of Edward's verbal bequest, and expected to become king when Edward died. William was well aware, however, that Earl Godwin of Wessex, the greatest of the

English lords, dominated King Edward and coveted the crown for himself and his heirs. Although he fully intended to reign in England, William was prudent enough to pave the way for a future alliance with the family of Earl Godwin by arranging the betrothal of his daughter Agatha to Harold, Earl Godwin's second son.

By the mid-1060s Duke William had become a hard, flinty, forceful man, active and dominant, and accustomed to being obeyed. He was physically imposing, tall and thickset and muscular with a grating, guttural voice which carried well. William was an exceptionally strong man, his arms and shoulders so well developed that he could draw a bow which no one else could bend while standing in his horse's stirrups.

No personal records survive to reveal his inner thoughts, but William impressed others as possessed of granite will and unswerving determination; perhaps, had he failed in his greatest enterprise, the judgment of his contemporaries might have been different. What is striking about William, when compared to his peers and to his successors, is his self-control. He did not allow anger, greed or vanity to force him into thoughtless action, nor did he let his expanding power make him egotistical or tyrannical.

If the monastic chroniclers of the time are to be believed, William was temperate and self-disciplined in his daily life, eating and drinking in moderation, observant of his religious obligations, faithful to his wife and an exacting (if sometimes mean and cutting) patriarch to his many children. In an age of aristocratic excess, surrounded by powerful men often carried away by grandiosity, and even oftener prey to vice, William seems to have stood out as unique. As to his follies and foibles, the records are silent.

Certainly Duke William was remarkable in his ability to do many things at once. To maintain order in Normandy, supervise his army of knights, oversee the day-to-day work of government, keep potential enemies at bay (William was ever alert to treachery, a legacy of his danger-filled childhood), while planning for the expansion of his rule into England must have required extraordinary dedication and fixity of purpose. He could not afford to grow lax, or to be careless; nothing short of vigilant, vigorous attentiveness would do if he was to retain his hold on affairs.

King Edward was aging. By 1064 William was making his preparations, planning how he would take his army of mounted knights and foot-soldiers across the Channel to England—an extremely expensive undertaking, and one fraught with risk. No doubt he anticipated a long and grueling process of subduing the English, stretching out over years. He added to his treasury by seizing control of the county of Maine, and added to his army by gaining a number of landowners and knights in Brittany. (Though the Normans were contemptuous of the Bretons, William now needed Breton support, while the Bretons, for their part, were eager to join any enterprise that promised to bring them land and wealth.)

A key step in William's preparation occurred in 1064, when by good fortune his principal rival for Edward's throne, Harold Godwinson, needed William's help. Harold had succeeded to his father Godwin's lands and title in 1053, and was the dominant English noble, wealthy and so influential with the mild-mannered King Edward that he had become a sort of "sub-king" himself. Yet when Harold came to Normandy in 1064, he swore an oath of loyalty to William, promising to do all in his power to secure William's succession to Edward's title of king. Harold's betrothal to William's daughter was one token of this pact. Later chroniclers, describing the events of 1064, embellished the story of Harold's oath by saying that William had tricked Harold, who never intended to pledge himself formally. But this tale was invented after the fact.

On January 5, 1066, King Edward died and immediately Harold, abandoning his oath to William and claiming that the late king had named him, Harold, as his successor, had himself crowned in Westminster Abbey.

Harold had good reason for haste. England was looked on as a prize for the taking, much the way Normandy had been seen in William's childhood. The Danish king Swein Estrithson and the Norwegian king Harold Hardrada both contemplated invading the country, and besides William of Normandy there were at least two other potential claimants: Edgar Atheling, King Edward's nephew, and Harold Godwinson's own brother and former ally Tostig, then living in exile in Flanders.

As soon as he knew that Edward had died, William was active. Discounting Harold's seizure of the crown, indeed dismissing Harold as a usurper and oath-breaker, William met with his principal supporters and summoned them to follow him to England, to claim the throne that he believed to be rightfully his. He solicited, and won, the backing of the pope. He hired mercenary soldiers from Poitou, Burgundy, Maine and especially Brittany; a few even came from southern Italy, among them boat-builders skilled in designing horse transports. Men were sent out from the ducal court to buy provisions, horses, carts, rope and arms. Shipwrights were assembled at Dives-sur-Mer to build a fleet large enough to carry the army and its supplies.

By August all was ready—but the winds were unfavorable for a Channel crossing. While William waited, another invasion fleet, under Harold Hardrada, landed in Yorkshire and Harold Godwinson met and defeated the Norwegian forces at Stamford Bridge on September 25, 1066. The Norman fleet embarked two days later, and landed at Pevensey on September 28. It was not until the morning of October 14 that William attacked Harold Godwinson's army at Hastings. William led his men himself, wearing saintly relics around his neck for protection and with the papal banner waving above his head. According to tradition, the Norman knights went into battle "singing a song of Roland," with a minstrel going before them, singing and juggling with his sword.

The English army was utterly defeated, and Harold was killed. Victorious, William camped that night on the battleground, surrounded by enemy bodies and abandoned arms and equipment.

He had won—but England itself, the land, the people, had yet to be conquered, and for the next twenty years William labored to subdue and consolidate his conquest. He used the same tactics he had adopted in Normandy as a young man. He built castles, nearly a hundred of them, often tearing down dozens of existing structures to make way for the defensive mound of earth, wooden tower and palisade ramparts. He dispossessed the Anglo-Saxon aristocracy and gave the lands to his Norman and Breton followers. He stormed towns and plundered them, killing many of the local inhabitants. He punished those who had fought against him and took hostages from among those he spared.

England had become a land under occupation, and the occupiers were hated. Normans were ambushed and killed, rioting and violence broke out. At William's coronation the guards standing at the doors of the cathedral, hearing shouts of acclamation from inside, thought that a riot was beginning; immediately they set fire to the houses nearby—their automatic reaction to any resistance—and caused panic among those attending the ceremony.

William must have been aware of the risks he ran in assuming the English crown, taking on leadership of a turbulent society, knowing that he himself might well become a target for assassins. England might be invaded again, or the undisciplined north or west might prove to be unconquerable. And there was a more personal risk: that William himself, who was thirty-eight in the year he claimed the English kingdom, might not have the strength or health to sustain the labors he would have to undertake. Shortly before his alarm-ridden coronation, William fell sick—and so did many of his fighting men. Camped in the open, in the drizzle and cold of late fall, they contracted dysentery, and had to rest for five weeks before attempting to move on to London.

William seems to have made an effort to learn English, "so that he could understand the pleas of the conquered people without an interpreter, and benevolently pronounce fair judgments for each one," the chronicler Orderic Vitalis wrote. But he made little progress, other than to learn to swear "By the resurrection and splendor of God!" With his closest advisers, Archbishop Lanfranc, whom he brought from the monastery of Bec in Normandy and made Archbishop of Canterbury, and William's half-brothers Bishop Odo of Bayeux and Robert of Mortain, the king spoke French, as he did with his family and servants. Even his jesters Berdic and Adelina joked in French.

For though he had become a king, and was the ruler of a large and prosperous realm, William was still duke of Normandy and conceived of his domains as a single unified political entity. His Norman barons owned lands on both sides of the Channel, their interests spanned the entire enlarged realm. When the king made the crossing to Normandy, as he did, by one historian's reckoning, at least seventeen times in the twenty-one years of his English reign, many of his barons went with him, along with an armed retinue.

Indeed William spent well over half his reign in Normandy, asserting and reasserting his authority, campaigning, checking the aggression of the counts of Anjou. Once Normandy had been temporarily pacified, the king returned to England, marching swiftly to crush rebellions in Wales, where Edric the Wild was in revolt, in Kent, where one of the French magnates, Eustace, Count of Boulogne, was defying royal authority, and in Dover, where the city of Exeter, in league with neighboring towns, held out against the king's army for eighteen days in 1067.

Only by ceaseless vigilance could the peace be maintained—and the keeping of peace and order was a prerequisite to good governance. Every time a rebellion was put down William built castles to secure his hold on the region. Exeter, Warwick, Nottingham, Lincoln, York, Huntingdon, London, Cambridge—the roll call of fortifications is long. Norman fighting men, supplemented by local levies led by Saxon military commanders, kept order, along with mercenaries hired from time to time. Those who did not cooperate were imprisoned, their relatives taken hostage and often maimed or killed, their possessions seized. Through coercion, sheer terror and the force of the stern king's dominant personality, a brittle peace was achieved—until shattered by fresh acts of defiance.

Peacekeeping was expensive, and to pay for it William taxed the English (as he did his subjects in Normandy) very severely. He relied on the Anglo-Saxon sheriffs to collect revenues and imposed extraordinary taxes from time to time over the entire kingdom. Together with the lands of his half-brothers Odo and Robert, William owned, as his direct property, nearly half the land in England; his personal annual revenue was extremely large. In addition, he drew income from trade, from tolls imposed in towns, and from judicial fines—all of which subsidized the costs of rule.

The English perceived their Norman king as an oppressor. In his reign, the Anglo-Saxon chronicle reads, "things went from bad to worse." The former ruling class was all but exterminated, dead in battle or forced into peasant poverty. To his English subjects, the new king seemed a cruel, ruthless and fearsome lord who "expelled bishops from their sees, and abbots from their abbacies; he put thegns [Anglo-Saxon barons] in prison." Yet even the most outspoken of William's English critics acknowledged that he had an exceptional measure of majesty and regal dignity, and was "stronger than any predecessor of his had been." "Any honest man could travel over his kingdom without injury with his bosom full of gold," the monastic chronicler wrote, "and no man dared strike another."

It was, of course, an exaggeration—or rather, an idealized image. No English roads near York were safe when in 1069 the Danish king Swein Estrithson invaded with a force of 240 ships and a large army, and the Norman garrisons surrendered, and parts of Dorset, Somerset and East Anglia were unsafe when in rebel hands in the late 1060s. William managed to bribe the Scandinavian invaders and send them back to Denmark, but further assaults came in 1075 and 1085, proof that to outsiders, England did not appear to enjoy stable Norman rule.

His energies divided between England and Normandy, and his authority threatened by frequent invasions and rebellions, William needed to be able to rely on his sons to be his deputies. But the oldest and most promising of his sons, Richard, was dead, the victim of a hunting accident in the New Forest. And William's second son, Robert, the one on whom he most needed to rely, was a severe disappointment.

Short and stout, brave and adventurous, Robert was an attractive character, but he lacked the calculated prudence that was such a marked trait in his father. Robert was rash, thoughtless, prodigal with money, impetuous and cocksure. Many of the young barons and knights were drawn to him, for he was generous and gave them gifts and promised more gifts, plus lands and favor, in the future. But William found little to admire in Robert and treated him with malice and mockery. (The queen, on the other hand, lavished all her affection on her second son.) William called Robert "Curthose" ("Short-Boot") and sneered at his companions— entertainers, hangers-on, prostitutes of both sexes; William preferred his third son and namesake, Prince William, who though he lacked Robert's charm and popularity, was a solid fighter in his father's mold.

In 1077 King William suffered his first serious military defeat, losing many men and horses and much treasure during an unsuccessful attempt to besiege the castle of Dol in Brittany. He was forced to retreat— something he rarely did—and the loss signaled a major reverse in his military fortunes. He was nearly fifty, becoming tired and slow. Once fit and strong, William had become very fat—the French king taunted him, saying he was as fat as a pregnant woman—and no longer the feared campaigner he had once been.

William's enemies, perceiving his decline in vigor, began to close in, the Scots king Malcolm raiding on the ill-defined northern border of England, and Norman, Angevin and Breton opponents making war on the continent. Robert Curthose, ambitious and resentful, demanded that his father turn over control of Normandy and Maine to him, and when William refused, Robert led a rebellion against him. In one hard-fought battle, against Robert's men, William was unhorsed and wounded, probably by Robert Curthose himself, and would have died had not one of his English knights rescued him at the cost of his own life. In order to restore peace William had to retreat and promise the right of succession to Normandy to Robert—a humiliating concession.

William's domains were beginning to slip from his control. A second rebellion by Robert Curthose, acts of disloyalty by William's half-brother Odo (whom William imprisoned), and a major invasion of England from Denmark called for all the king's remaining force; he mustered men in Normandy and brought them across the Channel to fight, forestalling the loss of his English realm.

To raise money to pay for this immense effort, William undertook an ambitious land survey. He sent men to every county in England to find out exactly how much land each landowner held, how many beasts he owned, how many serfs labored on his estates. "His inquiry was so strict," the chronicler wrote, "that there was not a hide nor a yard of land nor even an ox or cow or pig that was omitted from the record." The results of this detailed survey, still preserved in the Public Record Office in London, became known as Domesday Book, or the Book of Doomsday, the biblical Last Judgment. Though full of omissions and inaccuracies, the Domesday survey constitutes the most ambitious statistical undertaking of any medieval government. To the English of 1086, the Domesday surveyors were messengers of catastrophe. William's subjects were well aware that the purpose of the inquiry was to increase taxes, and King William's taxes were already rapaciously high. The English rioted, they resisted—but in the end, they were forced to pay.

Now nearing sixty, William went campaigning once again. He pillaged and burned the town of Mantes, and while riding through the ruins of the town, he was mortally injured. He was taken, in great pain, to the priory of Saint-Gervais in Rouen where, with his sons William and Henry, his brother Robert of Mortain and a group of clergy and servants around him, he lay on his deathbed. Robert Curthose was not present, he was in revolt and was at the court of the French King Philip.

Though it must have pained him to bequeath his duchy to a faithless, rebellious son, William passed Normandy on to Robert, giving the English kingdom to William—along with his crown and scepter—and giving his youngest son Henry a large sum of money from his treasury. Both William and Henry left, even before the old king died, William to secure his kingdom and Henry to claim his funds.

William had hardly taken his last breath before all his friends and attendants had gone, the servants of his bedchamber stealing all his arms, his goblets and plates, even the clothes off his dead body and the linens from his bed, "leaving the corpse," the chronicler Orderic Vitalis wrote, "almost naked on the floor of the cell."

The funeral was delayed, to allow time for the king's body to be transported to Caen, to the Abbey of St. Stephen. Unfortunately, by the time the funeral rites could be held, the body, swollen and bloated, had putrefied and the mass had to be hurried, so overcome were the mourners by the terrible stench.

In death William was all too mortal—but in the minds of his subjects he was something more, a man of superhuman energies and charisma. When they learned that he was dead they cowered in fear, expecting vast natural catastrophes to follow. For nothing short of great disasters, they felt, could mark the passing of so fearsome a king.

WILLIAM II

(1087–1100)

+⊰⊹⊱+

"WHOEVER KNEW A TALL MAN WHO WAS WISE,
A REDHEAD WHO WAS FAITHFUL, OR A SMALL MAN
WHO WAS HUMBLE?"

—TWELFTH-CENTURY PROVERB

T he third son of the Conqueror, who became king as William II in 1087, was a short, heavyset, thick-necked man, combative yet jocular, with a wild, unpredictable temperament and an air of danger that made people fear him. There was something feral about William, he would not be tamed. He did what he pleased, said what he liked and behaved with fierce—many said outrageous—independence. Archbishop Anselm, who was old enough to be William's father, likened him to a wild bull.

Rough in manner and bitingly, even wickedly, outspoken, William dressed like a dandy in luxurious, brightly colored silk garments of extravagant cut and let his reddish hair grow long down his back like a woman's; the contrast between his soldierly bluntness and loud voice and his effeminate image confused and ultimately angered his critics. Perhaps he was homosexual, more likely he was bisexual—and certainly lusty, if not lascivious. The monks who wrote the chronicles of his reign held William responsible for a widespread general corruption of morals. But his disregard for conventional morality went hand in hand with efficient kingship, exceptional military skill and the ability to command the loyalty of his fighting men, so that overall, as even his opponents conceded, William was a successful and strong king.

Because he had a red beard and a reddish complexion, William was called "William the Red," or William Rufus. In manner he was sometimes offhand, jokey, loose and good-humored, and often hot-tempered and bullying. He took offense easily—but could just as easily be pacified. Emotionally labile, he kept his servants off guard; just when they were expecting to be shouted at, they might find their master moved to tears.

Though he had a recurring stutter, William Rufus said memorable, or in any event startling, things, from his favorite oath—"By the Holy Face of Lucca!"—to his repertoire of blistering insults (some of which he heaped on envoys of foreign courts) to his forthright opinions and frank blurted reactions. Vehemently anticlerical, the king remarked, on learning that a new pope, Paschal II, had been elected, "God rot him who cares a damn for that!"

A chronicler wanting to expose William Rufus's vanity and extravagance recorded an anecdote about one of the king's chamberlains who brought him a new pair of shoes.

"What did they cost?" the king asked.

"Three shillings."

"You son of a whore! Since when has a king got to wear shoes as cheap as that? Go and buy me some for a mark of silver [13 shillings 4 pennies]."

The servant returned with an even cheaper pair, which he swore had cost a mark of silver.

"Now these are more fitted to our royal majesty," William is supposed to have said.

As a boy William Rufus would have been bred to war, like his older brothers Richard and Robert. Riding, learning to throw a spear and fight with a sword, playing at castle-building and castle-defending: these were the pastimes and studies of a duke's son. Very likely William was illiterate, or nearly so, even though he was put into the household of the learned Archbishop Lanfranc for his upbringing. Sometime after reaching the age of thirteen he would have been knighted, and allowed to accompany his father on campaign, taking part in sieges and—much more rarely—in battles. His younger brother Henry went along, and in the lulls between military activity the two brothers played at dice.

Sometime in William Rufus's adolescence, his oldest brother, the handsome and capable Richard, died in a hunting accident. From then on, if not before, William became his father's favorite son, and no doubt the confidence this gave him added to his innate self-regard, as did his natural proficiency at arms.

During William I's last years William Rufus remained loyal to his father, and although his faithless older brother Robert Curthose was given the duchy of Normandy, it was William to whom his father bequeathed the kingdom of England (then perceived as the lesser of the two patrimonies).

William Rufus was crowned on September 26, 1087, and quickly showed himself to be a worthy successor to his energetic, dominant father, to whose memory he raised a costly monument in gold and silver studded with jewels. When a number of powerful landowners rose in rebellion, among them William's uncle Odo of Bayeux, whom he had freed from prison, the king faced a serious threat to his authority. From Kent to Northumbria, disloyal barons ordered their knights to burn and waste the king's vast estates and those of his chief tenants. Rebel castles were fortified, rebel armies raised.

The king acted swiftly and decisively to crush the rebellion, confronting the magnates and their armies, storming Tonbridge, seizing Odo and, when fresh opposing forces arrived from Normandy, driving them back across the Channel. From his headquarters in London, William summoned his loyal supporters—and found their number to be great. His English subjects did not turn against him, and one by one the disloyal Normans were won over by a combination of military intimidation and bribery. The church stood behind the king. Within six months, by the fall of 1088, the throne was secure.

William emerged from his first serious challenge with a reputation for great personal courage, and for good luck. He had never yet lost an engagement, and it was beginning to be said that he never would. An atmosphere of superstitious awe began to surround him, and his reputation for victory fed on itself, for potential opponents were reluctant to offer battle to one who was perceived as bearing the charm of luck. At the same time, the king was becoming more and more popular with his soldiers, bestowing on them generous gifts of money and land and treating them with a coarse, jovial bonhomie that sealed their fidelity. Clearly the son of the great Conqueror was a soldier king, a warrior king. A man to be followed and obeyed.

And if he knew how to make himself admired, William also knew how to make himself feared. He punished those who were disloyal with the utmost severity, imprisoning them and starving them to death, mutilating the family members they were forced to give him as hostages, never hesitating to disinherit and utterly destroy his enemies. He could be implacable. When subjects came to plead for leniency, he ignored them, saying simply that they had to obey or die. His word was law, his will was of iron; but at the same time, he was the font of all benefits, the giver of lands and goods. His subjects were well advised to fear him, but they also could look to him to make them rich.

Villagers in the countryside dreaded the king, and even more his large mobile entourage of servants and household members, for when they passed by, on their way from one castle to another, they were like a cloud of locusts, destroying and consuming all in their path. It was not just that the royal purveyors seized all the foodstuffs, slaughtered all the beasts and took horses, carts and wagons; they treated the English peasants as if they were enemies to be despoiled. "Wherever the king went," one chronicler wrote, "his retinue harried his wretched people, burning and killing." The village women were raped, village churches robbed of their few valuables. No one and nothing was spared.

If the peasants resented King William II for plundering their crops and goods, the great landowners resented him for sending out judges to oversee the work of local courts in the name of the king, and for overseeing the work of the shire councils. William extended the reach and range of government, improving its efficiency and making it possible to collect taxes more effectively, though medieval tax collection remained a haphazard business at best.

Throughout most of his reign, the king was aided in this undertaking by his financial agent, Ranulf Flambard. A priest from an obscure family, Ranulf had been brought to William I's court and after his death had stayed on as William Rufus's chaplain, given greater and greater authority until as chief justiciar, he became the principal financial officer in the realm—and also Bishop of Durham.

Volatile, self-willed, often sarcastic, Flambard had panache, and the sort of personal daring, in speech and action, which the king himself possessed in full measure. Like William Rufus, Flambard dressed expensively, spent a great deal of money and was a devotee of sensual pleasures. His bisexuality—besides male lovers he had a wife and at least one mistress—offended critics of the court almost as much as his administrative abilities made him hated by the magnates. He was made a scapegoat, blamed for the oppressiveness of his royal master's government, and he feared the vengeance of William's subjects.

An impetuous assault nearly resulted in William Rufus's death in 1091. During a siege in Normandy, the king dashed off on horseback, chasing enemy knights. In the resulting skirmish his horse was killed under him, but not before he had been thrown off and dragged along the ground. While he lay helpless, his attacker dismounted and was about to finish him off—not realizing who he was—when Rufus shouted, "Stop, you fool! I am the King of England!"

Filled with dread, the knight disentangled the injured king and set him on another mount.

"By the Holy Face of Lucca, from now on you'll be my man," said the king, "and in my service get a proper reward for your courage and spirit."

The king recovered but the tale of his mishap spread, and there were murmurs among the monks and secular clergy that God was punishing William Rufus for his sins, and that his scrape with death had been a divine warning.

William Rufus's anticlerical attitude, his contempt for religious observance and his open mockery of bishops and archbishops invited retribution, as did his expropriation of church revenues for the crown and his heavy taxation of his subjects. Worst of all, however, was the louche immorality of his court, where a tawdry eroticism prevailed.

According to the monastic writers who recorded their impressions of the royal court, William Rufus encouraged the young men who served him there to grow their hair long and curl it with tongs, to shave their foreheads in brazen sexual invitation (previously men had hidden their foreheads under cropped, inverted bowl-shaped haircuts), and to develop a mincing, effeminate walk exaggerated by revealing robes slashed to the thigh.

Such dress and behavior had only one object: seduction. The court, William of Malmesbury wrote, was "more a brothel of catamites than a house of majesty." No lamps were lit at night, "unspeakable vice" went on in the darkness. The sex, revelry and gambling went on all night, the debauchees slept all day.

"All things that are loathsome to God and to earnest men were customary in this land in [William Rufus's] time," wrote an English chronicler, "and therefore he was loathsome to all his people, and abominable to God." Some clerics were so outraged at the long-haired young men that they cut their flowing locks with scissors. Others, like Archbishop Anselm, preached against homosexuality. The archbishop asked the king to join with him in a general council of the church to combat the practice. William Rufus was offended, and refused.

The Norman courts were hedonistic and worldly, populated by ambitious men, many of whom dressed flamboyantly and were full of bravura. Everything from flirting to romance to adulterous sex was commonplace; most courts had special marshals to govern prostitutes of both sexes, and everpresent homosexuality, though invariably condemned by the church, did not in itself trigger tirades of condemnation.

But William Rufus's critics detected something uniquely unsettling at his court, a degree of practiced, habituated sordidness that set it apart. Even when allowances are made for the monastic writers' moralizing, something elusive yet chilling remains in their accounts. Some behavioral threshold had been crossed at William's court, some profound shift in values had occurred. And the historians of the time, naturally enough, associated this change with the king himself.

In March of 1093, when William Rufus was thirty-three years old, he became ill. He grew worse rapidly, and, surrounded by monks and clergy who told him that God was punishing him and urged him to repent, he became convinced that he was dying. In great fear, and chastened by the momentousness of all that he was undergoing, William Rufus had a change of heart. He who had always been contemptuous of faith, actually confessed his sins, and promised to change for the better. He promised to take the church under his protection and not to exploit its revenues any longer. He promised to abolish all of his unjust laws. And, in order to wipe the slate completely clean, he gave orders that all those he had imprisoned should be released, all those who owed him money should be forgiven their debts, and all those who had injured him should be pardoned.

He recovered.

But the change of heart he had experienced was not lasting. Soon all his promises and good intentions were forgotten. And another baronial rebellion arose, the magnates intent on replacing William Rufus with his cousin Stephen of Aumale, the son of William I's sister Adelaide. The Welsh chose this moment to try to throw out their Norman overlords, and once again, the throne tottered.

William rose to the challenge. He rode swiftly to meet the conspirators in the north, took Newcastle and besieged Tynemouth. Next he drove into Wales, seizing, imprisoning and torturing those who had turned against him. Intimidated, the remaining rebels submitted themselves to the king and asked his pardon. The crisis had been averted and William Rufus retained his reputation as unbeaten.

When the king's brother Robert Curthose decided to go on crusade, he left his dukedom of Normandy in William Rufus's care—greatly adding to Rufus's responsibilities, for Robert had been a lax overlord and Normandy was disintegrating into a chaos of rival small lordships. Rufus made strenuous efforts to restore Normandy to centralized rule, but many of the Norman barons resented him, and wanted Robert back. Yet again, resentment against William Rufus arose, though no combination of opponents was willing to fight him, so formidable was his reputation for overcoming his military foes.

In May of 1100, Robert Curthose's illegitimate son Richard was killed in a hunting accident in the New Forest. Hunting accidents were far from rare, but this incident may have suggested to William Rufus's many enemies a way to rid themselves of their king without having to confront him militarily.

On the morning of August 2, 1100, the king and a party of his friends, including his brother Henry, his inseparable companion Richard FitzHaimo, and several others, including one Walter Tirel, count of Poix, went into the New Forest and took up their positions at shooting stands, waiting for the huntsmen to drive the game past them. (Later, inaccurate accounts of the hunt describe a chase.) William Rufus waited with Tirel, both of them armed and ready to shoot.

It was the "grease season," the time for hunting red deer and stags. There may have been a number of hunters in the forest that day, among them an assassin.

Suddenly, when the shooting began, the king was struck in the heart by an arrow, and died immediately. Walter Tirel fled, as did most of the others in the royal party, including Henry. They scattered out of fear—and superstition, for the king, as the chronicler later wrote, had "departed in the midst of his unrighteousness, without repentance and without expiation." There was no one to care for the royal corpse; a handful of servants lifted the body onto a wagon kept nearby for carting off game, and took it to the closest great church, Winchester Cathedral.

Questions must have been raised about the death, as they have been since. Could Walter Tirel have committed murder? And if so, at whose behest? William Rufus had no children, legitimate or otherwise. His brother Henry was his presumptive heir to both England and Normandy, though William Rufus distrusted Henry and had expressly disinherited him, and Henry, immediately after the king's death, thought it necessary to hurry to Winchester to secure the royal treasury, thus securing his succession.

Historians are divided in their assessment of the circumstances of

William Rufus's death. It may have been an accident—clearly the New Forest was a dangerous place for members of the ruling family. Or it may have been an assassination, following which Henry I usurped the throne, as many contemporaries believed.

Though he died without having made his confession or receiving the last rites, William Rufus was not denied Christian burial. His burial was hasty and his funeral simple. There were few enough to mourn him at Winchester; indeed it was said that those who mourned him most sincerely were the soldiers to whom he had been so notably generous.

To his critics, William Rufus's sudden, violent end was an appropriate conclusion to his wicked and unworthy life. Yet he had been a strong and, on the whole, a successful king. And when, a generation later, Geoffrey of Monmouth wrote his description of the legendary King Arthur, he based his ideal fictional king in part on what he knew of William Rufus. ("By the Holy Face of Lucca!" William Rufus might well have exclaimed, had he known.)

HENRY I

(1100–1135)

———◆❧❊❧◆———

"KING HENRY, IF IT IS RIGHT TO SAY SO, WAS A MAN OF
THE DEEPEST DISSIMULATION AND INSCRUTABILITY
OF MIND."

—HENRY OF HUNTINGDON

enry I was crowned king under a cloud of suspicion. Only three
days before his coronation, his brother King William II had died
under mysterious circumstances, shot in the heart by an arrow
while hunting in the New Forest. Henry had been present. And it was
noted that Henry had left the forest at once, without attending to his
brother's body, and had gone to Winchester where the royal treasure was
kept, claiming the treasure and the throne for himself.

It was almost as if he had known that the crime—or accident—was
about to occur, so people said. Certainly he had a motive for arranging his
brother's death. For William Rufus had not wanted Henry to succeed
him, indeed William Rufus and his brother Robert Curthose had jointly
made a pact, ten years earlier, to exclude Henry from the succession to
both Robert's dukedom of Normandy and William Rufus's kingdom of
England. By eliminating William Rufus, and seizing the treasury, at a
time when Robert Curthose was out of the kingdom, Henry assured his
own unhindered succession—or so it was widely presumed.

Henry was crafty and clever, so it was believed—and cruel. He was capable of coldblooded murder, or of inciting murder. Henry had once punished an oath-breaking supporter of his brother Robert by flinging him
headfirst off the top of Rouen Castle. Another time, according to rumor,

he tore out the eyes of a captive with his own hands. Men who displeased him were chained to the walls of dungeons and left to starve.

Knowing that he was under suspicion, and that he was greatly feared, Henry took immediate steps to put his throne on a more secure footing, to build his good repute among his subjects. He invited the exiled Archbishop of Canterbury, Anselm, to come back to England, improving his relations with the church. He married an exceptionally worthy wife, the good-hearted Matilda, daughter of King Malcolm Canmore of Scotland. The marriage pleased the new king's English subjects, as Matilda claimed descent from the Anglo-Saxon royal line. He promised to overturn his late brother's oppressive laws and reinstitute the just laws of his father William I.

On the day he was crowned, August 5, 1100, King Henry was in his thirty-second year, a brawny, stout, bright-eyed man with a "thunderous voice" which none could resist, thinning black hair and an outwardly pleasant demeanor. He had none of his brother Robert Curthose's charm, nor his late brother William Rufus's feral electricity; physically Henry was stolid and fleshy, with a tendency to corpulence, and at the same time sensual and virile, with a strong libido.

Unique among the Norman kings, Henry was literate. He had been educated for a clerical career, and so learned to read Latin and French, and may have learned English as well. "He was early instructed in the liberal arts," the chronicler William of Malmesbury wrote, "and so throughout imbibed the sweets of learning that no warlike disturbance and no pressure of business could erase them from his noble mind." According to the chronicler, Henry's learning helped him in the work of ruling. Medieval historians writing long after Henry's reign ended gave him the soubriquet "Beauclerk," but the nickname was not used in Henry's lifetime.

Henry had been the youngest and least prepossessing of William I's four sons, and the only one, he liked to point out, to be "born in the purple"—i.e., born after his father became king. Knighted at eighteen, in the year before his father's death, Henry had no lands of his own to manage and defend, but was given an inheritance of five thousand pounds—a very large sum indeed.

During William Rufus's reign, Henry engaged in intrigue, now aligning himself with Robert Curthose against King William, now joining with William Rufus to attack Robert Curthose in Normandy. Neither of his brothers trusted Henry, and with good reason; he was constantly engaged in intrigue, was devious and deceitful, and broke faith with nearly everyone.

In the early months of his reign Henry faced a serious challenge from his popular brother Robert, who returned from his crusading venture to find William Rufus dead and Henry anointed as king of England—and effective ruler of Normandy as well. Robert immediately galvanized the opposition, gathering around himself dissatisfied barons in England and those faithful to him in Normandy. William Rufus's justiciar Ranulf Flambard, whom Henry had imprisoned in the Tower of London, managed to escape by means of a rope smuggled in to him inside his water jar, and joined Robert.

Robert, an able fighter and a charismatic leader, had the additional advantage of having married a wealthy wife. He had the means to build a fleet of ships with which to ferry his army across the Channel, landing at Portsmouth in July of 1101. Henry was waiting with an army of his own; when the two met, at Alton in Hampshire, Robert saw that victory, if it came, would be very hard fought and decided to opt for a truce. With Archbishop Anselm as the negotiator, Henry and Robert came to terms. Henry retained his kingdom but agreed to pay Robert a large annuity. Robert resumed control of Normandy. In addition, the two brothers agreed to make one another their heirs.

The truce did not last, and before long Henry and Robert were at odds again, with Henry spending the majority of his time in Normandy, engaged in sieges and local skirmishes. (So frequently did Henry make the crossing to Normandy that he organized a regular ferry service, from Southampton to Barfleur and Dieppe.) England was stable, but Normandy was a chaos of competing lordships, with the Flemings a threat on the north and the French expanding into Norman territories on the east. The rising power of the neighboring counts of Anjou was a constant irritant and preoccupation.

When Robert Curthose proved to be a weak overlord, unable to control the turbulence of the Norman barons, Henry embarked on a campaign to seize the dukedom, and in 1106, at the Battle of Tinchebrai, Henry defeated his brother, captured him, and put him in prison where he was to remain for the rest of his long life.

Henry was able to pursue his aggressive policies in Normandy because England was on the whole peaceful, the magnates intimidated into submission. Maintaining peace and order was among Henry I's principal achievements as king; the other, which was only possible in a peaceful realm, was his extension and improvement of his brother's and father's administrative, financial and legal systems.

Henry brought to his court dozens of "new men" of low birth but high ability who served him as clerks, household officers, exchequer and legal officials. He recruited "every youth on this side of the Alps whom he heard of as desiring the renown of a good start in life." Through them the king governed, collected revenues, heard petitions and enforced the law. His regime was exacting, but not unduly harsh. On the whole, the magnates benefitted, and slowly England and Normandy were melded into a unified kingdom under uniform rule. Peasant cultivators praised King Henry for disciplining his purveyors and servants, so that when the royal party passed through the countryside, there was no more robbery or devastation. If any royal servants committed crimes, they suffered the king's swift summary justice: amputation of hands, feet or genitals—or blinding.

The king's edicts were enforced, and his governance was efficient. But that meant that his tax collectors were also efficient—and ruthless. "They showed no regard for piety or pity," the monk Eadmer wrote. Their "extortion, frightful and cruel, beat down like a raging storm upon all." Poor peasants with no money were driven from their huts, their furniture seized, reduced to utter wretchedness by the tax gatherers. For them, the reign of King Henry meant peace and order, but at the price of misery and want.

A large household staff served King Henry, from chaplains to cooks to chamberlains to ushers and grooms. Butlers looked after the royal drink, stewards the royal food. Constables were in charge of the stables and kennels and mews, while the chancellor was in charge of the clerks who prepared documents and sang masses. Marshals policed the court and kept order. In all there were at least a hundred servants—plus fifty more who managed and conducted the king's hunts.

Unlike the court of his late brother William Rufus, King Henry I's court impressed observers as a relatively wholesome place—though no royal court was ever free of the greed, jealousy, anxiety and ceaseless intrigue of the ambitious men who served the sovereign. A regimen was maintained, with the king taking counsel with "those who were ripe in age or wisdom" in the forenoon, the voice of the herald calling petitioners and those desiring an audience to state their business. In the afternoon the king and his servants napped, then recreated, devoting themselves, as the chronicler Walter Map wrote, to "hilarity and decent mirth."

On many mornings the king and his companions were up before dawn, preparing for the hunt. Huntsmen were out in the woods, taking up positions from which to drive deer toward the waiting hunters; fewterers with their greyhounds stationed themselves high on the hills. Butchers, knives out and aprons fastened on, waited to slaughter the game and clean and skin the carcasses. Henry I had several large packs of harriers, wolfhounds and greyhounds, and also liked to hunt with hawks along the rivers and marshlands. The best hawks, falcons and gerfalcons, came from Iceland and Norway, and Henry had hundreds of these birds delivered to his court from time to time, specifying a preference for rare white falcons.

King Henry and his wife Matilda had three children, a son who died in infancy, a daughter, Matilda, who was betrothed to the Holy Roman Emperor Henry V and was sent away, at the age of eight, to the imperial court and a second son, William Audelin, who was heir to his father's kingdom and, after 1106, to the dukedom of Normandy. In addition to his two surviving legitimate children, the king had upwards of two dozen acknowledged bastards, many of whom lived at his court and were accorded high status.

Henry's queen devoted herself to works of piety and became renowned for her generosity and self-sacrifice. Wearing a hair shirt under her royal gown, she washed the feet of lepers and looked after the sick and dying. When Matilda herself died in 1118, she was known as "the Good Queen," and Henry memorialized her through benefactions which fed the poor and paid for thousands of masses to be offered for her soul.

In Henry's forties and fifties, he continued to live a life of constant movement and ceaseless conflict. In Normandy he faced the combined forces of the French, Angevins and Flemish, and after seven years of warfare, defeated them. To seal the peace he married his son William Audelin to the daughter and heiress of Fulk V of Anjou, and had all his barons swear an oath of loyalty to William as his designated heir. Henry was feeling his mortality; in 1118 he had been the victim of an assassination attempt, and though of a strong constitution, he had grown fat and unwieldy. He could not be sure of living much longer, wearing himself out in the demanding labor of feudal warfare and the vigilant tasks of ruling and peacekeeping.

In the late fall of 1120, one twilit evening, a fleet of small ships carrying King Henry and his entire household set off from Barfleur. All set sail save one, which lingered on into the night hours, hovering near shore. It was the swift White Ship, the ship on which William Audelin and other young people of the court were to travel, including the king's natural son Richard and several of his natural daughters.

The young people stayed on shore, drinking and enjoying themselves, the crew of the ship having broached the wine barrels and shared in the general tipple. Finally, long after dark, the White Ship drew up anchor, and it had not gone far out into the bay when it struck a rock and began to sink.

In a futile effort to prevent disaster, the crew and some of the passengers tried to push the vessel free of the rock with boathooks and oars. But it kept sinking. Some of the passengers got into the dinghy and rowed away, but came back to get one of the king's daughters. It was a fatal error, for by now everyone was desperate and the dinghy was swamped as too many people tried to climb into it. Both the dinghy and the White Ship sank. The wreckage floated in the bay, and only one man, who clung to the mast all night, survived to relate what had happened.

William Audelin, his half-brother and half-sisters and one of his cousins, plus the Earl of Chester and many nobles, and a number of sons of important Norman and French barons, lost their lives. Some of the household members too were drowned.

In one night of tragedy Henry lost the heir to his throne, several of his other children and many of the familiar faces at his court. The intensity of his grief is not recorded, but it did not hinder him from taking the practical step of remarrying almost at once so that he could father another heir. However, his second wife, Adeliza of Louvain, remained childless.

Knowing that King Henry was aging, his enemies in Normandy now began to make fresh assaults on his castles. The county of Anjou was growing in territory and influence, and had become the rising power in the region. Count Fulk struck at Henry's lands, as did Henry's nephew, the son of the imprisoned Robert Curthose, William Clito. William became allied with King Louis VI of France and soon Normandy was embroiled in war. Relying heavily on Breton and other mercenaries, Henry managed to contain and capture the magnates who came against him, and even drove into the territories of the French king and camped there "as securely as if he were in his own kingdom." When in 1127 William Clito was killed while fighting in Flanders, there was a welcome lull in the aggression.

Henry was by this time nearly sixty, yet he still led his fighting men, often on foot, tirelessly moving from one region to another to intimidate, devastate, take hostages and, when all else failed, offer battle.

His sturdy, fleshy body continued to serve Henry well, but his mind tormented him. He felt beleaguered, constantly ringed with enemies. His mercenaries went on strike, objecting to being paid with English coins which had too little silver in them. His clergy, influenced by the movement for reform begun a generation earlier by Pope Gregory, were bent on reducing the king's authority over them and undercutting his control. He became frightened for his life, anxious that his bedchamber servants might attack him in the night. To prevent this he slept in several different beds, moving often, and increased the number of guardsmen who watched over him while he slept.

According to one of Henry's physicians, he had nightmares in which he was attacked by peasants with pitchforks and knights and churchmen with swords; he kept a sword and shield beside his bed every night in case of need. Clearly Henry was extremely ill at ease, and his physician suggested that he increase his almsgiving in order to redeem his sins. Perhaps his conscience troubled him, when he remembered what had gone on long ago in the New Forest on the day William Rufus died.

When Queen Adeliza failed to become pregnant, Henry realized that he needed to designate an heir in order to strengthen the throne. His daughter, Matilda, had been living at her husband's court for the past seventeen years, speaking German, her early Norman upbringing only a distant memory. In 1125 her husband died and King Henry decided to summon her back to England to become his heiress.

Matilda, who had grown into a handsome, self-willed, rather unpleasant woman of twenty-three, resisted. She knew what was in store for her if she returned to her father's court: submission to his will under threat of punishment, and, most likely, marriage to a man he chose for her, whether she was compatible with him or not. She had already endured one arranged marriage and wanted to avoid a second one.

But there was no resisting Henry for long; the reach of his long arm and the sound of his thunderous voice of command were compelling even in Germany. So Matilda came to England, and in January of 1127, underwent a ceremony of oath-taking in which each of her father's barons swore to uphold her as Henry's heir. They were to swear the same oath twice more, once after she married her new husband, the fourteen-year-old Geoffrey Plantagenet, and again six years later, after she gave birth to a son.

The succession had been arranged, but the barons were dissatisfied, and Henry must have known it. England had never been ruled by a queen, only by kings. If Matilda succeeded her father, it would not be she who ruled but her husband Geoffrey—for it was well understood in Norman society that married women had no property rights of their own, that everything they possessed belonged to their husbands, including, presumably, kingdoms—and no Norman would willingly put himself under the rule of a despised Angevin.

Furthermore, Henry was dismayed to find that his son-in-law Geoffrey was intriguing against him, making common cause with dissident barons, preparing for war. When Geoffrey demanded that Henry turn over to him certain strategic castles in Normandy, and Henry refused, war broke out—and even though Matilda and Geoffrey were at odds in their unhappy marriage, she took his side against her father.

By 1135 Henry, whom his subjects called the "Lion of Justice," was worn out, a toothless, clawless old beast who had retreated to his lair, the hunting lodge of Lyons-La-Fôret near Rouen. There, according to tradition, he unwisely ate too many lamprey eels, which made him fatally ill. He was sixty-seven, he had reigned longer than any previous king of England. On his deathbed Henry was still preoccupied with his ongoing struggle against Geoffrey, planning how he would seize Geoffrey's lands and shore up his own castles against future assaults.

The Archbishop of Rouen came to hear the king's confession and give him the last rites. Then, without the comfort of close relatives near at hand, he yielded to his illness and died on December 1, 1135.

Henry had given a generous endowment to the monks of Reading Abbey, which he had founded, to pray for the salvation of his soul and the souls of his father, his brother William Rufus, and "all of his predecessors and successors." It was to Reading that his body was taken, without his vital organs which were removed at Rouen and buried there. The king's embalmed body waited for a month at Caen before the Channel winds allowed for a favorable passage to England.

"A king is like a fire," Henry I's doctor Petrus Alfonsi once said. "If you are too close, you burn; if you are too far away, you freeze." The burning intensity of Henry I's majesty had singed many among his subjects, while others, distant from his attention, had withered in the cold. Henry's dominant will and relentless striving had made him the paramount force in his kingdom, a force that, once extinguished, would long be missed.

STEPHEN

(1135–1154)

————◆ ☙✳❧ ◆————

"A MAN OF LESS JUDGMENT THAN ENERGY, AN ACTIVE
SOLDIER, OF REMARKABLE SPIRIT IN DIFFICULT
UNDERTAKINGS, LENIENT TO HIS ENEMIES AND
EASILY PLACATED, COURTEOUS TO ALL."

—WILLIAM OF MALMESBURY

That Stephen of Blois was a pleasant, courteous man who was an apt and courageous soldier nearly all his contemporaries agreed. He was good-natured and easygoing, people liked him, he enjoyed convivial banquets, gatherings and hunts with his peers and his social inferiors alike. Though he was the nephew of William I, and a cousin of William Rufus and Henry I, he did not put on airs; though he was very rich, one of the richest men in England by the time he reached middle age, his wealth did not make him any less accessible, or any less affable.

In short, Stephen was a paragon: but he was not cut out to be a king.

Stephen spent nearly his entire childhood at the Norman royal court, as a favored young protege of Henry I. Because Stephen's own father had died while on crusade in Palestine, the much older Henry was a surrogate father to him, endowing him with extensive lands and arranging for Stephen to marry, in 1125, a great continental heiress: Matilda, only daughter of the Count of Boulogne, a spirited woman descended from Charlemagne and the Scottish kings.

It must have looked to all the English barons as though King Henry, whose son and heir William Audelin had died in 1120, was preparing the way for Stephen to succeed him, and indeed Stephen may have assumed this also. But Henry, who knew that the task of governing England and Normandy required not only stamina and courage (which Stephen had) but an almost maniacal aggressive toughness and ruthless brutality (which he lacked), saw that Stephen could not succeed as king. So he summoned his daughter Matilda, his only surviving legitimate child, to his court and forced all his barons to swear to uphold her rights as heir to his kingdom and his continental lands.

Stephen was the first to swear. He gave no outward sign that he was dissatisfied at having been passed over by King Henry, and when the king requested, several years later, that all his vassals swear loyalty to Matilda again, Stephen again complied. In all, three separate oaths were sworn to uphold Matilda's rights before King Henry died in 1135.

Yet almost immediately after the king's death, Stephen, disregarding his oath, made his way to England where he hurried to London and won the support of the most influential Londoners. Next he went to Winchester, to secure the royal treasury, all without opposition from Matilda or her supporters. The barons preferred Stephen—or his brother Theobald—to Matilda; they were content to allow him to take possession of the realm, especially after one of their number, Hugh Bigod, swore that on his deathbed King Henry had changed his mind about the succession, releasing his barons from their oath to Matilda and naming Stephen as his successor. Another objection to Matilda was raised; it was said that her birth was illegitimate, her mother having been a professed nun before her marriage to Henry I. This was in fact a spurious allegation, but it appeared to strengthen Stephen's claim.

In acting as he did, quickly and decisively, Stephen was prompted by his brother Henry, Bishop of Winchester, a much more commanding personality than Stephen and a leading churchman. Henry secured the support of the higher clergy for his brother by assuring them that Stephen would allow the church to retain the considerable independence it had won in Henry I's reign. Besides Bishop Henry, Stephen had the support of Roger of Salisbury, Henry I's most important official, who put the royal government in his hands.

Unopposed, shored up by the support of the clergy and the barons, in possession of the court and the treasury, Stephen was crowned king in Westminster Abbey on December 22, 1135, only a few weeks after the old king's death.

Matilda, in Anjou, made no immediate move to confront Stephen, although she did petition the pope, unsuccessfully, to reverse his recognition of Stephen as legitimate king. In early 1136 Matilda was pregnant with her third child, and though her claims were backed by her husband Geoffrey, the Scots king and her respected half-brother Robert of Gloucester, natural son of Henry I and himself a compelling choice to succeed his father, Matilda did not at first come forward. It was evident that the majority of the barons were behind Stephen, and Matilda was as aware as anyone that queens regnant were unknown in England and indeed throughout Western Europe in the twelfth century. By law and custom the property of a married woman became the property of her husband. The magnates assumed that, if Matilda became queen, her husband Geoffrey would be the actual ruler—and no Norman wanted to put himself under the rule of a hated Angevin.

Stephen had secured the English throne, but he immediately discovered that it had to be defended. A few bold barons challenged him right away, seizing royal castles and pillaging towns. Scottish lords defied him—and instead of marching northward to crush them militarily, as Henry I or William Rufus would have done, Stephen bribed them to submit—which left him looking vulnerable. A general rising in Wales, rebellions in the West Country and in Normandy quickly revealed that Stephen did not have the forces, the finances or the sheer determined drive to be a masterful leader.

In truth he was facing, not only fractious magnates and the hostility of the Scots, but a major conflict with the rising power of Anjou. Anjou and Normandy had been rivals for generations, but since 1100, the Angevins had been growing in strength, adding territory, expanding through political alliances and through advantageous marriages. Geoffrey of Anjou, a clever and heroic figure, had charisma and dash—both of which Stephen lacked—and was poised to move into Normandy to confront Stephen where he was weakest. Geoffrey's raids and seizures of Norman strongholds led Stephen to mount an expedition to Normandy in 1137, but once he landed his army began to unravel, the Norman barons melting away or becoming bogged down in conflict with his Flemish mercenaries. No effectual campaign could be waged, and Stephen wound up making peace with Geoffrey in exchange for a large annuity—something he could ill afford.

Fighting on many fronts, and increasingly beleaguered, Stephen was losing ground, his resources of fighting men and money greatly overtaxed. In the fourth year of his reign, 1139, Matilda landed in England and reached the protection of Arundel Castle in Sussex. Stephen, rather than besiege the stronghold, allowed Matilda to travel to Bristol unimpeded— forgoing an opportunity to capture her and either try her for treason or imprison her for life—and once she reached the southwest she and her supporters turned the area into a center of opposition.

Now, for the first time, England was the scene of civil war. Matilda relied on three experienced commanders to lead her forces: Robert of Gloucester, Miles of Gloucester and Brian FitzCount. Thanks in part to a growing dissatisfaction with Stephen's leadership on the part of the barons, Matilda's support expanded, and by 1141 the area under Stephen's control had greatly diminished.

When the two armies met at Lincoln in February, Stephen fought courageously. "His heavy battleaxe flashed like lightning," wrote the chronicler Henry of Huntingdon, "striking down some, beating back others." He fought on, continuing to grapple with the enemy in hand-to-hand combat until, with his battleaxe shattered and his sword broken, he was struck by a stone and crumpled in a heap, unconscious.

The battle was lost, Stephen was captured and taken to Bristol, where Matilda imprisoned him. His brother Henry, who was now papal legate, called a council at Winchester and declared, on behalf of the pope, that Stephen had lost the right to claim allegiance from his subjects. He was therefore deposed—and Matilda, by default, was the new ruler.

Such declarations aside, the actual political situation was confused. In truth, neither Stephen nor Matilda commanded a sufficient following to dominate England. (In Normandy, Geoffrey was rapidly making himself undisputed master.) Dissatisfied as they were with Stephen, the barons were equally unaccepting of Matilda. They did not want a queen, any queen. And they reacted unfavorably to Matilda's imperious personality. The very qualities they feared and respected in her father Henry I, they found repugnant in Matilda herself—her wrathful demand for obedience, her hardened, punitive attitude toward her followers, her harsh, unwomanly assertiveness. "She, with a grim look, her forehead wrinkled into a frown, every trace of a woman's gentleness removed from her face, blazed into unbearable fury," wrote the chronicler.

What Stephen's attitude toward Matilda may have been, other than competitiveness, no source records. But he must have been relieved to hear that when Matilda entered London, expecting to be crowned queen there, she encountered much opposition. Her demands for high taxes, her acts of retribution and vengeance, coupled with Londoners' growing distaste for her haughty persona led to her swift ejection from the city. She was not crowned, and her army, met at Winchester by an army of Stephen's regrouped followers led by Stephen's stalwart wife, was defeated.

The civil war had reached a stalemate. Stephen was liberated from his captivity but could not entirely eliminate Matilda—nor was she able to confront him decisively a second time. The papal legate Henry, who only a few months earlier had declared Stephen deposed, now called for Matilda's excommunication and returned to Stephen's camp. Matilda, besieged in Oxford Castle where she had taken refuge, was lowered by a rope from the castle wall late one night and, with only four companions, made her way to safety.

After nearly seven years as king, Stephen had steadily lost ground. He had shown personal courage, but neither political nor military sagacity. Instead of acting, for the most part he vacillated; instead of confronting, he appeased. He did not command sufficient awe or respect to inspire his fighting men, and he ran out of money to pay his mercenaries.

When Stephen's contemporary Walter Map wrote that the king was "a fine knight, but in other respects almost a fool," he was exaggerating, yet he had hit on a truth. Stephen knew how to conduct his personal affairs, but was unable to grasp the broader complexities of rulership or muster the qualities needed to sustain it. "Because of the king's undue softness," wrote the monk William of Newburgh, "public discipline had no force."

It was because of this woeful lack of public discipline that Stephen's reign is often referred to as "the Anarchy." Order broke down, government operated fitfully at best. Many areas of the countryside endured unprecedented suffering and disruption, with local lords, answerable to no one, extorting money through kidnapping and torture, and bands of renegade knights scouring the rural areas, looting and killing and pillaging. "For nineteen long winters," a monk of Peterborough Abbey recorded, "God and his angels slept."

Authority was localized, power decentralized. Every landowner built a castle—or rather, he forced the peasants to build it for him—and fortified it against all comers. Over a thousand new private castles were scattered across the landscape of England by the early 1150s; despite improvements in siege warfare, many were all but impregnable. The existence of so many small power bases encouraged predation. The result was a devastated countryside and a wretched and demoralized peasantry.

Anarchic conditions lasted for years, with very limited authority exercised by Stephen in the east, Matilda in the west and the Scots king David in the north. Apart from inconclusive sieges and brief skirmishes, warfare was all but moribund. Neither Stephen nor Matilda was decisively defeated, and in fact Stephen remained active, suppressing local revolts and containing local raiders by building castles of his own to counterbalance theirs. For all but two of his nineteen years as king, Stephen labored valiantly to be a military leader, but could never succeed in becoming paramount.

It was a paradox of Stephen's reign that the longer he fought, ineffectually, for preeminence, the more his reputation for personal honor and gallantry grew. It was as if he were too noble a character to inspire fear, and command obedience. Stories were told of how, when Matilda's impetuous fourteen-year-old son Henry came to England to defend his mother's interests, and lacked the money to pay his fighting men, Stephen generously gave the boy enough funds to pay what he owed and to return to Anjou without dishonor. On another occasion, it was said, Stephen had been besieging a rebel castle. The knight who held the castle had given up his five-year-old son as a hostage, and some of Stephen's advisers urged him to put the boy into a catapult and hurl him over the castle wall to his death, as a fitting punishment for his father's defiance. Stephen refused. (The boy, who grew up to be William Marshal, was to play a prominent role in future reigns.)

In 1147, in his fifty-first year, Stephen was wounded in small-scale fighting and never completely recovered. In the same year Matilda's most important commander Robert of Gloucester died, and in 1148 Matilda went back to Anjou, looking to her son to uphold her claims. Stephen too was looking more and more to his son Eustace to succeed where he had failed. Eustace had come into his own, having married the sister of King Louis VII, and joining with his brother-in-law to attack Angevin-held Normandy.

Now a widower, in poor health and tired of his long labors, Stephen was ready to consider a peaceful settlement to the wars which had reached an unprofitable stalemate.

Fortunately, a way to peace had begun to emerge. Matilda's energetic, athletic red-headed son Henry, whom Stephen had aided when Henry made his valiant, impetuous invasion of England in 1147, had grown into a wealthy young man who controlled vast territories in France. Henry had inherited Anjou and Normandy from his father, who had died in 1150, along with Maine and Touraine. Henry's marriage in 1152 to Eleanor of Aquitaine brought her enormous duchy under his governance. Fortified by the riches his territories brought him, and calling upon his very consider-able skills in the art of war, Henry had defeated Louis VII and, in the win-ter of 1152/3, was preparing to invade England, which he looked on as his rightful inheritance.

When Henry landed on January 6, Stephen opened negotiations with him which culminated in an understanding. Stephen agreed to make Henry his heir (Eustace having died suddenly), provided he be allowed to retain the throne during his lifetime. Henry agreed to keep the peace for the remainder of Stephen's life. Matilda was not mentioned.

Together Stephen and Henry traveled to London, where the war-weary citizens greeted the present and future kings with cheers of joy. The end of the Anarchy was at last in sight.

Another year remained to King Stephen, but whether he faced his last months with a sense of relief, or with regret, no contemporary recorded. He died at Dover on October 25, 1154, and was buried beside his wife and oldest son at the monastery of Faversham.

HENRY II

(1154–1189)

✦ ✥✪✦ ✦

"HE WAS IMPATIENT OF REPOSE, AND DID NOT
HESITATE TO DISTURB HALF CHRISTENDOM."

—WALTER MAP

When he became King of England in 1154 at the age of twenty-one, Henry II was a whirlwind of dynamic energy, constantly in the saddle, riding to war or to the hunt, his officials and household servants striving breathlessly to keep up with him.

Henry seemed to be everywhere at once, now besieging a castle, now riding to the borders of Wales, now turning north to face the Scots. "He does not linger in his palaces like other kings," one observer remarked, "but hunts through the provinces inquiring into everyone's doings, and especially judges those whom he has made judges of others."

So swift were King Henry's journeys, and so unpredictable his destinations, that he left others openmouthed in wonder. "He must fly rather than travel by horse or ship," the French King Louis VII said. Other travelers were slowed by muddy roads, or swollen rivers, but not Henry. Dressed in riding clothes, a short tunic and hose, and with a short cloak around his broad shoulders, he rode mile after mile like a fast courier, overtaxing his horses and himself, as if determined to overcome all obstacles to forward progress.

In this as in virtually all his undertakings, King Henry showed his central characteristic: his indomitable strength of will. From boyhood on, he had believed that enough willpower could force a solution to any problem—and very often he was right, though it was as much the power and intensity of his presence, his overwhelming life force, that resolved dilemmas and broke logjams as it was his clarity of purpose and determination. With his large frame, his forward-thrusting leonine head and steely gray eyes which seemed to "glow fiercely and grow bloodshot in anger," as one who knew him wrote, Henry appeared larger than life. In his expansive presence others seemed insignificant, hence his ability to persuade, argue, bully or demand obedience.

The England that Henry inherited from his ineffectual predecessor King Stephen was a realm prostrated by nineteen years of intermittent warfare and political chaos. Hundreds of castles had been built illegally, as bastions of independence from the late king and his rival for power, Henry's mother Matilda. Government barely functioned, the land had been ravaged by Stephen's mercenaries and the population plundered and battered by oppression.

Into this disorganized wasteland Henry rode, creating order, reducing the defiant to submission and overawing the barons. He sent the mercenaries back to the continent and, through his sheriffs and other officials, rounded up the roaming bands of outlaw soldiers which had terrorized the countryside. While never acknowledging that Stephen had ruled legitimately (for Henry's grandfather, Henry I, had designated Matilda to be his heir), the young King Henry forgave those who had opposed Matilda and thus began the process of restoring harmony.

What was remarkable about this rehabilitation of England was how rapidly it was accomplished. Within six months of his coronation, Henry had virtually restored order—though maintaining it would require constant vigilance and labor on his part and by his trusted underlings. He showed great skill in the art of war, making efficient use of mercenaries (and keeping them well controlled, as Stephen had not), giving them special training and equipment for siege warfare. His subjects were amazed at the swiftness with which he assaulted and destroyed castles, sometimes breaching their seemingly impregnable walls within days of beginning the siege.

Buoyant with self-confidence, Henry charged ahead against the forces of disorder: the Welsh and Scots, the Bretons and Poitevins, the king of France. He made his authority felt in every corner of his far-flung empire, which stretched from Ireland to the Auvergne, and from the Scottish border to the Pyrenees. For the better part of five years, from 1158 to 1163, Henry was in France—indeed he was gone so long that his English subjects began to believe that he would never return. Besides being King of England, Henry was Duke of Normandy, Count of Anjou, Duke of Aquitaine, Count of Brittany and overlord of countless other territories, nearly all of which were independent of one another, their only connection being their common rule by Henry. Policing these extensive domains would have overtaxed a dozen sovereigns, yet somehow King Henry, ever active, ever in the saddle, kept each one in line.

Henry had a gift for governance. His was a shrewd mind that grasped abstractions easily, and he turned the unruly jigsaw puzzle of overlapping jurisdictions into an exercise in logic. English military institutions were a congeries of regional practices, administration a shambles, finance and tax collection haphazard, and the legal system archaic. A start at reform and restructuring had been made under Henry I, but under Stephen things had worsened.

Now Henry II stepped in, and within a decade he had reversed the disintegration and put in place a truly royal bureaucracy, centralized, streamlined, and answerable to the king himself. Sheriffs regulated military and judicial affairs, exchequer officials supervised tax collection. Traveling legal officials brought the king's impartial justice to every part of the realm, establishing jury trials in place of the traditional trials by ordeal and combat. The king's judicial officials began to build a framework of common law which replaced the idiosyncracies of regional custom.

At the head of all, directly beneath the king and the chief justiciar in authority, was the chancellor, the king's close friend Thomas Becket. For the first eight years of Henry's reign, Becket, who was fifteen years the king's senior, ran the highly efficient royal secretariat, guarding the Great Seal, supervising the preparation and preservation of government records—the heart of government—and implementing the king's orders. Able, shrewd, a formidable man of business, the lowborn Becket was also vain, proud and self-centered. Henry looked up to Becket as a mentor, confided in him (as he did to very few) and gave him his trust. They worked together well, and when the work was done, they played together with the uninhibited exuberance of children.

"When business was over," wrote William FitzStephen in his biography of Becket, "the king and [Becket] would sport together like boys of the same age." They sat together at the long dining table in the great hall. They went to mass together, the king, ever restless, whispering to Becket or writing notes during the service. They rode to the hunt together, and afterwards, Henry would ride his horse into Becket's hall and join him in a goblet of wine. "Never in Christian times," wrote FitzStephen, "were there two men more of one mind or better friends."

Henry and his chancellor shared a common zest for feats of arms. When the king was marching on Toulouse in 1159, Becket equipped and led a host of seven hundred knights, and during the same campaign he fought a celebrated French champion in single combat and defeated him. Knightly renown, wealth, worldly glory: Becket savored them all. But when in 1162 King Henry decided to make Becket Archbishop of Canterbury, everything changed.

It was a fateful error, moving Becket into a role where his ascetic, unbending side came to the fore. He had always been a man of rigid views; compromise was not in his nature. And there were thorny issues to be settled between the royal government and the English church, chief among them the question of jurisdiction for the church courts. In Henry's view, ecclesiastical courts were taking lucrative business away from the royal courts. Becket disagreed, and adamantly defended all forms of clerical privilege. Henry, who had appointed his friend to the highest position among the English clergy in order to have his support, now found himself with a formidable opponent. Henry turned on Becket, fined and threatened him. In 1164 Becket appealed to the pope and fled to France.

By this time the king was in his thirties, ready to cast off his mentor Becket, his character maturing and gaining in complexity. After losing Becket's friendship he became indrawn and secretive, his goals and drives all but impenetrable except to those few who were in his small inner circle. He had considerable intellectual gifts—as a boy he had studied with renowned men of letters and had learned to speak and read Latin fairly fluently—and enjoyed reading and conversing with scholars.

"With the king of England it is school every day," one of his courtiers said. Henry enjoyed the challenge of unraveling philosophical issues, airing his views on history (of which he had considerable knowledge) and practicing his several languages. His learning was most likely that of a well-read and curious dilettante, but he had a searching, penetrating mind and a keen intelligence, combined with a retentive memory, and observers found him impressive.

Though clearly superior to most of those around him in ability and perception, not to mention in his exalted rank, Henry was the least pretentious of kings. He cared nothing for how he looked or what impression he gave, dressing casually, his person unkempt, paying no attention to court etiquette designed to foster awe in others.

An official once went in search of the king, needing him on some urgent matter of business, and found him in the forest, sitting comfortably on the ground surrounded by members of his court, occupied in stitching a leather bandage for his injured finger. Henry was at home among soldiers, thinkers, tavern-keepers (with whom he enjoyed getting companionably drunk) and especially, among the monks of the austere order of Grandmont, with whom he often took counsel. Yet though he was able to put himself at ease among a variety of companions, Henry remained fundamentally alone, isolated by his originality, an enigma to his contemporaries and, to an extent, an enigma to posterity.

In his thirties Henry found love. His marriage to the beautiful, vital and strong-minded Eleanor of Aquitaine, which had produced eight children, had gone stale, and Henry's frequent adulteries had led to rancor between husband and wife. But when Henry met Rosamund de Clifford, he found the sum of all his desires, and the discovery must have affected him profoundly.

The ceaseless work of peacekeeping and warmaking, subduing rebels and enforcing his lordship continued to preoccupy King Henry, as he traveled throughout his domains, invading Wales, policing the turbulent borderlands of Brittany, attempting to impose order on unruly Aquitaine, even attempting the conquest of Ireland. He spent the majority of his time in France, leaving England under the control of his chief justiciar Ranulf Glanville, called "the governor of the kingdom and the eye of the king." Henry's relations with the church remained poor. Becket was still in exile, and efforts on the part of the pope to reconcile the king and his Archbishop of Canterbury were fruitless.

The year 1170 was a watershed year in King Henry's life. His oldest surviving son, Prince Henry, was approaching fifteen and the king wanted to have him crowned King of England, to assure the succession. As the day of the ceremony approached, many of the magnates and their families traveled from the continent to London. Henry and his household were crossing the Channel with a large convoy of ships, when a sudden violent storm arose and many of the ships foundered. Five were sunk, though the ship carrying the king and his companions made it safely to shore.

For days the beaches were littered with debris, bits of cloth and lumber, dead horses and human corpses. The disaster was severe, four hundred died in all, but at least the king was spared. Henry, with his knowledge of history and his particular reverence for his grandfather Henry I, must have mused on that earlier disaster in 1120, the wreck of the White Ship, which had taken the life of the heir to the throne. Compared to his grandfather, Henry II was fortunate. His heir survived.

The coronation of the "Young King," as Prince Henry was known, took place in May of 1170, with a sadly diminished crowd of magnates in attendance. So many had perished, along with their wives and children, that it was whispered a curse lay on the Young King's prospective reign. As if to confirm these whispered fears, "Old Henry" became gravely ill only three months after his son's crowning.

The illness struck quickly and severely, prostrating Henry and laying him so low that rumors soon spread throughout his French domains that he had died.

What the nature of the king's illness was, no chronicler noted. But it began when Henry was under great strain. The tensions between the king and queen had led to a public rupture; they had not shared a bed for some time, but now they no longer shared even a domicile. And on top of this disruption, Henry had met, under intensely pressured circumstances, with Thomas Becket, whom he had not seen during the latter's six years in exile.

The king and his former friend and mentor met, and underwent a formal reconciliation—but beneath the surface, old grievances rankled, made more corrosive by Henry's sense that Becket had betrayed him. He had once trusted his former intimate to be his ally; instead, Becket had become an enemy, an unreasonable, overzealous advocate of church rights who had threatened him with excommunication. Now they were attempting a forced—and feigned—accord. Within days of their meeting the king was gravely ill.

For nearly six weeks Henry lay prostrate, weak and unresponsive to the attentions of his physicians. Then, gradually, he began to recover, thanks to his strong constitution and sheer force of will. As soon as he was able to ride, he made a pilgrimage, journeying hundreds of miles to the shrine at Rocamadour in Quercy, to give thanks for his survival.

He had survived shipwreck, and he had survived mortal illness. But as the year 1170 drew to a close, Henry was beginning to believe that he might not survive Becket. For the archbishop, restored to his see, was once again brandishing the weapon of excommunication, this time against several English prelates. The king was inevitably drawn into the quarrel.

Feeling ensnared, frustrated by Becket's maddening propensity to create discord, Henry vented his irritation publicly. According to John of

Salisbury, he remarked "that they were all traitors who could not summon up the zeal and loyalty to rid him of the harassment of one man." England was not big enough to hold both himself and Becket, he had said earlier.

Henry did not customarily guard his tongue, but there is no reason to believe that he meant his rash comments to be taken as commands to his subordinates to eliminate the archbishop. Still, four knights of his household, hearing what Henry had said, took it upon themselves to threaten Becket and put an end to his harassment of his royal master.

The four may not have meant to kill the archbishop, only to warn and frighten him or possibly send him into renewed exile. Certainly they meant to give him a sharp reminder of the king's power. But when they confronted Becket, accused and threatened him, he responded with scorn and went into Canterbury Cathedral to hear vespers. The knights armed themselves and followed him, heedless of the fact that they stood on holy ground. They tried to drag the archbishop out of the church, and when he resisted, they struck him repeatedly with their swords, killing him.

Henry's reaction to the news of Becket's death was extreme. He withdrew from everyone and everything for three days, causing alarm in his household; his servants wondered whether he meant to do himself an injury. His remorse went deep—though he denied any complicity in the crime—and in time he was to pay heavily for what his knights had done.

But Henry's reputation was permanently tainted, his honor stained by the shocking assassination, for which he was blamed throughout the Christian world. The sacrilege of Becket's death, the holiness of the murdered man (who in death took on the exalted stature of a martyr), the brutality and cowardice of the murderers, attacking an unarmed churchman as he was at his devotions before the high altar, stunned and grieved all Christendom, and the repercussions of the crime affected Henry for the rest of his life.

The pope laid an interdict on Henry's lands, so that no masses were said, no marriages or funerals performed. Apart from the baptism of infants and the administration of the last rites to the dying, there were no sacraments, and all the church doors were locked. Henry himself narrowly avoided excommunication. Meanwhile Becket's posthumous reputation mushroomed. Canterbury became a place of pilgrimage, the archbishop's tomb a shrine where miracles reportedly occurred. Christians from all over Europe prayed to St. Thomas. And the more Becket was revered, the more Henry was detested.

The king repented publicly in the spring of 1172, two years after the murder. He underwent flogging. He paid a large sum of money to the See of Canterbury and vowed to go on crusade. He did what he could, but nothing he did could restore his good name—or the full extent of his former power. There was a permanent chink in his armor.

Taking advantage of his father's vulnerability, Henry the Young King led a rebellion in 1173, allying himself with King Louis VII. Two of Henry's three other sons, sixteen-year-old Richard and fourteen-year-old Geoffrey, joined young Henry, and Queen Eleanor (who some said was the chief architect of the uprising) gave support to her disloyal sons. It was the signal many magnates had been waiting for. The revolt spread rapidly, to all corners of the king's immense territories. His authority was crumbling, and for once he was unable to be everywhere at once, to shore it up.

Momentarily Henry faltered—but quickly recovered. He seized his troublemaking estranged wife—who was on her way, disguised as a man, to join the Young King in France—and put her in prison. He sent couriers to all his castellans with orders to place the royal castles in a state of war-readiness. He hired Brabançon mercenaries and summoned his knights, bribing many of those who had joined the revolt to return to his army. After eighteen months of dogged confrontation the Young King and his brothers conceded defeat.

Henry was still the paramount leader, the strongest commander in his domains. But he foresaw that his sons were only biding their time, waiting for him to become feeble so that they could devour him. In Windsor Castle Henry commissioned a wall painting which showed an eagle, with four young eaglets perched on its wings and on its back. The young birds were pecking at the old one, tearing its flesh with their sharp talons. "The four young ones are my four sons," Henry told one of his courtiers, "who will not cease persecuting me even unto death." Two of the eaglets died in their father's lifetime, Henry the Young King (who was once again in rebellion when he died of a sudden illness) and Geoffrey (who was trampled during a tournament.) Of the two remaining, Richard and John, Henry much preferred John, but did not delegate to either son any portion of his power.

During the last ten of his fifty-six years, King Henry II enjoyed a considerable measure of fulfillment. His great love Rosamund de Clifford had died in 1176, much mourned and commemorated by a special shrine at Godstow Abbey, her tomb kept swathed in silken cloths. But Henry found other female companions. Queen Eleanor was perpetually shut away, and Richard, ever restless and occasionally rebellious, was little more than an irritant. Henry knew how to dominate his would-be rivals, and they did not trouble him for long, nor did the church present further obstacles to his sovereignty.

"He is great," Bishop Arnulf of Lisieux wrote of his king, "indeed the greatest of monarchs, for he has no superior of whom he stands in awe, nor subject who may resist him." As if to underscore his greatness, and to acknowledge the reputation he had gained, after decades of fighting, as a peacemaker, in 1185 Henry was offered the crown of Jerusalem.

The Patriarch of Jerusalem, Heraclius, came to Henry's court and offered him the keys to the Holy Sepulchre. The crusader kingdom was in need of a strong sovereign, for the current king, Baldwin IV, was dying and his heir was still a child. Would Henry, the patriarch asked, take up this holy burden and assume the throne?

That the presumed murderer of the Archbishop of Canterbury should be asked to become the sovereign of the Holy Land was in itself remarkable, and the full meaning of the gesture was not lost on the astute Henry. But he declined, after meeting with his barons. England and Anjou, Normandy and Aquitaine all needed him too much. Besides, he was beginning to feel the weight of his years. Like his grandfather and great-grandfather, he was growing heavy, and chronic illnesses slowed him down. He left it to Richard, his hotheaded, warlike son, to make the effort to rescue the Holy Land.

Henry died much as he had lived, while actively engaged in imposing his will and crushing those who challenged it. In the summer of 1189, he had been sick for six months, and was growing weaker. Though he could still ride, his legs were too shaky to permit him to stand, and others had to support his bulk when he tried to walk. Richard was making war on him, and to the king's great sorrow, he discovered that John, his favorite, had joined Richard. Only his natural son Geoffrey remained faithful.* Henry died in Geoffrey's arms at Chinon in Anjou, vowing vengeance on Richard with his final breath.

At last the ceaseless energy of Henry II was stilled. But the legend of the dynamic, forceful king lived on for at least a generation. Monastic writers imagined the king in hell, tortured for his sins, still fighting and dressed in full armor on a pitch-black steed, his armor "flashing out a fiery rain, like white-hot iron." Not even death, they imagined, could quench his ferocious energy.

---

*Henry had two sons named Geoffrey, one legitimate, one illegitimate.

RICHARD I

(1189–1199)

❖❖❖

"HIS VALOR COULD NO THRONG OF MIGHTY LABORS
QUELL . . . NO ABYSS OF THE DEEP, NO MOUNTAIN
HEIGHTS . . . NO FURY OF THE WINDS, NO CLOUDS
WITH SHOWERS DRUNK, NO THUNDERS, DREADFUL
VISITATIONS, NO MURKY AIR. NONE OF THESE
DANGERS PREVENTED HIM FROM MAKING TRIAL OF
THE PROWESS OF THE SICILIANS, OF CYPRUS,
OF SALADIN, OF THE PAGAN NATIONS IN ARMS."

—ROGER OF HOWDEN

Richard grew up amid the soft, balmy air of the south of France. The musical French of Aquitaine was his first language, the songs of Aquitaine his first tunes. He was raised at the refined court of his mother Queen Eleanor of Aquitaine, a court in which poets were honored and courtly love celebrated. Eleanor surrounded herself with artists, and took pleasure in cultivated conversation. She saw to it that her favorite son Richard was well educated and he was taught Latin and tutored in the writing of poetry and the composing of songs.

It was an environment appreciative of beauty, where ease and abundance bred languor. The warm sun beat down on the rich, lush countryside, with its fertile fields and broad rivers. Among the olive groves and vineyards, in the flowering meadows and tree-shaded courtyards, love flourished, fantasies blossomed, lofty ideals took shape.

From early childhood, Richard was steeped in the highminded values of chivalry, values which were cultivated with more fervor in Aquitaine than elsewhere. He grew up believing that the most important goal in a man's life was to achieve valorous deeds. In pursuit of that goal, he was taught, a wellborn man had to devote himself to learning feats of arms and performing them superbly, and to shaping his character around knightly honor, in order to protect the defenseless and seek out and vanquish the wicked.

He also grew up believing in himself and in his own uncommon worth. As his mother's favorite, and the only one of her four surviving sons to be raised at her own court at Poitiers—instead of at the court of his father Henry II—Richard felt singled out, unique among his brothers. Though he was not the oldest son, his brother Henry being two years older, Richard was in fact the bravest, the strongest, the best looking and by far the most charismatic of the children of Queen Eleanor and King Henry, and he knew it from a very early age.

He excelled at the basic military skills: horsemanship, fighting with spear and shield, mace and war-axe, shooting with the bow, scouting, analyzing terrain and choosing optimum sites for defense and points to attack. Tall and long-limbed, muscular and agile, Richard was made for warfare, able to withstand the punishing shock of encounter when an opponent's lance struck his armor and able to deal deadly blows with deadly accuracy.

Even in his teens he stood out, not only for his courage, strength and ability but for an intangible quality that made him the natural leader of other boys. His ambitious and competitive brothers, resenting Richard's capability, struck out at him where he was most vulnerable, exploiting his tendency to be overly trusting, his impetuosity, his intense devotion to their mother and his emotional distance from their father.

Queen Eleanor, it would seem, had kept Richard away from his father as much as possible, and father and son were at odds. There may have been an inherent antipathy between them, worsened by Richard's close attachment to his mother and resentment of his father's adulteries. Too little evidence survives to reveal the causes of their mutual antagonism.

But then, King Henry was at odds with all his legitimate sons, even his favorite son John. (The king's natural son Geoffrey remained loyal and dutiful.) When Richard was fifteen he joined his older brother Henry in rebelling against their father, with Eleanor's support and perhaps at her connivance. For eighteen months Henry and Richard did battle against their father, attacking his castles and striving to woo his barons away from him. They allied themselves with King Henry's principal enemy, King Louis VII of France, and it was King Louis who knighted Richard, girding him with the ceremonial belt of knighthood in the name of God and handing him his sword and shield "for the defence of the kingdom."

Young though he was, Richard made some headway in gathering allies in Aquitaine for his fight against his father, but when King Henry launched a strong counterattack against his sons, the rebellion crumpled. Richard and his brother Henry quarreled with each other, and neither felt adequately supported by the French king. Soon after his seventeenth birthday Richard went to his father and prostrated himself on the ground before him, asking his forgiveness. King Henry pardoned Richard, raising him up and giving him the symbolic kiss of peace.

He was forgiven—yet an undercurrent of enmity remained. Henry mistrusted and disliked Richard, and Richard resented Henry's mistreatment of Queen Eleanor, whom he imprisoned for her disloyalty in aiding the rebellion.

The royal family was profoundly scarred in the aftermath of the rebellion, disunited and full of mutual hostility. Richard returned to Aquitaine, where he had been made duke, and devoted himself to extending the duchy's southern borderlands, campaigning in Gascony and in the foothills of the Pyrenees. Soon word of his successes spread, stories were told of the bravery and prowess of the young Duke of Aquitaine, how he could assault seemingly impregnable castles and force them to surrender. There were also stories about his ruthlessness, how he brought to Aquitaine the harsh military methods of Anjou and Normandy, burning villages and devastating large areas of land in order to starve entire regions into submission. Richard's reputation grew, inspiring admiration and dread in equal measure.

In 1183, when Richard was twenty-six, his brother Henry died. Though Richard was the oldest of King Henry's three remaining legitimate sons, he did not automatically become heir apparent; primogeniture was not yet the governing principle of succession among the Angevins. Richard feared that his father would leave his best lands to John, who was only seventeen. Henry did in fact give Aquitaine to John, even though it had been Richard who had brought the duchy from near anarchy to some semblance of order. Richard angrily declared that he would not surrender any of Aquitaine to John, and stalked out of his father's court. The king was wrathful and condemned Richard as a fool and a knave.

"Invade Aquitaine!" Henry shouted to John, heedless of how his words sounded. "Take what you want!" John prudently declined, unwilling to face his indomitable brother in battle. But Henry remained angry.

Among the accumulating grievances between father and son was the fate of Richard's fiancée Alice, daughter of Louis VII. Richard and Alice had been engaged since they were children, and Alice lived at King Henry's court. But years passed and no marriage took place. In time

Henry took Alice as his mistress, and according to rumor, Alice bore the king a child that did not survive. Richard cared nothing for Alice, but he cared very much for his reputation, and his father's seduction of his fiancée dishonored Richard.

It dishonored him—and underscored the truth about Richard's sexuality, which was that he preferred male lovers. Sometime in his teens Richard had a mistress, by whom he had a natural son, Philip of Cognac. Apart from this one liaison, Richard seems to have avoided women—as he avoided marrying Alice—while confessing at several different times in his life before groups of clerics that he had had male sexual partners, and promising to amend his life. At the age of thirty-four, Richard finally made a political marriage, to Berengaria of Navarre, but the marriage was childless and the couple spent most of their time living apart.

In the Middle Ages, male homosexuality was considered to be an unspeakable vice and a criminal offense punishable by death. Richard's homoerotic preference was something to be kept hidden, and among his contemporaries it was never discussed, alluded to, when necessary, only in whispers. When Richard and the young King of France, Philip Augustus, developed a brief intense relationship in 1187, becoming inseparable companions and sharing the same bed, the pairing was observed with tacit acceptance.

It was in November of 1187 that Richard, then staying in the vicinity of Tours, heard the electrifying news that the great Muslim warrior and sultan of Egypt, Al-Malik al Nasir Salah ad-Din Yusuf, called by the Christians Saladin, had annihilated the armies of the crusader kingdom of Jerusalem at Hattin near Tiberias. The entire crusading venture was in peril. The Christian holy places, the tomb of Jesus and the sites of his passion and resurrection, were under Muslim domination. Even that holiest of relics, the true cross, was no longer in Christian hands.

No worthier object of Richard's knightly energies could be imagined. The morning after he learned of Saladin's victory and conquest, Richard vowed to go crusade to liberate the Holy Land from the infidel.

The crusade was still in preparation when, in the summer of 1189, Richard received the news that his father had died. Just then the two were at war with one another, their ever-simmering enmity having reached a boiling point yet again. Richard went to visit his father's coffin at the abbey of Fontévrault to pay his respects, but did not linger. Henry's inheritance was his to grasp, and he was quick to claim it.

The new king came to England to be crowned in a solemn ceremony at

Westminster Abbey, but he devoted little attention to affairs in England. The first months of his reign were almost entirely given over to raising funds for the support of his coming crusade. Offices were sold, taxes collected, loans acquired. Richard is said to have joked that he would have sold London itself had a buyer been found. The cost of the crusading enterprise was astoundingly high, yet Richard did not consider abandoning it. After all, he was prepared to pay an even higher price—the price of his life itself—in the holy cause if need be.

Having released his mother Eleanor from her captivity, and naming his late brother Geoffrey's son Arthur as his heir, Richard set sail from Dover in December of 1189, bound for the Holy Land. It was to be the grandest venture of his life.

He sailed in the flagship of the hundred-vessel fleet, the *Deulabenie*, or *God Bless Her*. Aboard his barge, *Portejoie* (*Joybringer*), were his warhorses and arms, chests of coins and siege equipment, along with goods and provisions for himself and his household. Three monarchs were joining together in the crusade, Richard of England, Philip Augustus of France and Holy Roman Emperor Frederick Barbarossa. The emperor accidentally drowned in midjourney, leaving Richard and Philip to carry on without the German knights. The French and English kings quickly became rivals for glory. Having once been on intimate terms, they developed an uneasy hostility, with the clever and intriguing Philip eager to encroach on Richard's territories for his own gain.

Territorial rivalry was far from Richard's thoughts. He believed himself to be on a divine mission, and was caught up in the grand drama of the crusade. He broke his journey in Italy to consult with the mystic Joachim of Flora, who taught that the end of the world was at hand and that Saladin was the forerunner of Antichrist who, Joachim believed, would begin his earthly reign in the year 1199. Richard saw himself as part of an unfolding sequence of events foretold in biblical prophecy; this conviction provided the framework for his endeavors and spurred him on to greater aspirations.

Everywhere Richard went, he inspired awe. When he sailed into the harbor of Messina in Sicily, intent on rescuing his sister Joanna from an unjust captivity there, he arrived in magnificence, "splendidly dressed and standing on a raised platform, so that he could see and be seen." Trumpets blew a fanfare as he stepped ashore, a conquering warrior. In Cyprus, where a local tyrant oppressed the populace, Richard conquered the island in three weeks, inspiring more tales and elevating his reputation further.

When he went into battle, a "terrible dragon banner" went before him, like the golden dragon banner King Arthur was said to have borne. Richard carried what he believed to be Arthur's sword, Caliburne (the Excalibur of later legend).

Once arrived in Palestine, Richard led the Christian forces in the taking of the great fortress of Acre, and won a major victory over Saladin's troops at the Battle of Arsuf, going on to occupy Jaffa and a chain of coastal fortresses. He went from victory to victory, always in the thick of the fighting, swinging his heavy sword with phenomenal strength, slaying the enemy right and left, rallying his men and leading them, blood-spattered and weary, to triumph. On long marches, even in the freezing cold of mid-winter, Richard rode up and down beside his men, encouraging them and urging them forward. He seemed to go beyond the limits of ordinary human endurance in his unceasing efforts, going without sleep, carrying heavy siege machines, bearing with ease the rigors of a long campaign.

Richard outshone Philip Augustus, who soon returned to France. He outshone the Muslim armies, and won Saladin's respect. But instead of capturing Jerusalem—the object of the crusade—Richard showed his visionary, idealistic side: he proposed that the Christians and Muslims share the city sacred to both. He suggested that his widowed sister Joanna, whom he had brought with him from Sicily, be married to Saladin's brother Saphadin. Together they would reign over a Christian/Muslim kingdom, a kingdom whose advent would coincide with the advent of the reign of Antichrist.

But Richard's grand ecumenical vision foundered. Joanna refused to marry Saphadin unless he converted to Christianity, and the project was abandoned. Jerusalem remained in Muslim hands, and Richard, after sixteen months in the Holy Land, prepared to return to the West.

His luck was running out. He had already had at least two narrow escapes from death, once when a party of knights attacked him and very nearly killed him and once when, after the Battle of Arsuf, he was set upon while hawking by a band of Turks and barely survived. Now, on his homeward voyage, a fresh series of adventures challenged him. In the storm-tossed Adriatic, Richard's ship was attacked by pirates who put him ashore near Venice. Separated from his entourage, and with only two companions, he started out for France overland, traveling incognito. But in a village near Vienna he was recognized, captured and delivered to Duke Leopold of Austria, who imprisoned him and held him for ransom.

It was a most uncharitable, not to say dishonorable, act, for Leopold had been a fellow crusader. But Leopold held a grudge against Richard; he had not received what he considered to be a fair share of the spoils when Acre fell. So he took his revenge and demanded a very high ransom—one hundred and fifty thousand marks, equivalent to thirty-five tons of silver.

It took several years for the English to raise enough money to ransom their king. A special government department was set up to collect the silver, which was stored in the crypt of St. Paul's Cathedral. Finally in 1194 Richard's mother Eleanor, now over seventy years old and wryly embittered at the course her life had taken (she signed herself "Eleanor, by the wrath of God, Queen of England"), made the journey to the continent to deliver the money and redeem her beloved son.

There was much rejoicing when the king, with his mother at his side, rode into London. His English subjects had pledged fully one-quarter of their annual incomes to raise his ransom, the churches had given their silver altar plate and the royal treasury was emptied. The kingdom had nearly bankrupted itself for their ruler's sake—and for the sake of the holy cause he had defended.

Yet Richard did not stay in England long. Within months he had returned to France, where for the next five years he was virtually continuously at war with King Philip Augustus. England was on the periphery of his concerns and he left its governance to others. His gifts were for fighting, not ruling; he devoted himself to an endless round of sieges, skirmishes, and occasional battles, punctuated by brief truces. Meanwhile in England, the barons and administrators found that they could govern quite effectively in the king's absence—a lesson they would keep actively in mind during the following reign.

By the time he was forty, Richard's vital, muscular body had turned to fat but his zeal for combat, and his legendary courage, remained as strong as ever. He was inspecting the walls of Chalus Castle in the Limousin, heedless of his personal safety, when an archer firing from the parapet above struck him in the shoulder. The wound became infected, and the king quickly succumbed. Within days he lay near death. He barely had time to send a message to his mother, who came at once. He died in her arms on April 6, 1199.

Eleanor gave orders that her son's body be buried beside that of his father at the Abbey of Fontévrault in Anjou. His entrails were removed and buried separately at Charroux, his heart "of great size," at Rouen. No part of him was sent to England. It may have been Eleanor who encouraged Richard's natural son, Philip of Cognac, to avenge his father's death, which he did by killing the lord of Chalus Castle.

Historical writers of the present age, seeking to deflate the extravagant praise of Richard by his contemporaries and the romanticized image created by nineteenth-century novelists, point out that he was a cold and brutal man, with a full measure of the Angevin ruthlessness. There was a savagery in his fighting prowess, he ordered throats slit and eyes burned from their sockets, he was given to violent rages and episodes of instability. In the aftermath of his great victory at Acre, Richard ordered twenty-seven hundred Muslim prisoners, chained together and helpless, marched out onto a plain and cut to pieces while he watched. They were, he said, "useless mouths" which he could not feed.

Even if he had not committed such atrocities, Richard may fairly be adjudged a neglectful king, a king who on his death left his realm poor and his subjects drained of much of their personal wealth. He spent only a few months of his ten-year reign in England, never learned English and left no legitimate heir, inviting turmoil after his death.

Yet to those who knew him, or who heard of his exploits, Richard was quite simply "the finest knight on earth, and the most skilled to fight." He was all nobleness rolled into one, "the courageous, the well-bred, the generous and the good giver, the enterprising, and the conqueror." Had he lived longer, his contemporaries believed, he might well have made himself master of the world.

In the ardor and jubilation of his fighting spirit, the renown of his triumphs, and the breadth of his vision, Richard embodied the personal and collective aspirations of his age—and in so doing, transcended it, as few English or British monarchs have. Something of his charisma lingers still.

JOHN

(1199–1216)

——✦❧✵❧✦——

"HE WAS INDEED A GREAT PRINCE BUT LESS THAN
SUCCESSFUL. . . . HE WAS GENEROUS AND LIBERAL TO
OUTSIDERS BUT A DESPOILER OF THE NATIVE
SUBJECTS. SINCE HE TRUSTED MORE IN FOREIGNERS
THAN IN THEM, HE HAD BEEN ABANDONED BEFORE
THE END BY HIS PEOPLE, AND IN HIS OWN END HE
WAS LITTLE MOURNED."

—BARNWELL CHRONICLE

King John's reputation has always suffered because he is inevitably compared to his greatly admired brother Richard. The monastic chroniclers of the thirteenth century hated John and wrote the worst about him. And it was during John's reign that the most famous—if not the most significant—document in English history was produced, the Magna Carta or Great Charter, a document often characterized as representing popular resistance to tyranny: therefore it is assumed that John must have been a tyrant.

Attempts by modern historical writers to rescue John from the condemnations of his contemporaries and of posterity have been only moderately successful. Although he was intelligent, shrewd and at times just, and had abilities as a governor and administrator, John failed to win the trust and loyalty of that small group of magnates, the principal landholders of the realm, on whom all medieval English kings depended. This signal failure triggered a host of other difficulties which made effective rule all but impossible.

John was a stocky, red-headed man of moderate height—about 5'5"—who like his brother, put on weight as he aged. He wore splendid clothes and rich jewels and surrounded himself with the pomp of majesty. Two trumpeters saluted him wherever he went. His tomb effigy, thought to be an authentic likeness, shows a handsome bearded face full of sly humor, and indeed John was said to be fond of coarse jokes, and given to making cruelly devastating remarks which wounded people by their brutal accuracy.

In personality King John was unpredictable, at times affable and welcoming, at times distrustful and dangerous. His cleverness was intimidating, his greed and underlying suspicion alarming, his rage as terrifying as it was ungovernable. When his chancellor, William de Longchamps, dared to oppose him John became "more than angry, his whole body unrecognizable," wrote the chronicler Richard of Devizes. "Rage furrowed his brow, his eyes glowed with flame, his rosy face became livid; I know what would have become of the chancellor if he had fallen like a ripe apple into those gesticulating hands in the hour of his anger."

John had the good fortune to be his father Henry II's favorite son, and almost from the year of his birth in 1167, King Henry heaped honors and wealth on him, granting him castles, lordships and estates throughout his dominions. Henry was disappointed in his three older sons, and estranged from them; when they rebelled against him in 1173, King Henry kept the six-year-old John near him, treasuring him as the only faithful prince.

While greatly favored by his father, John seems to have seen little of his mother Eleanor of Aquitaine, whose favorite son was Richard and who for most of John's early life was kept in confinement on her husband's orders.

John was apparently destined for a career in the church, and to that end was raised at the royal abbey of Fontévrault in Anjou until he was seven years old, along with his sister Joan. He was cared for by a tutor, a group of servants and a nurse, Hodierna, whom he loved; when he became king he granted Hodierna a generous pension. But the atmosphere of Fontévrault was uncongenial to him, possibly because, as the king's favorite, he grew up conceited and vain and was not catered to by the religious.

A story is told of young John playing chess with another boy, Fulk Fitz-Warenne. When the two quarreled, John "took the chess board and struck Fulk a great blow with it." Combative he surely was, though when he began his training in horsemanship and fighting with sword and lance, John did not distinguish himself.

Seven years spent in the household of his oldest brother Prince Henry, heir to the throne, may have given the young John a taste for intrigue; certainly he found his brother's court more agreeable than he had the abbey.

But there was still the question of his training. If he was not to become a churchman, and lacked military ability, there was another path open to him, that of royal governor. At the age of fifteen John's father placed him in the household of his leading minister, the justiciar Ranulf de Glanville. There he observed the workings of Henry II's efficient, well-run royal government at close range, while improving his mind. John had a liking for literature, his only inheritance from his cultivated mother; three years spent among the well educated clerks serving Ranulf de Glanville must have enlarged his mental horizons.

By the time he was eighteen John's tastes and character were formed. His father still favored him over his brother Richard (only the two brothers were left, Prince Henry having died of illness and Prince Geoffrey having been trampled to death in a tournament), but to others John appeared unworthy and flawed, a dandified, extravagant youth who was idle and overly self-regarding. Compared to the imposing, masterful Richard, who was earning great repute as a fighter in Poitou, John seemed to have little to recommend him.

King Henry knighted John himself at Windsor Castle, and then sent him to Ireland (John had been nominal lord of Ireland since the age of ten) at the head of a costly expedition. Not surprisingly, the expedition was a failure; John spent his time in Ireland carousing and hunting, and after nine months returned to England having accomplished nothing—a poor start to his princely career.

In 1189 John married an English heiress, Havisa of Gloucester, and in that same year he joined his brother Richard in making war on King Henry, who died soon after learning of John's disloyalty.

Now the childless, unmarried Richard was king—but instead of making John his heir, Richard chose his nephew Arthur of Brittany, who though still very young, was much more warlike and aggressive. Richard disliked John; whether the dislike was mutual is unknown. The brothers spent little time together, for almost immediately after his accession Richard went on crusade to the Holy Land, leaving England in the hands of capable officials and ordering John to stay out of England during his, Richard's, absence abroad.

John was slighted, and began referring to himself, despite his brother's caveat, by the title of "Highest Governor of the Realm." When Richard was captured on his way home from Palestine, John allied himself with King Philip Augustus of France and, with Philip's backing, went to England intent on usurping the throne for himself. He failed. The English, loyal to their absent sovereign, were devoting themselves to accumulating his ransom and could not be roused to rebellion.

In 1199, when Richard died, John was thirty-two, and still unproven. His brother's death provided him with an opportunity at last. John bestirred himself, claiming the duchy of Normandy at Rouen, seizing the royal treasury, and having himself crowned King of England at Westminster, all in swift succession. His mother gave him her duchy of Aquitaine, and key magnates in England stood by the new king despite the misgivings of those who criticized him as unwarlike and "somewhat slack of spirit."

A barbed nickname clung to John from this time on: Mollegladium, "Softsword." A king who preferred ease and comfort to the hardships of war was not worthy of his crown, so it was said. Knowing well that the late King Richard had once chosen Arthur of Brittany as his successor, many of the magnates pledged themselves to Arthur, who also had the backing of the ever-changeable King Philip Augustus.

The lords of Anjou, Maine and Touraine declared themselves for Arthur, and war began. For more than five years, from 1199 to 1204, John sought to establish his suzereignty in his continental possessions, showing himself to be a capable if not overpowering strategist. In 1202, when the embattled dowager Queen Eleanor was besieged by Arthur at Mirebeau—commanding the defense of the castle herself—John rode to her rescue, relieving the siege and capturing Arthur and several dozen of his principal followers.

The capture of Mirebeau was the apex of John's military endeavors in France. But what he did in the aftermath of victory made him notorious. Arthur's supporters were imprisoned at Corfe Castle and starved to death. Arthur himself, still in his teens, was imprisoned at Rouen and, according to the most credible contemporary account, became the object of John's personal vengeance.

One night in 1203 John, "when he was drunk and possessed with the devil, slew Arthur with his own hand, and tying a heavy stone to the body cast it into the Seine."

The murder of his nephew, his reputation for military slackness, his arrogance and suspicious nature combined to lower John's prestige among his followers; desertions began, and accelerated as Philip Augustus aggressively reconquered the Angevin lands. The death of Eleanor of Aquitaine weakened John's hold on the duchy, and many magnates, losing faith in John, pledged themselves to Philip.

By June of 1204 Normandy was lost, the last of the very extensive continental possessions once ruled by John's father. For the remainder of John's reign he made fitful, and ultimately futile, efforts to recover them.

For a time England too was under threat. Philip Augustus made preparations to cross the Channel with his army, and was expected in 1205. John showed his mettle in organizing a vast militia to repel the invaders, ordering that every male over the age of twelve take up arms and join a communal militia. Had the French invasion come, and had John led his forces in opposition, his prestige might have increased; as it was, Philip Augustus backed off from his invasion plans, and instead John faced a new threat from the church.

What began as a dispute over a clerical appointment soon developed into a struggle that undermined John's royal authority. Pope Innocent III, a forceful defender of church rights, rejected John's preferred candidate for Archbishop of Canterbury and gave the office to Stephen Langton, a learned English theologian and cardinal. The rebuff was a direct assault on John's authority, while triggering his deep-seated anticlericalism, and he refused to accept Langton, seizing the Canterbury revenues for himself and also the revenues of the Archbishop of York for good measure.

Now the full panoply of ecclesiastical sanctions was brought to bear, and England was laid under a papal interdict. No sacraments could be performed, other than baptism for infants and the last rites for the dying. The dead were denied Christian burial, and had to be interred in woods or ditches. Worshippers were locked out of churches, many clergy fled the country. In 1209 John himself was excommunicated—which threatened his sovereignty, since it meant that his subjects were released from their oaths of loyalty to him.

In retaliation John seized all the clerical property in England, but no amount of church wealth in the royal treasury could blunt the terrible force of the interdict—a force difficult for those of us living in a secular age to fathom. In medieval Europe, belief was the fundament, the sacraments the defining guideposts of life; for the populace to be denied access to churches and to the mass, to weddings and funerals, to the celebrations of the great church feasts and the shrines of the saints imposed an intolerable psychological burden. And John's subjects blamed the imposition of this burden, not on the pope, but on the king.

Meanwhile the king, in his forties, was becoming more secretive and suspicious, and more cruel. He maintained a network of informers to tell him what his most influential subjects were doing and saying, and was alert for talk of plots and conspiracies. He called off an expedition to Wales when he learned that two of his magnates were planning to depose and murder him. Instead of subduing the Welsh militarily, he turned to terror, ordering the hanging of twenty-eight Welsh hostages, all of them the sons of noblemen.

John sought to force loyalty from his chief subjects through an intricate web of coercion. Hostages were taken from among the English nobles, usually wives and children. Large landowners were deliberately enticed into going into debt to the crown and securing the debt with their lands, which meant that should they rebel, their property would be forfeit. In addition, some magnates were made to sign charters promising that if they were disloyal to the king, their estates would become his property.

Beyond these coercive measures, John showed by example what would befall anyone who turned against him. His murder of his nephew had provided a chilling illustration. Another was the fate of Matilda de Braose and her son, imprisoned by John and starved to death after Matilda unwisely spoke of the king's murder of Arthur.

In such an atmosphere of mutual suspicion and outright terror, it was no wonder that the populace seized on any message of hope. Apocalyptic prophecies began to circulate, predictions of the advent of Antichrist, of the approaching end of the world. And of the approaching end of John's reign, which, according to the ascetic and visionary Peter of Wakefield, would end on Ascension Day in the spring of the year 1212.

Peter traveled through the country, preaching to increasingly large crowds and announcing that the king's reign was about to end. He became the sensation of the day, much as Thomas Becket had been two generations earlier; his reputation grew rapidly and his predictions were repeated again and again, not only by villagers and the unlettered but by nobles and the learned.

John imprisoned Peter, along with his son, but the ascetic's prophecies continued to be repeated, and new ones were invented. Feeling against John was strong, and the prophecies enshrined this popular hatred—which only grew deeper after the king hanged the prophet and his son.

Ascension Day 1212 came and went—and still John reigned. He continued to be active, mounting costly campaigns against Philip Augustus and paying for them by levying ever higher taxes on his subjects, who despised him for impoverishing them to fund continuing military losses. In 1213, under threat of deposition, John finally came to terms with the pope, and was released from excommunication, the realm released from the interdict. But early in the following year, at Bouvines in Flanders, the English forces were resoundingly beaten on the battlefield by the French and John returned to England, defeated and supine.

Circumstances forced John to yield to the demands of the rebellious magnates in June of 1215 and make sixty-three written promises to them, promises which limited his authority and in addition to a list of minor grievances acknowledged, in essence, that excessive taxation ought not to be imposed without some form of communal assent, that the law was superior to the king's arbitrary will, and that the monarch was obligated to observe due process.

The promises were contained in a charter which later came to be known as the long, or great charter, in Latin Magna Carta.

In essence the Great Charter was an anachronistic feudal document, attempting to restore baronial rights lost—if indeed they had ever fully been won—in the previous century. Yet it was something more than this, because it gave voice to a sense of community among the baronial elite, and hinted at collective responsibility for the entire realm.

The rebels of 1215 called themselves "the army of God" and claimed a superior mandate for what they did. They declared that "they were of one voice and one mind, that they would place themselves as a wall before the house of the Lord and take a stand for the liberty of church and kingdom."

King Richard's long years of absence, and John's years of ineffectual rule had brought to maturity a commonality of purpose and a solidarity among the magnates that was never again to be entirely dissolved. In that sense the drafting of Magna Carta may be seen as a turning point in the history of the English monarchy. It was John's misfortune that this turning point was reached during his reign.

John's promises made at Runnymede in June of 1215 did not end his warfare with his magnates, and the pope declared him absolved of his promises shortly after he made them. Warfare resumed, with the magnates, still hopeful of victory, appealing to the ruling house of France to provide them with a more just and effectual king. The result was invasion by the dauphin Louis.

Nothing is known of John's reaction to these tumultuous events. He still had some supporters, and the government, for the time being, was his to command. But the great landholders who opposed him were powerful, each with a small, usually well equipped army of knights garrisoned in castle fortresses; they controlled large areas of the countryside. And John was forty-nine, no longer vigorous enough, or popular enough, to rouse the kingdom against the invading French. Evidently John was under enormous strain; it was making him ill. Yet he forced himself to continue the battle.

By the autumn of 1216, however, he must have been weary indeed. He was no longer master of his kingdom. In London, the dauphin Louis, Philip Augustus's son, held court, claiming to rule England in right of his wife Blanche of Castile, who was a granddaughter of Henry II. Louis was steadily gathering more support, John was losing it. And in the north, the Scots king Alexander had been welcomed. His army dominated the northern counties of England.

Forced from his capital, John wandered with his cumbersome household from one safe resting-place to another, guarded by mercenaries. At King's Lynn in Norfolk he fell ill with dysentery, but did not stop to rest. While his baggage train was crossing the Wash at low tide, a muddy expanse nearly five miles wide, the sea began to flood in and horses and carts foundered in the treacherous sands. "The ground opened,... and whirlpools sucked in everything, men and horses." The king himself was spared, but his servants, his treasures, even the coronation regalia and his grandmother Empress Matilda's crown and jewels, were lost.

Dispirited and impoverished, John rode on to Swineshead Abbey, then to Sleaford and finally to the Bishop of Lincoln's castle at Newark, growing more and more ill at each stop. At Newark, too sick to go on, he submitted to the ministrations of the Abbot of Croxton, a doctor. After receiving the last rites John died on October 18, 1216, and his body was taken to Worcester Cathedral for burial at the shrine of St. Wulfstan.

John was buried with his sword, as befitted one who had spent most of his reign at war. But he was remembered by his subjects, not as a warrior but as an oppressor and despoiler, a king whose reign had brought suffering and defeat, and who had, by his failure to wield the sword to good effect, lost the Angevin inheritance.

HENRY III

(1216–1272)

—❖❖❖—

"... THE SIMPLE KING WHO SAT BY HIMSELF."

—DANTE

Woe to thee, O land, when thy king is a child!" So wrote the author of the biblical book of Ecclesiastes. Minorities are precarious times in the life of any kingdom, and in the case of early thirteenth-century England, the dangers of a royal minority were especially pressing.

When the nine-year-old King Henry III was crowned in October of 1216, hastily and with minimal ceremony, in a makeshift ritual at Glouces-ter Cathedral, the realm was in peril. The oppressive and divisive reign of Henry's father, King John, had ended in disaster, the crown jewels were lost in the quicksands of the Ouse, and a foreign invader, the French dauphin Louis, had established himself in London.

Young Henry relied, of necessity, on his capable guardians William Marshal and Hubert de Burgh to lead the country, and fortunately he and the realm were well protected by these strong and able men. But having developed habits of dependence as a minor king, Henry never outgrew his tutelage. To an extent he remained dependent, childlike in his judgments, unable to act on mature instincts throughout his long life. The qualities medieval subjects admired in a ruler—military success, forcefulness, reso-lution, vigor and drive—were lacking in both the docile child-king Henry and the pliant, irresolute, shiftless adult; virtually all his actions were governed by a crippling weakness of character, which made him vulnerable to the influence of stronger personalities and undermined what limited rulership he sought to provide.

At the time of his accession, King Henry had the nominal loyalty of only the Midlands and parts of the West Country. Prince Louis, who had succeeded in capturing the richest and most populous part of England, awaited reinforcements from France with which he expected to conquer the rest. In the view of the French, the Angevin rulers of England had failed, and England could be easily added to the growing Capetian domain. But the stalwart Hubert de Burgh forestalled this outcome when he met the French fleet in the Channel and, though greatly overmatched, inflicted a decisive defeat, killing most of the invaders.

Together with William Marshal, who died in 1219, de Burgh proceeded to restore royal authority, reducing rebel-held castles, negotiating with the dauphin and persuading him to drop his claim to the throne in return for a large payment, and reviving the mechanisms of local government to ensure their smooth functioning. Within a year of the young king's accession, stability and order had been reestablished.

But the king, as he grew out of childhood, increasingly saw his principal minister as a hindrance rather than as the rescuer of the realm. Reacting petulantly to de Burgh's governance, Henry tried to strike out on his own, encouraged by his mother, the dowager Queen Isabella, and goaded by his tutor, the Poitevin Peter des Roches and a cluster of des Roches' relatives and hangers-on.

At twenty-two, the callow Henry, at the head of an incompetently prepared military and naval force, attempted a campaign in Brittany. His ships never left Portsmouth harbor—for which he held de Burgh responsible. In the following year he made the same attempt, this time humiliating himself and his men, overwhelmed not only by lack of preparations and his own inept oversight but by sickness and severe shortages of supplies. Once again the king sought to blame his justiciar, who was soon disgraced and removed from office.

Throughout his twenties, King Henry was the dupe of court factions, unable to assert—or even clearly to discern—his own will amid the clamor of voices around him. To others he must have seemed transparently immature, all strut and fret and shallow irascibility, while underneath remaining a frustrated and ineffectual youth. He had his father's vanity and arrogance, along with John's extravagance and his love of finery and gems, but he lacked John's intelligence, energy and naked cunning. Politics, and the realities of political maneuvering, eluded Henry completely. Without personal charisma, charm or military prowess, the king was at a loss. He foundered, clinging to those around him and to the church as he went forward into an uncertain future.

In one arena the king distinguished himself. He had an appreciation of art and a refined taste, combined with a fertile artistic imagination. Though not an artist himself, Henry patronized fine craftsmen and commissioned paintings, sculpture and decorative art of high quality for his palaces, and devoted much time to overseeing the implementation of these commissions. Culturally, England flowered during Henry's reign, and in his patronage of the arts the king reflected that thriving expansion.

In his personal life Henry was more fortunate than his father, his uncle Richard or his grandfather Henry II. His marriage to Eleanor of Provence, made when he was nearly thirty, seems to have been a compatible union and produced nine children. Contemporary records mention no royal bastards or mistresses, and Henry appears to have been a highminded and loyal husband.

When Henry married Eleanor, he gained not only a compatible life partner but a counselor to whom he often turned. He also gained an array of in-laws from Savoy and Provence, from among whom he chose deputies to run his household and court. He appointed three of his wife's uncles to be his ministers, and also showed great favoritism toward his four half-brothers, sons of his mother and her second husband Hugh of Lusignan. Lands and offices were heaped on these relatives, whose only merit—or so the king's critics alleged—was that they were in-laws or blood kin.

In addition to the many foreigners at the royal court, there was an abundance of papal representatives, legates and nuncios, who involved themselves, sometimes directly, in the governing of the realm and levied church taxes and contributions. Many English episcopal sees were filled by absentee Italian bishops, appointed by the pope. Ever since the years of struggle between King John and Innocent III, the papacy had gotten the upper hand where ecclesiastical and temporal rights came into conflict. King Henry's piety and deference toward the church accelerated the one-sidedness of this relationship, which was in fact part of a Europe-wide growth in papal influence.

Increasingly careworn and unable to come to grips with the realities of his diminishing power, Henry stumbled through his thirties and forties, seeking in vain to insulate himself against mounting criticism by shutting the magnates out of his government and ruling through those he trusted. Among these was Simon de Montfort, earl of Leicester, Henry's brother-in-law and a capable fighter and diplomat. Like most of those on whom Henry's favor rested, de Montfort was French, not English. He had been born into the lower ranks of the Norman nobility, and had inherited the earldom of Leicester.

Henry's feelings toward his Norman brother-in-law were ambivalent. On the one hand, the king needed de Montfort and acknowledged his ability, commending him for the way he carried out the assignments he was given and complimenting him on his skills. On the other hand, Henry was aware that de Montfort was coming to the fore as a leader among the English nobles, and this made him fearful and suspicious. He often shouted at de Montfort, accusing him of treachery, disloyalty and crime. Few men were in as advantageous a position to observe the king's changeable, unstable and untrustworthy nature as Simon de Montfort, and this gave de Montfort added force when he eventually emerged as the baronial spokesman.

The longer Henry reigned, the more his English subjects came to view his reign as barren of achievement, marked by repeated failures in warmaking (expeditions to France in 1242 and 1253 had ended unsuccessfully) and by what they regarded as the king's incapacity and lack of good judgment, his perverse inclination to shun his natural advisers and look to others for counsel.

"He did not keep his promises," the chronicler Matthew Paris wrote, "having little regard for the keys of the church and for the tenor of his Great Charter so many times paid for. Also he exalted his uterine brothers in a most intolerable manner, contrary to the law of the kingdom as though they had been born in this country."

Again and again the Great Charter was looked to as a benchmark for good governance and good lordship. It was issued and reissued during Henry's reign, a stabilizing force in an increasingly unstable political situation. Civil war had been avoided in 1234 when the disaffected magnates had demanded the dismissal of the hated Poitevin minister Peter des Roches, Henry's old tutor. The king had backed down. In the late 1250s another crisis loomed, this time in the aftermath of Henry's ill-advised involvement with papal aspirations in Sicily.

King Henry had vowed to go on crusade in 1250, but never actually started out for the Holy Land. The funds he had collected for his crusading venture went instead to the papacy, to finance its aggressive campaign against the German Hohenstaufens, Holy Roman Emperor Frederick II and his successors, who had conquered Sicily. In return for his contribution, Henry was granted the kingdom of Sicily by the pope; his intent was to place his second son, the deformed Edmund "Crouchback," on the throne.

The entire scheme was ill-advised and ill-timed, for Sicily was held by the late Emperor Frederick's son Manfred, and to dislodge Manfred would require a large and expensive campaign. Moreover, King Henry had allowed himself, and England, to be exploited; he had agreed not only to finance the conquest of Sicily—which would ultimately benefit only the papacy—but to pay all the pope's existing debts, which had reached the staggering sum of 135,000 marks.

To the magnates the disastrously ill-judged Sicilian venture seemed to signal a new low in the king's imprudence and misgovernance. That he appeared before Parliament, with Edmund, both wearing the plain tunic and trousers of Sicilian peasants, was an added insult to the native baronage of England.

At this point the magnates declared that the king had "acted imprudently and without advice of his nobles," the chronicler wrote, "alike rejecting all deliberation and prudence." He had had nearly thirty years of adult rule in which to demonstrate his ability to govern; for nearly thirty years he had demonstrated only folly, inadequacy and lack of foresight. It was time the nobles themselves came to the fore, as they had in his father's reign in 1215.

When King Henry summoned a great council or parliament of his barons to meet at Oxford in 1258, they arrived carrying lists of grievances, wearing full armor and ready for confrontation. Henry, out of money and facing excommunication unless he met his obligations to the pope, demanded that the council vote him a high tax. The nobles in their turn insisted that the king address the issue of reform before any tax was considered.

According to Matthew Paris, the king "on reflection," acknowledged that the realm had been misgoverned and "humbled himself, declaring that he had been too often beguiled by evil council." He swore before the shrine of Edward the Confessor "that he would fully and properly amend his old errors, and show favor and kindness to his natural subjects."

Specifically, Henry swore, in the Provisions of Oxford, to in effect turn over his powers to a new council, which would devote itself to the restoration of good government.

The new arrangements were, in all but name, a regency—but a regency established, not for a minor king or one incapable of ruling, but during the reign of an adult king in full possession of his faculties. As such it was a blatant usurpation of royal power.

Had any of Henry III's hotheaded Angevin predecessors been presented with so radical a political upheaval he would surely have exploded in anger. Henry responded, outwardly at least, with meekness, and for the better part of two years allowed the country to be ruled by the great nobles. But the experiment in baronial rule began to unravel as individual ambitions clashed and factions formed; some of the magnates remained loyal to the crown, others looked to Henry's oldest son, twenty-year-old Edward, as an alternative to his father, while most supported Simon de Montfort.

Amid the turbulence the most respected ruler in Europe, Louis IX, pronounced judgment on the Provisions of Oxford in 1264, declaring Henry free of their restrictions. Soon afterward, fighting broke out between the baronial army and the royal forces. King Henry, at the head of an army made up chiefly of mercenaries, was active, relieving de Montfort's siege of Rochester Castle and, drawing support from nearby castle garrisons, capturing Tonbridge and Winchelsea.

When Henry and his army arrived at Lewes, tired from the long march across the Weald, they were ten thousand strong; de Montfort had only half as many men. Yet momentum was with the baronial army and when the two forces met de Montfort drove the king's men off the field and into the town of Lewes itself. There, engulfed in street brawling, King Henry eventually broke free and took refuge in Lewes Priory. The defeat of the royal army was complete. Henry had no choice but to surrender, and to hand over Prince Edward to de Montfort as a hostage.

It was by far the most serious crisis of Henry's reign. De Montfort was in charge, and Henry was nothing more than an aging, defeated king regnant under the control of his enemy. The Welsh were in rebellion and the perpetual threat of invasion from France loomed.

Now Henry had reason to rejoice in his courageous oldest son. For Prince Edward, a vigorous, resilient fighter, became the champion of his father's cause. Showing himself to be more than a match for the opposition, he escaped from captivity, raised a large army, and, within a few months of the defeat at Lewes, met de Montfort's army at Evesham near Worcester in August of 1265.

Still a captive of de Montfort, King Henry was brought onto the battlefield, and was wounded in the shoulder while the fighting swirled around him in a driving rainstorm. At the end of the day Prince Edward and his forces had inflicted heavy losses on the opposition, and de Montfort lay dead on the field.

The Battle of Evesham effectively resolved the problem of King Henry's weak rulership. Without any formal transfer of power, Prince Edward took charge and Henry became a background figure—perhaps to his relief.

For the remaining years of his reign, until his death in 1272, Henry let his son manage the affairs of the kingdom, and pursue the ongoing war with the magnates—which did not end for several years. He seems to have been content to remain in the background, devoting himself to the remodeling of his palaces and to his most ambitious undertaking, the rebuilding of Westminster Abbey where, in 1269, the remains of King Edward the Confessor were enshrined.

The adjective most often used to describe Henry by those who knew him was "simple." Like a child or a simpleton, Henry was one-dimensional in his thinking, unable to fathom subtleties and complexities. Simplicity can confer a certain purity and nobility, but Henry had neither. Far from possessing saintliness of character, he was deceitful, untrustworthy, elusive. (Indeed he eludes modern biographers, and is among the most difficult of British monarchs to characterize.) Henry's fundamental cowardice made him sly; he could not be trusted. Fickle in his allegiances, mercurial in temperament, he was ultimately a shadowy figure, who left a weak imprint on his times.

And, one suspects, Henry was a very lonely man. His poignant effigy in Westminster Abbey, in the chapel of Edward the Confessor, looks unutterably sad. His subjects had come to despise him. For the last seven years of his life he occupied a political limbo, a cipher relegated to the margins of his court. The chroniclers of his reign, particularly the malicious Matthew Paris, omit mention of him. He no longer counted.

Whether Henry gained any satisfaction from observing his capable son Edward assume his role and begin the rebuilding of the shattered polity is unknown. Henry's attitude toward Edward was ambivalent, as his attitude toward Simon de Montfort had once been; he loved his son, yet was suspicious of him.

As he watched the rebuilding of the great cathedral which was to be his lasting monument, Henry may have ruminated on the parallels between his reign and that of his venerated ancestor Edward the Confessor. Like

Henry, Edward had preferred foreign favorites to English advisers, and had been overwhelmed and ultimately reduced to political impotence by the stronger personalities around him. Like Henry, Edward had devoted his old age to the enlarging of Westminster Abbey. Edward had been an ineffectual king, but was revered as a saint; here the parallel did not hold true, for Henry did not have the compensation of being widely venerated.

In poor health in the last two years of his life, King Henry absented himself from court and turned more and more to the town of his birth, Winchester. When he finally died at the age of sixty-five he was all but forgotten.

Amid the soaring gothic vaults of Westminster Abbey, surrounded by the graves of many of his royal descendants, King Henry lies entombed, a king who had the stubborn temper of the Angevins but a will as weak as water and, in the judgment of Matthew Paris, "a heart of wax."

EDWARD I

(1272–1307)

—◆◦◦✦◦◦◆—

"IN BUILD HE WAS HANDSOME AND OF GREAT
STATURE, TOWERING HEAD AND SHOULDERS ABOVE
THE AVERAGE. . . .HIS BROW WAS BROAD, AND THE REST
OF HIS FACE REGULAR, THOUGH A DROOPING OF THE
LEFT EYELID RECALLED HIS FATHER'S EXPRESSION.
HE SPOKE WITH A STAMMER (OR LISP), BUT DID NOT
LACK A READY POWER OF PERSUASION IN ARGUMENT."

—NICHOLAS TREVET,
ANNALS OF SIX KINGS OF ENGLAND

Though he was named after the meek, saintly Edward the Confessor, Edward I had none of the Confessor's gentler attributes. Six feet tall, with a sinewy body and an abundance of energy and stamina, Edward seemed a throwback to his fearless, intrepid great-uncle King Richard. He combined robust athleticism with self-confidence and an air of mastery; his physical presence alone was enough to intimidate and command.

As a young man Prince Edward threw himself energetically into knightly exercises, excelling in tournament competition. He liked rough hunting, riding at breakneck pace after hounds. The sheer thrill of the sport satisfied something in his emotionally turbulent nature, for he was quick-tempered and restive, and his overabundant physicality demanded an outlet.

Handsome and black-haired, with a slight stammer, Prince Edward showed early that he had the power to sweep all before him. But it was also evident that he could be handicapped by the same forces that made him masterful and self-assured. Carried away by his pride and vehemence, he was capable of vindictive anger, and of striking out violently against servants, companions, even members of his own family. Though he dreamed of going on crusade, and emulated the knights of the previous century, Edward was conspicuously unchivalrous; he was a bully, he went back on his word and did not hesitate to use trickery, rather than sheer skill and courage, to win over his opponents.

Still, when in 1254 Edward reached the age of fifteen and was endowed by his father Henry III with extensive lands in England, Wales and Gascony, he gave promise of becoming, in time, a strong king—and England was in dire need of strong monarchy. Weak and ineffectual, King Henry was locked in combat with his nobles, and the kingdom was sinking into a state of civil war.

Young as he was, Edward set off across the Channel to take possession of his duchy of Gascony, and to get married. At the Cistercian convent of Las Huelgas, near Burgos, he married Eleanor of Castile, half-sister of Alphonso X of Castile. It was a political union, whose intent was to protect the southern border of Gascony. However, Edward became devoted to his child-bride, who in time grew into an intelligent, dark-haired beauty, and they were to have sixteen children together.

Edward returned to England in 1255 seasoned by his sojourn in France, and eager to prove himself further. A more ambitious prince might have allied with his father's adversaries, the baronial opposition led by Edward's uncle and godfather Simon de Montfort. Rebellion by the heir to the throne was, after all, an Angevin tradition. But Edward chose a less risky course, remaining loyal to his father while using his growing influence in an effort to mediate between the two camps and to persuade wavering would-be rebels to remain loyal to the crown.

When civil war broke out, Edward was twenty-five years old, and eager to be in the thick of the fighting. At the Battle of Lewes in 1264 he rode boldly into combat, encountering the enemy and riding on in rash pursuit, unwisely abandoning his position and weakening the royal battle lines. Partly as a result of Edward's indiscipline, the battle was lost, and Edward himself was taken into captivity.

Undaunted, Edward escaped from his captors, raised an army and, at the Battle of Evesham in 1265, won a major victory. It was a turning point, not only in the civil war but in his father's reign; from 1265 on, Edward, not Henry, was the de facto ruler of England. There had been no usurpation, no formal handing on of the crown. But the magnates now looked to Edward for leadership, and his father became a cipher.

Edward met the challenge of leadership, though he had forfeited a measure of respect. At Evesham, it was said, he had dishonored himself by falsely disguising his soldiers, displaying an enemy banner as if it were his own and using the deception to lure the baronial army into a vulnerable position where he could destroy it. As a result of Edward's trickery, de Montfort was killed.

His knightly reputation tarnished, not only by his battlefield deceit but by a tendency to evade the truth and to serve his own interests first, Edward was able nonetheless to make his will obeyed and to begin the process of restoring good government, peace and order to the realm. Within a few years he had made enough progress to think of leaving England once again, and in 1270 he fulfilled his long-held hope of becoming a crusader, traveling to the Holy Land with a party of knights and a host of servants and camp followers.

Edward's timing was poor. The crusading ideal, which a century earlier had been an exalted vision of Christian overlordship of the Holy Land, had declined into undignified squabbles over trade rights, lands and money. Moreover, the enemy had changed. In the time of the great crusader King Richard, the cultivated, chivalrous Ayyubite dynasty had held the sacred shrines, and Saladin had regarded Richard as a respected peer. In Edward's time the harsh, fanatical Mamelukes were in control of Jerusalem, Caesarea, Arsuf and Antioch, led by their fiercely daring sultan Bibars. No chivalrous courtesy was extended to Christians, who were regarded as vermin to be exterminated.

When Edward left England on his way to the Holy Land, he expected to join the crusade mounted by King Louis IX. En route he learned that the French king had died in Tunis, and that a peace had been concluded with the Muslims. The crusade was over. Disappointed but tenacious of his purpose, Edward decided to pursue his own crusade, and took his men to Acre, the last remaining major Christian stronghold. He stayed there for sixteen months, defending the city, conducting raids in the vicinity, negotiating with the invading Mongols in an effort to make common cause with them against the Muslim enemy.

None of Edward's military or diplomatic initiatives led to significant outcomes, but his reputation for personal prowess greatly increased. He became known as "the greatest lance in the world," the foremost fighter, the supreme combatant. When he narrowly avoided death at the hands of a Muslim assassin, his status grew even higher, and he carried the mark of a grave wound as a symbol of valor. By the time Edward and his knights returned to England in August of 1274, he was no longer seen as a self-serving young prince whose word was unreliable and who won battles through deceit: he had become Edward the warrior, battle-scarred and courageous, admired and talked of throughout Europe.

And he had become King of England.

Henry III had died late in 1272, giving Edward the throne whose powers he had long been exercising. On his arrival in England Edward was given a magnificent coronation. The realm had not witnessed such pageantry, such feasting and genuine rejoicing, in living memory. At the dramatic climax of the coronation ceremony, Edward lifted the crown off his head and made a solemn vow. He would never wear the crown, he swore, until he had recovered all the royal lands his father had given away.

Restoration of lands, restoration of royal rights, restoration of the rule of law: such was Edward's avowed agenda as king. He had a gift for organization; it irked him that the existing law prevailing in his realm was an untidy congeries of feudal customs, local practices and enclaves of special power and jurisdiction. The weakness of his father and grandfather, and their confrontations with the great magnates, had led to corruption and abuses. Edward made it his primary task as king to bring order and coherence to law and lawmaking.

Edward began by sending commissioners to tour the entire country—much as William I had done two centuries earlier—to bring back reports on local conditions. Then, acting with the advice of his council, or Parliament, he enacted a series of sweeping statutes which set out the rules of landholding, military recruitment and obligation, and civil and criminal procedure. Nothing like this had ever been done before in England, and the statutes created under King Edward formed the enduring foundation of the British legal system.

Thanks to the royal statutes, justice became more swift, trial by jury (instead of the feudal practice of trial by combat or by ordeal) became the norm, and local courts came under the scrutiny of the royal court. For the first time since 1066, there was one royal law common to the entire realm. The law, which had been, to a large extent, under the private control of major landholders, now became public, and under the control of the king. Local officials became the king's officials, not puppets of local magnates. Local governance, with its inevitable abuses, shrank as the king's administration spread out into nearly every corner of the realm.

Along with regularizing and clarifying the legal system, Edward established the precedent that changes in the laws governing the realm had to be made with the assent of Parliament—the term coming into general use to define the lawmaking and advisory body that met when the king sum-

moned it. In summoning the Parliament of 1295, the king's clerks included in the writ of summons the Roman legal maxim "what concerns
all should be approved by all." This was not yet an established principle,
but Edward thought it desirable, and perhaps unavoidable; when it came
to important matters, and in particular extraordinary taxation, the
monarch needed to meet with representatives of the community of the
realm and obtain their agreement.

After decades of clashes between monarch and magnates, the idea that
the king ought to rule with the aid of a representative, advisory body was
finally taking institutional form—though Parliament was still embryonic
in form and would continue to be so for decades to come.

That Edward presided over these significant changes in law and governance was a tribute not only to his clarity of thought and administrative
capability but to his confidence. He did not fear the broadening of parliamentary influence, any more than he feared rebellion. He seems to have
felt certain that if his supremacy was challenged, he would be fully able to
meet the challenge. Indeed, far from being apprehensive about maintaining his authority in England, he mounted a vigorous campaign to extend
English rule into Wales.

From the remote fastness of Snowdonia, the Prince of Wales, Llewelyn
ap Gruffydd, was claiming complete independence from the English king,
while in South Wales, semi-independent marcher lords maintained a restless vigil over Llewelyn and each other. In a carefully organized campaign,
Edward began by building a road into North Wales, along which his large
force of fifteen thousand fighting men marched, from Chester to De-
ganwy, intimidating the Welsh prince but not defeating him; campaigning
was difficult given the arduous terrain and it was not until 1284, after
Llewelyn had been killed, that the king declared Wales to be annexed and
united to the crown. The Statute of Wales, passed in that year, extended
English law to the king's Welsh subjects, though the marchlands of the
south were to remain semi-independent until the sixteenth century.

King Edward's fourth son and eventual successor, Edward, was born in
Wales in 1284 and seventeen years later was given the title Prince of Wales.
The infant Edward's birth was welcome, for King Edward and Queen
Eleanor had lost three older sons, John, Henry and Alphonso, to childhood illness, and had only daughters. To his children Edward was, at
times, a stern father. On at least one occasion he became so angry with his
daughter Elizabeth that he plucked the coronet off her head and threw it
into the fire. At his daughter Margaret's wedding, the king became en-

raged, not at Margaret, but at one of his pages; he struck the man a mighty blow, injuring him severely.

As he aged, Edward's toughness rigidified into a hardened intolerance which, when added to his pride and emotionality, made him vindictive. But he did not let this vindictive streak dominate him, or make him unbalanced. Edward remained a towering, often terrifying figure even into old age, with snow-white hair and craggy features. But he had his vulnerable side. He listened when his elderly mother, who lived until 1291, sent him letters advising him on how to deal with continental princes and cautioning him to avoid catching cold. He was attached to his hounds and horses, and in particular to his falcons; when one of the falcons was ailing, he had a wax image of the bird made to place before the shrine of St. Thomas Becket, in hopes that the saint would assure its recovery.

Edward's human side was evident with special poignance when his wife Eleanor died in 1290. "My harp is turned to mourning," he wrote. "In life I loved her dearly, nor can I cease to love her in death." The grieving Edward ordered that, as a lasting testimony to his love for Eleanor, elaborate stone memorial crosses be erected along the route from Harby, near Lincoln, where she died, to Westminster Abbey where she was buried. Two tombs were built to contain her remains, one at Lincoln and one in the cathedral.

Despite his sincere regret at the loss of Eleanor, Edward did not remain a widower long. He married Margaret of France, the French king's sister, by whom he had two sons. He was tenderly attached to Margaret. Once when she was ill, the king wrote to her physician, instructing him to ensure that the queen did not travel until she had recovered. "And if you allow her to travel too soon," Edward warned, "by God's thigh you will suffer for it."

In his fifties, King Edward faced an unprecedented range of challenges. Revolts in Wales and warfare with the Scots necessitated his swift response. When the French king confiscated Edward's lands in Gascony, the resulting warfare lasted for nearly four years, from 1294 to 1297, forcing the elderly king to cope with fighting on three fronts at the same time.

Raising funds to pursue his war-making was the greatest challenge of all. Nearly three-quarters of a million pounds were needed to finance the wars, and the king's own revenues were far from sufficient to cover the cost. In the past the crown had turned to Jewish moneylenders, and to the Ricciardi bankers, for loans. However, in 1290 Edward had expelled all the Jews from England, and the Ricciardi firm was no longer willing to advance funds. In desperation Edward seized all the money that individuals and organizations had deposited in churches, arousing an outraged response.

In July 1297, the king was preparing another campaign in France, but his subjects, heavily taxed and suffering from years of scant harvests and high prices, were on the verge of rebellion. The magnates, gathered at Westminster to swear oaths of fidelity to young Prince Edward, heard their chastened king beg their forgiveness, and tearfully promise to return all that he had taken.

Edward was persuasive, but not persuasive enough. Both the king and the magnates began fortifying their castles, readying themselves for war. Fortunately, under the pressure of renewed Scots aggression, civil war was averted. But the king's financial problems remained, and he had to turn to another Florentine banking house, the Frescobaldi, for aid. By the end of the reign, some two hundred thousand pounds had been borrowed.

When Edward turned sixty, in 1299, he was locked in a prolonged and seemingly intractable struggle with the Scots. He had won a great victory at Falkirk the previous year, but his nominal overlordship of Scotland was still disputed, and the outlaw William Wallace led a rebellion that went on for years. By avoiding pitched battles, and harrying the English from their mobile camps in the hills and forests, the Scots effectively thwarted Edward in his effort to control the country. William Wallace was captured and executed, but Robert Bruce inherited what had become a patriotic resistance movement, and seized the Scottish throne.

In the summer of 1307 Edward, aged sixty-eight, resolved to take the field and lead his armies once again, to vanquish Robert. He had been ill throughout the previous winter, and his great strength had begun to fail. But his determination was unwavering. Shakily, he made his way north. When he reached Burgh-on-Sands, on the Solway Firth near Carlisle, he faltered. His heart gave out, and he died.

Even in death Edward's will made itself felt. He asked that his corpse be boiled, and that the bones, stripped of flesh, should be taken with the army every time an expedition against the Scots was made. Neither this request, nor his wish that his heart should be taken to the Holy Land, were carried out.

Few medieval kings possessed Edward's toughness of mind and body, or his record of achievement. Despite the disappointments and crises of his last fifteen years, Edward left a remarkable legacy. He had succeeded at the preeminent tasks of a king: to be an effective military leader, and to make himself obeyed. His statutes and legal reforms were of lasting value. Though he failed at the thing he cared about most—the conquest of Scotland—and though he left the realm deeply in debt, he had undeniably strengthened the kingdom, and reversed the decline of monarchical power.

Something of Edward's own strength remains in the ring of castles he built in Wales: Beaumaris, Caernarfon, Flint, Conway, Rhuddlan and Harlech, massive stone piles whose thick walls, impenetrable and forbidding, have endured the centuries.

EDWARD II

(1307–1327)

———✦✦❈✦✦———

"... A HANDSOME MAN, OF OUTSTANDING STRENGTH,
BUT HIS BEHAVIOR WAS A VERY DIFFERENT MATTER ...
HE WAS DEVOTED TO CHORISTERS, ACTORS, GROOMS,
SAILORS AND OTHERS SKILLED IN SIMILAR
AVOCATIONS.... HE WAS PRODIGAL IN GIVING,
BOUNTIFUL AND SPLENDID IN LIVING,
QUICK AND UNPREDICTABLE IN SPEECH ...
SAVAGE WITH MEMBERS OF HIS HOUSEHOLD,
AND PASSIONATELY ATTACHED TO ONE PARTICULAR
PERSON, WHOM HE CHERISHED ABOVE ALL ... "

—RANULF HIGDEN, *POLYCHRONICON*

In his fierce old age, King Edward I was a savage father. His only surviving son, the future Edward II, was an intense disappointment to him, and the king despised him. Prince Edward was a tall, strapping young man, handsome and intelligent. But he was weak-willed and indolent, preferring music, plays and rustic crafts to the knightly arts. With his intimate companion Piers Gaveston, "Brother Perrot," the prince made fun of the solemn, self-important court officials and magnates (and probably of King Edward as well), sending the king into paroxysms of rage. In the last year of the king's life, he lost his temper and attacked the prince and his lover, banishing Gaveston from the realm and assaulting Prince Edward so severely that he tore out handfuls of his hair.

Soon after the attack took place, the battered prince became king, and it was not long before he recalled Brother Perrot from his exile. The two became inseparable once again, and the new king made Gaveston Earl of Cornwall and showered him with gifts, lands and wealth. Edward arranged a lucrative marriage for Gaveston, to his niece Margaret, even though Gaveston was far below Margaret in social standing, being the son of a Gascon knight.

The king's preoccupation with his lover, and the jealousy to which it gave rise, became the besetting preoccupation of the royal court. Nothing else seemed to matter, or to be talked of, not King Edward's own marriage to Isabella of France, sister of the French king (he gave away most of the wedding presents to Gaveston), not the royal coronation (Edward spent the night with Gaveston, and not with the queen), not the ongoing war with the Scots (Edward abandoned his father's military campaign against Robert Bruce, and amused himself with Gaveston), not even the king's ineptness at the craft of rulership, an ineptness which became more evident with every passing month.

The royal friendship might have mattered less had Edward been able to manage his royal duties adequately. But as king, he was far from adequate—indeed, he was appallingly inept. Though grave matters of war and finance demanded addressing, Edward avoided coming to terms with them and instead devoted his time to farming, horse-breeding (he was a fine rider), swimming and boating. A note in the court records reveals that once while disporting himself in the water with "Robert the Fool," he caused injury. Sums were set aside from the royal treasury for the purchase of pleasure boats, small craft in which the king, Gaveston and perhaps Robert the Fool and others amused themselves.

Kings and sons of kings were bred to martial arts, exercises with lance and sword, wrestling and jousting, but Edward avoided these pastimes, preferring to spend his time the way the humblest of his subjects did, thatching roofs and trimming hedges, maintaining his own workshop for which he ordered large quantities of iron and plaster, possibly for erecting stage sets. Music and plays were among his favorite diversions. He maintained a small orchestra of two trumpeters, a horn-player, a harpist and drummer, and his chancellor, Walter Reynolds, was said to be skilled at arranging theatrical entertainments.

But players were low company, as were the singers, acrobats, farmhands, grooms and sailors who were Edward's preferred companions. The king seems to have avoided noble young men—or it may be that his noble companions were simply upstaged by the flamboyant Gaveston, who, at the king's coronation, strutted regally in purple robes decorated with pearls.

The contrast between Edward I's tough, masterful rule and his son's weak negligence gave renewed force to the rumor, begun in the senior Edward's reign, that his son was a changeling, put into the royal nursery under false pretenses. And it was not only the courtiers and noble class that half-doubted the king's lineage; his humbler subjects too had their doubts and kept their distance.

It was customary for those afflicted with the disease of scrofula (tuberculosis of the bones and lymph glands) to come to the royal court so that the king could lay his hands on them and heal them; kings had ritually touched for the "king's evil" of scrofula for centuries. In Edward I's time, upwards of two thousand of his subjects had availed themselves of this hoped-for cure. But in Edward II's reign, the stream of scrofulitic supplicants diminished to a trickle; even those desperate for a cure were skeptical of the king's healing abilities.

Edward II had ruled for only a year when the magnates, incensed by the gifts, privileges and honors the king had heaped on Gaveston, and by Edward's reliance on his favorite to advise him and even to be Regent of the kingdom in his absence, demanded that Gaveston be removed from the kingdom. Edward sent him to Ireland as royal lieutenant.

But in 1309 Brother Perrot was back at court, restored to his former position of favor and influence and full of mockery toward his noble opponents. He had given the principal magnates derisive nicknames; Gaveston and the king laughed long and hard at their expense. Gaveston had committed another unpardonable offense: in a series of tournaments, he had beaten the leading jousters of the court, and they burned for revenge.

In 1310 King Edward, under financial pressure because of the failure of the Scots war, had no choice but to summon a great council, to which the magnates came in full armor. They insisted that the king place himself under the governance of a baronial committee, the Lords Ordainer, which was to oversee the reform of the government.

But Edward, though outwardly compliant, resisted this check to his authority—and the continuing calls for Gaveston's permanent exile. The nobles prepared for war, and the king, feckless and seemingly incapable of organizing the forces of the crown, fled northward with his lover.

Gaveston went to Scarsborough Castle, where he was captured and turned over to the earl of Pembroke, who swore to protect his life. But Pembroke was unable to fulfill his vow; as Gaveston was being taken back toward London, the earl of Warwick, whom Gaveston called "the black dog of Arden," kidnapped him and took him to Warwick Castle. There, after a hasty trial, he was convicted of treason.

The pent-up hatreds were unleashed as Gaveston was led to Blacklow Hill near the town of Warwick for his execution. A carnival atmosphere greeted the executioner and his victim and a noisy, shouting crowd gathered to watch the death of the hated royal favorite. Horns blew, cheers rose as the axe was raised. A few quick chops and Brother Perrot was no more.

The king, who had been powerless to prevent Gaveston's execution, now showed himself equally powerless in guiding the realm. Deprived of Gaveston's support and advice, he allowed himself to be shunted aside entirely by the wealthiest of the magnates, his cousin Thomas of Lancaster. Thomas was the son of Edward I's brother Edmund "Crouchback," whose expensive candidacy for the Sicilian throne had become the occasion of civil war between Henry III and his barons in 1258.

Though he had a great fortune, with five earldoms, strong castles, a large personal retinue and the wherewithal to buy and maintain a substantial private army, Thomas was no leader. He desired power but lacked the capability to use it effectively. As a result, after 1311 the kingdom was adrift, with King Edward still nominally in charge, but in actuality unable to free himself from the hobbling control of his nobles.

In 1314, with the Scots raiding the border counties and Lancaster unable to protect them, Edward bestirred himself to resume his father's war against Robert Bruce. He raised an army of twenty-one thousand men—an army which neither Lancaster nor the other leading magnates joined—and set out with despatch for the north.

Edward was not a novice at war. With his father and on his own, he had taken part in four campaigns against the Scots, and was a competent fighter. But he was no general, and lacked sound military advisers. Prudence would have dictated that he wait to offer battle to the Scots until he had secured expert commanders. But Edward was never prudent, and so he marched his army northward, trusting to fate.

At Bannockburn near Stirling he drew up his forces, keeping them under arms all night waiting for the Scots to attack. Edward had very substantial numerical superiority—there were three English soldiers to every one of Bruce's men—but when the two armies engaged, he squandered this advantage through inept tactics. The Scots came on in clusters of spear-carrying footsoldiers; the mounts of the English cavalry were impaled on the spears, the force of the English archers was blunted, and the entire array fell like dominoes, those at the rear falling into a deep ravine.

It was a very great disaster, indeed an unprecedented one. No Norman or Angevin king had ever lost so many men so quickly, or had presented so feeble a resistance to the onslaught of the enemy. For Edward, when he saw defeat coming, did not attempt to rally his troops but fled the field, riding hard for safety. It was said that he did not spare his successive mounts until he reached Dunbar fifty miles away. With his flight, the rout was complete, the dishonor beyond measure. One chronicler called the king Edward the Chickenhearted, and denounced him as "luckless in war."

For three years following the battle of Bannockburn, England reeled on the edge of chaos. The king had been utterly discredited, and the Lords Ordainer imposed new restrictions on him. Thomas of Lancaster, appointed commander against the Scots, was ineffectual and the victorious soldiers of Robert Bruce continued to harry the northern counties of England, holding towns for ransom and committing fearsome atrocities. The Welsh were in revolt. With the police power of the government moribund, warfare between private armies broke out, plunging many regions of England into confusion. And, to compound the kingdom's miseries, crop failures resulted in famine conditions, the worst famine to strike England—and Europe—in centuries.

Edward, who in the year of Bannockburn was thirty years old, was caught up in an ongoing struggle to regain the authority he had forfeited. Slowly, over a period of years, he began to build up support by buying the loyalty of individual barons, a process aided by the growing disillusionment with baronial leadership.

While misgovernment and incompetence flourished, and Thomas of Lancaster was accruing a large private army, Edward was relying more and more on two new advisers, the Despensers, father and son. The Despensers held lands in the Welsh marches, and were eager for more; Hugh Despenser the younger, capable but entirely self-serving, had political ambitions. He became Edward's chamberlain, and before long Edward was turning to him, as he once had to Piers Gaveston, as his chief adviser, and rewarding him with gifts, lands and honors.

In 1322, at the Battle of Boroughbridge, King Edward finally won his first and only victory, defeating Lancaster and his private army. In the aftermath of the battle, Edward had the satisfaction of supervising the execution of his cousin, who was beheaded along with twenty of his followers.

At last the death of Gaveston had been avenged. Yet Edward, once he regained power, did not turn to Parliament and distrusted the nobles. He seemed unable to rule except through a few familiar advisers, and the Despensers, along with a small group of household administrators, were the only advisers he trusted. The Ordainers were dismissed and their authority rescinded.

At last Edward ruled, unrestrained by others. He gave full vent to his long-held anger at those who had tried to circumvent him, ordering dozens of executions and over a hundred of his former enemies killed, imprisoned or sent into exile. Those who escaped death were required to purchase their freedom by paying large sums to the royal treasury.

England had suffered much since the king's accession, and the scars of conflict, poor governance, famine and coup and counter-coup were evident. Nearly every town in the realm displayed, over its main gate, the rotting remains of executed traitors. King Edward was not respected, but he was feared, for he was known to be vindictive and capricious in his vengeance.

Meanwhile the wealth and influence of the Despensers grew. Hugh Despenser the elder was made Earl of Winchester, while Hugh the younger received nearly forty grants of land, plus cash gifts to strengthen his castles and buy arms for his soldiers. The king named one of his ships *La Despenser*, and showed other marks of his personal favor. Both the earl and his son were becoming very wealthy, and both were abusing their power, sometimes extorting money and lands from noble widows under threat of imprisonment and starvation.

Once again, as at the start of his reign, Edward was allowing himself to be dominated and exploited by ambitious, often unscrupulous men. His household was riddled with them, including men indicted for murder, robbery and assault. One of his knights, Gilbert de Middleton, attacked and robbed a bishop and two cardinals; one of his military constables, Robert Lewer, who rose to influence and wealth as a result of Edward's particular favor, was a convicted murderer ultimately condemned to death for his crimes. The crown, already greatly lowered in popular esteem, sank to fresh depths.

In 1325 new opposition to Edward arose, and from an unanticipated source. Queen Isabella, who along with many others hated the Despensers for their corrupt and arrogant influence over her husband, became the focus for dissatisfaction.

Isabella and Edward had been married for seventeen years, and the marriage had produced four children, two boys and two girls, of whom the eldest, Prince Edward, was a vigorous, strong boy of twelve. But the royal marriage, corroded from the start by the king's preference for Gaveston and, more recently, for the younger Despenser, had grown not only stale but hostile, the partners embittered to the point of loathing. Edward's hatred for his queen was well known; he told others that he carried a knife with which he meant to stab his wife, and vowed to "crush her with his teeth" if no weapon was available.

Isabella had suffered deprivation and humiliation ever since the king's victory over Lancaster and the Ordainers in 1322. Edward suspected her of conspiring with his enemies, and he and the Despensers seized her lands and dismissed many of her servants. Perhaps because of the worsening mutual enmity between the king and queen, Isabella, who was the sister of the reigning King of France, Charles IV, was sent to Paris in 1325 to try to settle the future of Gascony, which England still claimed and France had seized.

Many of those whom King Edward had banished had settled in France, and now that the queen was in Paris, they came to her court, looking for succor and no doubt for encouragement to launch a rebellion. Among the exiles were the Earl of Richmond, the king's half-brother the Earl of Kent, and three English bishops. Also among the English exiles was Roger Mortimer, an intensely ambitious, rich and influential Marcher lord. Mortimer had been imprisoned in the Tower by King Edward but made a dramatic escape; condemned to die, he gave a final farewell banquet for his jailers, drugged the guards and made his way to safety.

Isabella and Mortimer seem to have been well matched in strength of personality, boldness and hostility to the prevailing English regime. They became lovers, and together they plotted King Edward's overthrow, though it was Isabella who was in the vanguard of the venture.

Isabella had flung down the gauntlet to her husband, vowing never to return to England unless the Despensers were dislodged from their favored position at court. Now she strengthened the force of her opposition by sending for young Prince Edward, ostensibly so that he could do homage to King Charles for his French lands, Ponthieu and Aquitaine. Foolishly, King Edward sent his son to France.

Once they had the heir to the throne under their control, Isabella and Mortimer possessed a formidable advantage. They were able, in effect, to hold young Edward hostage, and to use him to further their own plans. Banished from France by King Charles, who was offended at his sister's brazen cohabitation with her lover, Isabella and Mortimer went to Flanders and struck a bargain with the Count of Hainault. The young Prince

Edward would marry the count's daughter Philippa, and in return the count would allow the conspirators to raise an army of mercenaries in his domain.

In England, King Edward heard rumors that an invasion was being planned and might soon be carried out. But he seems to have done nothing to forestall it, or to prepare a defense. Possibly he was pessimistic, aware that most of his subjects would welcome an invading force as a deliverance. Possibly he hoped that his queen and her lover would be unable to raise the enormous sum needed to fund the ships, men and provisions necessary to invade. It could be that he trusted the Despensers to arrange for the defense of the realm. Or possibly, as had been the case with his failed invasion of Scotland in 1314, Edward simply neglected to take adequate precautions against disaster, and once again, trusted to fate.

The queen and her army landed in Essex in September of 1326, accompanied by Mortimer and Prince Edward. Almost at once King Edward's fighting men deserted him en masse, and the invaders met with no resistance. Proclaiming that she had come to avenge the murder of Thomas of Lancaster and to expel the king's evil councilors, Isabella led her forces on unopposed.

Edward fled to the west with Hugh Despenser the younger, the two setting out from Chepstow by sea and landing in Glamorgan, where Hugh had estates. But escape was futile; Henry, brother of the late Thomas of Lancaster, captured both men and sent King Edward into captivity at Kenilworth. Both Despensers met sorry ends, the elder captured at Bristol and executed, the younger tried and executed at Hereford as a heretic and sodomite, his genitals cut off and burned while he still lived.

Edward II was formally deposed by Parliament in January of 1327. In the articles of deposition, his defects were spelled out: he had been incompetent, he had rejected good advice and sought evil counsel, he had lost Scotland, Ireland and Gascony, he had broken his coronation oath. The litany was long—and it was justified. Edward III became king, and Isabella and Mortimer in effect ruled.

Of Edward's last months little is known with accuracy, except that by the fall of 1327 he was dead. (Even this was disputed at the time; there was a story, widely repeated, that he had escaped to Sicily and lived on there, hoping to regain his crown.) After agreeing to give up his throne to his son, Edward became an inconvenience—and a potential danger to the stability of the new king's reign, should conspirators arise to fight for his restoration. He was shunted from one castle to another under guard, finally coming to Berkeley Castle in Gloucestershire.

There, according to the chronicler Geoffrey le Baker, who was writing decades after the event, Edward was kept under insufferable conditions, and virtually starved, in hopes that he would die a natural death. When he stubbornly refused to die, he was murdered. But his death could not look like murder, there could be no marks on his body. So, according to the chronicler, his jailers killed him by thrusting a red-hot plumber's iron into his vital organs via his anus. True or not, this gruesome tale has caused shudders of horror for centuries, and evoked a measure of sympathy for the hapless Edward.

From the outset of his reign, Edward had been under the control of others, in thrall to Gaveston, then to the Lords Ordainers and his cousin Thomas of Lancaster, then to the Despensers and finally to his wife and her lover. He seemed incapable of attaining true maturity; instead he remained, despite his advancing years, an immature boy, self-centered and weak, unable to separate private indulgence from public responsibility and incapable of ruling.

Edward died unmourned, but was viewed as a martyr nonetheless, and pilgrims came to his tomb in St. Peter's Abbey in Gloucester, hoping that he could perform posthumous miracles. To prevent their numbers from growing too large, guards were placed at the doors of the church, and stories that miracles did in fact occur there were stifled.

EDWARD III

(1327–1377)

**"HIS LIKE HAD NOT BEEN SEEN SINCE THE DAYS OF
KING ARTHUR."**

—FROISSART

Edward III came to the throne amid an environment of coercion and fear. His father, Edward II, was an inept king and had made many enemies, among them the queen, Isabella, and her ally and lover Roger Mortimer. Together Isabella and Mortimer planned to use young Edward to carry out a coup d'etat.

Edward, Prince of Wales was only twelve years old when his father sent him to France to do homage to his uncle King Charles IV for the duchy of Aquitaine and the county of Ponthieu. Isabella was there already, gathering supporters and making preparations for a daring invasion of England. What attitude the young prince had toward his mother's treachery is unknown, nor did the contemporary chroniclers record whether Edward II and the Prince of Wales got on well or were estranged. Wherever the prince's loyalties lay, the queen, spurred on by her ally Mortimer, had determined to take bold action.

Her first step was to refuse to permit her son to return to England. She kept him with her, first in France and then, after her brother Charles IV banished her for breaking her marriage vows and plotting disloyalty, in the Flemish county of Hainault. While in Hainault Isabella arranged the betrothal of the Prince of Wales to the Count of Hainault's daughter

Philippa—the price of the count's permission for Isabella to raise an army of Flemish and Dutch mercenaries.

Deprived of his freedom, forced into a position of rebellion against his father, his betrothal and future marriage forfeit to his mother's grand designs, Edward was a pawn. If he resisted, his resistance went unreported. The queen and Mortimer landed in England in September of 1326, Edward II was coerced into abdication, and early the following year, the prince was crowned as Edward III.

The coronation was genuine enough. Edward was crowned, recited his oaths and received the homage of his vassals—including Mortimer—and was anointed with the sacred chrism. But he was still being held hostage, his every move choreographed by his mother and her lover. The coronation could not proceed until the young king promised, under duress, to take a special oath to observe "the just laws chosen by the community of the realm"—a way of putting him under an obligation to the magnates.

And the coronation itself was an anomaly, because the old king was still alive, and had only agreed to abdicate because he was told by his captors that if he did not, his son's rights as well as his own would be taken away.

It is presumed that Edward III had nothing to do with the subsequent murder of his father at Berkeley Castle, but no surviving record exists of his reaction to his father's death, whether he felt outrage, grief or perhaps even guilt. That he blamed Mortimer is clear from later events. But Edward's personal response to the callous murder can never be known.

Only fourteen when he was crowned king, Edward matured rapidly over the next few years. A vigorous, aggressive young boy, strong and skilled at feats of arms, he clashed with the overbearing Mortimer, who kept power to himself and yielded little authority to the council of barons set up to guide the new king. As he watched Mortimer, who took the title Earl of March, seize more and more lands and treasure, including the ample treasury that had belonged to the late king, Edward must have realized that the earl intended before long to seize the ultimate prize: the crown itself. Mortimer presided, king-like, over costly tournaments and arranged prestigious marriages for his daughters. He presided at great councils and issued orders as if he ruled all. And because he distrusted Edward, he placed spies in the royal household.

But when, at a council meeting held at Nottingham in 1330, Mortimer challenged Edward directly, humiliating him in front of his vassals, Edward decided to act. With the blessing of the baronial council Edward and a small group of knights slipped secretly into Nottingham Castle and seized Mortimer, taking him to London where he was tried for his crimes and soon executed.

"The king's affairs and the affairs of his realm have been directed until now to the damage and dishonor of him and his realm," announced the proclamation Edward issued. "He will henceforth govern his people according to right and reason, as befits his royal dignity." He was not quite eighteen.

Tall and handsome, with red-blond hair and a keen glance, King Edward was the ideal knight, hearty and courteous and with more than enough bravado to cause excitement. He liked magnificence in dress and kept an opulent court, well aware of the value of appearing to be a wealthy and successful ruler, even if the throne was in fact none too secure.

Edward had had no instruction in kingship, but observing his father and Mortimer had taught him what not to do, and reading had exposed him to good models. He liked to collect chronicles of English history, and admired the kings he read about, especially his predecessors Henry II and Edward I, both active, energetic kings who aggrandized their kingdom through conquest. He also liked the Arthurian tales, and saw himself in the mold of the heroic Arthur of legend, a king with courage and spirit who lavished gifts on his knights. Like Henry II and Edward I, Arthur had been a great conqueror, and Edward burned to make conquests of his own.

But first he had to settle matters in Scotland where Mortimer, a weak commander, had spent a great deal of money and gained nothing. Edward intervened in the Scottish succession dispute, backing Edward Balliol against Robert Bruce's infant heir David. He led his men vigorously, and experimented successfully with an innovative military strategy, a combination of footsoldiers and bowmen. The result was a significant English victory at the Battle of Halidon Hill in the summer of 1333. Balliol became king and did homage to Edward as his overlord, and at the same time Edward's lust for territory was sated; he claimed eight lowland shires for England.

In the course of campaigning against the Scots Edward even found an occasion to enhance his growing reputation for chivalry, rescuing a woman in distress—the Countess of Atholl—from the siege of Lochindorb in the highlands in 1336.

War with Scotland led to conflict with France, Scotland's ally. The French king Philip VI positioned his fleet to attack southern England and in 1337, confiscated the English-held duchy of Aquitaine. Edward's response was to claim that he, and not King Philip, was the rightful king of France.

No one could have foreseen, at the outbreak of war, that this conflict would last, with interruptions, for more than three generations or that it would bring such luster to English arms. The early years of the war brought nothing but frustration and expense. Levies were raised, arms and victuals amassed, captains arrayed—all at enormous cost. But not a single major engagement was fought and the king was condemned as a self-aggrandizing adventurer.

By 1340 taxes and customs duties had been increased to such an extent that the English were on the verge of revolt. Edward was not only failing to make territorial gains in France, he was proving to be a tyrant, dismissing officials and judges, imprisoning financiers, while continuing to take more and more of his subjects' money and goods.

When Parliament met in 1341, the Lords and Commons insisted that the king's finances be examined, a turning point in the political relations between crown and subjects and a hindrance to the ongoing pursuit of the war. Edward was conciliatory to the Lords and Commons, while at the same time altering his tactics in France. Instead of confronting the French royal forces directly, he undermined them by allying himself with enemies of Philip VI in various regions, until eventually he was able to launch a large-scale campaign.

In the course of that campaign, the English and French armies met at Crécy near the Somme in August of 1346. The French host was far larger, and expected victory. But Edward put heart into his troops, riding up and down their ranks on a warhorse with a white rod in his hand, "desiring every man to take heed that day to his right and honor. He spake it so sweetly," the chronicler Froissart wrote, "and with so good countenance and merry cheer that all such as were discomfited took courage in the seeing and hearing of him."

Again and again the French attacked, only to encounter such a hail of English arrows, "let fly . . . so wholly together and so thick that it seemed snow." A great wall of French dead rose before the English army. Amid great rejoicing, the English declared victory.

King Edward returned to England after the Battle of Crécy laden with wagonloads of treasures, the spoils of victory. There were jewels, furs, costly furnishings, featherbeds, silken cloaks and gowns without end. Knights who came home from the wars were showered with largesse by their generous prince, until every household had some piece of fine linen or silver, every wellborn woman some ornament, all souvenirs of victory. The feasting and merrymaking never seemed to end. King Edward presided over banquet after banquet, with spiced meats and freely flowing wine, and even ordered a new circular stone hall built at Windsor where his nobles could gather for these celebrations. Tournaments were held, with knights competing in the lists for royal prizes.

There had never before been so lavish a ruler, so splendid a court, so great a king. "Without doubt this king had been among all the kings and princes of the world renowned, beneficent, merciful, and august," the historian Thomas Walsingham recorded. He was called "the Favored One" and compared again and again to his idol King Arthur. In this season of success Edward built palaces, castles, chapels and hunting lodges. With his wife Philippa he patronized musicians and writers. There seemed no end to his bounty, no limit to his vision of the ideal court.

With his chosen knights around him, Edward swore to "begin a Round Table, in the same manner and estate as the Lord Arthur," and in 1348 he inaugurated the Order of the Garter in which he was joined by twenty-four Knights Companion.

In that same year of 1348, at the hour of his greatest success and satisfaction, King Edward and his realm began to suffer catastrophic loss. The king's thirteen-year-old daughter Princess Joan suddenly became ill, and soon died. Others in her household were stricken, and before long there were outbreaks of pestilence in every town in England and on the continent. King Edward's infant son Thomas also died, along with dozens of the royal servants and many in their families.

It was the plague, the Black Death, that terrifying wave of mortality that seemed to contemporaries a visitation from God. Bubonic and pneumonic strains of plague fused with exceptional virulence, and carried off one person in every three. Death became the obsessive concern, the burying of bodies the preoccupying task. In the villages, the fields lay fallow and in the towns, death-carts rattled over the cobblestones at all hours, while church bells tolled incessantly.

King Edward buried his children and called off his war, and in the aftermath of all the devastation, he seems to have thought of trying to negotiate a permanent peace. His longtime foe Philip VI died in 1350, and the new king, John II, had not yet declared his intentions. With the military reputation of the English monarchy at a new high, and his country depopulated and exhausted, Edward could have abated his ambitions abroad. But his honor was at stake, and his five surviving sons, now of an age to pursue victories for themselves, were eager to renew the long quarrel with the French. When Edward's cousin Charles, King of Navarre, appealed to Edward for help in his dispute with John II, Edward began preparing his armies once more.

The next great English victory, at Poitiers, was won by Edward's son and namesake, called "the Black Prince" from the shade of his dusky armor. Six thousand of the English overcame a larger French force, and this time the French king John was captured and sent to England to await payment of an immense ransom. But by now the French were in no position to redeem their king. The countryside, much of it burned and destroyed by the English, was in grave disorder, given over to plundering gangs of mercenaries. A widespread peasant revolt added to the chaos.

Pressing his advantage, Edward invaded France in 1359, leading his large army toward Rheims, intending to be crowned king of the realm he had claimed for a quarter of a century. But his men froze in the harsh winter weather, and the expedition failed. Edward made peace, gaining Aquitaine in return for renouncing his claim to the throne.

Edward was now nearly fifty, still vigorous, his reputation as a distinguished military leader intact. Over the next decade he was to stabilize England's finances and consolidate administrative control by the crown—something his father had been unable to accomplish. Edward's achievements in war had necessitated making political concessions; in the interval of peace the king improved his relations with his subjects, ending direct taxation and reducing the wool subsidy.

Peace had come, yet it was a troubled time. The plague returned, and with it the pervasive atmosphere of decay and mortality. The French king languished, captive, in London and died unransomed in 1364. Aquitaine rebelled against its English overlord, and the French, revitalized by their new king Charles V, raided Portsmouth and burned it. Meanwhile King Edward, slowly declining, began to withdraw from affairs, delegating authority to his sons.

The English had overreached themselves. Conquered territories required guarding and governing, and there were not enough men or resources. Town by town, region by region, the lands Edward had won slipped out of his control, until by 1370, only Calais and some coastal territories were left under English rule. Whether Edward reacted with dismay or resignation is unknown. He planned an expedition in 1372, but could not carry it out. His ablest son, the Black Prince, was mortally ill, and his second son, John of Gaunt, was proving to be an ineffectual commander.

Edward had the misfortune to outlive his glory. In his last years, weak and feeble-minded, he fell under the control of his chamberlain and steward, who enriched themselves at his expense and tarnished the high repute of the court. By the king's side was his grasping mistress, Alice Perrers, by whom he had three children; she too took advantage of him. In 1376 the Black Prince died.

King Edward is said to have died virtually alone, with only a single priest to give him the last rites. The greedy Alice Perrers was there to steal the rings from the old king's stiff fingers.

For a king who had surrounded himself with such grandeur, and won the loyalty and devotion of so many comrades-in-arms, it was an unexpectedly sad passing. But in the memory of his older subjects Edward was still the Favored One, the scourge of the French, a just ruler to his people.

"The gallant and noble King Edward III departed this life to the deep distress of the whole realm of England," Froissart wrote, "for he had been a good king for them. His like had not been seen since the days of King Arthur." When the royal bier was borne at a slow march through the streets of London, carried by two dozen black-clad knights, thousands of the late king's subjects wept at the sight. "To witness and hear the grief of the people," wrote Froissart, "would have rended anyone's heart."

RICHARD II

(1377–1399)

————————◆◆◆◆————————

"SIRS, WILL YOU KILL YOUR KING . . ."

—SHAKESPEARE, *RICHARD II*

At the great Christmas feast held at Windsor in 1376, King Edward III sat at a raised table in the vast banqueting hall, his sons, his knights and barons arrayed below him. The old king was growing physically weak, and mentally wandering, but of one thing he was sure: he intended that his nine-year-old grandson Richard should be king after him.

Richard's father, the Black Prince, was dying and would not live long enough to reign. The boy, Richard, must be recognized as the rightful heir. Edward had required all his magnates to swear to uphold Richard as their "only lawful lord and undoubted sovereign." Now, at the Christmas banquet, Edward exalted the prince by placing him at his side at the high table, so that no one in the huge hall could mistake his status as heir.

It was with a strong sense of his high destiny that the ten-year-old Richard II was crowned seven months later, following his grandfather's death. Richard was by this time accustomed to being acclaimed. His grandfather had given him a place of honor on many ceremonial occasions. He had even sat on the late king's throne at the opening of Parliament. At his coronation Richard carried himself like a miniature king, a slender, good-looking, blond young boy in a crimson robe, surrounded by prelates and dignitaries, prominent among them his uncle John of Gaunt, steward of England, the most powerful man in the realm.

That John of Gaunt supported his nephew Richard's accession was re-assuring to the English, for there had been rumors that the new king's uncle would usurp the throne himself. After the crowning Richard was lifted high on the shoulders of one of his knights and carried, wearing his full regalia, through cheering crowds to the palace. The crown appeared to be stable, the king's position secure.

Then in June of 1381, when Richard was fourteen, a dangerous tumult arose. Rebels in Kent and Essex formed huge marauding bands and began attacking manors and monasteries, burning crops and buildings, harassing entire districts. Focussing on the inequalities that divided society, the rebels attacked the wealthy monks, rich landowners and the lawyers who wrote the documents perpetuating social distinctions. They demanded an end to serfdom, low rents on all lands and an amnesty for themselves.

Day after day the scale of violence widened, with local peacekeeping forces overwhelmed and the royal council hampered by lack of men to send against the rioters. Most of the army was away on campaign, in Scotland and France. John of Gaunt was far to the north of the capital, at-tempting to arrange a truce with the Scots. Emboldened by their unhindered success, and growing in numbers, the rebel armies marched on London, shouting "Death to all lawyers!" and "King Richard and the true commons!"

Like a horde of locusts the embattled villagers, armed with scythes and pitchforks, knives and thick cudgels, swarmed into the capital, breaking into houses, stealing food and plundering churches, "howling like men possessed," one chronicler wrote, threatening and terrorizing house-holders and merchants. Many in the city fled, but not the young king, who withstood the onslaught even after the rebels ransacked the Archbishop of Canterbury's Southwark mansion and the palace of John of Gaunt.

The night sky was red with the flames of burning buildings, and there were reports of murders and mayhem, of severed heads impaled on pikes, of criminals loosed from the city's prisons and of bands of looters break-ing into the private apartments of the king's mother, Queen Joan, and de-stroying her possessions.

Taking a group of armed nobles, King Richard rode to Mile End where the rebels from Essex were milling in disorder. They cheered him, and did not try to waylay or assault him. Showing great courage—for the rebels, at any moment, could have turned against him—Richard listened to their grievances and promised to give them what they wanted.

The following day he met with another huge crowd of rebels at Smithfield, and here the situation became much more dangerous. When the rebel leader Wat Tyler came too close to the king, the Lord Mayor struck him and killed him. Now the angry crowd began to close in. But Richard, firm in his authority, and with the courage of a seasoned commander, rode toward the advancing rioters.

"Sirs, will you kill your king?" he shouted. "I am your captain. Follow me."

And follow him they did, as far as Clerkenwell, where he convinced them that all their grievances would be redressed. Trusting in the king's promise, the mob dispersed.

It had been a remarkable feat of bravery, worthy of Edward III or the Black Prince. Richard had succeeded in halting a wave of mayhem almost single-handedly. And afterward, when he rode through Essex and Hertfordshire, supervising the trials and brutal punishment of the rebels (for he had no intention of genuinely granting them amnesty or ending serfdom; his promises had been a ruse), the magnates commended Richard as a worthy leader and protector of the public peace.

By the time he was seventeen, however, opinions had changed. The brave boy had grown into a seraphically handsome, narcissistic, dissolute young man, contemptuous of his elders and full of ridicule and hauteur. With his impudent young friends he mocked the knights of the court, his insolence an insult to the chivalrous ideals of his father and grandfather. Richard thought highly of himself, and demanded, as his grandfather never had, that others kneel before him. He lashed out, verbally and physically, at anyone who criticized him and he slighted his advisers discourteously.

With his "fair, round and feminine" face often flushed with irritation, his "abrupt and stammering" speech, his capriciousness, Richard gave offense. He was not manly, he was not kingly. Though capable of exertion, he was not warlike and his liking for extravagantly fashionable clothing and jewels seemed to his elders excessive. His refined tastes grated on more conventional sensibilities; in an age when garbage was thrown on the floor and hands were wiped on the tapestries, Richard carried small squares of linen with which to wipe his nose—an unheard-of daintiness.

But it was above all the air of languor and sensuality, the dissipation of

Richard and his friends that worried his uncles and other critics. The court had been turned into an erotic pleasure palace, and at the center of it all was Robert de Vere, earl of Oxford, the king's favorite and chamberlain. De Vere had cast off his wife and formed a liaison with one of the court ladies, but that was only the beginning of scandal; de Vere was said to be guilty of "obscene familiarity" with the king, and Richard was rumored to be so besotted with his favorite that he was planning to make him king of Ireland.

Chroniclers condemned the king and his friends as "more knights of Venus than of Bellona, worthier in chamber than in field, sharper in tongue than in lance." They stayed up all night drinking. They emulated the ancient Romans, wearing togas and reclining on couches to eat. They cultivated effete mannerisms and indulged their palates and their lascivious urges—meanwhile neglecting the kingdom and its welfare.

The king's critics watched in deepening dissatisfaction as the eighteen-year-old Richard led an expedition to Scotland. He advanced as far as Edinburgh, then quickly retreated, having spent a great deal of money and accomplished nothing. It was time for intervention.

Taking advantage of the fact that Richard's powerful protector John of Gaunt was out of the country, a group of lords led by the king's uncle Thomas, duke of Gloucester, chastised the king and insisted that Robert de Vere and others be deprived of their offices and punished. The demands of the five Lords Appellant, as the king's opponents were called, were enforced by the Parliament of 1388, but their real force lay elsewhere. Each of the Lords Appellant had a large private army. In addition, there was the precedent of the events of 1327, when Edward II had been guilty of misgovernment and forced to abdicate.

Though he never fully realized it, Richard had always held his throne on suffrance. As long as John of Gaunt, with his army, backed Richard, none dared move against him. But without Gaunt's support he was, and always had been, vulnerable.

Richard gave in, and was forced to acquiesce in the dismissal and execution of several of his friends and officials. Robert de Vere was not among them; he escaped capture, raised an army and attempted to defy the Lords Appellant and Parliament. But his effort failed, and he went into exile in France, where he died in 1391.

The king was chastened, but not humbled. He was contemptuous of the new council placed in authority over him, and determined to regain his preeminence by raising a strong private army of his own. He traveled through the west country and the north, gathering longbowmen and men-at-arms, sworn to be loyal to him, men to whom he gave his insignia, the badge of the white hart and a golden badge of the sun.

Instead of maturing under the tutelage of his elders, Richard became embattled against them, and narrowly preoccupied with his own eminence and destiny. He commissioned sculptors to create images of the thirteen kings who had ruled from the time of Edward the Confessor to Richard's own time, to be placed in Westminster Hall. He took the Confessor as his particular patron, identifying himself with his saintly predecessor whose powers were not only regal but spiritual. Richard sent an embassy to Rome in an effort to have his predecessor Edward II canonized, and investigated the reports of miracles experienced at the late king's tomb.

More and more Richard was drawn toward exploring the sacred powers of kingship. His close identification with Edward the Confessor was a sign of this preoccupation. When Richard discovered, in the Tower, a golden eagle with a stone ampulla containing holy oil—oil which he believed had been given to Thomas Becket by the Virgin Mary—he wanted to repeat his coronation in order to be anointed with it. He wore the gold eagle, believing that its wonderworking powers would assure him success and abundance. He began consulting astrologers, and collecting prophecies and writings on magic; his physician, a monk of Winchcombe, was known not only as a healer but as a "weaver of spells."

Richard's fascination with the occult may well have been a sign of fear. At twenty-two, he declared his independence of councils and advisers, and began to reign on his own. But he knew that the older men of the court (with the exception of his faithful uncle John) neither approved of him nor respected him, and he was afraid of them. He dreaded becoming the victim of poison or sorcery, as he believed King Charles VI of France had been.

The king was concerned about his health, and was continually consulting physicians and taking medicine. He had a painful stone in his urinary tract, and may have had other chronic complaints. His queen, the tiny, ill-favored Anne of Bohemia, was childless. Whether this was due to her infertility, or to the king's impotence (or homosexuality) or some physical defect, is unknown. Some historians have suggested that Richard and Anne actually made a pact to have a chaste marriage—a mode of piety commonly met with at late fourteenth-century courts.

All across England, crops failed in the summer of 1390, and the harvest was meager. By spring 1391 there was famine in many districts, and at the same time, wool prices fell, causing great hardship. Plague revisited the towns, once again the bells tolled incessantly for the dead and mass graves had to be dug to hold the corpses.

The king, his treasury depleted, refused to cut back on his expenditures. With borrowed funds he staged costly tournaments to which he invited knights and magnates from abroad, feeding and housing them at his expense, handing out generous prizes and purses of coins to the champions. Gowned in magnificence, glittering with gems, Richard sat on his high golden throne, surrounded by precious hangings embroidered with blazing suns.

"The more we bestow honors on wise and honorable men," he announced, "the more our crown is adorned with gems and precious stones." There was a purpose behind his generosity, for the king had a new goal. Among the prophecies revealed to him by flatterers was one which claimed that he was destined to be more than a mere king: that he would become Holy Roman Emperor, and as such, "the greatest among the princes of the world."

The office of Holy Roman Emperor was elective, not hereditary, and by the 1390s it had become largely ceremonial. Seven imperial electors met to choose the emperor, and Richard approached a number of them in hopes of winning their votes. As Holy Roman Emperor, Richard would no longer have to be concerned about his critics in England; he would belong to a realm beyond criticism, beyond nationality. He would be on a par with the other lord of Christendom, the pope—though the papal office, in the 1390s, was disputed between rival claimants, its prestige lowered and its moral authority greatly reduced.

The more Richard's vanity increased, the more he aspired to act on a larger, Europe-wide stage. He dreamed of going on crusade to the Holy Land, in concert with other sovereigns, of subduing the enemies of Christ. An entourage of astrologers and soothsayers encouraged his ambitions and fed his grandiose dreams.

By the time King Richard reached his late twenties many of those in his household feared for his mental balance. His wife Anne died in 1394 and in the months following her death the king's behavior became erratic and extreme. He ordered the palace where she died, Sheen Manor, torn down, so that not a single brick or stone was left standing. He made a dramatic declaration that for a year he would enter no building where he and Anne had been together. And at the queen's elaborate funeral he became violent.

The earl of Arundel (one of the Lords Appellant from years earlier) arrived late at the cathedral and got up to leave before the service was over. Richard seized a wooden rod from one of the attendants and struck the earl on the head. He crumpled at the king's feet, bleeding, yet the berserk Richard went on beating him until restrained by members of his household. Aghast at the desecration, the clergy stopped the service until the blood could be washed away and rituals of purification carried out.

Richard's next project was to negotiate his remarriage—to the six-year-old daughter of Charles VI of France. On a windswept plain near the town of Ardres, near English-held Calais, the English and French kings met. (Over a century later, Henry VIII and Francis I would meet on the same ground, and call their splendid encounter "The Field of Cloth of Gold.") Amid elaborate pageantry, the two kings embraced, and Richard's child-bride Isabella was brought to him, a tiny figure on a great war-horse, a small jeweled crown on her head.

That Isabella could not be expected to have children for many years concerned Richard less than that she brought him a dowry of eight hundred thousand francs, and that with their marriage, in November of 1396, a long truce in the war with France began. Richard had hopes of joining his new father-in-law on crusade, realizing his lifelong dream, but his hopes came to nothing when an advance force of French knights was slaughtered by the Turks at Nicopolis.

Disappointed as a crusader, trying harder than ever to attain the imperial crown, Richard intensified his dealings with the German electors, sending them gifts and receiving their representatives in England. At the same time, he seems to have become convinced that his enemies in England were plotting to dethrone him. Partly to forestall the danger in which he saw himself, partly to convince the electors that he was master of his kingdom, and partly on the advice of an astrologer he brought to court from Paris, Richard decided to act.

He ordered the arrest of three of the five Lords Appellant—his uncle Thomas of Gloucester, the earl of Arundel (who had survived the king's ferocious beating), and the earl of Warwick. Gloucester was murdered on the king's orders at Calais, Arundel was beheaded and Warwick exiled to the Isle of Man. The two remaining former Appellants, John of Gaunt's son Henry Bolingbroke and Thomas Mowbray, earl of Nottingham, were also exiled.

The king's sudden, seemingly unprovoked action against the five lords disturbed the realm, especially when it was learned that Gloucester had died. No one believed the king when he insisted that the men were pun-

ished for present crimes and not for their past opposition to him. Gloucester, who had earned a reputation as "the good duke," was mourned. The
punishments raised alarm. Would the king's wrath fall on others? Would
there be warfare within the realm, between the magnates' private armies?
King Richard was known to have a large force of Welshmen and immediately after the arrests of Gloucester, Arundel and Warwick he began to
fortify his castles and to seize other strongholds where he garrisoned his
troops. A new force of two thousand longbowmen was raised in Chester,
and to pay for it, and for his other men-at-arms, Richard forced his subjects to make him new loans.

"Savagery held sway by the sword," wrote John Gower about this troubled season. King Richard trusted no one, and confided to Albert of
Bavaria that since his childhood, "nobles and members of the royal household had traitorously conspired to disinherit our crown and usurp our real
power." Now, at last, he had begun to take his revenge, "to the destruction
and ruin of their persons." The traitors were destroyed, he told Albert.
"We have threshed them out even to the husks."

Richard had destroyed his enemies, yet he was still fearful. Night and
day, everywhere he went, the king was accompanied by a bodyguard of
soldiers, "armed as for war." They stood outside his bedchamber at night,
their huge battleaxes at the ready, watching for enemies. Should the worst
happen, and the king's life be threatened, he had prepared a safe place to
go, Holt Castle in Chester, where he had chests of treasure stored away
and where his faithful archers would protect him.

In November of 1398 a comet blazed across the night sky, an omen of
disaster. "Burning with extraordinary intensity," the comet was thought to
foretell the death of a king, or a great transformation or upheaval. The
king consulted his occult advisers, and received disturbing confirmation
that an event of major significance was about to occur. All the laurel trees,
he was told, had withered—and then mysteriously revived. A river in
Bedfordshire had suddenly changed its course, indicating that nature herself was being altered, just as alterations were about to occur in the political realm.

There was a death, in February of 1399, but it was not the death of a
king; it was the death of John of Gaunt. Richard seized his uncle's wealth
and redoubled his guard, knowing that his cousin Henry Bolingbroke,
John's heir, would try to seek revenge. With the death of John of Gaunt the
last pillar of stability in the realm fell. The king lost the loyalty of his sub-

jects. In the words of one chronicler, "all the good hearts of the realm clean turned away from him."

Richard was in Ireland, pursuing rebels there, when he learned that Henry Bolingbroke had landed at Ravenspur on the Humber with a small band of men and was marching south. The king hesitated, then took refuge at Conway castle in Wales. The number of Henry's supporters steadily grew, while the king's men deserted him. Richard was captured and taken to the Tower, where he was forced to abdicate in September 1399. Parliament declared Henry Bolingbroke king, as Henry IV.

The swift reversal of fortune that swept Richard II from his throne revealed how fragile his rule had always been. The shadow of his grandfather, the great King Edward III, had always hung over him, at once a validation and a reproach. For if Richard was Edward's chosen heir, he was also Edward's opposite, shallow and dissolute where Edward had been valorous, weak and vain where Edward had shown inner strength, ineffectual on the battlefield (indeed Richard had never gone near a battlefield) where Edward had won renown through military might. Richard's slender authority could not survive once Edward's powerful son John of Gaunt was no longer there to defend it.

Henry Bolingbroke was accepted as king, but as long as the deposed Richard lived, there were bound to be those who rallied to him, to make him a focus of rebellion. To prevent this he was killed, either by starvation or smothering, in February of 1400, and his body was brought to London and displayed, so that no impostors could claim his identity.

HENRY IV

(1399–1413)

"IN THE NAME OF THE FATHER, SON AND HOLY GHOST,
I, HENRY OF LANCASTER, CHALLENGE THIS REALM OF
ENGLAND AND THE CROWN . . . THROUGH THAT RIGHT
THAT GOD OF HIS GRACE HATH SENT ME WITH THE
HELP OF MY KIN AND OF MY FRIENDS TO RECOVER IT,
THE WHICH REALM WAS IN POINT TO BE UNDONE FOR
DEFAULT OF GOVERNANCE AND UNDOING OF THE
GOOD LAWS."

—HENRY BOLINGBROKE

On a large open field outside the English-held town of Calais in 1390 a great tournament was held. The finest jousters from England, France, the Italian and German states and even as far away as Hungary came to test their skills and fight for the generous prizes being offered. For thirty days the contest went on, with a large crowd watching and cheering on their favorites.

Among the English knights, one stood out: the stocky, redheaded Henry Bolingbroke, son of the great English magnate John of Gaunt. Henry was twenty-four, at the peak of his strength and agility. One who saw him called his performance "exceedingly strenuous," and others noted how generous he was, off the field, giving gifts and throwing handfuls of coins to his admirers with hearty abandon.

Henry was an attractive figure, chivalrous and courteous, vigorous and wholesome and full of valor. Again and again he pitted his solid, muscular body against those of taller and stronger men, splintering lances in the harsh shock of encounter, always emerging victorious. With each victory a roar went up from the onlookers. "Bolingbroke! Bolingbroke!" He was the man of the hour, the champion, the popular hero.

The great Calais tournament established Henry as a leading international competitor on the field of arms. His fame spread. Invitations to other tournaments in faroff lands came to him, and other invitations to travel. The Duke of Bourbon was preparing an expedition to Barbary in North Africa, and asked Henry to join it; he wanted to, but the time was too short to allow sufficient preparation, and he had to decline.

Henry was swiftly becoming a knight of international repute, but his roots were firmly planted in England. He was heir to both his father's and his late mother's extensive lands and titles, which included dozens of castles and manors, the vast estates and ducal title of Lancaster, and the earldoms of Derby, Lincoln and Leicester. He had a wife in England, the heiress Mary Bohun, and a growing family. He was the King of England's cousin, and had been raised with King Richard at the English royal court. And he had played a role in English politics, though not out of ambition; his ambition was concentrated on being the best jouster in the realm.

Henry had been born at his father's castle of Bolingbroke in Lincolnshire in 1366 (not 1367, as was formerly thought), and spent his earliest years with his two sisters Philippa and Elizabeth. Their mother, Blanche of Lancaster, died when Henry was only three years old, and a stepmother, Constance of Castile, took her place. But John of Gaunt was never attached to his second wife Constance, and was in love with Katherine Swinford, with whom he had six children, Henry's half-brothers and sisters.

At the age of nine Henry was sent to live at court, in the household of the future King Richard, then the eight-year-old Prince of Wales. For the next six years the boys were together a great deal. At Richard's coronation in 1377, Henry bore the ceremonial sword of mercy. When Richard married Anne of Bohemia, Henry was present at the ceremony. With other young nobles, Richard and Henry learned to ride, fence, joust and fight— and Henry was clearly the toughest and most skilled of them all.

Overshadowing whatever rapport, or lack of rapport, there was between the young king and his companion was the king's dependence on Henry's father. With John of Gaunt King Richard had an uneasy relationship; he relied on John's immense power and personal influence to prop up his shaky throne, yet at the same time he resented his dependency, and constantly quarreled with John. (So menacing did Richard become, in fact, that from time to time John wore an iron breastplate under his gown, to protect himself against an assault by his royal master.)

Richard distrusted both his uncle John and his cousin Henry, and the older he became, the more his distrust grew. Late in his reign he confided to a correspondent that he had always feared he would one day be deposed. And if his throne were to be taken from him, it would most likely be by either his powerful uncle John or his clever, athletic, personable cousin Henry.

For those who saw the two boys at court could not but favor Henry over his royal cousin. Richard grew into a haughty, dissolute adolescent, vain and self-absorbed, effete and unmanly. Henry, on the other hand, was confident and outgoing, open-handed and likable and full of daring. Richard shunned the warlike arts, Henry eagerly embraced them. Richard surrounded himself with decadent, pleasure-loving companions while Henry sought the more robust company of other aggressive young knights, eager to prove themselves on the field of honor.

The contrast between the two young men could hardly have been sharper. Unfortunately, the writers of the time recorded almost nothing about how they got along—except for one telling incident.

In June of 1381, when Richard was fourteen and Henry fifteen, peasant rebels invaded London and the king, showing unexpected courage, confronted them. Members of his court, including some of the royal ministers and Henry Bolingbroke, took refuge in the Tower, which was poorly defended, the drawbridge being left down.

The mob swarmed in, seized the ministers, and summarily executed them. They also seized Henry, and would have killed him had he not been rescued and taken to safety by an obscure knight, John Ferrour—to whom Henry was forever grateful.

At the time it was said that King Richard deliberately left Henry at the mercy of the murderous peasants, and this may have been true. What Henry made of the terrifying incident, and how he interpreted his cousin's behavior, is unknown. However, he did not return to live at Richard's court.

At the age of twenty-one, Henry Bolingbroke was among the five Lords Appellants who took it upon themselves to confront the king and rebuke him for misgovernment. Led by Henry's (and Richard's) uncle, Thomas of Gloucester, the Appellants demanded that Richard remove his unworthy favorites from office and that they be punished. It is possible that the Appellants discussed, and decided against, attempting to depose the king. When they made their demands, Richard acquiesced, removed his hated favorites, and submitted to the rule of the Appellants, who in effect were in charge of the government until the king reached his majority and declared himself independent of them.

Henry had been called in late to the Appellant challenge, valued by the other four Appellants for his prestige and for the large number of soldiers and retainers he could put into the field to intimidate the king. He was not eager to enlarge his influence, or to continue to exercise political power, and once Richard declared his liberty from the Appellants' governance, Henry returned to his family and to the adventure-seeking life he preferred.

Not long after the Calais tournament in which he excelled, in the autumn of 1390 Henry set out with a party of some two hundred knights, squires, grooms and servants for Lithuania, where the Teutonic Knights were attempting to conquer and convert the pagan Lithuanians. It was the last remaining area in the West where Christianity had not yet penetrated, and Henry, a crusader at heart and a devout, observant Christian (though hardly a saint in morals), meant to do his part to spread the gospel.

Thanks largely to Henry and his knights, the Lithuanians were defeated at Kovno and the city of Vilna was besieged. Though the siege later had to be abandoned, and the English knights returned home in the spring of 1391, their contribution had not been insignificant, and Henry had fought valiantly.

In the following year Henry set out once again with a party of some two hundred knights and servants, this time bound for Prussia. This expedition turned into a pilgrimage to the Holy Land for Henry himself. He visited the Holy Sepulchre (the only medieval English king ever to do so; even Richard I did not get to Jerusalem) and along the way, spent time at Rhodes, Cyprus, Venice, Milan, Pavia, Frankfurt and Paris. Everywhere Henry went, his reputation preceded him, and he was welcomed and feted by such dignitaries as Duke Albert of Austria, the Doge of Venice, and the Duke of Milan.

In the early 1390s Henry was at the pinnacle of his repute, as famed for his crusading piety and chivalrous charm as he was for his fighting skills. He was an international celebrity, a paragon; young men emulated him, young women, such as Lucia Visconti, fell in love with him and swore they would marry no one else.

Returning to England in 1393, life must have seemed tame, and indeed by 1396 Henry was eager to go on another adventure, this time to Friesland. But John of Gaunt intervened to prevent his son from leaving. By this time Henry had become a widower with six children, Mary Bohun having died in childbirth in 1394, and the mundane affairs of a great aristocrat— land disputes, estate supervision, overseeing the nurture and education of his children—preoccupied Henry, as did the worsening political situation in England.

In 1397 King Richard, who was increasingly tyrannical and showed signs of being mentally unbalanced, suddenly turned on three of the former Lords Appellant. Thomas of Gloucester was murdered, the earl of Arundel executed and the earl of Warwick forced to forfeit his goods and leave the realm. The remaining two Lords, Henry Bolingbroke and Thomas Mowbray, earl of Nottingham, became embroiled in a quarrel whose precise nature is a matter of debate among historians. A court of chivalry at Windsor ordered that the two should meet in formal combat to decide the outcome of their quarrel, and the combat was set to take place on St. Lambert's Day, September 16, 1398.

No doubt eager to appear in the lists once again, Henry prepared carefully, and was ready to meet the challenge. A large crowd assembled at Coventry to watch the fighting, expecting Henry Bolingbroke to emerge the victor. He made his appearance, a magnificent figure on a white warhorse, his armor gleaming against a backdrop of blue velvet embroidered with gold swans and antelopes. Mowbray too, gorgeously caparisoned, took up his position.

But at this point the king, presiding from a high dais, threw down his baton and stopped the combat from proceeding. He announced that both Bolingbroke and Mowbray were to be banished from the realm.

It was a stunning turn of events, but Henry, for the moment at least, did not protest. He obediently left England and went to Paris, where he was taken in by the French royal court—indeed his reception was so enthusiastic that it alarmed Richard. For four months Henry enjoyed himself in Paris, no doubt participating in tournaments, hunting, renewing acquaintances he had made earlier, and waiting to see what course events would take in England. He sometimes went to the University of Paris to attend debates and lectures, remarking that while the English clerics were more subtle, those of Paris were more learned in theology. Henry was both learned—for an aristocrat—and well-read; having the time to devote to his intellectual interests must have been welcome.

Still, exile was uncomfortable, all the more so because Henry had had to leave his promising oldest son, Prince Hal, with the unstable and vengeful King Richard, as a hostage.

In February of 1399, Henry learned that his father John of Gaunt had died—and that King Richard had seized the immense inheritance that would otherwise have been Henry's, at the same time banishing him for life.

Taking the king's unacceptable actions as a challenge, Henry made preparations to return to England against the king's express orders, to regain the inheritance that he believed was rightfully his. In doing so, he would be breaking the law, as well as his feudal oath of obedience to his royal overlord. The venture would be morally as well as physically perilous. Yet he went ahead.

Henry might have hesitated, had he not known that King Richard was in Ireland, campaigning in remote areas where news would not reach him for days, perhaps weeks. Richard's regent in England, his brother the duke of York, was not likely to mount a formidable opposition; Henry did not fear him. However, Richard had taken Henry's son Hal with him to Ireland, and Hal would be at risk, once Richard learned that Henry had broken faith with him.

On July 4, 1399, Henry landed at Ravenspur in York, a region where he knew he could count on strong local support. He had three hundred men with him, and soon acquired more, as all the servants and retainers of his late father came to join him. Within days of his landing, Henry had acquired more support, from his brother-in-law the earl of Westmorland and from the even more powerful Henry Percy, earl of Northumberland. The Percies dominated the north. With their adherence to his cause, Henry achieved control of an important part of the country, and at this point, though he swore to the Percies that his intent was only to claim his inheritance, he may have begun to envision a larger goal.

Events were moving quickly. As Henry went south toward London, magnates from many parts of the realm came to join him, and by July 27 even the regent, the duke of York, brought many of his soldiers and threw his support behind Bolingbroke. Whatever loyalty Richard had once been able to command was simply melting away, and Henry, who may well have been surprised at the extent of his triumph (or perhaps he had expected it; the contemporary records reveal nothing of his expectations), saw that the throne was his for the taking.

By late July, he had decided to take it.

Entering Bristol with his army, Henry seized the king's most unpopular councilors, and ordered the arrest and beheading of the royal treasurer William Scrope. Then he sent Northumberland and others to capture the king.

Richard, who as noted above had feared usurpation throughout his reign, was now confronted with the fate he had long dreaded. His cousin, his boyhood rival, his nemesis had come to seize his realm.

Richard returned from Ireland as quickly as the contrary winds in the Irish Sea would permit, but could not persuade his fighting men to stand with him against the usurper. Betrayed by those he trusted, he was ambushed by Northumberland near Flint, captured and brought to London. On the way to the capital, Richard nearly escaped, eluding his captors and going out through an open window at night, but was recaptured before he had got far. Once he was under lock and key in the Tower of London, he was forced, under threat of death, to give up his throne.

Henry Bolingbroke now held the royal power, but he was not yet king. Richard had designated as his heir the seven-year-old earl of March, Edmund Mortimer, whose claim to the throne was stronger than Henry's. (Young Edmund was descended from Edward III's second son Lionel, while Henry's father John of Gaunt was Edward III's third son.) With the advice of lawyers, Henry drafted a carefully worded statement of his claim, in which he said that he "challenged" the crown "through the right that God of his grace hath sent me, with the help of my kin and friends to recover it."

No one was convinced by the ambiguous wording; Henry Bolingbroke, though a descendant of the late King Edward, and therefore of royal blood, had usurped the throne.

Because he had attained the throne by force (by "challenge," in his knightly phrase) and not by legal means, Henry's grasp on the crown remained precarious. The deposed King Richard languished in the Tower, awaiting rescue. Ambitious opportunists could overthrow King Henry in Richard's name.

Only a few months after Henry IV's coronation, at the Christmas festivities of 1399/1400, conspirators indeed plotted to overthrow him. They planned to pose as jousters come to Windsor for the Epiphany tournament the new king was holding. They would mingle with the crowd, and then, at a favorable moment, seize the king and his sons and kill them all.

Fortunately for Henry and his sons, one of the conspirators revealed the plot—just in time for Henry to gather up his sons and, with only two attendants, gallop away to safety. The conspirators took possession of Windsor Castle and proclaimed Richard king once again. But the same momentum that had propelled Henry to the throne now allowed him to raise an army once again, and with it he intimidated the conspirators into surrendering. Soon their heads were displayed on London Bridge.

As long as he lived, Richard was a threat to the stability of the realm. Sometime early in 1400, he died in captivity, probably either starved or smothered. His death was to haunt King Henry throughout his reign.

It was one thing to take the crown, it was quite another to hold it. Invading Scots threatened in the north, and for the first three years of his reign Henry and his magnates, the Percies of Northumberland, fought them. Not until 1402, at the Battle of Homildon Hill, were the Scottish armies pushed back and defeated. But in the following year the Percies, who had been the king's staunchest allies, rebelled against him, joining forces with the Welsh under their strong, seemingly unconquerable leader Owen Glyn Dwr (Glendower) and with insurgents from Cheshire and Shropshire who believed that King Richard was still alive and hoped to bring about his restoration.

Henry Hotspur, Northumberland's son and the principal conspirator, intended to capture Prince Hal, defeat the king and put the young earl of March on the throne. King Henry, informed of the plot, marched swiftly to Shrewsbury to rescue his son, then confronted Hotspur. On July 21, 1403, in a day-long battle of unusual ferocity and with high casualties, he won over the rebels and Hotspur was killed.

That the king survived the Battle of Shrewsbury was considered remarkable, given his insistence upon charging recklessly—many thought valiantly—into the forefront of the fighting and given the determination of the enemy to kill him. Many of those fighting to Henry's left and right were cut down; Prince Hal was severely wounded when an arrow struck him in the face.

It was the king's second narrow escape. Earlier, while campaigning against the Welsh, his tent had collapsed on top of him during a windstorm. Had he not been sleeping in his armor, he would have been crushed to death.

The longer he reigned, the less secure Henry felt. His enemies seemed to be hydra-headed, no sooner had he met the challenge of one rebellion or conspiracy than another, even more formidable, arose to take its place. To add to his anxieties, despite his vast personal wealth he was constantly in debt, and his military endeavors were at times undermined by lack of funds. When he sought to raise taxes, the Commons accused him of extravagance.

In 1405 a new crisis arose when, in addition to the ongoing Welsh menace, the French harassed the south coast and a group of magnates planned a new conspiracy to seize the throne. Among the conspirators was the Archbishop of York, Richard Scrope, who denounced the king for having taken the crown illegally and murdered King Richard. Henry acted quickly to prevent the conspirators from acting on their plans. He executed the principal plotters, and did not spare the archbishop—which horrified many of his subjects.

About a month after Scrope's death as Henry was out riding he suddenly felt a pain, as if he had received a blow from an opponent in combat. That night he felt as if his body were on fire, and woke up screaming.

It was the beginning of a long nightmare of pain and debility, which afflicted Henry for the remainder of his life. The nature of his illness has never been discovered; contemporaries believed it to be leprosy, because like a leper, his face and hands became disfigured and covered in weeping sores. It may have been syphilis, which was not unknown in the fifteenth century, or it may have been a combination of venereal disease and tubercular gangrene, or a series of blood clots in the brain. Whatever it was, it was chronic, and progressive. After 1405 King Henry was never again able to regain his full capacity.

Ill, worn out, old before his time, Henry had no choice but to turn over more and more of his responsibilities to his son Prince Hal and to his trusted associate Archbishop Arundel, who became chancellor in 1407. The king's illness darkened his mind. He became depressed, suspicious—especially of his son, with whom he was often at odds—and racked by guilt. Henry's last will, written in 1409, began with the words "I, Henry, sinful wretch . . ." and alluded to "the life I have misspent." At times he was completely incapacitated. From 1410 on, he withdrew more and more from court and had lost effective control of his government, and before long had become a complete invalid.

On March 20, 1413, Henry IV died at the age of fifty-five, full of remorse, repentant but no doubt fearful of eternal punishment. He who had ordered the execution of an archbishop was laid to rest in the chapel of the martyred archbishop Thomas Becket, where his second wife, Joan of Navarre, built him an altar tomb.

HENRY V

(1413–1422)

————— ✦ ⚜ ✦ —————

**"I AM THE SCOURGE OF GOD SENT TO PUNISH
THE PEOPLE OF GOD FOR THEIR SINS."**

—SHAKESPEARE, *HENRY V*

There is something chilling about the man who is arguably the best known and most widely admired of medieval English kings. Henry V was a cold and ruthlessly self-disciplined man, with an implacable singleness of purpose; his remarkable military gifts, coupled with his unswerving belief in his right, made him an invincible foe, and a great king. But his humanity suffered, and he was beset by fears and constrained by a rigid self-denial and a gloomy piety, and his life was shrouded by pessimism.

Henry was born into difficult circumstances. His father, the heroic jouster and tournament athlete Henry Bolingbroke, was at odds with the king, his cousin Richard II; eventually, when young Henry was twelve, King Richard sent Bolingbroke into exile.

Young Henry was caught up in the family discord, for though he was loyal to his father, he also admired his Uncle Richard, who had taken him to Ireland on campaign. There amid the dense forests and bogs, with the fearsome, long-haired, half-naked Irish warriors attacking the royal camp every night, the boy and his uncle forged a bond. King Richard knighted Henry, telling him to "be gallant and bold" and conquer.

While in Ireland Henry learned that his father had returned from his exile at the head of an army, and was taking over the kingdom. King Richard left Henry and the other highborn hostages at Trim Castle in County Meath, and crossed the Irish Sea—to be captured and imprisoned by Henry Bolingbroke (now Henry IV) and ultimately executed.

Now young Henry was heir to his father's usurped throne, and he gave evidence of a precocious ability in the knightly arts. Already at the age of ten he had appeared at a tournament in Essex, wielding a sword and riding a fine horse. He enjoyed hunting and falconry, was attracted to armaments and, apart from one serious childhood disease, was physically robust.

Prince Henry was much better educated than most heirs to the English throne. At the age of eight he was studying Latin, and he became an avid reader and book collector. He played the harp and gittern, "delighting in songs and musical instruments" as one of his biographers wrote. He may even have studied for a time at Queen's College, where his uncle, Henry Beaufort, was chancellor.

Emotionally, however, Henry may have been shortchanged, losing his mother at the early age of seven and his favorite uncle at thirteen, forced into a precocious maturity by his father who gave him his first military command, at the head of a band of seventeen men-at-arms and ninety-nine archers, when he was barely into his teens.

The Welsh campaign against Owen Glendower hardened as well as toughened the young prince, who was thrust into the midst of the fighting and who, in the course of doing battle with Glendower, ordered and watched gruesome beheadings and disembowellings. Another harsh initiation in the dangers of wielding power came when Henry was sixteen. Conspirators captured the prince, who had to be rescued by his father; in the resulting battle between King Henry and the plotters, young Henry was badly wounded when he was struck in the face by an arrow. Bravely he fought on, refusing to leave the field to treat his wound.

At sixteen, Prince Henry was made royal lieutenant of the Welsh marches. With energy and vigor he pursued the elusive rebel Glendower and his mountain fighters, capturing Glendower's captains, burning crops and terrorizing settlements, surmounting severe cold and coping with constant money shortages that forced him at times to sell his jewels to pay his men. He became an expert tactician, skilled at siegecraft and in the use of the giant guns that shot heavy stones against the walls of fortresses to devastating effect. In 1407/8 Prince Henry besieged Aberystwyth, and in the following year Harlech. Both surrendered, though Glendower himself remained at large.

In Wales, Prince Henry showed that he was not only an exceptionally talented commander but a strenuous, dogged fighter who would not give up. "I will do all that in me lies to withstand the rebels and preserve the English land," he wrote to his father in 1404. He did his best—but ascribed the outcome not to his own efforts but to divine will. "It is known," he said, "that victory is not in the multitude of the people but in the power of God."

Henry had grown into a handsome, slim, slight young man with an air of command and an unmistakably aristocratic posture and carriage. Though he wore his thatch of brown hair in a soldier's cut—long on top and shaved at back and sides—he seemed more an austere priest than a fighting man. There was an asceticism about him, a fastidiousness that belied his soldierly persona. He drove himself tirelessly, worked extremely hard and never lost sight of his primary purpose, whatever it was.

Yet there was another side to the prince. When he allowed himself to relax, he played cards and chess and backgammon, strummed his harp and listened to his minstrels, his goblet filled with his favorite Burgundy wine. Poets and actors looked to him for patronage, as did students and poor clerks. He had a weakness for low, loud company, and with his brothers, sometimes became involved in raucous tavern brawls or mildly criminal escapades. He was reputed to lie in wait, at night, for couriers coming to and from the palace, and then rob them.

The most thorny challenge Henry faced was dealing with his angry father, whose mind became clouded by illness and who was increasingly suspicious of his gifted son. Confrontations between Henry IV and his heir apparent became more and more frequent as King Henry's mental and physical health broke down and his son's impatience with the status quo increased.

For five years, from 1405 to 1410, while Prince Henry continued to wage war in Wales and the royal council, dominated by King Henry's preferred deputy, Archbishop Arundel, supervised the everyday running of government, the situation deteriorated.

Meanwhile France, England's traditional enemy, was showing renewed signs of hostility and when the French king, Charles VI, became insane (an odd parallel to Henry IV's own periods of mental incapacity), two political factions began a struggle for preeminence.

The way was open for the English to profit from the resulting turmoil. Ever since King John lost Normandy in the early thirteenth century, English kings had dreamed of recovering the old Angevin inheritance, and the Hundred Years War had been fought over the English kings' claim to the throne of France. But Henry IV and Prince Henry disagreed over how this should be accomplished, with the king, when lucid, preferring to back the Armagnac faction, and Prince Henry favoring an alliance with the other faction, the Burgundians.

The civil war in France became an ongoing source of friction at the English royal court, and Prince Henry, backed by a growing number of council members and nobles, pushed hard for a more aggressive policy toward the French. After several rocky years, during which Henry IV alternated between minimal competence and a comatose state, the prince forced an ultimate confrontation.

In September of 1412 Prince Henry, backed by a very large entourage, went to see his father at Westminster. The king was ill, unable to ride, barely able to sit; his mind wandered, sometimes leading him into a fantasy-world, sometimes able to retain a hazy grasp of affairs. But he still clung to his authority.

The prince, dressed, according to the chronicler, in an odd but symbolic blue satin robe full of hanging needles, stood before his father and poured out all that was in his heart. Clearly he was in torment, caught between those who urged him to force an abdication and his own conscience, which guided him to remain loyal. He knew that the king was angry and antagonistic toward him, and that the anger arose, at least in part, from incapacity. Perhaps he thought that by making an extravagant gesture he could jar the king out of his state of impotent hostility.

In any event, at the conclusion of his long speech the prince knelt in front of his father, took out his dagger and held it out toward the king.

"Father, I desire you in your honor of God, for the easing of your heart, to slay me with this dagger."

The king, appalled and mortified, threw the dagger away and tearfully forgave his son. Six months later Henry IV was dead, and the accession of Henry V was proclaimed.

In a blinding snowstorm, Henry V was crowned King of England in April 1413. But at the coronation banquet that followed, the new king seemed to ignore the splendor, the tables laden with heaping platters of meat and fish and sweets, the fantastic decorations in the shape of antelopes and eagles made of spun sugar. He had undergone an inward metamorphosis, and was all but indifferent, for the moment, to the outer world.

On the night his father died, conscious that the crown was now his, Henry had gone to the cell of an anchorite who lived in the south transept of Westminster Abbey. He stayed there all night, according to a chronicler, and "confessed himself of all his offenses, trespasses and insolencies of times past." Having purified himself in order to make himself worthy of the throne, Henry sent away his unsavory companions and "reformed and amended his life and manners." From the opening of his reign, his old occasional wildness was gone; suddenly "all his acts were changed into gravity and discretion."

It was a startling change—and apparently a sincere one. Henry was preparing himself, not only for the responsibilities of kingship, but for the great venture he meant to undertake: the conquest of France.

Almost from the first weeks of his reign, Henry was preparing for a massive cross-Channel invasion. He was carrying on negotiations with the French, ostensibly in an effort to prevent war. But he did not expect the negotiations to be fruitful. The Armagnac faction offered him lands in Aquitaine plus Charles VI's daughter Catherine as a bride, along with a dowry of six hundred thousand crowns, if he would agree to suspend his invasion plans, but he refused this. Nothing less than all of France would satisfy him.

Narrowly escaping assassination by two groups of plotters, Lollard heretics and aristocratic conspirators, Henry coolly went ahead preparing his army, raising loans from every possible source, including wealthy merchants, nobles, city corporations and great churchmen, and using the funds to buy guns, arrows, siege towers and battering rams. While overseeing the assembling of men and equipment, he found time to fulfill family obligations. He commissioned a copper statue of his late mother Mary Bohun, to be placed on her tomb in Leicester, and had the body of King Richard II brought to Westminster for burial. In arranging an honorable burial for the deposed King Richard, Henry was hoping to remind his subjects, many of whom believed Richard was still alive, and some of whom plotted to retake the throne in his name, that there was no uncertainty about his being deceased.

On August 11, 1415, King Henry set sail with the afternoon tide aboard the *Trinity Royal*, bound for Normandy. In his great armada were some ten thousand men-at-arms and archers, sixty-five gunners, many hundreds of armorers, farriers, bowmen and fletchers, engineers and sappers—and a band of trumpeters and fiddlers led by the king's master minstrel. Three of the ships caught fire and foundered, but the rest arrived safely on the rough stone beach at Clef de Caus on the Seine estuary near Harfleur.

As soon as the boats were unloaded, Henry began besieging Harfleur, bombarding the thick town walls with thousand-pound gunstones shot from immense, huge-bore bombards and culverins. Filled with energy and purpose, Henry was an active commander, working alongside his men, going without sleep in order to direct the placement and laborious loading of the guns. His efforts were rewarded when Harfleur surrendered late in September, and Henry, dressed in cloth of gold and seated on a throne, watched the formal ceremony from a hilltop opposite the town.

But the English army, camped on the flooded salt marshes surrounding the town, was swept by an epidemic of dysentery and many of the soldiers died. Others, fearing to die, deserted in large numbers. Henry led the sick and fatigued remnant on a march northeastward, intent on besieging Calais. But at Agincourt they encountered a very large French force, three times as large as the English army, and battle was joined.

Bringing to bear all his experience from years of fighting the Welsh, Henry chose his positions with great skill, and massed his lethal archers with their strong six-foot longbows and steel-tipped arrows behind a wall of sharpened stakes. The French crossbowmen, with their heavier weapons and much slower rate of fire, were outmatched, and the French cavalry could make no headway against the deadly firepower of the English arrows, which could pierce plate armor.

The bloodbath took only a few hours, and when it was ended, some six thousand of the French lay dead, while the English lost only a few hundred. While the English were stripping the helpless French prisoners, Henry became alarmed by a rumor that another French attack was imminent. To prevent the prisoners from escaping, he ordered them all put to death, except for those with the highest ransoms. It was a calculated, and profoundly unchivalrous, decision, but the sight of the coldblooded slaughter deterred the French from launching a second attack.

Agincourt was as stunning a victory as English arms had ever achieved, and the king himself, young and agile, a striking figure (and an easy target) in his gleaming burnished armor, velvet surcoat and jewelled crown was the most furious fighter of all. He led his men-at-arms personally, encouraging and heartening the tired soldiers, dashing in to save the life of his brother Humphrey, risking his life again and again—and emerging victorious.

Duke William and his fleet cross the Channel to Pevensey.
Musée de la Tapisserie, Bayeux, France/Bridgeman Art Library

Thomas Becket, at top right, taking leave of Henry II to go into exile.
British Library, London/Bridgeman Art Library

Edward I pays homage to
the King of France, Philip IV.
*Bibliothèque Nationale,
Paris/Bridgeman Art Library*

Effigy of King Henry IV, Canterbury Cathedral.
Canterbury Cathedral, Kent/Bridgeman Art Library

Portrait of King Henry V.
National Portrait Gallery, London/Bridgeman Art Library

Edward IV landing in
Calais, 1459.
*Musée Thomas Dobrée–Musée
Archéologique, Nantes/Bridgeman
Art Library*

Portrait of King Richard III.
Private collection/Bridgeman Art Library

Bust of King Henry VII.
Victoria and Albert Museum/
Bridgeman Art Library

Portrait of
King Edward VI.
Collection of the Earl of
Pembroke, Wilton House,
Wiltshire/Bridgeman
Art Library

Queen Mary I.
Isabella Stewart Gardner Museum, Boston/Bridgeman Art Library

Idealized portrait of
Queen Elizabeth I.
*Palazzo Pitti, Florence/
Bridgeman Art Library*

King Charles I in
garter robes.
*Wallace Collection,
London/Bridgeman Art
Library*

Inspired by his genuine valor, Henry's men gave their utmost.

"Sirs and fellows," the king had told them before the battle began, "as I am true king and knight, for me this day shall never England ransom pay."

"Sir," they shouted back, "we pray God give you a good life and victory over your enemies!"

The news of the magnificent Agincourt victory electrified the English, and the rejoicings that followed, when King Henry returned from France, were intense and heartfelt. Agincourt, and its heroic royal victor, were beginning to become legend; the stirring Agincourt song, still sung today, reverberates with something of that long-forgotten joy:

Owre Kynge went forth to Normandy,
With grace and myght of chivalry;
The[re] God for hym wrought marvelously,
Wherefore Englonde may calle, and cry Deo gratias:
Deo gratias Anglia redde pro victoria.

Yet Henry, in the aftermath of his triumph, was sober and modest. Amid the shouts and cheers and pageantry of his triumphal parade in London, he maintained "an impassive countenance," and a "quiet demeanor," attributing the success of the battle to divine intervention.

The bookish, withdrawn private Henry was an enigma, scrupulous, idealistic, driven and utterly ruthless. He seemed to live in his own carefully constructed inner world where strict moral rules constrained him and where, as time went on, a deeply rooted fear of the demonic assailed him. In common with many of his subjects, Henry had a dread of dark occult forces, and the more worldly success he achieved, the more he feared to be struck down by them.

In 1419, four years after the Agincourt victory, the king asked that special prayers be said by all the English clergy, for divine protection against necromancers. He was convinced that black magic was being used against him, and that he needed to counteract it by every weapon in his spiritual arsenal.

By this time he had completed a second successful invasion of France, with an even larger army, conquering most of Normandy and well on his way to achieving his goal of conquering the whole of France. Yet he was compelled to devote himself to obsessive religious seeking, consulting hermits, visiting and revisiting the shrine of a wonderworking Yorkshire holy man, John of Bridlington, who had a reputation for casting out demons. He heard mass several times a day and spent hours at his devotions, refusing to allow anyone to disturb him while at prayer.

In an age of extremes, Henry was a man of extremes: exaggerated piety, exaggerated ambition, an exaggerated degree of success. And exaggerated fears.

By the Treaty of Troyes, signed in May of 1420, Henry V became heir apparent to the throne of France. King Charles was to keep his crown for as long as he lived. But after his death, Henry would become King of France, and in the interim he agreed to continue the war—for most of the kingdom still lay out of Henry's control. He married Charles VI's daughter Catherine in June, and in December of 1421 a son, the future Henry VI, was born at Windsor. The infant was heir to both kingdoms.

When he became a father Henry was only thirty-four, but looked older. Strenuous campaigning, and the strain of his overregimented inner life had aged him prematurely and made him chronically ill. Always dour, he had become grim, and observers noticed that he dealt out ever more savage justice to his soldiers when they broke his regulations and treated the French victims of his sieges with ever more pitiless inhumanity.

During the siege of Meaux, in the winter of 1422, the king contracted a chronic illness. He fought off the weakness that invaded his body as he had fought the enemy, resolutely and with determination. But this battle he could not win. By summer he had become too feeble to ride. He continued to direct his men in the work of war even as his body failed him, having himself carried from place to place in a litter. But he grew more and more frail, and in late August he lay near death.

On his deathbed, instead of reflecting with satisfaction on his remarkable achievements Henry lamented that he had left so much undone. In particular, he was worried about his baby son, and made arrangements for his minority rule. The great work he had envisioned, the dual kingdom he had meant to leave to the infant prince, was unfinished, and might not survive a regency. All that he had worked for could be overturned quickly by a resurgent French army.

Had he lived, the king said, he would have brought all of Christendom together in a great fight against the Turks. He would have rebuilt the walls of Jerusalem, and made it a Christian city once again. But the forces of mortality had triumphed, and Henry, given his fear of the demonic, may have believed that his mortal illness was the work of the necromancers who had succeeded despite his clergy's prayers.

Henry died peacefully, "like one who fell asleep," on August 31, 1422. His corpse, boiled to separate muscle from bone, was sealed in a casket and taken to Calais, and then across the Channel to be buried in Westminster Abbey. During the long final journey mourners paid tribute to Henry as an extraordinary hero, "of whose superior in all nobleness, manhood and virtue" his biographer wrote, "it is not read nor heard amongst the princes of England since William of Normandy." His funeral was more magnificent than that of any king for many generations, and his legend continued to grow.

Stories were told of how the lithe, muscular young king, at the great battle of Agincourt, wore his heavy armor "like a light cloak" and fought with fearsome agility. Of how personally ethical he was, and how reverent. Of how he was cut down by an unkind fate while still young and valiant, and how he would have extended his conquests like another Alexander the Great had he been granted a longer span of years.

In actuality, had Henry lived longer, his shining repute might have been tarnished. For the French did resurge, and become formidable; he might not have conquered the remainder of the realm after all. His dream of reconquering Jerusalem would have been nearly impossible to achieve given the rising power of the Ottoman Turks. Eventually Henry would have had to confront the reality of England's near bankrupt state, a condition brought about by his costly warmaking. And the king himself, lonely and isolated, could in time have fallen prey to the derangement that bedeviled his father and would befall his son.

As it was, Henry lived on, resplendent in memory, the scourge of France and the victor of Agincourt, a troubled man but forever England's champion.

HENRY VI

(1422–1461, 1470–1471)

———◆꞉ꞏ✳꞉ꞏ◆———

KINGDOMS ARE BUT CARES,
STATE IS DEVOID OF STAY,
RICHES ARE READY SNARES,
AND HASTEN TO DECAY.

PLEASURE IS A PRIVY PRICK
WHICH VICE DOTH STILL PROVOKE;
POMP, IMPROMPT; AND FAME, A FLAME;
POWER, A SMOULDERING SMOKE.

WHO MEANETH TO REMOVE THE ROCK
OUT OF THE SLIMY MUD,
SHALL MIRE HIMSELF, AND HARDLY SCAPE
THE SWELLING OF THE FLOOD.

—KING HENRY VI

In his poem King Henry VI distilled his outlook on life: He looked on rulership as an anxious burden, disdained pomp and notoriety and distrusted pleasure. Wealth and power were impermanent and illusory at best, he thought; at worst they invited wrongdoing.

Such views were eccentric in a king, but then, Henry was unique in a number of ways, not least the fact that he became king as an infant.

The future Henry VI was born December 6, 1421, the son of King Henry V and Catherine de Valois, daughter of King Charles VI of France. When his illustrious father, conqueror of much of France, died in his mid-thirties he bequeathed to his baby son not one throne but two, the kingdom of England and also that of France, to which the father had been made heir by the humbled and defeated French king. Thus young Henry, half French and half English, entered a momentous inheritance, and at only nine months old he was being compared to the Christ child, the savior of his realms.

Perhaps no royal child could have met the expectations that went along with such a legacy. Young Henry, intelligent and curious, was an overly sensitive boy, gentle in manner and innocent in character, utterly lacking in the combative, self-assertive, warlike traits valued in a prince. Neither his quarrelsome uncles, the Duke of Gloucester and Cardinal Beaufort, nor his governor Richard Beauchamp, Earl of Warwick, were able to harden him, though the youthful king did not lack outspokenness. He once questioned his guardian whether, as a ruler, he ought to be exempt from punishment for misbehavior.

Lacking a father, and with his mother Catherine a remote figure, preoccupied with raising a second family with her new husband, the Welsh squire Owen Tudor, Henry did not develop strong affective ties. His mind was trained but his emotions seem to have been stunted, though he had a generous and compassionate heart.

At only eight years old King Henry was taken to France in an effort to defend his claim to the French throne. The lands his father had conquered were in danger of being lost, for a new leader had arisen in France, a charismatic peasant girl known as Joan the Maid, and her claims to supernatural revelations filled the English soldiers with dread.

Henry's tutors and confessors apparently convinced him that Joan, who claimed to hear the voices of saints, was nothing more than a witch, an instrument of the devil. (Henry later referred to her, with precocious eloquence, as "a repository of pestilent error.") He was housed in Bouvreuil Castle in Rouen, across the courtyard from a tower where Joan was imprisoned. After Joan's trial and execution the boy-king, now nine years old, was robed in magnificence and taken to Paris, where on December 16, 1431, he was crowned King of France.

The ceremonies were impressive, the banqueting sumptuous—despite some disappointment with the food, which had been cooked three days earlier and had spoiled—but the Parisians resented their half-English king and were loyal to the Valois claimant Charles VII, whose coronation at Rheims had preceded Henry's coronation at Paris. Henry returned to England having achieved a hollow triumph.

Henry entered adolescence a tall, slight boy of tender conscience with delicate features which "shone with goodness of heart," as a later chronicler wrote. Still in thrall to his disputatious uncles and Cardinal Beaufort, his occasional efforts to reconcile them to one another lacked force, and it was more and more apparent to all that the young king had none of his father's drive or authority, not to mention ambition. Instead of distinguishing himself as a conqueror, he seemed doomed to preside over the disintegration of the domains Henry V had seized. One by one the conquered territories were retaken by the French. When in 1435 Henry learned that Burgundy, England's ally against the French, had thrown its support to King Charles, he burst into tears.

On reaching his majority Henry stood out from among his courtiers for the singularity of his traits and tastes. He did not share other young noblemen's enjoyment of either hunting (he deplored bloodshed) or sex; indeed, when offered an entertainment of "a dance or show of young ladies with bared bosoms," he left the room, offended. The vulgarity and promiscuity of his servants and courtiers revolted his sensibilities, and he was said to have had hidden windows made through which he would spy on them, to prevent "any foolish impertinence of women coming into the house."

Most likely Henry was less a prig than an idealist, high-minded and personally pure. No doubt he suffered ridicule and isolation (beyond his isolation as king), and if some in his household admired him, many more denied him respect. For his values were not those of the ruling class. In an era of flamboyant and fantastic dress for both men and women, Henry wore only sober black gowns, "rejecting expressly," his biographer wrote, "all fashion." He wore a stiff, scratchy hair shirt next to his skin to mortify the flesh. He scorned jewels, avoided merrymaking and sought privacy in which "to refresh himself," complaining to his confessor that his hours of refreshment were constantly being disturbed by clerks and officers bringing him urgent business.

The things that mattered to Henry were not administrative or political affairs, but relieving suffering, alleviating want and promoting education and the arts. He founded Eton and King's College, Cambridge and watched over the building of these foundations with particular concern for the morals of the students. He pardoned criminals and deplored torture, even for traitors.

Once when riding through Cripplegate into London, Henry glimpsed part of a severed torso impaled on a tall stake. He asked what the gruesome thing was, and on being told that it was the quartered body of a traitor, he remarked, "Take it away. I will not have any Christian man so cruelly handled for my sake."

When he was twenty-one Henry began searching for a bride, and sent a portraitist to foreign courts to paint likenesses of possible candidates. The young woman he eventually chose, fifteen-year-old Margaret of Anjou, was the niece of Henry's enemy Charles VII and their marriage was intended to promote peace between England and France. Unfortunately, Margaret had a passionate, headstrong nature and a tendency to bully and dominate her gentle husband. Her vehement likes and dislikes became a disruptive force at court and what was worse, the queen had no children. For the first eight years of the royal marriage the king and queen were apart much of the time, and when they were together, the king's confessor encouraged Henry's natural inclination to chastity.

As a personal and political force, Henry VI was proving to be a nullity, much to England's detriment. He delegated authority to a trusted few, chief among them William de la Pole, Earl of Suffolk and later Edmund Beaufort, Duke of Somerset. Unable or unwilling to prevent divisive rivalries among his advisers, Henry neglected affairs and let his government drift. Monarchical power retreated, factional infighting increased.

Meanwhile England's military humiliation at the hands of the French reached its climax with the loss of all English-held territories save Calais. Parliament stepped in to impeach Suffolk, who was subsequently executed, and Somerset, unpopular with everyone but the king and queen (whose lover he was rumored to be), became locked in a struggle with his bitter personal rival, Richard, Duke of York.

The combat between the dukes of Somerset and York took center stage, with York invading London with armed followers and Somerset responding with an armed force of his own. All-out fighting was narrowly avoided, but the contest for power continued, and the people backed York. With the queen childless, and both York and Somerset claiming royal descent from brothers of King Edward III, the succession itself appeared to hang in the balance.

Amid the chaos a popular uprising in Kent, Cade's Rebellion, broke out and threatened the precarious position of the monarchy. The rebels blamed the destructive course of events on the king's ministers, not the king himself. False counselors had led King Henry astray, they said, and so impoverished the royal treasury that the king himself lacked even the money to buy food. The realm was "all out of good governance," and the common people faced ruin.

The Kentishmen were subdued, but the accusation of the rebel leaders, that good governance was not to be had in England, was uncomfortably accurate. Whether through naivete or neglect, King Henry had placed his trust in unworthy deputies, whose mismanagement of the French war, incompetent administration, and greedy pursuit of wealth and court preeminence had led to corruption, deep popular dissatisfaction and a state of near anarchy. Only the natural conservatism of the rural populace (Londoners were restive) and a strong tradition of loyalty to the anointed monarch prevented worse evils.

That the king chose his advisers unwisely was beyond dispute. Why he did so is harder to understand. From earliest childhood Henry had been dependent on others to govern his realm and make decisions on his behalf. Possibly he never outgrew this habit, and was inherently malleable and hence a prey to unprincipled power-seekers. His own unworldliness was undoubtedly another factor. He was genuinely indifferent to power himself—as he was to fame, wealth, and the prestige of high position. The virtues he admired, simplicity, profundity, spirituality, belonged not to the sphere of government but to private life. His own charitableness worked against him as king in causing him to forgive the blunders and crimes of his deputies.

Clearly Henry either lacked any deep grasp of his role as king, or he found his role so distasteful, so contrary to his nature, that he shunned its responsibilities. To him, as his poem quoted above indicates, the monarchy was simply a burden ("kingdoms are but cares"), a weight of anxieties and a ceaseless source of strain. Quite possibly his mental health had never been strong, and the multiple pressures of rulership, which to a sturdier man would have seemed challenges to be surmounted, caused Henry intolerable strain.

That strain grew unbearable in the summer of 1453. The king suffered a complete mental collapse, and became unresponsive.

Now the realm was truly in crisis. The queen was at last pregnant—her son Edward was born in October—ostensibly solving the problem of the succession, but the more immediate problem of who was to wield power on the king's behalf was to prove intractable.

The Duke of York was named Protector, the king's deputy Somerset was arrested and imprisoned. Though Henry recovered, temporarily, from his attack of melancholia he had permanently lost any vestige of true authority, and from 1455, when Richard of York's army defeated the royal forces at the first Battle of St. Albans, the king was nothing more than a figurehead.

For the next five years, the royal forces, inspired and led by the fierce, determined and often embattled Queen Margaret, were pitted against the followers of the Duke of York. The emblem of the royalists, or Lancastrians (so called from King Henry's descent from Henry IV, Duke of Lancaster), was a red rose, that of the Yorkists a white rose; their long quarrel became known as the Wars of the Roses.

King Henry alternated between periods of incapacity and periods of lucidity. Always a pacifist, he was able, in 1458, to preside over a charade of reconciliation between the warring factions, but the gesture was futile. In 1461 York's eldest son and heir Edward (York had been killed in battle) seized the throne and was crowned King Edward IV at Westminster Abbey.

In his fortieth year King Henry, once the monarch of two kingdoms, had now lost both realms.

The royal army was no match for the forces of the vigorous nineteen-year-old King Edward and his powerful supporter and ally, his cousin Richard Neville, Earl of Warwick (known to history as "The Kingmaker"). A bloody defeat at the Battle of Towton forced the royals to flee to Scotland.

Now Henry, lacking a throne, guarded by his wife and with a small entourage, became a fugitive. While Margaret attempted to rebuild the decimated royal army, hoping to gain allies among the Scots and the French, Henry languished, moved from one castle to another, protected by the remoteness of the bleak Northumberland hills and misty Scottish lakes. In 1463 Margaret left for France, and Henry, friendless and witless, reached his nadir. He was brought to London as a traitor and criminal and imprisoned in the Tower, where his jailers, according to his biographer, mocked and abused him.

It was nothing short of a martyrdom—or so Henry's admirers thought. An exalted king brought low, a humble and good man subjected to constant mistreatment. Ill fed, ill housed, "not cleanly kept as should seem such a prince," one contemporary wrote, wandering in his mind and denied all respect, abandoned by his erstwhile supporters, Henry languished for five years, a prisoner of King Edward.

But then abruptly, in the fall of 1470, his fortunes appeared to change. Once again there was unrest in England and in the resulting turmoil a new alliance had been forged, between Henry's wife Margaret and the earl of Warwick. The Lancastrian cause was revived, and Edward IV was forced to take refuge in the Burgundian Netherlands.

Now it suited Warwick to restore the bedraggled prisoner Henry to the throne. To his astonishment, Henry was brought from his cold, cramped

Tower quarters to the royal palace and addressed by the title of king. He was made to understand that his years of deprivation and suffering were at an end, and that King Edward had abandoned his crown and kingdom. Henry's old enemy Warwick begged to be forgiven, and sealed his pardon by betrothing his daughter to Henry's son Edward.

The year 1470 ended with Henry enjoying something of his former status and comforts—but not his former authority. For Warwick still governed all, and controlled Henry's every movement, where he lived, whom he saw, even what he wore and what he ate. He was nothing more than a puppet king, serving Warwick's interests, and when in March 1471 Edward IV came back from France, intent on retaking the kingdom for himself, Henry became a prize to be fought over. Once again Lancastrian and Yorkist forces took the field, and Henry was forced to join Edward's army, which prevailed over both Warwick and forces raised by Margaret.

Lest Henry become the focus of rebellion, Edward gave orders for him to be killed. Toward midnight on May 21, 1471, Henry was put to death, his body put on display afterwards so that there could be no mistaking his fate.

The circumstances of Henry VI's death, and his reputation for piety and generosity in life, combined to make the late king revered. As a ruler he had been a failure, but as a martyr he was looked on as a saint. His tomb in the Lady Chapel at Chertsey Abbey became a shrine to which pilgrims came seeking cures for their illnesses and help in their troubles. Miracles were reported, and the number of pilgrims steadily increased.

The late King Henry's posthumous fame, and the reverence his remains attracted, threatened the Yorkist kings who succeeded him. King Richard III moved Henry's body to St. George's Chapel in Windsor Castle in an attempt to control Henry's growing cult and counteract the rumors of miraculous cures occurring at his tomb. But when the Lancastrian Henry VII became king in 1485, he promoted the popularity of the late King Henry, and even made efforts to have him canonized—efforts which ultimately failed.

Henry VI never became a saint, but in popular memory he remained a crowned martyr, a good man who had the misfortune to live in turbulent and evil times. For generations after his death Henry was portrayed in church windows and carvings with a halo as well as the crown, orb and scepter of monarchy, and was remembered as an extraordinary king whose achievements spanned both this world and the next.

EDWARD IV

(1461–1483)

—◆+▷+✳+◁+◆—

"MEN OF EVERY RANK, CONDITION AND DEGREE OF
EXPERIENCE IN THE KINGDOM MARVELLED THAT
SUCH A GROSS MAN SO ADDICTED TO CONVIVIALITY,
DRUNKENNESS, EXTRAVAGANCE AND PASSION COULD
HAVE SUCH A WIDE MEMORY THAT THE NAMES AND
CIRCUMSTANCES OF ALMOST ALL MEN . . . WERE
KNOWN TO HIM JUST AS IF THEY WERE
DAILY WITHIN HIS SIGHT . . ."

—*THE CROWLAND CHRONICLE*

Edward IV came to power amid the turmoil of the disastrous reign of Henry VI. A weak and sensitive man, and a complete political incompetent, King Henry allowed the realm to unravel, while he drifted into madness. The power of the monarchy withered, good governance became only a distant memory and civil war broke out between the royal, or Lancastrian, forces and the rival Yorkist faction.

Edward was in his early teens when the so-called Wars of the Roses (a term unknown to Edward and his contemporaries, coming into general use only in the nineteenth century) began, and his father, Richard, Duke of York, assumed leadership of the Yorkist army. For five years, from 1455 to 1460, the two sides struggled, with Edward's father commanding the Yorkist forces and the queen, Margaret of Anjou, defending her feeble-minded husband's Lancastrian cause.

Young Edward was an active observer of events, a tall, good-looking, manly boy, somewhat coarse in his habits but outwardly devout. He had been born in Rouen in 1442, while his father was serving King Henry as Governor of Normandy. Later Edward lived on the Welsh marches, or borderlands, where rebellion was endemic and the overlordship of the king—an overlordship that was crumbling under Henry VI—had to be maintained by force.

As Richard of York's eldest son Edward was given military responsibilities at an early age, and proved to be an exceptionally able fighter and clever strategist. Though only seventeen, he joined his father when the latter was driven into exile in 1459, and helped to organize and lead the successful Yorkist invasion of England from Calais in the following year.

Throughout 1460 the warring factions continued to contend with each other, until in December, Richard of York met the Lancastrians at Wakefield; the Yorkists lost, and both Richard and Edward's younger brother Edmund were killed. Edward was not present; he was away in Wales, raising troops.

With Richard of York's death, Edward became the richest and highest-born nobleman in England—and the leader of the Yorkist forces. He was only eighteen years old.

Edward lost no time in demonstrating the effectiveness of his leadership. Within weeks of his father's death, he led his men against a Lancastrian army under Owen Tudor—the Welshman who had married Henry V's widow Catherine—and Owen's son Jasper Tudor at Mortimer's Cross in Herefordshire. Edward's vigorous and courageous assault carried the day, and Owen Tudor was executed.

Before the battle, a contemporary chronicler wrote, a remarkable vision was seen in the heavens: three suns appeared. In an age exceptionally alert for omens and portents, the awesome sight led to much speculation. Edward, the chronicler wrote, believed that the three suns were symbolic of the Christian Trinity, and meant that he and his men enjoyed divine favor. From then on, Edward used the "sun in splendor" as his personal badge.

Buoyed up by this supernatural sign, and at the urging of his cousin Richard Neville, Earl of Warwick, who now came to the fore as his dominant partner and political manager, Edward took steps to have himself declared king.

To be sure, the reigning king, Henry VI, was still very much alive, though no longer in his right mind. (At the Battle of Wakefield, Henry VI had sat under a tree, laughing and singing, while the rival armies surged around him.) But in the view of many, King Henry had forfeited the loyalty of his subjects by his well established incompetence; the realm required a new monarch. As to who had the legal right to select the new king, no one knew for certain.

On March 1, 1461, a ceremony was held in London at which Warwick's brother George Neville, Bishop of Exeter, asked the assembled crowd of Londoners whether King Henry was worthy to be king.

"Nay!" went up the cry from hundreds of throats.

Then Neville asked whether Edward was lawfully heir to the throne, being in the direct line of descent from Lionel, second son of Edward III.

"Yea!" came the shout of assent.

Edward was informed that the people had chosen him to be king. He solemnly put on royal robes and presided in Westminster Hall, acting the part of monarch. But it was not until his overwhelming victory over the Lancastrian army at the bloody battle of Towton on March 29, 1461, that his supremacy was assured. Margaret of Anjou took her weak-witted husband and fled to Scotland, leaving no one to challenge Edward's claim to the crown.

At last there was an end to all the turmoil, or so it appeared to the new king's subjects, who greeted his coronation in June of 1461 with joy and a pervasive sense of relief. Preceded by his two young brothers, eleven-year-old George and eight-year-old Richard, King Edward rode in procession to Westminster where, with all solemnity, he was crowned king. "Words fail me to relate how well the commons love and adore him," wrote an observer, "as if he were their God."

At last a competent, regal figure sat on the throne, a strong young man who had proven himself in battle. Edward brought his subjects hope; they trusted that he would restore order and just rule.

Edward's appearance alone was reassuring. Over 6'3" tall, golden-haired and handsome, with a royal bearing and an open, affable disposition, he could not have been less like the slight, delicate, vacant-eyed Henry VI, with his neurasthenic air and his aversion to conviviality. King Henry wore a hair shirt, scorned jewels and dressed in sober gowns; King Edward loved finery and adorned himself with jewels and sumptuous, colorful clothing. In personality the two kings were opposites, with Edward jovial, high-spirited and unbuttoned in contrast to Henry's prudish, fastidious and highminded air.

Even though Parliament confirmed Edward IV's title in November of 1461, his situation was in fact precarious, for there were still two anointed kings. Henry VI was not declared formally deposed; it was simply assumed that his right to rule had been nullified by his incompetence— coupled with the stigma of his descent from the usurper Henry Bolingbroke. As long as King Henry lived, the potential for future discord remained.

None of this appeared to trouble Edward in the least at the start of his reign. He enjoyed being king. The public role satisfied his instincts for self-display—he liked to dress in the latest fashion, and enjoyed being admired—and was at ease with all his subjects, from stable boys to bishops to great nobles. Getting along with people was one of Edward's most outstanding gifts. And he had a gift for enjoying himself, liking to stay up late, drinking and carousing with his favorite companions.

"In food and drink he was most immoderate," a contemporary wrote. "It was his habit . . . to take an emetic for the delight of gorging his stomach once more."

Sensual and self-indulgent Edward certainly was, yet he seems not to have been criticized for his behavior, probably because it did not interfere with the restoration of good government that was under way. Nor did Edward's other besetting vice, an apparently inexhaustible sexual appetite, lead to any lessening of his popularity.

The French chronicler Commynes wrote that Edward "thought upon nothing but women and that more than reason would." Young or mature, noble or lowborn, married or unmarried, women attracted Edward—and he "overcame them all by money and promises." If they were compliant, he took his pleasure—and then, "having conquered them, he dismissed them," handing them over to his friends. If they resisted him, as the widowed Lady Eleanor Butler did, he offered marriage—injudiciously, since the royal marriage was a matter of state.

Though undeniably indolent, the king had ambition. He was immensely wealthy, and sought to become more so through trade. Investing part of his fortune, he added to it through the profitable buying and selling of wool and cloth abroad, thus building up both the English woolen industry and the crown treasury. After the penury of the Lancastrian kings, the wealth of the Yorkist Edward IV was very welcome, especially to Parliament, which had been urging kings to "live of their own" so that no need for extraordinary taxation would arise.

While Edward was absorbed in merrymaking and money making, Warwick defended the throne and consolidated the Yorkist royal power. Tough and choleric, personally ambitious and very much aware that, like his cousin, he too had royal blood, Warwick seemed to court observers to be the true power in the realm, with the young and self-indulgent king a mere figurehead. It was an erroneous impression, for Edward, when he chose, could and did exert the superior authority. But Warwick, with his many offices, his influential family connections, and his omnipresence at court, gave the appearance of ruling Edward and making all important decisions—which made it all the more startling when Edward, in effect, declared his independence of Warwick in the fall of 1464, when he was twenty-two.

The issue, not surprisingly, was Edward's marriage.

Warwick had chosen a suitable potential bride, Bona of Savoy, sister-in-law of King Louis XI of France. But Edward was in love with the beautiful Elizabeth Woodville, a commoner, the widow of John Grey, Lord Ferrers, a Lancastrian knight. And Edward was intent on marrying for love.

His mother, Cecilly Neville, tried to dissuade him, saying that it was "not princely" to marry one of his own subjects "for a little wanton dotage on her person." His royal dignity required that he marry into another royal family, as nearly all his predecessors had done.

But Edward was stubborn. God had made the two of them love one another, he insisted. It was better to follow God's will than to seek a different marriage merely for the sake of advancing the interests of the throne. And besides, he added, since Elizabeth had already had two robust sons, she had proven her fertility, which was a crucial attribute in a queen.

On May 1, 1464, very early in the morning, Edward IV and Elizabeth Woodville were married, with only the priest, an altar boy, and three witnesses present. The marriage was so secret that it was not performed in a church, but in a small private room; not even Edward's servants knew about it, they thought he had gone out hunting. Since the newly married pair could not live together openly, they had to rely on intrigue in order to be together. Late at night, after all the king's servants were asleep, Elizabeth was brought into Edward's apartments; she must have left again long before dawn.

For five months this clandestine, romantic marriage continued, until in September 1464, Edward, "in right merry guise," revealed the truth to his council. He enjoyed the joke, but his councilors did not. Warwick was angry—and deeply embarrassed, as he had been negotiating in good faith on Edward's behalf for the hand of Bona of Savoy and was about to leave for France to finalize the terms of the marriage contract. Not only would England's interests be damaged by the loss of the foreign alliance, but Warwick's own prospects were sure to be harmed, for Louis XI had promised that Warwick would profit as the diplomat who negotiated the Savoyard marriage.

Edward's alliance with Elizabeth Woodville embittered his relations with his cousin Warwick, and indeed with most of the magnates, who regarded the new queen as not only unworthy to be her husband's consort but as greedy and manipulative. The fact that she was poor, and that she had a large and hungry family—five brothers and seven unmarried sisters in addition to her two wastrel sons—deepened their suspicions.

The Woodvilles quickly took advantage of their rise in status; Elizabeth's sisters married into wealthy titled families, and one of her brothers, the twenty-year-old John Woodville, took as his bride the eighty-year-old Duchess of Norfolk. ("A diabolical marriage," in the view of one contemporary chronicler.) Not all the Woodvilles were ambitious. Elizabeth's brother Anthony Woodville, Earl Rivers, was a man of culture as well as a fine jouster; he translated books from French to English and was a model of good taste and chivalric manners. But her dissolute sons, Thomas and Richard Grey, were a disgrace. Along with their uncle Edward Woodville, Thomas and Richard joined the young king—who was nearer their age than his wife's—in drinking and overeating and late-night debauchery, and had few redeeming qualities.

Edward IV's crown was strengthened in 1465 when Henry VI was captured and brought to London. He was delivered to the Tower and imprisoned there, uncomfortably, to prevent any revival of Lancastrian resistance. Opposition arose, however, from the alienated Warwick, whose advice Edward ignored with increasing frequency. Warwick began plotting with Edward's brother George, Duke of Clarence, persuading the foolish, egotistical eighteen-year-old George that he could become king; all that was required was for Parliament to declare Edward IV deposed.

In July of 1469, Warwick stirred up rebellion in the north and midlands, then sailed with George to Calais, where George married Warwick's daughter Isabel, against King Edward's explicit prohibition. Edward was preoccupied with the rebellion, and soon found himself overwhelmed. Gambling on his subjects' loyalty, Edward surrendered to Warwick—who promptly discovered that the king was indispensable. It was impossible to keep order in the realm, much less to govern, without him.

But when Warwick rebelled a second time, in 1470, Edward was forced to flee to the Low Countries, taking only a few supporters with him. The sudden reversal of fortune found him unprepared. He had neither money nor treasure and was forced to pay for his passage across the Channel by giving the master of the ship a costly fur-trimmed gown.

In London, Warwick celebrated his triumph by bringing the poor bedraggled prisoner Henry VI out of captivity and restoring him as king—an abrupt and thoroughly bewildering transition. George of Clarence was rudely forgotten as Warwick paraded the frail, pallid former royal prisoner before the Londoners, controlling his every movement and audaciously announcing that the restored king would marry Warwick's daughter Anne.

Meanwhile in Flanders, Edward, not overly perturbed by the course events had taken, turned to his brother-in-law Charles the Bold for protection and help, and also to his business contacts among the Flemish merchants. His own vast fortune no doubt also helped to sustain his confidence. He stayed with the governor of Holland, Louis of Bruges, and during his sojourn, interested himself in Louis's impressive collection of manuscripts and also in the new art of printing with movable type.

By March of 1471 Edward had assembled a fleet of thirty-six ships, most of them hired or lent to him by the merchants of the Hanse, and a force of twelve hundred men. He set sail from Flushing on March 11, and immediately encountered storms which dispersed the small fleet and threatened to thwart the entire undertaking. Surviving the extremely rough Channel crossing, the ships limped into port, only to discover that Warwick had fortified the eastern coast of England and had sent armed supporters to defy the invaders.

At this perilous juncture Edward managed to bring his ships into harbor at Holderness and to land his men safely. Neither Warwick nor the restored King Henry had gained the loyalty of the kingdom, and as soon as Edward landed, his former subjects began to declare themselves loyal to him. Tentatively he moved his men southward, toward London, expecting resistance. But Warwick did not at first offer battle and the march south continued. Soon Edward was joined by his contrite brother George, who asked his forgiveness. "Armor and weapons laid apart on both sides," a chronicler wrote, "the brothers gladly embraced one another."

Two battles now determined the contest for the throne. At Barnet, Edward defeated Warwick, who died in the fighting. A few weeks later, at Tewkesbury, Edward's army routed the forces of Margaret of Anjou, and shortly thereafter, on May 21, 1471, King Henry VI was killed—almost certainly on Edward's orders. There could be no leniency toward the Lancastrians, no rival to King Edward around whom they could rally. Once Henry VI was dead, and with the only child of Henry VI and Margaret of Anjou having died in the Battle of Tewkesbury, the Lancastrian claims were at an end.

After ten years, the throne at last appeared to be secure. With relief Edward settled down to enjoy his respite. His subjects were content, the great nobles loyal, Parliament gratified by the king's continued solvency. Though extravagant himself, Edward paid his own bills, and curtailed the costs of his household while continuing to encourage England's recovering prosperity through attention to foreign trade.

On the troubled borderlands of Scotland and Wales, two reliable deputies kept order, the king's brother Richard, Duke of Gloucester and the queen's brother Earl Rivers. No rebellions arose to mar the tranquillity of the 1470s, and it seemed to contemporaries that the number of robberies and murders, though still high, had gone down.

The responsibilities of rulership, which had weighed so heavily on his predecessor Henry VI, seem to have weighed lightly on the genial, amiable Edward IV. He chose his servants and deputies carefully, and made certain that they obeyed him and did not abuse their power. Only in the case of his brother George, whose restlessness and ambition made him a constant source of annoyance, did the king become exasperated; in 1478, after years of continual troublemaking, George was attainted of treason and executed.

Throughout his thirties King Edward devoted himself to the enthusiastic pursuit of drink and women. "Addicted to conviviality," as the author of the *Croyland Chronicle* wrote, the king happily indulged his appetites, feasted and "grew fat in the loins," and spent his time in the company of his many mistresses. His favorite, Jane (or Elizabeth) Shore, a goldsmith's wife, enjoyed his favor the longest ("For many he had," wrote Thomas More, "but her he loved"). But he also seems to have loved his wife Elizabeth Woodville, with whom he had ten children, mostly girls.

However intense his pleasures, Edward never allowed them to distract him so thoroughly that the business of the realm was forgotten. He had a grand design in mind, the perennial goal of the English kings: to conquer France.

In 1475, after much preparation, Edward led a well-equipped army of some ten thousand men to France, expecting to be met there by his brother-in-law Charles the Bold and by another ally, the Duke of Brittany. Confident of victory, the English landed at Calais and began making their destructive way south toward Amiens, devastating the countryside and reviving fears of the ruinous times of the Hundred Years War.

But both Edward and his foe Louis XI were shrewd, and neither was a chivalric visionary, mad for glory in arms. Edward knew that Louis had a large and strong army, and Louis respected Edward's proven skill in battle. When his two allies failed to come to his aid as promised, Edward was amenable to negotiating with King Louis—who saw a way to buy off his rival. A deal was struck, amid much wine and feasting on venison pies. There would be a truce for seven years. Edward would take his army home, and Louis would pay him seventy-five thousand gold crowns, plus another fifty thousand every year.

In what should have been his prime, Edward began to decline physically, worn down by late nights and drink, and by the fat that slowed him down. He was still a magnificent figure, but as he approached forty his resistance became low. In 1481 he planned to lead a large army to the Scots border, where war threatened, but because of poor health and waning strength he was forced to send his brother Richard north instead. Two years later, when Louis XI failed to make his annual payment to the English treasury, Edward wanted to raise another army to invade France, but lacked the strength.

Finally in the spring of 1483 Edward became seriously ill, weakened, it was rumored, by a chill which he caught while fishing. He declined rapidly, and by the first week in April he knew that he did not have long to live.

No one had expected the robust, hard-living king to die at forty, least of all himself. His son and heir, Prince Edward, was only twelve, far too young to be burdened with kingship. The Woodvilles were at odds with the rest of the nobility, and especially with the king's brother Richard. Summoning the last of his strength, Edward sent for all the members of his council to come to his sickbed in an effort to bring about a reconciliation and lay the foundations for his son's reign.

Sitting up in his bed, propped up by pillows, the dying king made a poignant speech. The young prince would need their help, he told his councilors. "In these last words that I ever look to speak with you, I exhort you and require you all, for the love that you have ever borne me, from this time forward, all griefs forgotten, each of you love other."

It was indeed a heartrending moment, and the councilors, in tears, joined hands and forgave each other. But the distrust and rivalry among them became more intense after the king died on April 9, 1483, and in fact Edward's positive legacy was clouded by the mutual suspicion between his brother and his wife's relatives.

Throughout his life the tall, commanding Edward had been something of an anomaly: a king relatively unscathed by anxiety, a king who seems to have enjoyed himself to the full without paying a harsh personal price for his self-indulgence. He died loved and mourned—and within a few months was to be sorely missed, as his brother, full of fears and lacking the ease of enjoyment, strove by unconscionable means to make himself secure on a tottering throne.

RICHARD III

(1483–1485)

"A MIGHTY PRINCE AND A SPECIAL GOOD LORD."

—JOHN ROUS

A short, slight, handsome man with dark hair and an energetic manner, Richard of Gloucester might never have entered the foreground of English history had his commanding brother, Edward IV, not died in 1483 at the age of forty.

Until the abrupt end of his brother's reign, Richard had been content to stand in Edward's shadow, his loyal supporter and deputy. Unlike their ambitious, restless brother George, Richard had never rebelled against Edward and indeed had stood by him and fought beside him, sharing his exile and afterwards supporting his return to power.

A competent general and capable administrator who, according to a contemporary, "kept himself within his own lands and set out to acquire the loyalty of his people through favors and justice," Richard had a good reputation throughout Edward's reign. From his estate at Middleham in Yorkshire, he defended the borderlands, fought the Scots when necessary and toured the north as a fair and impartial judge, dealing out justice "to all who sought it, were they rich or poor, gentle or simple." York, England's second largest city, was indebted to Richard as a benefactor; its citizens looked to him for leadership and were loyal to him, as were many other northerners.

Even though Richard had been the victim of his brother George's machinations, he seems to have borne no enduring grudge against George. The brothers were married to Isabel and Anne Neville, the older and younger daughters of the extremely wealthy Earl of Warwick; after vainly attempting to prevent Richard's marriage to Anne Neville, George tried to reduce Anne's share of the Warwick inheritance. Richard's response was reasonable, and moderate, and with the aid of King Edward, the dispute was settled.

Richard's temperance and moderation were in contrast to George's increasingly reckless scheming. He plotted with King Edward's enemies, he stirred up rebellions and spread false rumors. When his wife Isabel died, George attempted to marry a second wealthy heiress, though the king expressly forbade it. After a decade of such provocations, King Edward ordered George executed (perhaps by drowning, in a butt of malmsey wine), and Richard, crushed and sorrowful, mourned and grieved.

After George's execution, Richard stayed away from King Edward's court. He blamed George's death, not on Edward, but on Edward's wife Elizabeth Woodville, who wanted revenge. Elizabeth's father and brother had been killed as a result of George's disloyalty, in the rebellion of 1469/70; she wanted George to pay the price of their deaths with his own.

Indeed Richard blamed—and hated—all of his Woodville in-laws, who in his view had advanced themselves shamelessly, acquiring wealth and titles by exploiting Elizabeth's exaltation to the rank of queen.

Richard's dark view of the Woodvilles was shared by many of the great magnates, who resented King Edward for marrying a commoner and allowing her grasping relatives to take an undeserved place among the aristocracy.

The bad feeling intensified during the last years of Edward IV's reign, but did not affect Richard's relationship with his brother the king. Richard remained King Edward's loyal deputy, fighting the Scots, holding court, carrying out the royal orders in the north. He lived up to his motto, "Loyauté me lie" (Loyalty binds me), carrying out his duties conscientiously, while living a conventional life.

Personally pious, Richard interested himself, as his mother had, in the movement toward a more inward-turned, introspective devotion developing within the late fifteenth-century church. He deplored gross sensuality and, when compared to his hard-drinking, sexually freewheeling brother Edward, with his many mistresses, Richard appeared positively puritan.

Richard attracted admiration and loyalty—but not liking. In this respect he could not have been more unlike King Edward, who had always been an attractive figure. No matter what he did or how he lived, Edward continued to be generally beloved. But Richard, whether because of his innate austerity, or because he appeared straitlaced and priggish, or for some other reason not recorded in contemporary accounts, seems to have repelled people. This flaw was to prove to be a serious handicap.

In 1483, fate thrust Richard into a grave situation which tested his judgment and strength of character to their limit.

His brother King Edward died, leaving as his heir his young son Edward, then twelve years old. The death of the king was unexpected, and created a power vacuum. Now the bad blood between Richard (and most of the magnates) and the Woodvilles was thrown into stark relief. Who would control the direction of events?

Before he died, Edward had named Richard to be Protector of his heir, but young Edward was actually under the guardianship of the queen's brother Anthony Woodville, Earl Rivers, living in faroff Ludlow in the Welsh marches. Richard too was far away from court, in Yorkshire, while the queen and most of her relations were in London, which gave them a considerable advantage.

Disregarding the late King Edward's wishes, the queen and those around her, with the support of the royal council—dominated by the Woodvilles—began issuing orders and taking matters into their own hands. Prince Edward was proclaimed king, as Edward V, on April 11, 1483, two days after his father's death. Preparations were begun for his coronation, to be held in early May. The queen sent a message to her brother Earl Rivers to deliver the new king to London as quickly as possible. In the meantime, the Woodvilles seized the royal treasury, secured the Tower of London, and prepared their defenses against the possibility of a military assault. Sir Edward Woodville took to sea with a fleet to guard the coasts.

Clearly the queen and her relatives planned to exclude Richard from the new regime, which they hoped to keep under their tight control. They expected opposition, and were attempting to forestall it—which might well lead to civil war.

At this juncture, the late king's Lord Chamberlain, Lord Hastings, sent a message to Richard informing him that King Edward had died, and that the Woodvilles were rapidly securing the government for themselves. Hastings added that Edward had named Richard as Protector of his son.

Cautiously, Richard gathered three hundred men and began traveling south toward the capital, having taken the precaution of swearing fealty to his nephew as Edward V and also having written a reassuring letter to the queen.

What his plans were at this point it is impossible to say, since no letters or recorded conversations survive to offer a glimpse of Richard's thoughts or plans. His actions were in keeping with his previous behavior: considered, deliberate, loyal to the crown. But not loyal to the Woodvilles. With his ally the Duke of Buckingham, Richard intercepted Anthony Woodville and his party as they were escorting young Edward to London. The earl was arrested and his armed force disbanded.

Now Richard was in possession of his nephew, and immediately the Woodville resistance began to crumble. The queen took refuge at Westminster Abbey with her younger son, the Duke of York. Edward Woodville left the country. Others scattered.

On May 4, Richard arrived in London and the royal council acknowledged him as protector of the young king. Londoners accepted him, as did Parliament. But over the course of the following month, two significant things happened. First, young Edward was not crowned. And second, a conspiracy arose (or so Richard believed) to oust Richard as protector.

Early in June 1483, Richard wrote to the city of York, asking the city fathers to send troops south to support him. The queen and her allies were intent on destroying him, he said. Would the men of York come to his aid?

In London, Richard arrested a circle of conspirators, among them Hastings (who had warned him of the Woodville coup) and the late king's mistress Elizabeth (Jane) Shore. Hastings was put to death, as were Anthony Woodville and others. Gravely alarmed, and apparently convinced that the only way to end the unsettled, dangerous situation and to restore order was to take power himself, Richard canceled the arrangements for his nephew's coronation and began planning for his own.

At what point he decided to usurp the throne can never be known with certainty. But once his decision was made, Richard became both methodical and ruthless. His nephews, lodged in the Tower, disappeared; most likely he ordered them killed, though no firm conclusion about their fate is possible. (Two bodies discovered in the Tower in the seventeenth century were not those of Edward IV's sons.) When his former ally Buckingham proved unreliable and rebelled, he eliminated him too.

On July 6, King Richard III was crowned, with most of the nobility present to acclaim him. Parliament had formally petitioned him to accept the throne a week or so earlier, and there were no voices raised in opposition to the new state of affairs.

Nearly three months of uncertainty and apprehension were at an end. The Woodville threat had been suppressed. At least some of the new king's subjects were pleased by the outcome; after all, a minority reign would have invited continuing turmoil and intrigue, and Richard had already made a reputation for himself as a competent governor and military commander. But the temporary security of the throne had been achieved at a high cost, and Richard would never enjoy permanent safety.

Outwardly confident as he began his reign, Richard set up a splendid court and extended lavish hospitality. He seemed comfortable and at ease in the purple robes of monarchy, presiding over court ceremonial, entertaining distinguished guests, showing himself to be efficient in attending to the business of governing.

But beneath his apparent calm he was almost certainly apprehensive. Among the books in his surviving library is a Book of Hours containing fragments of a handwritten private prayer, added during Richard's reign. "More doubting than trusting in his own cause," reads one passage, "vexed, wrested, and tormented in mind with fear . . . whence he had a miserable life." Again and again the prayer refers to ongoing trials and difficulties, and exhorts God for aid. "Defend me from all evil and from my evil enemy," the unknown writer says, "and free me from all tribulations, griefs and anguishes which I face."

The poem may stand as an emblem for Richard's brief reign, for he was never free from worry and retaining his crown took all his energy.

Small risings erupted in the early months of the new reign, in Devon, Kent and Dorset. By the following year, 1484, opposition to Richard had coalesced around Henry Tudor, descended from John of Gaunt and hence a claimant to the throne in the Lancastrian line. Henry was in exile in Brittany, but was known to be preparing an invasion force.

King Richard's insecurities increased after his only son, ten-year-old Edward, died in April 1484. As a usurper he was vulnerable to being overthrown, but as a usurper with no direct successor he was even more vulnerable, and to counteract the threat he ordered his military forces to be on the alert, ready to muster on half a day's warning when the need arose.

In the summer of 1484 the king attempted to persuade the Duke of Brittany, through the duke's treasurer, to capture Henry Tudor and send him to England so that he could be tried as a traitor. This effort very nearly succeeded, but at the last minute Henry was forewarned and escaped to France, where the king, Charles VIII, gave him not only protection but encouragement.

Threatened from all sides, and aware that his support from within England was eroding, Richard was beleaguered. His subjects suspected him of ordering the deaths of his nephews, and condemned him for it, and there were whispers that he might soon order his wife to be killed also, for he had been overheard to complain to the Archbishop of York that she was "unfruitful."

The Christmas festivities at the end of the year 1484 were exceptionally opulent, with much dancing and celebration—and libidinous merrymaking. Restraints were loosened, and the behavior of the king, who until then had apparently been a faithful husband, gave rise to gossip and speculation. People began to whisper that Richard was looking around for another wife to replace the unfruitful Anne, and suspected him of wanting to marry his niece Elizabeth of York. A marriage to his late brother's oldest daughter would strengthen Richard's claim to the throne, and Elizabeth, young and healthy, would be likely to provide a male heir.

Shortly after Christmas, early in the new year 1485, Queen Anne began to grow sickly and by February was too weak to get out of bed. Richard kept his distance from her, on the advice of his physicians—which led to further gossip. When Anne died on March 16, it was widely believed that Richard had poisoned her, in order to remove her as an obstacle to his marriage to Elizabeth. A total eclipse of the sun which occurred on Anne's death day seemed to underscore the prevailing suspicions.

By now Richard was struggling to overcome the ill effects of incriminating rumors. In what one chronicler called a "uniquely shameful spectacle," the king appeared in the great hall of the Priory of the Knights Hospitallers and made a solemn statement that he was innocent of causing his wife's death. The statement was unconvincing, and in fact members of the king's own council were certain that the rumors were true.

Believing that he was, as he wrote in a letter, the victim of "false and abominable lies," Richard felt beleaguered. His opponents were eagerly awaiting Henry Tudor's invasion, which was becoming more likely with each passing month. Henry had in fact come close to invading in 1483, his plans thwarted by bad weather which scattered his ships. It was only a matter of time before he made another attempt.

In August of 1485 the long-expected invasion came. Richard heard of Henry Tudor's landing at Milford Haven in south Wales when he was at a hunting lodge in Sherwood Forest. He sent for his commanders, and ordered the swift muster of his fighting men, who had been on alert for months.

It was a season of danger. A plague had broken out in London, and was threatening to spread into nearby villages and towns. The sweating sickness—influenza with pulmonary complications—was a frightening disease which struck the strongest and hardiest in the population and against which there was no known defense. Victims sickened, wasted and died within hours. The king and his courtiers had left London in haste in hopes of avoiding getting sick, but some of Richard's fighting men were not so lucky, and a good many were buried before the military summons was issued.

The fearsome eclipse, the devastating plague, and now the arrival of a foreign army: it was enough to unnerve any king, let alone one whose hold on his throne was already tenuous. But Richard showed no outward hesitation. Assembling his forces, he rode out from Leicester on August 21, riding a white horse, clad in the steel armor in which he had fought successfully at the Battle of Tewkesbury fourteen years earlier. Richard was a seasoned veteran, stalwart and confident, while Henry Tudor had never been in a battle. Richard had the larger army, and was fighting on home ground; his opponent, having been raised in Wales and Brittany, was in foreign territory. Richard knew he had the advantage.

The English army camped near Sutton Cheyney, near the town of Market Bosworth, intent on giving battle the following day. That night, according to one contemporary account, the king had a frightening dream in which he "imagined himself surrounded by a multitude of demons." Whether or not the story is true, it has resonance. Commanders and men alike slept uneasily the night before a battle, and Richard had more reason for troubled sleep than most.

Early on the morning of August 22 Richard put his men in an advantageous position on the slopes of Ambion Hill, overlooking the White Moors where the opposition forces had made their camp. He expected the Earl of Northumberland and Lord Thomas Stanley, steward of the royal household, to form a rearguard, adding their thousands of men to his when ordered into the fray. But when battle was joined both Northumberland and Stanley held back, failing to commit their men until they were certain they would be joining the winning side.

When the forces engaged, fighting was concentrated in the vanguards of the two armies. Richard's commander, the Duke of Norfolk, led a charge against the Tudor van. During the fierce hand-to-hand combat, Norfolk was killed, and it became apparent that both Northumberland and Stanley were going to remain on the sidelines.

At this point the king himself, a conspicuous figure wearing his battle crown atop his helmet, led his household knights in a bold charge. Shouting "Treason! Treason!" he spurred his horse toward Henry Tudor's standard, and managed to kill the standard bearer, Sir William Brandon, before he himself was cut down.

Richard's last fierce gesture won him grudging admiration. In the words of a chronicler generally hostile to him, "he bore himself like a noble soldier, and despite his little body and feeble strength, honorably defended himself to his last breath, shouting again and again: 'Treason! Treason! Treason!'"

With the king dead, the battle was soon lost. The royal forces surrendered. According to tradition, a soldier found Richard's battle crown hanging from the branches of a hawthorn bush. He snatched it up and placed it on the head of the victor, Henry Tudor.

In death Richard's last heroic assault was quickly forgotten and his naked, blood-smeared corpse was unceremoniously removed from the battlefield on the back of a horse. Soldiers contemptuously tugged at his hair, taking lengths of it as souvenirs. For two days the body, stinking and decomposing in the summer heat, was exhibited at the convent of the Grey Friars in Leicester, to prove that Richard was indeed dead so that anyone who might claim the contrary in the future could be discredited.

Richard was buried in the Franciscan church of St. Mary's, where after his accession, Henry VII ordered a marble tomb to be built with a statue of the late king in alabaster. A half century later, when Henry's son Henry VIII ordered England's monasteries secularized, the tomb was desecrated and the statue destroyed. Richard's bones were thrown into the river Soar.

With the advent of the Tudor dynasty, the memory of the last Yorkist king was bound to be besmirched. In the rich imagination of Thomas More and others, the historical Richard was transmogrified into a freakish ghoul, a hunchback with a withered arm and bloody gnawed lip who murdered not only his nephews but his wife, his brother George, King Henry VI and Henry's son Prince Edward. In the hands of Shakespeare, Richard became a deliciously evil villain, "a hellhound that doth hunt us all to death," as the dramatist has Margaret of Anjou say.

But these fanciful imaginings, and the numerous books endeavoring to rehabilitate Richard and present him as a blameless victim of Tudor vilification, are equally distorted. Were Richard alive today, he would undoubtedly shout "Treason!" to both camps, and lay about him with his valiant sword.

HENRY VII

(1485–1509)

—✦⊷✱⊶✦——

"HIS BODY WAS SLENDER BUT WELL BUILT AND
STRONG; HIS HEIGHT ABOVE THE AVERAGE. HIS
APPEARANCE WAS REMARKABLY ATTRACTIVE AND HIS
FACE WAS CHEERFUL, ESPECIALLY WHEN SPEAKING;
HIS EYES WERE SMALL AND BLUE, HIS TEETH FEW,
POOR AND BLACKISH; HIS HAIR WAS THIN AND WHITE;
HIS COMPLEXION SALLOW. "

—POLYDORE VERGIL

Henry Tudor's disadvantageous childhood made it improbable that he would ever become king. At the time of his birth, in January of 1457, Lancastrians and Yorkists were vying for power. Henry's father, Edmund Tudor, Earl of Richmond, had fallen victim to that power struggle and had died, a prisoner in Carmarthen Castle, while his son was still in the womb. Henry's mother, Margaret Beaufort, was a girl of thirteen, dependent on the chivalrous protectiveness of her brother-in-law, Jasper Tudor, for her safety.

Margaret gave birth in Jasper's Welsh fortress, Pembroke Castle, in the dead of winter, and despite her youth and the strain she was under the baby survived. The hardy infant grew into a robust and precocious boy, quick-witted and adaptable. Because he had royal blood (his mother was the great-great-granddaughter of Edward III), Henry was a valuable dynastic pawn, on the Lancastrian side, in the ongoing contest between Lancaster and York. Throughout his boyhood his fortunes rose and fell with those of his kin and lineage.

Never secure, young Henry was passed from hand to hand. His Uncle Jasper watched over him until the age of four, when political upheaval brought the Yorkists to power. From age four to twelve Henry was under the guardianship of William Herbert, who supplanted Jasper Tudor as earl of Pembroke. Because of his unusual intelligence, Henry was given a somewhat better education than most gentlemen's sons received—perhaps thanks to his mother's influence, for Margaret Beaufort was herself a woman of high intelligence and some cultivation.

The widowed Margaret had remarried, and Henry hardly ever saw her, but she watched over him from a distance, and was ambitious for him and affectionate toward him.

There were to be two more sudden reversals in Henry's fortunes. With the brief return of the Lancastrian king Henry VI, Jasper Tudor regained royal favor and William Herbert, who had supplanted him, was executed. Young Henry Tudor came to London with his uncle and visited the royal court. He might well have had a promising future there, but Henry VI was soon overthrown and put to death and the Tudors, uncle and nephew, were forced to leave England. They sailed from Tenby in June of 1471, headed for France. Their barque was blown ashore in Brittany, however, and there they stayed.

The Duke of Brittany, Francis II, harbored Henry and his uncle but more as captives than honored guests. They had no money, and were entirely dependent on Duke Francis's hospitality; he kept them in separate residences and restricted their movements. The duke was well aware that the fourteen-year-old Henry was a valuable asset to control, because in 1471, Henry had become the sole remaining male heir to the English throne descended from John of Gaunt. (The Yorkist King, Edward IV, was also descended from a younger son of Edward III.) As Henry grew older, opponents of Edward IV looked to Henry to lead them; as long as Duke Francis continued to keep Henry in Brittany, he could use him to bargain with his own opponents.

For Henry, the years in exile in Brittany seem to have been relatively sterile ones. He had little to do. He received letters from England, and must have tried to stay informed about King Edward. He knew that there were those who looked to him to overthrow the Yorkist regime, and that the king, aware of the threat that Henry represented, wanted to put him in prison—or execute him for treason.

Yet in his more reflective moments, Henry must have realized what a minor threat he actually represented. He had never been a ruler, and knew nothing about governing. He had no money with which to launch an invasion. And what was more important, he had no experience of battle. If and when the opportunity arose for him to return to England and make a bid for the throne, it would be as an untested leader.

In 1475 Edward IV invaded France, and Henry and his uncle were in danger of being captured. Although the English and French kings came to terms quickly, preventing all-out warfare, Henry was still in peril. Edward requested that Duke Francis send Henry to England, ostensibly so that he could marry one of Edward's daughters. It was a ruse, but the duke did not at first perceive this. He ordered Henry to embark for England and had him escorted to St. Malo.

Henry, now eighteen, was in much "agony of mind," a chronicler wrote. He got sick—or perhaps he was feigning illness so that he could avoid departing for England. While he lay in bed at St. Malo, one of Duke Francis's advisers took it upon himself to become Henry's advocate. He persuaded the duke that King Edward had no intention of making Henry his son-in-law, but meant to imprison or kill him. The duke's eyes were opened, and with his connivance, Henry was delivered from his would-be captors.

Throughout most of his twenties, Henry remained in Brittany, gathering around him an ever growing number of discontented English exiles. In 1483 Edward IV died, and his brother Richard usurped the throne. Though he was a competent ruler, Richard was disliked and distrusted and did not command the loyalty of the English. Henry gathered troops, ships and equipment and sailed for England in the summer of 1483, only to be turned back by rough seas. In the following year, he was preparing another invasion force when he received word that he was about to be delivered into Richard's hands by treachery.

As soon as he received the warning message, Henry took five attendants and rode toward the frontier of Anjou, disguising himself as one of his own servants. He barely made it to safety, pursued by his betrayers. Once across the French border, however, Henry put himself at the mercy of the French king, Charles VIII, who was willing to loan him the funds, soldiers and ships he needed to make another attempt to conquer England.

By August of 1485 all was in readiness. The armada crossed the Channel in safety and landed at Milford Haven in south Wales. It was not an imposing force, many in Henry's army of some two to three thousand men were criminals and vagrants recruited in Normandy. Henry knew that Richard would have a much larger force, and worried over rumors he had heard in France, that Richard intended to marry the princess he himself had promised to wed, Edward IV's daughter Elizabeth of York. Henry needed to make this marriage in order to shore up his claim to the crown; worry over this matter, wrote the historian Polydore Vergil, "pinched him in the very stomach."

But Henry need not have worried. By the time he met Richard's army near the town of Market Bosworth on August 22, many more Englishmen had come to march beneath his banners. When battle was joined, key commanders on the Yorkist side held back, weakening King Richard's fighting strength. And when Richard made his desperate attack on Henry, killing many of Henry's knights including his standard bearer, his valiant effort proved to be futile. King Richard was cut down, and following his death, his men soon capitulated.

According to tradition, Richard's battle crown was found on the field and placed on Henry's head. Henry had won the kingdom; henceforth he would be acclaimed as King Henry VII.

Tall and slender, blond and blue-eyed, with a long pale face and a prominent wart above his chin, Henry Tudor was an attractive figure, especially when garbed in gowns of violet velvet or cloth of gold and with flashing diamonds in his hat and around his neck. What struck observers most about Henry were his "quick shining" eyes, and the alertness in his animated features. Those who knew him best were aware that he was prudent, and had a large share of common sense. When his subjects turned out to see King Henry, a few days after the Battle of Bosworth, as he made his way through the London streets from Lambeth to the Tower, they cheered him lustily, and rejoiced once again when he was crowned.

Though he was careful to surround himself with a grand entourage and all the symbolic accoutrements of royalty, and though he adopted the style "Most Christian and Most Gracious Prince, our Most Dread Sovereign Lord," Henry was well aware that his throne was not yet secure. Like his predecessor Richard III, he was a usurper. And a landless, rootless refugee besides. He had few possessions of his own, and those he had he guarded zealously, especially his crown. When he went to sleep at night, he kept his crown beside his bed on a cushion, lest anyone try to snatch it away from him. To guard his person, Henry formed a bodyguard of two hundred tall, strong men, the "yeomen of the guard."

The first grand celebration of the reign was Henry's marriage to Elizabeth of York, the wedding that symbolized the reuniting of Lancaster and York and the end of a generation of bloodletting. Wedding guests dined on roasted peacock and swan, lark and quail, sugared almonds and rich tarts in a banquet of surpassing richness.

The fragile stability of the new reign was threatened when a pretender, an English boy claiming to be the son of Edward IV's late brother George, began to gather support in Ireland and the north of England. The boy, Lambert Simnel, was a plausible imposter and swiftly attracted a following among Irish lords and rebels in Yorkshire, always fervently anti-Lancastrian. Simnel also had the backing of Edward IV's sister Margaret, duchess of Burgundy, who sent two thousand battle-hardened Swiss and German mercenaries to form the core of a rebel army.

For a time it looked as though the pretender might succeed in over-throwing the Tudor regime. He was crowned in Dublin as King Edward VI in 1487, and some four thousand Irish soldiers were added to the European mercenaries in his army. King Henry raised a force of his own and marched north to meet the rebels, who were making their way toward the capital. On June 16, 1487, the two armies met near the village of Stoke, and the royal forces, weakened by desertions and low morale, broke before the onslaught of the Swiss and German professionals. Henry himself brought up reinforcements and drove the rebel line back, ultimately turning the battle into a rout. But the royal army had come close to defeat, and losses were very high on both sides. Young Simnel was captured and put to work in the royal kitchens.

In the 1490s another pretender attracted aid from the continent and menaced Henry's throne. Perkin Warbeck, a young Frenchman, was well prepared for his role. He learned a great deal about the family of Edward IV from Sir Edward Brampton, a former Yorkist official living in exile in the Low Countries. Warbeck posed as Edward IV's younger son, Richard of York. It was generally believed that Richard III had killed both of Edward IV's sons, Richard and Edward. But Warbeck insisted that he, Richard of York, had escaped from the Tower and was seeking aid to take his rightful place on the throne as his father's heir.

Warbeck was apparently believable. King Charles VIII of France backed him, his "aunt" Margaret of Burgundy recognized him as her nephew, and Emperor Maximilian patronized him and gave him funds. In the summer of 1495 Warbeck landed briefly on the Kentish coast and at Waterford in Ireland, but was unsuccessful in attracting support from the local population. He went on to Scotland, where the king, James IV, welcomed him and, apparently, believed he was indeed Prince Richard. James arranged a marriage for Warbeck with one of his relatives, and agreed to support him with soldiers and funds for yet another attempted invasion of England.

Fortunately for Henry, this final attempt came to nothing. Warbeck crossed the border into England with an army, but soon abandoned his effort; King James, no longer willing to be burdened with the ineffectual pretender, and engaged in negotiations with King Henry to marry his daughter Margaret, sent Warbeck back to the continent. A few years later Henry hanged the pretender as a traitor.

What was most disturbing about the rival claimants to the throne was their ability to attract support from foreign courts. It was evident that continental rulers were eager to overthrow the fledgling Tudor regime, and that Henry was vulnerable. At the same time, however, Henry was doing what he could to build alliances abroad. He succeeded in arranging the marriage of his favorite daughter, Margaret, to James IV of Scotland and that of his eldest son, Arthur, to Princess Catherine of Aragon, daughter of King Ferdinand and Queen Isabella of Spain. Increased security, widened trade and peace were his aims; by the time his reign ended, England was viewed, not as a feudal backwater, but as a significant member of the community of European states.

Crucial to this shift in perception was Henry's style of rule. He modeled himself on the Italian despots, wealthy rulers of small states who governed through financial control, treachery and intimidation, and who overawed others by their personal magnificence. The old style of chivalrous monarchy, of kings who led and inspired through personal strength and military might, was abandoned.

Visitors to Henry VII's court were impressed, for the king always seemed to be the glittering focus of a visual pageant, a feast for the eyes and ears. Trumpets blared and servants in colorful livery took their places in a scenic display whenever the king entered a room. He sat down under a golden cloth of estate to receive guests, surrounded by glowing tapestries and rich embroidered wall hangings, and with thick carpets underfoot. Elaborate ritual and ceremony accompanied his every act, from getting dressed to dining to going to bed, all of it designed to emphasize his distance, as king, from the ordinary mortals who were his subjects.

During Henry VII's reign, the voyages of Christopher Columbus and others were revealing the true shape of the earth and opening vast possibilities for evangelization (the professed purpose of the ventures) and trade. The king financed voyages of exploration by John Cabot (Giovanni

Caboto), a Genoese living in London, giving him royal license "to seek out, discover and find whatever isles, countries, regions or provinces of the heathen and infidels, which before this time have been unknown to all Christians." One-fifth of the profits from Cabot's voyaging was to go to the king. Cabot sailed from Bristol in 1497 and reached Cape Breton Island, wrongly believing that he had arrived on the northeast coast of Asia. On a second voyage he reached Newfoundland.

Henry's tastes were as international as his interests were global. From Burgundian Flanders he imported art works and books for his fine library at Richmond. Italian furniture decorated his palaces and the vestments of his chapel priests were sewn by Florentine embroiderers. His most striking likeness was a portrait bust by the Italian sculptor Pietro Torrigiano, who was also to sculpt the effigy on his tomb. Humanist scholars were brought to Henry's court to teach his children, humanist historians were employed to write England's history from the Tudor perspective—reducing the troubled years of Lancastrian-Yorkist conflict to nothing more than a dark preamble to the glorious present.

But the central feature of King Henry's court were the entertainments he offered, the sumptuous banquets for seven or eight hundred guests amid costly displays of silver salt cellars, drinking cups and basins, the festive entertainments with dancers, acrobats and tightrope walkers, magicians and fools and freaks ("the great Welsh child," "the little Scotsman," "the great woman of Flanders"), the jousts and balls and masks at which his courtiers amused themselves.

The king himself did not join in the jousting or the dancing, but he did like to gamble with his guests and courtiers, frequently losing large sums playing cards and dice, and betting on tennis games and archery competitions. In his private hours he collected relics—his prize possessions were a leg bone said to have belonged to St. George and a fragment of the true cross—and experimented with alchemy, the art of turning base metal into gold.

Gold, it seemed to many, was the king's besetting preoccupation. Starting his reign with little he could call his own, he became wealthy, greatly enlarging the royal treasury and leaving, on his death, a hoard of coins worth nearly two million pounds, as well as jewels worth over a hundred thousand pounds. Frugal by temperament, and with a taste for the minutia of finance, the king spent many hours "writing the accounts of his expenses with his own hand," a contemporary wrote. He kept a close watch on all the royal financial records, looking for ways to increase revenues by exploiting the right of the crown to collect fines and wardship rights. Under his scrutiny, the income from crown lands went up nearly threefold.

But it was in attaining control over his nobles that Henry showed his greatest capacity for financial creativity. Recognizing that an untamed nobility would soon undermine his authority, Henry ingeniously curbed his nobles' independence by forcing them to pay large sums of money "to keep their allegiance." If they rebelled, they forfeited these large bonds, which in the meantime sat in the royal treasury. The sums involved were very high; in one year alone, some sixty-five thousand pounds were paid.

In 1500, when he had been king for fifteen years, Henry seemed to have reached a plateau of success. His realm was rich, tranquil and well governed. "From this time forward," wrote the Milanese ambassador about Henry VII, "he is perfectly secure against Fortune."

The pronouncement was premature.

Prince Arthur, heir to the throne, sickened and died in 1502, and Henry's hopes that his wife Elizabeth might have more children were extinguished when she too died in 1503, giving birth to her last baby, Katherine, who also died. The king's efforts to remarry came to nothing, and he concentrated on his sole remaining son, Prince Henry.

But the king's relations with the prince were darkened by the physical deterioration which came over him in his early forties. He was not aging well; already at forty he looked like an old man, his thin hair white, his once strong body shrunk and weakened, his eyesight poor. He was often immobilized by gout.

Worst of all, his temperament changed. Where once he had been affable, alert and bright-eyed, an eager participant in court life, he now became reclusive, suspicious and prone to violent rages during which he lashed out, often at his son.

By 1506, when Henry was forty-nine, his physical and mental decline were so marked that his physicians did not expect him to live much longer. But his will was strong, and for another three years he lingered, afflicted ever more severely by recurring pneumonia, tonsillitis and crippling arthritis. With the king in no fit state to govern, at odds with his heir and mentally aberrant, the kingdom was adrift. But thanks to the indemnities put up by the great nobles, and with no immediate military threat from outside the realm, the hiatus passed uneventfully.

Prince Henry was at his father's bedside when on April 21, 1509, King Henry died in great agony. At the very end he had tried to bargain for his life. "If it pleased God to send him life," he swore, "he would be a changed man." Whether he repented of his violence, or of other transgressions left unrecorded, is unknown. After his death his special instructions were carried out. His two most precious relics, the leg bone of St. George and the fragment of the true cross, were placed inside the altar of his tomb, and small statues of himself, kneeling in golden armor, were placed by the shrines of his favorite English saints.

HENRY VIII

(1509–1547)

————— ✦❧❈☙✦ —————

"KING HENRY IS . . . MUCH HANDSOMER THAN ANY
OTHER SOVEREIGN IN CHRISTENDOM. . . . HE IS VERY
ACCOMPLISHED AND A GOOD MUSICIAN, COMPOSES
WELL, IS A CAPITAL HORSEMAN, AND A FINE JOUSTER,
SPEAKS GOOD FRENCH, LATIN AND SPANISH, IS VERY
RELIGIOUS. . . . HE IS ALSO FOND OF TENNIS, AT WHICH
GAME IT IS THE PRETTIEST THING IN THE WORLD TO
SEE HIM PLAY, HIS FAIR SKIN GLOWING THROUGH A
SHIRT OF THE FINEST TEXTURE."

—SEBASTIAN GIUSTINIAN,
VENETIAN AMBASSADOR

There is no finer youth in the world than the Prince of Wales," the Spanish ambassador wrote to his master, King Ferdinand, in 1507. Young Prince Henry was then sixteen, already taller than his father Henry VII, with the coordination and dexterity of a gifted athlete. He was good-looking, sociable, highly intelligent and well read, an exceptional jouster—in short, a paragon, with "limbs of a gigantic size."

Prince Henry was not only gifted, he was energetic. He seemed always to be in the tiltyard, practicing his riding, or pitting himself against another boy at wrestling, or teaching tricks to one of his horses. Those who saw him marveled at his agility and were charmed by his exuberant, outgoing personality. Unlike his father Henry VII, who had become dour and suspicious in his old age, young Henry was magnetic and likable. He reminded the oldest of his father's courtiers of his tall, strikingly handsome grandfather Edward IV. They commented on the similarities between the young prince and the fondly remembered King Edward, and looked forward to the day when the prince would ascend his father's throne.

But Prince Henry, at sixteen, was suffering. His father kept him in strict isolation, watched by bodyguards, kept away from all but a restricted circle of carefully chosen companions. His recreation was confined to a private park, his jousting partners limited to those the king trusted. Prince Henry was the king's only surviving son, his older brother Arthur having died five years earlier. King Henry, troubled and fearful, was keeping the prince safe, as he kept his immense treasure hoard and his relic collection safe, locked away from the world.

But it was not just that the exuberant young prince was forced to live a restricted life; he was subjected to his ill father's furious fits of rage, during which the king became so angry that he fought with the prince, as violently "as if he sought to kill him," observers thought. Young Henry never knew when these onslaughts might come, or whether, in his unbalanced state of mind, King Henry might resort to even harsher punishments, banishing him from the realm or imprisoning him in a dungeon where he might be left to starve.

The Prince of Wales spent his teens in an anxious state, until finally, in April of 1509, he was summoned to his dying father's bedside. Henry later said that among his father's last wishes was that he should marry his late brother's widow, Catherine of Aragon. Less than two months after Henry VII's death, he did so—against the advice of some of his churchmen and courtiers, who pointed out the dubious validity of such a marriage under church law.

Marrying a brother's widow was condemned as "an impurity" in the biblical book of Leviticus, where it was written that God would punish with childlessness those who made such a marriage. The pope had granted a special exemption, or dispensation, permitting Henry and Catherine to marry, nonetheless the union bore a stigma, and was to become the one weak point in the new king's otherwise triumphant reign.

For Henry VIII was, in most ways, a model ruler. Pious, virtuous, with splendid physical endowments, good-tempered, magnanimous, courageous: he seemed to sum up, in his person, all the qualities his subjects could desire in a king. The full treasury bequeathed to him by his wealthy father allowed him, at the age of twenty-two, to invade France. He insisted on leading the army himself, telling those who worried about his safety that his soldiers would fight more bravely when led by their king. Besides, he said, he was frankly eager "to create such a fine opinion about his valor among all men that they could understand that his ambition was not merely to equal but to excel the glorious deeds of his ancestors."

Henry VIII wanted to outdo his famous predecessor Henry V, to win a battle as great as the battle of Agincourt. If possible, Henry VIII wanted to be crowned King of France, as the earlier Henry had been.

"A noble heart in war is never afeared of death," Henry told his soldiers once they landed in France and began the campaign. Fearless Henry appeared to be, as he disdained shelter even when under fire from enemy cannon. He made himself a conspicuous target, standing out in the midst of his men in a golden tunic and a bright red hat with red feathers. The harness of his horse was hung with golden bells which jangled noisily, announcing his comings and goings. When besieging the fortress of Thérouanne, the king seemed to be everywhere, practicing with his archers, adjusting the positions of his guns, leading his men on foot across swollen rivers, keeping up their morale when they were enmired in mud (the summer was stormy) and succumbing to illness.

The climax of the French campaign was the Battle of the Spurs, a large-scale skirmish during which a few hundred English knights chased a French force twice its size off the field, capturing many French standards and taking over a hundred prisoners to be held for ransom. As victories go, it did not compare to Agincourt, and Henry did not attempt to follow it up by besieging Paris and pressing his claim to the throne of France. He was content to bask in the reputation he had earned, as one who had repeated some of the success of Henry V, and had won his renown at a younger age and earlier in his reign.

For though he emulated the flinty, single-purposed, ruthless Henry V, King Henry VIII was an entirely different personality, hedonistic and easygoing, with no sternness, no arrogance, above all no instinct for the jugular. When not taking his exercise in the jousting field or hunting, he liked ease, pleasure and comfort. He enjoyed dressing in exotic costumes and taking part in masques, he liked invading Queen Catherine's apartments dressed as an outlaw and insisting that the queen and her ladies join him in a dance. He enjoyed performing, as a very gifted amateur, on the recorder, flute and virginal. He set poems to music and wrote choral masses in the complex polyphonic style of the era that called for considerable musical sophistication.

King Henry did so many things well, and seemingly without effort. It was this effortlessness, combined with his sunny, apparently guileless nature, and his matchless panache, that captivated all who saw him.

But the diplomats from foreign courts who came to London and observed the king criticized him as an overgrown child, occupying himself with nothing but "the pleasures of his age." He put much more time into enlarging his stables and acquiring new horses—fine high-stepping Neapolitans, Spanish jennets, bounding Frieslanders—than he did into consulting with his councilors and meeting with diplomats. He neglected the tasks of rule and left them to trusted senior advisers. He neglected England's relations with foreign states.

In actuality Henry's boyishly eager style was deceptive. The king himself made all the important decisions, even though it appeared that others, especially his ambitious, overworked, haughty but astute chancellor Thomas Wolsey, were in charge. But there was one decision he was struggling with, and it had to do with the very important issue of the succession.

By the mid-1520s, King Henry and Queen Catherine had been married for sixteen years, and the queen, at forty, was at the end of her childbearing years. Yet despite numerous pregnancies and births, Catherine had only one surviving child, Princess Mary. England had never been successfully ruled by a woman; the one experiment with a queen regnant, when Henry I left his kingdom to his daughter Matilda in the twelfth century, had resulted in civil war and Matilda had never been crowned. Henry needed a son to inherit his kingdom, and it was beginning to look as though he would never have one.

His advisers were as worried as he was. Every time he suffered the least indisposition there was great concern, for what if he should die at a young age, as his grandfather Edward IV had? Every time King Henry entered the tiltyard there was anxiety, for he had already survived one serious accident—when sharp fragments from a shattered wooden spear flew into his unprotected face—and might not survive another. Without a male heir, it was hazardous for the king to lead soldiers into battle, yet he continued to campaign in France, risking his life.

At about this time, in the mid-1520s, when Henry was thirty-four or thirty-five, he seems to have convinced himself that his lack of a son was a divine punishment for his having married his brother's widow. Despite the papal dispensation, and despite Catherine's insistence that she and Henry's brother Arthur had never consummated their marriage (and therefore she was not truly Arthur's widow), Henry believed that he and Catherine had sinned; they were being punished.

Clouding Henry's thinking just at this time were two emotional stressors. For the first time in his life, he was suffering from an inner sense of defeat—and for the first time in his life he was helplessly besotted, with a lively, black-haired, sexually magnetic gentlewoman named Anne Boleyn.

Thanks to his intense infatuation with Anne, King Henry was able to lift himself out of his depression and to see his way past the snares of his vexing marriage. He decided to divorce Catherine and marry Anne.

At the outset Henry probably assumed that the entire issue would be settled in a matter of months. Rulers often discarded their spouses, usually by means of a technicality of canon law; accommodating popes granted dissolutions or made other legal arrangements to accomplish what was wanted. But when Henry appealed to Rome, he confronted only delays and disappointments. And Queen Catherine, relying on the political support of her powerful nephew, Holy Roman Emperor Charles V, showed herself to be a formidable adversary.

For years the divorce suit dragged on, while Henry waited and fretted and, for the first time, took on the full workload of monarchy. His chancellor Wolsey had died, leaving behind mountains of unfinished work and much confusion; Henry took all on himself, and, working harder than he ever had, began to feel the first assaults of age. Headaches, catarrhs, a chronic ulcer on his thigh that led to dangerously high fevers: all these and other ailments weighed down his once magnificent body and kept him inactive.

His divorce had become a cause célèbre throughout Europe, provoking Charles V to threaten war. Indeed all the Catholic powers of Europe stood against England, and Henry, seeking allies, turned to the followers of the rebellious monk Martin Luther. When Henry learned that even Luther had decided to support Queen Catherine, he suffered as never before, from insomnia, worse headaches and a growing sense of desperation.

Finally, after six years of frustration and seeming futility, the impasse was broken. In 1532, Anne, who had never before consented to become Henry's mistress, changed her mind and soon became pregnant with the king's child. Hoping that the baby would be a boy, Henry ignored the advice of his councilors and declared his marriage to Catherine dissolved, secretly married Anne, and then, very publicly, had her crowned—to the astonishment and disapproval of his subjects. His delight in his wife and the prospect of an heir turned to dismay when Anne gave birth to a daughter, Elizabeth, in September of 1533.

The repercussions of Henry's decision to marry Anne Boleyn spread throughout Europe. England left the community of Roman Catholics and, by fiat of the Reformation Parliament, King Henry VIII became head of the English church—a church which had yet to define itself theologically and institutionally. The same Parliament addressed England's outmoded administrative system and introduced sweeping changes in the way the departments of state were run. New currents were being felt in many aspects of English life, new learning in the universities influenced by Italian humanism, new vitality in the economy, new trends in dress and music, art and architecture.

To enhance his status King Henry built the palaces of St. James's and Nonsuch, the latter a unique structure bristling with turrets and pinnacles, and with a huge statue of the king in the center of the main courtyard. Wolsey's former mansion York Place was turned into the palace of Whitehall, whose extensive grounds and spacious halls were meant to impress foreigners and the king's English subjects alike.

In his forties King Henry, always confident, developed an unshakable inner certitude. He ceased to listen to any advice and relied on no one but himself, trusting his own opinions completely. To symbolize this transformation he wore a gold bracelet inscribed, in French, "plys tot morir que changer ma pensée," "to die rather than change my mind."

Others found Henry bewildering, full of contradictions and increasingly inclined to caprice. He was erratic in his behavior, argumentative with everyone, contrary and combative and full of exaggerated bravado. King Francis I called him "the strangest man in the world." Certainly he was childishly irrational at times, and more and more implacable toward those he distrusted. Spies searched out disloyal subjects, people were imprisoned for slight offenses. Bishop Fisher and Thomas More, once Henry's beloved friends, were put to death. And in 1536, Queen Anne too was beheaded, after miscarrying a male child, along with a number of her alleged lovers.

Anne had not presented the king with the son he needed, but his next queen, Jane Seymour, succeeded where Anne had failed. In October of 1537, Jane gave birth to Prince Edward, who in due course would succeed his father as King Edward VI.

But the birth of a son did not restore Henry to good humor. Rather he became even more combative, filled at times with murderous wrath. When in a fury his reason and understanding deserted him entirely, and he became, in the words of one of his courtiers, "the most dangerous and cruel man in the world." On the continent he was called "the English Nero." His subjects referred to him, in whispers, as "the Mouldwarp," a man/beast whose coming had been prophesied by Merlin centuries before. The Mouldwarp, according to the prophecy, was to be a heroic figure, praised by his people, but ultimately destroyed by sin and excessive pride. In youth Henry had been highly praised, but with the sin of his marriage to Anne Boleyn, and the excessive pride he showed as king, he was doomed.

It was in the mid-1530s, a time of religious upheaval, widespread terror and ever more frequent public executions, that the legend of Henry VIII took on a life of its own. The contours of that legend are familiar: the outsize Henry, at once stout and formidable, a royal satyr indulging his lusts and decapitating his discarded wives, a tyrannical ruler sweeping aside venerable institutions at his erratic whim. It is an image of power unleashed, of dark chthonic forces erupting into light—a Renaissance image of humanity unshackled.

The real Henry, the irascible yet vulnerable middle-aged king, is overshadowed by the legend. Yet vulnerable Henry certainly was. In 1538 he nearly died when the infected ulcers on both of his legs became blocked and, perhaps as a result of a blood clot traveling to his lungs, Henry came close to choking to death. He lay writhing in agony, unable to speak, spending all his energy gasping for breath. Veins straining, eyes protruding, he came to the point of suffocation again and again, each time barely managing to recover. He had grown prodigiously fat in his forties, and lumbered when he walked; the graceful, athletic body he had driven so hard in his younger years was long gone.

After Jane Seymour's death Henry at first announced that he would never remarry. But within a few years he changed his mind and chose a Protestant bride, the sister of the Duke of Cleves. To his everlasting regret, he agreed to marry Anne without ever meeting her; he had only seen portraits of her, and relied on these portraits plus the reports of envoys sent to Cleves. Though Anne was neither ugly nor objectionable in any obvious way, Henry found her physically abhorrent. On first seeing her, he was "marvelously astonished and abashed," overwhelmed by his "discontentment and misliking of her person." Though overwhelmed with misgivings, he married her—only to discover that he could not bear to consummate the marriage. Within six months he had it annulled, though the king felt no animosity toward his fourth wife and she continued to live contentedly in England after the annulment.

Within weeks of ridding himself of Anne of Cleves Henry had taken another wife, the young Catherine Howard. When they married, Henry was forty-nine, Catherine most likely still in her teens. The king doted on his young wife, "caressing her more than he did the others," as the imperial ambassador noted. Catherine was his thornless rose, the rejuvenating comfort of his old age. He ordered a French artisan to make a special bed for them, inlaid with mother of pearl. In it he hoped to find, at last, a woman who satisfied both his sexual desire and his need for long-term companionship.

When Henry learned that Catherine had been repeatedly unfaithful to him, he called for a sword to kill her, and mumbled "that wicked woman had never such delight in her incontinency as she should have torture in her death." He wept publicly over his ill fortune in marrying Catherine, and once again, declared that he would remain unmarried for the rest of his life. But those who saw him feasting and celebrating on the day of Catherine Howard's condemnation had no doubt that he was once again searching for a wife—and in the following year, 1543, he found one in Catherine Parr, a mature, highly educated, good-natured widow of thirty-one. Catherine was to stay by Henry's side, loyal and affectionate, until his death.

In July of 1544 King Henry, by now a rotund colossus whose belly all but burst out of his doublets, put on full armor and rode on a great war-horse out through the gates of English-held Calais and into French territory. Campaigning seemed to agree with him. His dark moods vanished, there were no outbreaks of savage anger. Henry's vitality and stamina confounded his captains, who thought he was far too old and unsteady to endure the hardships of a military camp. Each day he rose at daybreak and was active until evening, telling Queen Catherine in a letter that he was "so occupied, and had so much to do in foreseeing and caring for everything himself" that he had no time for rest or leisure.

The English succeeded in taking Boulogne, but then, after less than two months, embarked for England. Once they had gone, all the English gains were quickly reversed, and the king, looking old and tired, lapsed into low spirits and complained of ill health.

"No prince in the world more favoreth his subjects than I do you," he told Parliament in 1545. He had reigned for nearly four decades; for more than a generation his awesome presence had overshadowed his subjects' lives, inspiring affection, fear, awe—and not a little dissatisfaction and resentment. Many of his subjects wished him dead.

In his final years Henry became an invalid, living in a small suite of rooms, taking dozens of medicines to alleviate the pain in his sore legs, his severe itching and his ulcers. Among his final expenses were payments made for perfumes to freshen his rooms and scent his sheets, repairs to his velvet-upholstered, black-fringed "close stool" or toilet, and two pairs of large slippers to warm his feet. He continued to spend money on finery, however, ordering feather-trimmed hats and lace nightcaps and dozens of jeweled rings and so many other gems that he had to commission his cabinetmaker to make a new coffer "with drawers to put stones in." He had not lost all his vitality; there were rumors that he was seriously thinking of taking a new wife.

On January 28, 1547, Henry VIII died, leaving a much altered England to his successor, the pale, undersized Edward VI.

EDWARD VI

(1547–1553)

**"HE WILL BE THE WONDER AND TERROR OF THE
WORLD—IF HE LIVES."**

—BISHOP HOOPER

N o royal child was ever as welcome, at its birth, as Edward Tudor, son of Henry VIII and his third wife, Jane Seymour.

When Edward was born, in October of 1537, King Henry had been on the throne for twenty-eight years, and though he had two daughters, twenty-one-year-old Mary and four-year-old Elizabeth, he needed a son to succeed him, the accession of a queen regnant being thought too precarious to ensure the continuity of the dynasty.

Baby Edward had the appearance of a lusty, attractive child, and seemed likely to survive. Pageantry and feasting were ordered to celebrate the birth of the prince, and in every church in England, hymns of thanksgiving were sung. In London cannon were fired and church bells rang day and night.

At his elaborate christening, Prince Edward was wrapped in a fur-trimmed mantle of crimson cloth of gold and a miniature canopy of estate—the symbol of royalty—was held over his head. His half-sister Mary was godmother, his half-sister Elizabeth carried the holy oil in the christening procession.

Edward flourished, but his mother grew weak and ill in the aftermath of his birth. For eleven days Jane suffered before succumbing to fever and dying. Henry mourned her, "retiring to a solitary place to pass his sorrows."

Young Prince Edward was a continual comfort to his father in his grief. He was precociously strong, standing alone on his sturdy legs long before he was a year old and eager to walk. The ambassadors who saw him judged him to be "one of the prettiest children of his age that could be seen anywhere." They imagined that they could detect in his infant features the seriousness and "sage judgment" of a fledgling king.

But such transparent flattery could not disguise the fact that, as Prince Edward grew older, he seemed to grow weaker. By the time he was four years old he was being talked of as a "fragile child," and his doctors predicted that he was "not of constitution to live long." During one attack of illness he lay in his bed, fever-ridden and glistening with sweat, while physician after physician peered down at him and recommended medicines and therapies. Publicly they did not give up hope; privately they admitted that Edward was on the threshold of death.

After many days the prince recovered—but continued to be chronically ill. The king took every precaution to protect him, keeping away visitors from London, where plague was endemic, and surrounding him with watchful nurses and the everpresent physicians. There were those who attempted to harm the little prince through magic. A porter at the University of Oxford sent a message to the court about a wax replica of the prince he had seen with a knife through its heart.

Though King Henry married three more times, he had no more sons. His sixth and last wife, Catherine Parr, was an active and involved stepmother to Edward and his sisters, a pious, good-natured and affectionate woman who wrote devotional books and sincerely sought to live a good life. She gave Edward gifts of books and clothing and no doubt supplemented the education he received from the Cambridge humanist Richard Coxe and John Cheke, professor of Greek at the same university, with her own strongly held opinions on church reform.

If Edward was on affectionate terms with his stepmother, he was also fond of his sister Mary—or at least they were on cordial terms. Mary sent her half-brother gifts—embroidered coats, gold jewelry—and he sent her in return baskets of vegetables, accompanied by brief notes written in precise, precociously correct schoolboy Latin. He also wrote Mary occasional notes, urging her, rather primly, not to join in "foreign dances and merriments which do not become a most Christian princess." Sounding like his stepmother, at the age of eight Edward reminded Mary, who was of an age to marry, that "the only real love is the love of God."

By the time he was eight years old, the prince was being allowed to play important roles in court ceremonial. With his uncle Edward Seymour and an escort of eight hundred yeomen of the guard, Edward rode to Hounslow to meet the French admiral Claude d'Annebaut. His horsemanship was much admired, as was his speech, which was thought to be full of "high wit and great audacity" for a boy of his age.

For a child, the prince was indeed admirable. But as his father's reign drew to a close, the men around him, chiefly Edward Seymour and John Dudley, maneuvered their way into power, intending to take control of the realm themselves once the new reign began.

In Henry VIII's last months, his heir was kept at a country house at Ashridge, far from the court, troubled about his father's failing health and lacking the comfort of his stepmother or his half-sister Mary. While he waited for news from London, he celebrated Christmas and New Year's, writing formal notes of thanks for his gifts. He thanked Queen Catherine for the double portrait of herself and the king that she had sent him, receiving a reply suggesting that he "meditate upon the distinguished deeds of his father." To King Henry he wrote promising to follow his royal example "in virtue, wisdom and piety."

At last in January 1547 the waiting was over. Edward received word that King Henry had died and that he was now the sovereign. He was only nine years old.

Cheering crowds lined the streets to watch the coronation procession of King Edward VI, and banquets, tournaments and merrymaking went on for days afterward. In his doublet and mantle of cloth of silver embroidered in gold, his belt and cap sparkling with rubies, diamonds and pearls, the boy-king was a splendid, if hardly robust, figure, with a delicately beautiful face and a gravity of manner worthy of his high position.

He looked the part of a king in miniature, but given his age, others ruled for him. Before he died King Henry, in his will, had drawn up a plan for a regency for Edward, with a council of sixteen to guide the young king through his minority. But the will was altered, and the old king's wishes ignored. Edward Seymour took the role of Protector and exercised all but sovereign rule.

Yet Seymour—or rather, the Duke of Somerset, the title King Edward bestowed on him—proved to be an erratic ruler, inadequate to cope with the social turbulence the late king had left behind. Though he won a victory over the Scots at Pinkie in September of 1547, Somerset was unable to cope with the onslaught of the French. Tempted by the presumed weakness of Edward's minority government, the French king Henry II sent troops to Scotland and blockaded Boulogne. Rebellions in the West Country and in Norfolk added to the chaos, and led to Somerset's overthrow.

Two forces unleashed the domestic turmoil: resentment over the unsettled economy and the vagaries of the religious settlement.

Henry VIII's costly warmaking had drained the country of wealth and caused widespread hardship. The coinage had been debased, the value of the currency eroded. England's credit abroad had been all but exhausted, hampering enterprise, while the ongoing disruption of agriculture from the enclosing of common fields—on which the poor had always relied for their subsistence—reduced many in the country districts to destitution. County governments were overwhelmed by sporadic outbreaks of rioting and localized violence.

Equally disruptive were the deeply disturbing religious changes imposed by the government. In Henry VIII's reign, the English church became independent of the pope; the monarch became head of the church and an English liturgy was sanctioned. The monasteries were secularized and the time-honored seven sacraments were reduced to three. Many traditional beliefs and practices came under attack as anticlericalism spread.

Under Protector Somerset, this process was accelerated, causing a deep and wounding rent in the fabric of belief. It was not merely that, by order of Somerset and the privy council, the old altars were overturned, shrines demolished and statues and wall paintings mutilated; it was something more profound, something irreparable. Anticlericalism was nothing new, it was as old as the church. Shrines and altars had been pillaged, and clergy vilified, in past centuries. But faith itself—apart from the institution of the church—had been an immemorial pillar of English life. Now it seemed, especially to the mass of uneducated people, that faith itself was under assault, and they reacted with predictable panic and deep unrest.

During the reign of Edward VI England became Protestant. The Catholic mass, with its central doctrine of transubstantiation (the miraculous alteration of bread and wine to Christ's body and blood), was replaced by a Protestant service of Holy Communion, in which the bread and wine commemorated the biblical Last Supper but did not undergo any transformation. Other theological alterations were made. Many of the English resisted the radical shift in belief, and its imposition by law. The result was renewed unrest.

In October 1549 Somerset was removed as Protector and Dudley became President of the Council. Two years later he took the title Duke of Northumberland, and Somerset was executed. King Edward, who turned fourteen in the fall of 1551, was all but lost amid the intriguing of his councilors. Though he sat in on council meetings, and voiced his opinions on how his government was organized, he had no real influence. When he ordered the renaming of a ship, or made suggestions about some aspect of administration, his recommendations were noted, but often overlooked.

One ambassador wrote that Edward was "naturally gifted with a gentle nature" and lacked the strength of will and personality to defy his unruly councilors and assert himself. They dominated him, telling him what to say and how to think. Though he realized what was happening, and resented being exploited, he was powerless to prevent it. Pressured by his greedy and corrupt advisers, caught amid the push and pull of factional politics, Edward lost his peace of mind. One day he demonstrated to his attendants how he felt.

According to Cardinal Pole, who heard the story from "people whose testimony should place it beyond doubt," King Edward took the falcon he kept in his bedchamber and began plucking its feathers one by one.

When it was completely plucked, he tore it into four pieces as his attendants looked on in horror, "saying as he did so to his governors that he likened himself to the falcon, whom everyone plucked, but that he would pluck them too, thereafter, and tear them in four parts."

Clearly Edward felt himself to be trapped in his uncomfortable role, and meditated revenge.

As he grew out of childhood the king was a slight, delicate youth, who carried one shoulder higher than the other and had to squint to see at any distance. To his doll-like beauty was now added an incongruous pose of royal majesty—a wholly unconvincing image of his hearty, burly father. He put his hands on his hips and strutted about on his thin legs, frowning with regal dissatisfaction and piping out "thunderous oaths." He cultivated a bad temper that contrasted oddly with the religious doctrine that, under Dudley's coaching, came readily from his lips.

In his early teens, Edward was still very much an unformed boy, posing as a man, but he had the makings of an intellectually fastidious, pedantic king, impressive yet unappealing. "He will be the wonder and terror of the world if he lives," Bishop Hooper remarked, and others agreed. But the young king's physical frailty was becoming alarming, and it made his councilors, especially the Duke of Northumberland, attempt to entrench themselves more securely in power while they enriched themselves at the realm's expense.

Northumberland was a much better leader than Somerset had been. Under his ruthless command, domestic peace was restored, potential rebels kept in check through fear of his foreign mercenaries. Financial disorder was somewhat stabilized, and the wars with Scotland and France were brought to an end. But the underlying social ills remained, and good government was nowhere to be had. Northumberland himself was none too secure. King Edward, his health failing, was at the mercy of a coterie of opportunists that was gradually turning in on itself and devouring its own.

Thin and weak, King Edward lost his vitality and fell prey to a series of diseases. In the spring of 1552 he had measles and smallpox, and his convalescence was very slow. Those who saw him in July and August shook their heads, certain that he could not survive much longer. "It was observed on all sides how sickly he looked," wrote one observer, "and general pity was felt for him by the people." A Milanese physician who came to the English court noted that the king bore "an appearance on his face denoting early death," and added that "his vital powers will always be weak."

It was to be a long, slow decline. Edward lingered into the following year, with a "tough, strong, straining cough" and much feebleness and "faintness of spirit." There were rumors that someone—probably someone with political ambitions—had dosed the king with a slow-acting poison.

England was not only losing a king, it was losing a faith—and an insecurely rooted faith at that. Dying without an heir of his own body, the throne would pass to Edward's oldest half-sister Mary, who had refused to embrace Protestantism and remained a fervent Catholic. If Mary became queen, she would return England to the Roman fold.

In an effort to prevent this, Northumberland, in May of 1553, prevailed on the frail bedridden King Edward to name his Protestant cousin Jane Grey his heir, setting aside Mary's rights. (Jane was the granddaughter of Henry VIII's younger sister Mary.) Edward was only too glad to comply, not wanting to see any further alteration made in the realm's religion. A few weeks earlier, Northumberland had married his son Guildford to the fifteen-year-old Jane, in an effort to ensure that he would be able to hold on to his position of power when Edward died and Jane became queen.

Meanwhile the tubercular king withered into agonized immobility, kept drugged with opiates, his wasted body livid and bloated and covered with a scabrous growth. His attendants could not bear to come near him, he gave off such a stench of putrefaction.

The physicians gave up, and a wise woman dosed him with something vile which made him swell up and added to his pain. Surely no king ever suffered more in his last days. Finally on July 6, 1553, Edward was released from his sufferings and Jane Grey was proclaimed queen.

MARY I

(1553–1558)

"I KNOW THIS QUEEN, SO GOOD, SO EASY, WITHOUT
EXPERIENCE OF LIFE OR OF STATECRAFT; A NOVICE IN
EVERYTHING. I WILL TELL YOU HONESTLY MY
OPINION, THAT UNLESS GOD GUARDS HER SHE WILL
ALWAYS BE CHEATED AND MISLED EITHER BY THE
FRENCH OR HER OWN SUBJECTS, AND AT LAST TAKEN
OFF BY POISON OR SOME OTHER MEANS."

—SIMON RENARD

When Catherine of Aragon, Henry VIII's queen, gave birth in February of 1516 to Princess Mary, the court rejoiced, for Mary was the first of Catherine's many babies to be healthy and strong enough to survive. Both the king and queen hoped fervently that Catherine would soon bear a healthy son.

Baby Mary was given her own large household of servants, with a chamberlain, treasurer, and chaplain as well as a wet-nurse, a governess and four "rockers" to rock her carved wooden cradle. All wore uniforms in her colors of blue and green. Before she was three years old, Mary was given a small miniature throne, upholstered in cloth of gold and velvet, with gold cushions to go under her little feet.

King Henry adored his pretty daughter, carrying her in his arms, showing her off to visiting dignitaries at his court, calling her "the greatest pearl in the kingdom." He saw to it that she was taught to ride and to hunt with a goshawk. By the time she was six years old she was a good horsewoman.

But it was in the schoolroom that Mary excelled. Here she was taught according to a plan of education drawn up by the Spanish humanist Juan Luis Vives, who turned to the misogynistic Saint Jerome for his inspiration. Mary became proficient in Latin, Greek, Italian and French, learning

Spanish from her mother. At the age of nine visitors to her father's court were impressed by her ability to speak fluent Latin, and act in Latin plays. The princess was praised as "handsome and admirable by reason of her great and uncommon mental endowments."

But intellectual attainments were not, according to Vives, the principal goal of education; for a girl, the most important thing was training in virtue. And when it came to virtue, every female started life with a handicap, Vives believed. Females were "the devil's instruments," inherently sinful. Mary was taught to distrust and despise her flesh, to avoid "uncomely gestures" and quench any impulse toward sensuality. She was served bland food lest anything spicy "inflame the body." And she was kept all but cloistered like a nun, so that she could avoid the company of men and "quench the heat of youth."

Vives' program of claustration, cultivated prudery and complete avoidance of sensuality may not have been followed in strict detail, but Mary was carefully watched and guarded throughout her childhood, and remained innocent. Her role model was her strong, quick-witted mother, a proud and dignified Spaniard, never really at home among the English. Catherine knew how to retain her gravitas no matter what her circumstances, and Mary learned from her to do the same.

By the mid-1520s, when Mary was nine, it was apparent that Catherine would have no more children, and Mary was designated Princess of Wales. She was sent to Ludlow with a court of her own, and a council of advisers, to preside over the Welsh march. Mary was heir to her father's throne, but there were objections to her succession. If she became queen, it was argued, she would be either at the mercy of her councilors or of her husband. One way or the other, she would not rule, but be governed by others, and the result would be instability and perhaps even civil war. It would be better, some of King Henry's advisers argued, for him to designate his natural son, Henry Fitzroy, as his successor.

Henry Fitzroy, who was three years younger than Mary, was King Henry's son by one of his many mistresses, Bessie Blount. The boy was made a Knight of the Garter, created earl of Nottingham and duke of Richmond and Somerset. Henry was raising his son as a prince, so that, when the time came, he could substitute Fitzroy for Mary in the succession. The suggestion was made—and rejected—that the king marry his daughter to his natural son, despite their being half-siblings, so that both could succeed.

Mary was aware that Henry Fitzroy was her rival, but from the age of eleven she was much more concerned about a more serious threat to her own and her mother's future: the king's infatuation with Anne Boleyn.

When Mary returned to her father's court from Ludlow, she found it to be in turmoil. Her father had made up his mind to set her mother aside, declaring that their marriage, though sanctioned by the church, was no marriage at all. Before she married Henry, Catherine had been his late brother Arthur's wife (though Catherine claimed that her marriage to Arthur had never been consummated). To marry a brother's widow was an abomination in the sight of God. Therefore the union was invalid, and Henry and Catherine were living in sin; God was punishing them by denying them sons.

Such was Henry's logic—and he was convinced that he was right. But court observers speculated that the king was led astray in his reasoning by his intense infatuation for Anne Boleyn, and by his hope that, once Queen Catherine was set aside, he would marry Anne and she would give him sons.

Anne became Queen Catherine's nemesis—and Mary's. Anne took Catherine's place at court, and acted as if she were queen. Her threats, her growing influence over the king, and her eventual triumph were the dominant themes of Mary's life throughout her maturing years.

Queen Catherine was exposed to one humiliation after another, pressured to enter a convent (which she haughtily refused to do), insulted by her husband's wooing of Anne, removed from the court and kept in uncomfortable, undignified confinement. All this was wrenching to her daughter, who found herself the unwanted offspring of a cast-off queen.

Once his "pearl of the world," Mary was now ignored or mistreated by her father. Wounded and confused by the swift and sudden changes, in a constant state of uncertainty and suspended hopes, the princess prayed for her mother's vindication while living under constant strain. For the issue of the "king's great matter," as it was called, dragged out for years, a sequence of delays and disappointments. The pope refused to release the English king from his marriage, and all the Catholic powers of Europe stood behind Queen Catherine, especially her nephew, Holy Roman Emperor Charles V, who threatened Henry VIII with war.

Mary was seventeen when her father, despairing of a resolution, declared his union with Catherine dissolved, married the pregnant Anne Boleyn and had her crowned queen. The allegiance of the English church to the pope was withdrawn; the Reformation Parliament declared that henceforth King Henry was head of the English church.

Queen Anne's daughter Elizabeth was born in the fall of 1533 and Mary's degradation began. She was no longer princess but merely "the lady Mary, the king's daughter," and was deprived of her succession rights. Forced to live in shabby rooms in the household of the tiny Princess Elizabeth, and to defer to the baby princess in everything, Mary suffered—and protested. She agreed to call Elizabeth "sister," but would not acknowledge use of the title "princess" for anyone but herself.

Mary's stubborn resistance was as dangerous as it was courageous. Like her mother, she had great spirit and scruples of conscience, but she was only a seventeen-year-old girl, facing a powerful, increasingly vengeful king and his pitiless councilors. Had Mary not had the backing and protection of her cousin, Emperor Charles V, she would surely have been imprisoned or harmed.

As it was, Mary carried out a dogged campaign of defiance, objecting loudly every time she heard her half-sister Elizabeth called by the name of princess, or whenever she herself was called "lady Mary." She objected to her position at the dining table, to how she was lodged, to what form of transport she rode in—to everything, in short, that reminded her of her inferior status to Elizabeth. And as often as she protested, she was punished; all her jewels and most of her clothing were confiscated, most of her other possessions taken from her. When she continued to resist, she was manhandled and abused.

Visitors were kept from her—her governess locked her in her room and nailed the windows shut—and she was not allowed to see her mother. After months of tension, obstinacy and punishment, in the winter of 1535, Mary fell ill.

It was a sudden, grave attack of illness, and there were rumors of poison. The king was informed, but did nothing. After six days he allowed the imperial physicians to treat Mary, who did not die, as had been expected, but continued to be chronically ill for months.

Mary suffered from what was known as "strangulation of the womb," a cluster of symptoms that included headache, nausea, vomiting, "an ill habit of body, difficulty of breathing, trembling of the heart, swooning, melancholy, and fearful dreams." Possibly her severe illness attack in 1535 was yet another episode of this malady, or she may have eaten spoiled food that made her violently ill. Whatever it was, the episode of illness frightened her, and she began to think of escape.

According to the imperial ambassador, at nineteen Mary "thought of nothing else" than leaving England secretly, with the help of her cousin

Charles V. "Her desire for it increases every day," the ambassador wrote to the emperor, adding that Mary was certain that if she did not escape, she "considered herself lost, knowing that they wanted only to kill her." From this danger she was providentially delivered when in 1536, Queen Anne fell into royal disfavor and was executed by King Henry.

Now Mary's misfortunes were reversed. She was moved to a more honorable residence, recalled to court, restored to good relations with her father. Banquets were held in her honor and the jewels of the late Queen Anne were given to her. Mary's half-sister Elizabeth, who now bore the stigma of her mother's disgrace, was declared to be illegitimate. The king's new wife, Jane Seymour, was instrumental in the reconciliation of father and daughter.

Declaring that she "willingly forgave and forgot," Mary went on, rejoicing at her good fortune, though mourning the loss of her mother, who had died in lonely isolation.

At twenty, Mary was an exceptionally pretty young woman, judged by the French ambassador to be one of the beauties of her father's court. With a fresh complexion, slim figure and sweet, gentle manner, she seemed likely to marry as soon as her father could arrange a match for her. She was active and robust, exercising vigorously each morning and often walking two or three miles after breakfast. Her only disadvantages were a deep, mannish voice, short stature and the everpresent attacks of her chronic illness—which led to worries about her ability to have children.

Mary was nearing thirty-one when her father died, and the throne passed to her nine-year-old half-brother Edward, son of Henry VIII and Jane Seymour. No husband had been found for Mary during her father's last years, and as a spinster in her thirties, her prospects for marriage were slim. It was presumed that she would live out her life at her brother's court, in honorable retirement, perhaps devoting herself to good works, for her Catholic faith was strong and she had a reputation for benevolence.

But this placid future was to be denied her. With the advent of a minor king, the realm was once again plunged into chaos and the king's uncle, Edward Seymour, who exercised nominal rule as Protector for his royal nephew, was unable to keep order. A new religious settlement moved the country further away from Catholic tradition and established an unambiguously Protestant theology. As an outward sign of this shift, churches were vandalized, statues of the saints destroyed, stained glass windows smashed.

Mary's own unwavering Catholicism made her an important symbol to many of the English who were unsettled by the violent overturning of the old order, and who, like Mary, clung to the old ways. Mary believed implicitly that she had been spared by God during all the dangers she had lived through, and that divine providence would continue to deliver her. Her faith became deeper than ever during her thirties; lacking a husband and children to fill the emotional void in her life, and aware that Catholicism was under assault, she made it the cause to which she devoted her entire being. She heard three or four masses each day, and held prayer services in her chapel each night.

Though urged to give up the mass and conform to the new Protestant usages, Mary remained stubbornly Catholic. She continued to believe that providence was shielding her from the wrath of her brother's councilors— while failing to grasp the fact that she was spared persecution because her cousin Charles V warned the English government that further interference in Mary's affairs would result in war with the Empire.

It was a hazardous miscalculation, and a revealing one. Mary's character had been formed, and though she was admirable in her strength of will and nobility of conscience, she was lamentably naive when it came to worldly understanding. Her view of life was overly simplistic. To Mary, people were either wholly good or wholly bad, situations entirely perilous or entirely beneficial. The subtleties of politics, the thick tangle of motives, often contradictory motives, that drive human behavior eluded her. Lacking guile and subtlety herself, she failed to detect it in others and read them incorrectly. Rather than using her substantial intellect to unravel complexity, she denied it—and asserted the prepotence of the divine.

"This natural life of ours is but a pilgrimage from this wandering world, and exile from our own country," Mary wrote in 1549 in her "Meditation Touching Adversity." "Sickness, weepings, sorrow, mourning, and all adversities be unto us as spurs ... to remember our proper and true country."

King Edward, always a fragile child, had become a sickly adolescent. His health continued to fail, and by the time he reached the age of fifteen, it was evident that he could not live long. Mary was Edward's heir, and there was no doubt that when she became queen, Mary would undo the religious changes and restore Catholicism.

John Dudley, Earl of Northumberland, the most powerful member of the royal council, was determined to prevent her accession. Dudley prevailed on the dying King Edward, weak and bedridden with tuberculosis, to name his Protestant cousin Jane Grey as his heir, removing Mary from the succession. Northumberland had married his son Guildford Dudley to the fifteen-year-old Jane so that his family would be favored by the new queen.

On July 6, 1553, Edward died and Jane was proclaimed queen.

Without hesitating, confident that the throne was rightfully hers and that God would favor her cause, Mary went to Framlingham in Suffolk to rally her supporters. Her contingent grew, while in London, where Jane was precariously installed as queen, there was dissent and, before long, capitulation. Northumberland's attempt to manipulate the succession had failed. The English wanted no one but Henry VIII's eldest daughter, Mary, for their queen.

On her accession Mary was thirty-seven, still a striking woman, very slender, with auburn hair and hazel eyes. Her expression, an Italian observer thought, was of "great benignity and clemency," and her trusting nature, her own personal goodness were evident. Despite her age she still had the look of an unawakened girl, though her features, in repose, were somewhat set and grim. She had been through a great deal in her thirty-seven years, and it showed.

As queen she was determined to be conscientious, and set high standards for herself. She rose at daybreak, said her prayers, heard a private mass, and then worked at her desk until one or two o'clock in the afternoon, when she ate a sparing dinner. Much to the amazement of her councilors, conditioned to expect little of a queen regnant, Mary was present at every council meeting and heard "every detail of public business." She often worked until late into the evening, reading despatches, answering petitions, writing letters. Her intelligence and competence were apparent to all, but so were her weaknesses.

"I know this queen," the imperial ambassador Simon Renard wrote early in Mary's reign, "so good, so easy, without experience of life or of statecraft; a novice in everything." In Renard's view, Mary was doomed to be "cheated and misled" by all those around her, and sooner or later she would be "taken off by poison or some other means."

Pride was among Mary's besetting faults. She was "inclined to talk about her exalted station," and evidently inordinately proud of it. Her air of solemnity was meant to draw attention to her own majesty, and made her vulnerable to flattery.

Mary and her council made a start at improving some of the financial difficulties that had burdened the realm ever since the last years of Henry

VIII's reign. A survey of customs duties led to a considerable increase in crown revenues. With an eye to improving trade and restoring local government, which had suffered much disruption, roads were repaired and broken bridges reconstructed.

Mary's first priority, however, was reconciling England with Rome. She appointed Catholics to bishoprics and restored Catholic doctrine and practices. Broken altars were mended and dismantled shrines rebuilt. She gave up the title Supreme Head of the church and in November of 1554, Cardinal Pole, in a formal ceremony, absolved England of its sin of schism and brought it back within the Roman fold.

But though Catholics rejoiced, Protestants resisted. A generation of vilification of the pope and the mass had left many, especially among the young, in doubt, and Protestant sectarians were as staunch in their faith as the queen was in hers. She met with resistance in another quarter as well. When her father secularized the monasteries, he gave the monastic lands to his nobles and gentry—and now, when Mary asked for them to be returned, the nobles and gentry resisted.

Worst of all, Mary, true to her convictions, reimposed Catholicism on her subjects by force, punishing hundreds who refused to convert by burning at the stake, and giving the Protestants a handful of martyrs—Cranmer, Latimer, Ridley, Hooper—whose deaths became the stuff of legend. The queen's image was forever tarnished in the memory of the English; she was not Queen Mary, but "Bloody Mary" of infamous memory.

Mary's almost complete naivete in regard to sex and romantic love led her painfully astray, and ultimately proved her undoing. She had always dreamed of marriage, and it was only natural that when searching for a husband she should turn to her Hapsburg relatives. They were Catholic, they were faithful. They were the only ones who had consistently cared about her welfare.

The queen chose Prince Philip of Spain, a somber, stuffy, rather dull young man of twenty-six with large, mild eyes and a receding hairline. There was a noble sadness in his expression, or so Mary thought when she saw his magnificent portrait by Titian. In actuality, the dark circles under Philip's eyes were produced by mild stomach upsets and dissipation, but Mary was not to know this. She idealized him—and as in all other aspects of her life, she believed that she was divinely guided to choose him.

Mary confided to the imperial ambassador Renard that, before making her selection, she did not sleep for two days and nights, spending all her time in continual weeping and prayer, asking God to inspire her with the right decision about her marriage. And God, "who had performed so many miracles in her favor," inspired her to marry Philip.

For Mary, the marriage was a tragedy. She loved her husband, but though Philip showed her every courtesy, he had no feeling for her whatsoever and soon left England to attend to his continental affairs. "I confess I do unspeakably long to have him here," Mary wrote to her cousin Charles V. Believing that she was pregnant, Mary waited for her child to be born—and then, in an agony of disappointment and embarrassment, had to admit that it had been a false pregnancy. In fact she had ovarian cancer, and by autumn 1558 was near death.

Mary's reign, like her marriage, had been a failure. As she prepared herself for death she described to those who stood around her bed "what good dreams she had, seeing many little children like angels playing before her, singing pleasing notes, giving her more than earthly comfort."

Lost in her heavenly visions, and having sent her beloved Philip a ring as a sign of her undying love, Mary heard a last mass and died early in the morning of November 17, 1558. She was forty-two.

ELIZABETH I

(1558–1603)

❖ ⟐❈⟐ ❖

**"I KNOW I HAVE THE BODY OF A WEAK AND
FEEBLE WOMAN, BUT I HAVE THE HEART AND
STOMACH OF A KING."**

—ELIZABETH TUDOR

When the newborn Elizabeth Tudor lay in her great cradle of estate, swaddled tightly and watched over by her nurses and rockers, she was the object of widespread gossip. As the news of her birth reached the courts of Europe, she became the most talked-of child in Christendom.

For Elizabeth was the daughter of the infamous woman known as the Great Whore, Anne Boleyn, the fruit of King Henry VIII's scandalous and unholy second marriage. And instead of being the boy the king had wanted so badly, she was a girl—a sign, so it seemed to Henry's critics, that God was punishing him.

From her birth in September of 1533 Elizabeth was shrouded in scandal. And before she was three years old, her notoriety darkened when her mother Anne was executed, accused of treason.

Whether or not Elizabeth, as an adult, had any memories of her mother is unknown, but Anne Boleyn overshadowed her daughter's childhood in countless ways. Perhaps Anne's primary influence was merely the negative one that she was absent. Young Elizabeth lacked the comfort, security and nurture of a mother's love and the fierce tenacity of a mother's protection—something her half-sister Mary had in abundance.

Anne's disgrace meant that Elizabeth was declared illegitimate, and in fact, even her royal paternity came into question, for King Henry, full of spite against Anne, fostered rumors that Elizabeth was the child of one of Anne's many lovers. (Mary Tudor always believed that her half-sister resembled Mark Smeaton, a musician and groom of the chamber in the royal household who was executed along with Queen Anne.)

Because he associated Elizabeth with the wife he had loved most and whose alleged betrayal had wounded him most grievously, Henry ignored Elizabeth, rarely visiting her and leaving her upbringing to others. He gave her a large and comfortable household, but denied her his company.

Worst of all, Elizabeth bore the stigma of Anne's transgressions. It was assumed that she would grow up to resemble Anne, and Anne had been accused, not only of infidelity and promiscuity, but of incest and murder (it was said she had poisoned Queen Catherine), and of conspiring to kill her royal husband. Indeed the catalogue of Anne's crimes included transgressions so unspeakable that they had never been divulged—but were known to those who sent her to her death. That these terrible things were only hinted at, never disclosed, made Elizabeth's legacy even more sinister.

Thin and fair-skinned, with her father's coloring, as a girl Elizabeth had delicate features and eyelashes and eyebrows so light they were nearly invisible, giving her a perpetually startled look. At the age of six she impressed a visitor as possessing "great gravity," and a precocious maturity. Her self-possession was born of fear, for she had observed what a fearsome thing it was to bring down on herself her father's wrath. Her half-sister had displeased King Henry, and had been punished by Henry's deputy, the Duke of Norfolk, with shouts and curses and the terrible threat that her head would be dashed against a wall until her skull cracked and became "soft as a boiled apple."

As Elizabeth grew older the training of her gifted intellect was handed over to two learned humanists from Cambridge, Richard Coxe and John Cheke, and eventually to William Grindal and finally Roger Ascham. Study of Latin and Greek classics was supplemented by readings in theology, composition and French and Italian. Like other highborn young women, she was trained in deportment, learned to play the virginals, and practiced her needlework.

When Elizabeth was eleven years old, she sent her third stepmother Catherine Parr a handwritten book she had made, its cover skillfully embroidered in blue and silver with clusters of purple flowers. Inside, in admirably clear handwriting, was a treatise Elizabeth had translated from French into fluent, ornate English: a devotional work entitled "The Mirror of the Sinful Soul."

By the time of Henry VIII's death in 1547, Elizabeth was a slender, sloe-eyed girl with red hair and milk-white skin, with a steely vigilance in her unsmiling gaze. A contemporary, Jane Dormer, who knew Elizabeth well commented on her striking looks and "proud and disdainful" expression and manner. At thirteen, Elizabeth was already a figure to be reckoned with, though no one expected her to reign. Her half-brother Edward, son of Henry VIII and his third wife Jane Seymour, became king as Edward VI on Henry's death and it was assumed that Elizabeth and Mary would live out their lives in comfortable obscurity in the orbit of the new king's court. Once Edward grew old enough to marry and have children, his sisters would cease to have any dynastic significance.

Thomas Seymour bounded into Elizabeth's life just as she reached adolescence. Handsome, cocksure, thoughtless, devastatingly attractive, he was well connected politically—being the brother of Edward Seymour, Lord Protector and virtual ruler of England during King Edward VI's minority—and highly ambitious. A man of action, Seymour wanted to advance himself by marrying well, and when the royal council denied him permission to marry either of the king's sisters, he married the late Henry VIII's widow, Catherine Parr.

Elizabeth lived in her stepmother Catherine's household, and an emotional triangle developed between Seymour, Catherine and Elizabeth which put the latter very much at risk. Disregarding propriety, Seymour burst into Elizabeth's bedchamber early in the morning, "striking her upon the back or the buttocks familiarly" while she was dressing or still in bed. Elizabeth's servant Kat Ashley, who slept in her bedchamber, tried to keep Seymour in line (though privately encouraging the flirtation) but he was irrepressible, and eventually Seymour's wife Catherine "came suddenly upon them [Seymour and Elizabeth] when they were all alone." Her husband had her stepdaughter in his arms.

Elizabeth was sent away in disgrace, and once again became the subject of gossip. What could one expect, people said unkindly, from the daughter of Anne Boleyn, except sexual misconduct?

Precisely what went on between Elizabeth and her much older wooer can never be known for certain, but because Seymour was subsequently imprisoned for treason against the king, Elizabeth came under suspicion and was interrogated mercilessly. Though terribly frightened, she matched wits capably with her interrogators, evading and eluding, feinting and parrying their questions and avoiding arrest, which could have meant imprisonment and even death.

In the aftermath of her ordeal, she went out of her way to cultivate an image of innocent, sober piety to contrast with the widely received image of her as the morally compromised daughter of the late Queen Anne. Aligning herself with her brother Edward's soberly Protestant court, she wore only simply cut gowns of black velvet, and simple headdresses, shunning adornment. She found favor with Edward—but Edward, who had always been sickly, died at fifteen and there was a struggle over the succession.

When Elizabeth's half-sister Mary became queen, and returned England to Catholicism, Elizabeth came under suspicion. Elizabeth had associated herself strongly with Protestantism, and though she attended mass, and swore tearfully, during a painful audience with Mary, that she had adopted the Catholic usages from conviction and not out of "fear, hypocrisy, or dissimulation," Mary did not believe her.

Elizabeth's keen political instincts were sharpened by her experience living on the razor's edge of Marian politics. Unlike her unworldly half-sister, Elizabeth saw the subtleties, ambiguities and contradictions in human behavior; she knew how to be both flexible and devious. Self-preservation had become second nature to her, and unlike Mary, she looked to herself, rather than to providence, to save her.

Elizabeth's adroitness aside, she owed her survival during the dangerous years of her sister's reign at least in part to luck. When rebels rose in Elizabeth's name, Mary might well have had her put to death had the members of the royal council, and Mary's husband Prince Philip of Spain, not urged against it. It was Elizabeth's good fortune that Philip wanted her spared; he had plans for her future. For Mary, pursued by ill luck for much of her life, was unwell and Philip intended to marry Elizabeth as soon as he was a widower.

Mary's unhappy reign wound down amid disappointment and popular dissatisfaction. Mary's marriage to the Spaniard Philip was resented and her persecution of Protestants abhorred. The more unpopular the queen grew, the more her subjects looked to Elizabeth to deliver them from their aging, barren monarch. For in the absence of an heir of Mary's body, Elizabeth was her likely successor.

In November of 1558 Mary died, and the twenty-five-year-old Elizabeth, weeping with relief (or so she said thirty years later), became queen.

From the start of her reign, the Spanish envoy Feria noted, Queen Elizabeth I was "incomparably more feared" than her half-sister had been, and "gave her orders and had her way absolutely as her father did." Elizabeth prided herself on her resemblance to her father, spoke of him often, and "gloried in him," as a French observer wrote. She enjoyed it when people said she was much more like Henry VIII than Mary had been. Taking King Henry as her model, Elizabeth exerted a strong sense of command. She expected to be obeyed, and was.

She enjoyed the challenges of power, and boldly took control, making all decisions herself—though she expected her councilors to advise her exhaustively beforehand and blamed them vociferously when any decision proved ill advised. When factions formed, she played them off against one another rather than allowing her authority to be undermined. It was among Elizabeth's greatest skills that she was able to take the measure of each man who served her, calculate his strengths and weaknesses, and then use her insights to manage him, while benefiting from his counsel.

It was of the essence of Elizabeth's mystique that she was a woman—but "a very strange sort of woman," as the Spanish envoy Feria wrote. She was neither passive nor conventionally self-effacing, as women were taught to be; instead she was uninhibited, spontaneous rather than controlled in her emotions, free in her manners in the way that Henry VIII had been. Seemingly unconcerned about what others thought, she said what she thought and acted the way she felt.

It was baffling, a young and pretty woman—"a young lass, sharp, but without prudence," Feria wrote—who was at the same time commanding and personally enchanting. She lacked Mary's gravitas but possessed more valuable qualities in a ruler: unique political skills combined with a strength of character and a forceful personal presence.

Elizabeth inspired awe, yet at the same time she retained a capacity for girlish delight and pleasure, enjoying dancing the high-jumping, vigorous galliards and stately pavanes then in fashion, costuming herself magnificently in gowns of rich embroidered damask and cloth of silver, adorning herself with costly jewels. Gone was the image of maidenly simplicity she had once cultivated. Now that the kingdom was hers, Elizabeth became a royal peacock—but never gaudy, as Mary had been, always in exquisite taste.

"She is very fond of having things given to her," an ambassador noted after presenting her with an expensive ring. Vanity was prominent in her, and though she distrusted flattery, she could not help but like it and encourage it, as she liked and encouraged male admiration.

Elizabeth was very much a novice when it came to foreign affairs, and began her reign with no experience whatsoever in overseeing England's role in European affairs. But guided by her councilors, she learned quickly. The greatest potential threat came from a possible alliance of France and Spain to overthrow Elizabeth and place the Catholic Mary Stuart, queen of Scotland and wife (soon to be widow) of the French dauphin, on the English throne. Scotland was a potential source of danger, with its Catholic queen and with a restive nobility; traditionally, France had used Scotland as a staging area from which to invade England.

Complicating the foreign threats was the question of the succession. It was essential for Elizabeth to marry and have children, indeed, to most of her subjects, it was unthinkable that she would not. Parliament urged her to marry as quickly as possible, not only to protect the throne but to silence the gossip surrounding the queen and her horse master, Robert Dudley; it was widely believed that the two were lovers, and when Dudley's wife Amy Robsart died under suspicious circumstances, the queen's name was blackened.

Although Elizabeth entertained and encouraged a number of suitors for her hand, she allowed her potential childbearing years to slip away while she remained unmarried. That she loved Robert Dudley seems certain, but she knew that if she married him, factional jealousies would make her government difficult to operate. Beyond this, Elizabeth knew that marriage would inevitably bring with it subordination, and she liked too well being in command. Thus she continued, year after year, to play the dangerous game of appearing to be serious about the search for a husband, and dangling before foreign princes and archdukes the possibility that she might one day wed. But in the end all the maneuvering and negotiations, while they gained England diplomatic advantages, came to nothing.

By the time she reached midlife Elizabeth was truly formidable. Her colorful, unpredictable, usually indecorous behavior kept everyone at her court off balance. She swore, she shouted, she forgot her manners and swaggered unconscionably before the abashed visitors in the presence chamber.

"God's death!" she roared when a luckless councilor or official offended her; she swore, in fact, "by God, by Christ, and by many parts of his glorified body, and by saints, faith, troth, and other forbidden things," and she seemed to like it when those around her swore too—though they swore at her, surely, to their peril.

The queen loved the sound of her own voice. "It is her wont," wrote a diplomat much wearied by Elizabeth's torrent of language, "to make long digressions and after much circumlocution to come to the point of which she wishes to speak." "As a rule," wrote another, "she speaks continuously."

Truculent, violent (she sometimes struck her waiting maids with heavy brass candlesticks when they displeased her), disagreeable, arrogant, always majestic: such was the mighty Tudor queen, "the great lioness," as the hawkers of street ballads called her.

By the 1580s, when Elizabeth faced her greatest challenges, she was on the threshold of old age. Her nemesis King Philip II of Spain, once her brother-in-law and, after he became a widower, a suitor for her hand in marriage, was preparing to invade England and seize her throne.

In 1588 Philip assembled an immense fleet of 130 ships and twenty thousand fighting men, expecting to be joined by another huge army under the Duke of Parma. Once he landed in England, Philip expected that the English Catholics would rise in rebellion and join the Spaniards in overcoming the forces of the queen.

Against this onslaught Elizabeth had an efficient navy but no standing army, only local levies and the small bodies of troops raised by the nobility—a total of perhaps twelve thousand fighting men. The queen visited her troops, amassed at Tilbury, riding on a huge white warhorse, armed like a queen out of antique mythology in a silver cuirass and carrying a silver truncheon, plumes waving from her bright orange wig.

"My loving people," she shouted to the assembled troops, "we have been persuaded by some that are careful for our safety, to take heed how we commit ourselves to armed multitudes, for fear of treachery. But I assure you, I do not desire to live to distrust my faithful and loving people." Amid cheers, she told the men that she had "placed her chiefest strength and safeguard in the loyal hearts and good will of her subjects," and that she was resolved to live or die with them, "to lay down for my God and for my kingdom and for my people, my honor and my blood, even in the dust."

Her words were deeply stirring, as was the sight of her thin, aging, yet valiant figure.

"I know I have the body of a weak and feeble woman," she told them, "but I have the heart and stomach of a king."

The great Armada sailed slowly up the Channel, pursued by the English fleet, and dropped anchor off Calais. The English admiral sent fireships which did much damage and caused many of the Spanish vessels to cut their cables and run. Some two-thirds of the Spanish soldiers died, while English losses were negligible.

The defeat of the Spanish Armada was a great victory, as great, in the view of Elizabeth's contemporaries, as the battle of Agincourt in the fifteenth century. Twice more in the 1590s King Philip sent large fleets against England, and twice more the English were spared—by storms which wrecked many ships and made landings impossible for the others.

The English revered their victorious queen, yet as she entered her sixties she was confronted by mounting problems—poor harvests which left her subjects in want, financial pressures, a strident Puritan movement which complained about the religious settlement (a moderate Protestantism, which was to endure), and Parliamentary opposition. There were those who said that she had been queen too long, and looked forward eagerly to a change of reigns.

The elderly queen, now a grotesque and coarsened caricature of her former self, still dressing with outrageous coquetry, still whooping with loud laughter and stabbing at her councilors and others with her mordant wit, resisted the effects of her evident physical decline. Ignoring the pains in her hip and the mocking laughter of her chamber women, she danced alone in her bedchamber, tossing her head and stamping her feet with abandon to the music of whistles and drums. She went for long walks in her gardens and hunting parks, tiring out the attendant who marched unwillingly at her heels. She consulted astrologers and drank elixirs of perpetual youth.

Though assailed from time to time by depression, Elizabeth managed to overcome her morbid thoughts and showed remarkable resilience. But she could not go on forever, and in her seventieth year, worn down by pain in her joints, unable to sleep, her appetite gone, she succumbed to a listless sadness and died, leaving her throne to King James VI of Scotland.

Long before she died Elizabeth had entered the realm of myth. Poets had saluted her as Gloriana, the Virgin Queen, the mighty lioness whose stalwart leadership had roused England to defeat the might of Spain. Her quarrelsome nature, her deceit and dissimulation, her eccentricity were cloaked in a mantle of legend, and in that legend she was eternally serene, eternally youthful and beautiful. She had become the symbol of England's triumph.

Future generations, troubled by political and social conflict and dissatisfied with tyrannical or unappealing rulers, looked back on the Elizabethan era as a halcyon season, forgetting that it too was shaped by conflict and that Queen Elizabeth had many critics and left to her successor a fissured and unsettled realm. The mythic image of the queen was more appealing, and ultimately more useful, than the reality; her name became, and remains, a watchword for the glory of England.

JAMES I

(1603–1625)

————— ◆▷◆✳◆◁◆ —————

> "AWKWARD IN HIS PERSON AND UNGAINLY IN HIS
> MANNERS, HE WAS ILL-QUALIFIED TO COMMAND
> RESPECT. PARTIAL AND UNDISCERNING IN HIS
> AFFECTIONS, HE WAS LITTLE FITTED TO ACQUIRE
> GENERAL LOVE."
>
> —DAVID HUME

When King James VI of Scotland learned, late in March of 1603, that he had at long last become King of England he was beside himself with delight. He had known for years that the childless Queen Elizabeth would eventually look to him as her successor, but she had never formally named him as her heir. On her deathbed she did.

Within days James was on his way to his new kingdom, having borrowed ten thousand marks from the city of Edinburgh to finance his journey. As king of Scotland, James had been deeply in debt for years. But now that he had inherited the great and wealthy kingdom of England, his financial difficulties were certain to be over.

The farther south he rode, the greener and more fertile the land became. Stony, mountainous Scotland gave way to verdant England, with its lush meadows and fertile fields. Sparsely populated, widely scattered villages were replaced by prosperous towns, their streets bustling with traffic. Everywhere James went, crowds gathered to greet him, the women dropping curtseys of respect, the men throwing their caps in the air and shouting "Hurrah for King James!"

"The multitudes of people in highways, fields, meadows, closes and on trees, were such that they covered the beauty of the fields," wrote one contemporary. "And so greedy were they to behold the countenance of the king, that with much unruliness they injured and hurt one another, some even hazarded to the danger of death."

It was a tumultuous welcome, and James, savoring everything about his new kingdom, took his time making his way to London. He was entertained at several great country houses, where he enjoyed hunting—his favorite pastime—and was awed by the affluence of the nobles and the extent of their vast parks. One day when he was riding, in his usual reckless fashion, from Burghley to Exton, he fell from his horse, and lay as if lifeless. His companions panicked. Was it possible that the new king had died before he could be crowned?

But James was a veteran of hunting accidents. He fell off his horse frequently, and just as frequently staggered to his feet, bruised but otherwise unharmed. With a wave of his hand he dismissed the fears of those in his entourage and was soon on the road again.

In 1603 James was thirty-seven. He had never known what it was not to be king, having inherited the Scottish throne at the age of thirteen months. But his childhood had been violent and unsettled, making him wary and suspicious. His father Darnley, of whom he had no memory, had been murdered, with his mother, Mary, Queen of Scots, among those who conspired to murder him; she subsequently married Darnley's assassin. Mary, forced to abdicate, had fled to England where she was held captive. Of the four successive regents who ruled on James's behalf during his minority, two died violently and a third was rumored to have died of poison.

A portrait of young James at the age of eight shows a slight, grave, thoughtful child, dressed in the wide stuffed trousers, high ruff and plumed hat of an aristocrat, holding a falcon. He was already surprising his tutors with his exceptional mind and genuine curiosity and love of learning. At eight he was translating passages from French into Latin with ease, and would soon go on to show a talent for writing both verse and prose.

But James's classical education, while it guided his mastery of language, taught him nothing about such worldly matters as finance or politics. Because he was physically timid—the legacy of his turbulent childhood—he was not trained in military skills, and the idea of having to make war repelled him. As fighting, either in tournaments or on the battlefield, was the natural pastime of the noble class, this aversion, coupled with his "naturally timorous disposition," alienated James from his nobles, and made him an object of ridicule.

A physical weakling, as an adolescent James had shown himself to be a coward, who liked only to hunt, to read (which he did, prodigiously) and to talk. To protect himself he wore thick quilted doublets, so padded that they provided a kind of armor against any assassin who might attack him with a knife. When he revealed a sexual preference for men, falling in love with his cousin Esmé Stewart and elevating him to a position of authority on the royal council, some of his nobles kidnapped James and held him captive, banishing Stewart and controlling James's every move. After nearly a year James escaped, but continued to resent his jailers; after he began to rule on his own behalf, at seventeen, he made it a priority to bring the turbulent Scots nobles under control.

James's reign as King of Scotland had not been entirely successful. He had been able to dominate the church but had achieved only an imperfect dominion over the nobility. He had narrowly escaped assassination several times, most recently in 1600. By allying himself with Queen Elizabeth, he had kept peace with England, but at a cost; Elizabeth had ordered the execution of James's mother Mary in 1587.

But the greatest obstacle James had faced in his long reign in Scotland had been a chronic shortage of money, which had led him to depreciate the currency repeatedly, much to the despair of his subjects. He spent more than he took in, and was incapable of managing what funds he had—or of finding capable royal servants to manage them for him. James's perennial insolvency was to pursue him even in England, where it became a persistent theme of his reign.

No sooner had James installed himself in London than an epidemic of plague broke out with exceptional virulence. As the weather warmed, the disease spread, disrupting plans for the coronation and causing Londoners to murmur that the king had brought a curse with him from Scotland.

On July 25 James and his queen, Anne of Denmark, were crowned but without the customary pomp of a procession from the Tower to Westminster. Within weeks the entire court left the capital in an effort to escape the disease, traveling from one country house to another, "continually haunted with the sickness," as one royal official wrote, "by reason of the disorderly company that do follow us." Everywhere they went, it seemed, the royal party carried the plague with them.

It was an anxious time, but by the following spring the infection had abated, and the new king was able to ride in his ceremonial procession.

There had been no coronation procession for more than forty years, and when King James appeared, riding on his white horse amid his gorgeously appareled entourage of officials, clerics and soldiers, he was loudly cheered.

Seven specially built triumphal arches had been erected in various parts of the city, with pageantry, music and staged entertainment at each. For five hours the king, who disliked crowds and shunned the scrutiny of his subjects, endured the noisy applause, the intense excitement, the endless speechifying, singing and mumming. To judge from the high degree of popular favor, the new dynasty was secure.

James had lost no time adapting to his role as English sovereign. He sent away the rough servants of his former household and acquired a large new household, at considerable cost. He bought himself a fine wardrobe of velvet cloaks and suits of cloth of gold and silver, complete with boots, garters and gloves—and especially stockings, of which he had never had enough when King of Scotland. His extravagance drew comment; it was said that he bought a new pair of gloves every day, and other garments at frequent intervals. He was less generous with Queen Anne, expecting her to replenish her wardrobe with the outmoded garments left behind by the late Queen Elizabeth.

The initial enthusiasm that had greeted King James began to diminish as the English came into increased contact with the Scots. The English snubbed the Scottish courtiers as lice-ridden and "beggarly," greedy for money and advancement, unworthy and ill-bred. The king himself, when not riding in ceremonial splendor, seemed to his subjects appallingly unregal in his behavior, loutish and utterly lacking in dignity. He talked incessantly, and hardly ever listened; he wore down their patience with his endless harangues and his strongly held opinions.

The entire tone of the court deteriorated, or so it seemed to the king's critics. Where Queen Elizabeth had had first-rate troupes of actors performing a variety of plays, many of them works of rare genius, King James allowed his wife to act in masques, elaborately staged but culturally shallow pageants featuring sea-nymphs and tritons, mermaids and monsters. The queen participated enthusiastically, "appearing often in various dresses to the ravishment of the beholders."

James applauded the masques, but preferred what he called "fooleries," with the men of his chamber—Sir Edward Zouche, Sir George Goring and Sir John Finet—his "chief and master fools." With Sir George as the drunken master of the revels, and a troupe of fiddlers playing in the background, Sir Edward sang ribald songs and told obscene jokes. The royal fools rode one another like horses, staging mock tournaments, and making the king laugh helplessly when they fell off.

"I ne'er did see such lack of good order, discretion, and sobriety, as I have now done," said one of Elizabeth's former courtiers, who thought that the "king's own lax example" was entirely to blame. Where Elizabeth had always maintained a measure of dignity and distance between herself and her subjects, James was loose and informal, unbuttoned and louche.

The debauchery at Whitehall reached new depths when the queen's brother, King Christian IV of Denmark, visited the court in 1606 and a masque was held in which the Queen of Sheba was gorgeously enthroned amid a bevy of allegorical figures, including Hope, Faith and Charity, Victory and Peace. All the performers had had far too much wine—as had the monarch—and the performance was disrupted when the Queen of Sheba fell over drunk, Victory and Peace staggered off the stage and Hope and Faith had to be helped to bed, "both sick and spewing." King Christian, far gone in drink himself, had to be carried to "an inner chamber" to sleep off the night's excesses.

It all amused James very much—as did the discomfiture of the more puritanical members of the court. For James, at bottom, cared little what others thought of him. He knew who and what he was: physically ugly, uncouth, given to dissipation, but an anointed king, and therefore exalted beyond other men.

James's view of kingship—and of governance in general—was available in print for all who were literate to read. He had written two treatises, *Basilikon Doron (Royal Gift)* and *The True Law of Free Monarchies*, in which he set forth his staunchly held beliefs.

In the Bible, James wrote, kings are called gods, because they sit upon God's throne on earth and are responsible to God alone for their acts. To rebel against a king was therefore not only unlawful but blasphemous, since the king is God's representative. In James's view, a king had the obligation to protect his people, and to rule them well, but was not in any sense answerable to them for his deeds.

The idea of a ruler turning to his people, or to their elected representatives in Parliament, for approval or support was antithetical to this philosophy. A king's subjects, by definition, were inferior beings, the nobles "feckless and arrogant" and full of conceit, the merchants concerned only with their own profits, the craftsmen inherently lazy and given to rioting, the clergy troublemakers who led the people astray.

Such were King James's views, and when coupled with a stalwart Scots patriotism, they were offensive to the English. "England was famous, victorious and glorious," James once said in a speech, "but she had been conquered; Scotland never had." The kings of Scotland, when they bestirred themselves, were "ever victorious." Such tactless statements, made to men whose ancestors had fought at Flodden and Solway Moss and Pinkie Cleugh—all notable English victories over the Scots—were insulting, especially coming from a monarch who disdained war and lacked physical courage.

By 1610, when James had been King of England for seven years, he had alienated many of his subjects. England, far from being the Eden he had once thought it, had turned out to be a wilderness full of vipers. James found his English subjects to be unruly and ungrateful; they in turn found his constant loquacity, frequent drunkenness and exalted view of monarchy repugnant.

Rather than try to mend the breach, James avoided his responsibilities, spending his days hunting. "He seems to have forgotten that he is a king," the Venetian ambassador wrote, "except in his kingly pursuit of stags, to which he is quite foolishly devoted."

James pursued stags with a passion, galloping so recklessly after his hounds that he was often thrown from his horse, so eager was he to reach the fallen beast, tear open its belly and, as was the hunter's custom, thrust his hands and feet inside to cover them with the warm gore. He not only pursued stags, but anything that ran, flew or swam. At the end of his day's hunt, his servants would bring home braces of hares and baskets of larks and fish, to be prepared and eaten in the royal household.

Nor were blood sports limited to the hunting field. The king liked to watch cockfights and bulls mauled by vicious dogs. He ordered a special pit made for bear-baiting, and once even matched a lion with a bear—but was disappointed when the lion refused to fight.

As he aged James indulged his preference for handsome men, living apart from his wife. His doting fondness was part paternal, part erotic; he called his favorite George Villiers "sweet child and wife" and referred to himself as "your dear dad and husband." But to his courtiers, the sight of the aging, paunchy, balding monarch, who according to one court observer had a tendency to drool, leaning on his paramours was utterly repellant.

The first of the king's minions was Robert Carr, Groom of the Bedchamber, whom the king elevated to earl of Somerset and appointed Lord Chamberlain. After six years of favors and royal gifts Carr was brought low, accused of murder and sent away from court. The second and greatest royal favorite, the extraordinarily handsome George Villiers, rose from cupbearer to Gentleman of the Bedchamber and ultimately to Earl of Buckingham.

"I love the Earl of Buckingham more than anyone else," James announced to his councilors, "and more than you who are here assembled." He compared his love for the earl to Jesus's affection for the "beloved disciple" John. "Jesus Christ did the same," the king said, "and therefore I cannot be blamed. Christ had his John, and I have my George."

With such pronouncements King James seemed to reach a new level of outrage, especially when he compounded his offense, in the view of many, by heaping Buckingham with costly jewels, lands, and lucrative offices.

The king was bankrupting England, as he had all but bankrupted Scotland, with his excessive spending. "The royal cistern has a leak," observed one frustrated financial adviser, "which, till it were stopped, all our consultation to bring money unto it were of little use." Parliament voted funds, but they were soon spent. The costs of the royal household had doubled since the end of Elizabeth's reign, the royal guardsmen were unpaid, and were "clamoring and murmuring" in their discontent.

James made fitful efforts to raise funds and lower costs, selling titles of nobility, ordering the palace officials to reduce the number of dishes served at his table and even rationing wine (though not his own personal supply). But nothing could plug the leak in the royal cistern, and the disgruntled servants, unpaid and resentful, took to pilfering the silver from the dining tables and stealing linen and cutlery.

For most of his reign James had avoided entanglements in European affairs, but in the 1620s England was drawn into the conflict which became known as the Thirty Years' War. Spain, the most powerful of the continental states, attacked the territory of James's Protestant son-in-law Frederick, Elector Palatine; Frederick appealed to his father-in-law for help, and the House of Commons clamored for war. When the Commons protested that the "urgent affairs concerning the king, state and defense of the realm . . . are proper subjects and matter of council and debate in parliament," James became angry and tore the written record of this protest out of the Commons' journal, dissolving Parliament.

Now he was at odds, not only with Spain, but with the representatives of his own subjects. And there were other difficulties: the Puritan movement which pressured the monarch to purge the liturgy of all traces of Catholic tradition; the impeachment or execution of leading officials; and the strident complaints of James's deputies and servants who resented Buckingham's overriding influence on the king in all his political decisions.

"The end of all is ever the bottle," wrote the French ambassador in 1622, referring to James's evident alcoholism. He was fifty-six, in excruciating pain from stones in his bladder, his face a mass of ulcerated sores. His arthritis made walking unaided on his spindly, atrophied legs impossible, and even when he leaned on Buckingham, the king had an "odd twist" to his walk. Digestive miseries, insomnia, intermittent fevers added to the king's miseries, and his physician told the councilors that it was the king's great burden of illnesses that made him alternately melancholy and irascible. "He is of an exquisite sensitiveness and most impatient of pain," the physician went on. He did anything he could to avoid having to take medicine "which he detests."

Dosed with medicine or not, James suffered intensely, and kept a journal of his sufferings, writing down every bruise he received from his frequent falls, every attack of nausea and every "windy swelling" in his liver.

Mighty in his anointed royalty, possessing supreme power on earth, accountable to none but God, King James was succumbing to mortality.

In March of 1625 he developed a severe fever. Several doctors were quickly at his bedside, and both Buckingham and his mother prepared plasters to apply to his stomach and fed him medicinal drinks. Nothing could bring the fever down, and within days King James was dead.

No expense was spared to provide a lavish funeral. A magnificent catafalque made to resemble a classical temple, designed by Inigo Jones, was constructed to receive the king's embalmed body, which was borne in splendor along the Strand and through the Holbein Gate at Whitehall to Westminster Abbey. Black clothing was handed out to some nine thousand of the watching Londoners who lined the streets, so that the king's impressive cortege would be framed by mourners in appropriately somber garb.

In death, the king who had shunned crowds and on occasion shouted curses at those who stared at him was watched by thousands, and at his long funeral, was extravagantly praised. But James had left to his shy, prim son and heir Charles a troubled legacy—an impoverished kingdom on the threshold of war, a monarchy tarnished and lowered in public esteem, and a Parliament exceptionally jealous of its liberties and ready to challenge the prerogatives of the king.

CHARLES I

(1625–1649)

———— ✦ ⟐ ✲ ⟐ ✦ ————

"THE ESTATES ARE PERTURBED ABOUT THE TWO
GREAT CAUSES OF RELIGION AND THE DIMINUTION OF
THE LIBERTY OF THE PEOPLE. [KING CHARLES] HAS
PERTURBED BOTH, AND WILL BE VERY FORTUNATE IF
HE DOES NOT FALL INTO SOME GREAT UPHEAVAL."

—ANZOLO CORRER,
VENETIAN AMBASSADOR

Charles Stuart spent his childhood overshadowed by his older brother Henry, who was heir to the throne of their father, James I.

Henry, who was seven years older than Charles, was everything Charles was not: good-looking, strong, well made, with broad shoulders and an athletic physique. Everyone remarked on what promise Henry showed, what a good king he would one day be, for he combined courteous manners with a regal bearing and a regal disposition. Henry's gracious smile made the courtiers melt with pleasure; his terrible frown made them cringe.

Charles, by contrast, was an ill-favored weakling, slow to walk and talk, with such fragile bones in his legs and ankles that when, at the age of three, he managed to walk the length of a large room without holding his nurse's hand it was an occasion for rejoicing.

The royal physicians did not expect him to live, as his general health was delicate and he frequently succumbed to fevers. He also stammered when he talked, and had tantrums, and wept when Henry, who was not the kindest of brothers, taunted him and bullied him.

"Sweet, sweet brother," ten-year-old Charles wrote in a letter to Henry, "I will give anything that I have to you, both my horses and my books and my [handguns] and my crossbows, or anything that you would have. Good brother, love me . . . "

It was a cri de coeur, and indeed young Charles, who was never close to either Henry or his sister Elizabeth, or to his parents, suffered from lack of nurture throughout his childhood and did not have the toughness or resilience to find strength in himself.

With his louche, coarse father King James I, Charles was always shy and retiring. James talked incessantly, while to Charles, talking was a humiliating purgatory of hesitations, false starts, and failures. Nothing brought him more shame and embarrassment. Perhaps in an effort to force Charles out of his awkward disability, perhaps from sheer exhibitionist cruelty, James forced his younger son, at the age of nine, to take part in a theological disputation with his chaplains before an audience of hundreds of courtiers. The results were predictable, and the prince was in agony. Yet the experiment was not a total failure; a few years later, Charles was able to attend the House of Lords and take part in debates there, despite his persisting stammer.

Charles was an oddity in his extroverted family. His brother Henry was an outgoing athlete, his sister vivaciously friendly, his mother an actress of sorts, always taking part in masques and staged entertainments, and his father loved an audience and spent his days lecturing his servants and the officials of his court. Only Charles enjoyed solitude, had very few friends and possessed the sensibility of a studious introvert.

Charles was studious, but not brilliant like his gifted father, who had written lucid, trenchant books and treatises whose breadth of knowledge was much admired. In order to learn, Charles had to apply himself very diligently, which he did. With commendable self-discipline he learned his lessons, hoping to please his father, mastering Latin and Greek and attaining some proficiency in French, Spanish and Italian. In addition to his tutor, the prince was trained in theology by two earnest Puritans, Dr. George Hakewill and Dr. Thomas Winiffe, who had orders from the king never to leave Charles's side. Everywhere he went, Charles was shadowed by his two black-robed religious guardians, and Dr. Hakewill's book of sermons became his second Bible.

Yet for all his determination to be "settled right in religion," fulfilling his father's wishes, from a young age Charles was pulled away from Puritan austerity toward the sensual in the realm of art. The opulent nudes of Titian, the rich portraits of Raphael enthralled him, pulling him into a pagan world severely frowned on by the Puritan divines.

King James tried to foster a rivalry between his sons, teasing Henry and telling him that if he did not improve at his lessons, the crown would go to the more dutiful Charles.

"I know what becomes a king or prince," was Henry's scornful reply. "It is not necessary for me to be a professor, but a soldier and man of the world." On one occasion, exasperated by his father's cruel taunts, Henry grabbed the clerical cap off the head of an archbishop and jammed it roughly on Charles's head, saying that when he became king, he would have Charles as his archbishop.

But Henry was never to be king. At the age of eighteen the young Prince of Wales, who had always been so robust and energetic, was dying. Charles, who had just turned twelve, came to his brother's bedside, clutching his most precious possession, a small bronze horse. He put it into the delirious Henry's hands.

Charles's mourning for Henry was embittered by his conviction, which he was to maintain all his life, that his brother had been poisoned. As he walked behind Henry's funeral chariot Charles must have pondered the uncertainty of life, even as he contemplated his new role as heir to his father's throne.

Prince Henry's death changed everything for Charles. Now he was called upon to stand beside his father on ceremonial occasions, to meet the foreign ambassadors who came to the English court, and to attend the opening of Parliament. He was his sister's escort when she married Frederick, the Elector Palatine; he appeared in masques; he listened to MPs and to the scientists, writers and theologians who came to court. His world widened greatly.

In his teens, Charles was a prominent figure at his father's court. But as he grew toward manhood he remained a physical weakling, undersize, shy, and far less good-looking than his late brother. His manner was reserved, even restrained; unlike other young men, who enjoyed boisterous merrymaking and mayhem, and who considered the pursuit of sexual adventures to be a rite of passage into the adult male world, Charles avoided merrymaking, ate little and drank less, and never strayed into profligacy. He was modest, chaste and—to his peers—prudish. When others wenched and drank, he sent them away.

Ill at ease among his father's louche companions, especially his favorite George Villiers, Earl of Buckingham, Charles and Buckingham clashed—then reconciled, and, to the surprise of the entire court, became friends. The newfound amity between the short, nervously straitlaced

Prince of Wales and the angelically handsome, suave Buckingham was as warm as it was improbable. Charles seemed to be unaware that on Buckingham's side the relationship was at least partly, most likely entirely, self-serving; King James was drifting into drooling invalidism, and Buckingham wanted to ensure his future by attaching himself to the next ruler, knowing that the change of reigns could not be long delayed.

In 1623, Charles and Buckingham went off together on an adventure. For years James had been endeavoring to arrange a marriage between Charles and the Spanish infanta, but the Spanish kept escalating their terms. Charles thought that if he arrived in person, all could be settled quickly and decisively.

Disguising themselves as "Jack and Tom Smith," putting on false beards and dressing as ordinary Englishmen, the prince and Buckingham sailed for Spain. At first all went well; the two were welcomed at the court of King Philip IV, who, like Charles, had a passion for Italian painting. There were banquets and exchanges of costly gifts. But the Spanish were Catholic, and Charles was Protestant; before there could be a marriage, Charles was told, he would have to convert to Catholicism, which he could not consider.

Furthermore, Charles was not allowed to meet his intended bride, who was kept behind high walls and locked gates. When he boldly climbed one of the walls and tried to approach her as she was gathering flowers in an inner garden, she ran, calling for help, and the mortified Charles was ejected. At length a marriage agreement was signed, but then endless delays set in, and he began to doubt that the agreement would ever be implemented.

James, who was meanwhile missing Buckingham and his son, sent them a letter. "Alas, I now repent me sore that I ever suffered you to go away," the king wrote. "I care for match nor nothing, [sic] so I may once have you in my arms again; God grant it! God grant it!" (Buckingham wrote back, asking James to send him some jewels, and ending, "I kiss your dirty hands.")

After three months at the Spanish court, Charles had had enough. He abruptly left, having nothing to show for his adventure but a beautiful Titian, *The Venus of Pardo*, a gift from the Spanish king, and a stylish Spanish beard, which gave a slightly rakish look to his weak and indistinct features.

By the time the ill, chronically incapacitated King James died in 1625, Charles had in fact been ruling for him for at least a year. As king, Charles changed the entire tone of the court, imposing his own self-discipline, chaste habits and serious turn of mind on what had been a wasteland of disorder and rowdy dissipation. "The fools and bawds, mimics and catamites, of the former court, grew out of fashion," wrote Lucy Hutchinson, who had a relative at court, "and the nobility and courtiers, who did not quite abandon their debaucheries, yet so reverenced the king as to retire into corners to practise them."

Decorum reigned. Charles restored the court regulations that had been observed under Queen Elizabeth, setting out in detail the etiquette to be followed. Drunken servants were dismissed. No longer were the royal apartments under siege at all hours by demanding petitioners, dissatisfied nobles and a swarm of servants and officials. Grooms guarded the entrance to the king's apartments, and maintained order, assigning each visitor his appointed place.

Charles imposed rules on himself, setting himself a daily schedule which included prayers, private meditation in his bedchamber and liturgical readings as well as times for government business and audiences.

But though the new king was evidently pious, he was not particularly principled. And instead of addressing the pressing needs of the realm, he distracted himself with his favorite pastime, the acquisition of works of fine art.

That he was capable of duplicity was clear from Charles's handling of the Spanish marriage negotiations. Having agreed to exorbitant demands, he walked away, going back on his word. Diplomatic relations with Spain, already strained to the threshold of conflict, were worsened, and war broke out. His father's mismanagement of England's finances meant that Charles inherited high debts and an unbalanced budget. Yet instead of finding a way to repair the soured relations of crown and Commons, and restoring solvency through taxation, Charles let the entire situation fester.

Indeed he worsened it by going further into debt, buying up paintings and sculpture with enthusiastic abandon. Charles truly loved his acquisitions. Of one Tintoretto he wrote that "flint as cold as ice might fall in love with it." A Michelangelo painting reduced him to helpless adoration ("the most divine thing in the world. I have been such an idolater as to kiss it three times"). He had agents in France, Italy, anywhere there were great works of art on the auction block. From the Gonzaga family of Mantua he acquired 175 fine paintings at a price of sixteen thousand pounds, considering them a bargain. Works by Leonardo da Vinci, Correggio, Andrea del Sarto, Rembrandt, Dürer and others hung on the walls of his palaces.

By the mid-1630s Charles I had amassed the most magnificent collection of art ever in the possession of a single sovereign, with the possible exception of the contents of the Hermitage under Catherine the Great and her successors.

In the early years of his reign, the king went from crisis to crisis, as the kingdom was at war with both France and Spain and military losses led to ever greater conflict with Parliament. The Commons indicted Buckingham (who was assassinated in 1628), and withheld money grants from the king until he addressed their formal grievances, which he refused to do.

English Protestants, both in and out of Parliament, were terrified of a restoration of Catholicism, either enforced by continental powers or introduced through a conspiracy within the realm. Charles's marriage to Henrietta Maria, the Catholic sister of the French king, deepened these fears, arousing suspicion that the king himself would alter the church settlement.

"There is a general fear in your people of some secret working and combination to introduce into your kingdom some innovation and change in our holy religion," Charles was told by the Commons in 1628. But Charles's response was to imprison some members and to act, in general, with an aloofness which appeared to be disdain. He was king, he was in charge.

In actuality the king found Parliament "odious." He abhorred it, and could not even stand to hear the word Parliament spoken. He shared his father's view of the supremacy of monarchy, a supremacy that ought not to be weakened by any claims of representative government whatsoever. Kings were answerable only to God, not to men.

"Look not to find the softness of a down pillow in a crown," King James had written in his *Meditations on St. Matthew*, "but remember that it is a thorny piece of stuff and full of continual cares."

Charles's continual cares were only beginning. He dissolved Parliament and, from 1629, ruled without it, resorting to various unpopular expedients, among them the reimposing of archaic taxes and forced loans from wealthy individuals, to support his government. While he spent his time in the privacy of his court, amid his art works and surrounded by his family (his marriage to Queen Henrietta Maria, after an initial estrangement, had become a happy one), preoccupied with art patronage and connoisseurship, the grievances of Parliament rankled.

In 1640, after a long hiatus, Charles once again summoned Parliament but the result was the most serious clash yet over representative rights. Finally, after long and fruitless negotiations, the king raised his standard at Nottingham in August of 1642 and called upon all his subjects to support him in arms. The parliamentary forces were likewise summoned and the Civil War began.

Charles assumed the role of commander of the royalist army and proved to be a competent general, boasting that his presence on the battlefield was worth a thousand extra troops. Initial battles were inconclusive, however, and both sides settled in for a long war.

But the king, sensitive and ill at ease, was not warlike and was unnerved by the experience of battle. The shrieks and groans of suffering and dying men kept him awake at night and the shock and grief of losing so many friends and followers depressed him; he lacked the toughness to harden himself to these constant emotional onslaughts.

"It is a hard choice for a king that loves his people and desires their love," he was to write later, "either to kill his own subjects or be killed by them." In the midst of his distress he took comfort from his wife's constancy and support. "It is her love that maintains my life," Charles wrote, "her kindness that upholds my courage, which makes me eternally hers."

In June of 1645, at Naseby in Northamptonshire, the parliamentary forces led by Oliver Cromwell and Thomas Fairfax defeated a much smaller royalist army, which lost some five thousand men. After this major defeat Charles still had hope, and retired to Oxford to wait for French help, which Henrietta Maria assured him would come. But toward the end of April 1646, it was apparent that aid would not be forthcoming, and the king, disguised as a servant, left Oxford in the early hours of the morning and joined the Scottish forces.

"There was never man so alone as I!" Charles wrote to his wife while with the Scots. He was lonely, he was beleaguered—his captors tried to convert him to their version of Protestant theology, and constantly harangued him with sermons and arguments—and he was weary of waiting for a royalist victory. When finally allowed to see his children, Charles brightened considerably. He adopted as his motto "Dum spiro spero," "While I breathe, I hope." Even after the Scots turned him over to Parliament, he continued to be optimistic, knowing that Parliament was divided into factions and in need of a unifying leader; he saw himself as that leader, and sincerely believed that England could not survive without her monarch.

Charles was taken to his own estate at Holdenby in Northamptonshire, where he settled into a relatively comfortable state of house arrest. Talks went on with the parliamentary leaders in an effort to find a compromise that would allow the government to continue peacefully. Meanwhile the king spent his time reading, walking in the gardens or playing at bowls. He was allowed to visit the homes of the nearby gentry and whenever he went out riding, crowds gathered to cheer him and shouted that they were praying for him.

The show of support was heartening, but the king's political fortunes were on the decline. A second round of fighting broke out in 1648 and Charles, now a captive of the radically democratic parliamentary army, was kept in close confinement. His numerous well-wishers did nothing to rescue him, no force from abroad came to deliver him.

In November of 1648 the general council of the army insisted that the king be put on trial. The following month Colonel Pride emptied the House of Commons of all those members who had been in favor of peace and possible conciliation with the monarchy, leaving only a small minority of radicals.

The king was aware of his danger, and wrote of it to his son James. "We are sensible into what hands we are fallen," he told his son. "We have learned to busy ourself in retiring into ourself . . . not doubting but God's providence will restrain our enemies' power and turn their fierceness to his praise."

In the first week of January 1649 a High Court of Justice was called into being, to try the guilt or innocence of the king before a court of some fifty Members of Parliament. The action was unprecedented, and in Charles's view, it was completely contrary to every known law of God and man.

"I would know by what power I am called hither," he said when brought before his accusers.

"By the authority of the people of England," he was told. Despite the king's dignified protests he was sentenced to die as a "Tyrant, Traitor, Murderer, and public enemy to the good people of this Nation."

On a raw, cold morning, the 30th of January 1649, King Charles walked for the last time from St. James's to Whitehall, where a black-draped scaffold had been erected. He spent the morning in prayer, waiting to be called to his execution. Just before the summons came, he asked his servants to give him an extra shirt, to wear against the cold.

"The season is so sharp," he said, "as probably may make me shake, which some observers may imagine proceeds from fear."

He was not afraid, he had made his peace with God. Those who saw the king walk past on his way to mount the scaffold remembered his "cheerful look," and remembered too that the soldiers who guarded him were silent, with downcast expressions.

It was not just this king, Charles I, who was to be killed; monarchy itself was about to die, or so it seemed to those who shivered in the courtyard, awaiting the final act of the drama. An icon was passing, something sacred was being violated. Centuries of tradition were ending.

Charles stood before the crowd of onlookers, a small, neat figure with carefully trimmed hair and beard. "Death is not terrible to me," he told them, his voice even. "I bless God and am prepared."

After making a declaration of his faith, he knelt and put his head on the block. The sharp sword rose, then fell, severing the head with a single blow.

There was a collective gasp, then a hush. Many were in tears. Others rushed forward, holding handkerchieves to dip in the king's blood as it spread in a widening pool. The blood of a murdered criminal was reputed to work miracles; why not that of a king?

CHARLES II

(1660–1685)

———— ✦ ❧ ✠ ❧ ✦ ————

"ALL APPETITES ARE FREE, AND GOD WILL NEVER
DAMN A MAN FOR ALLOWING HIMSELF
A LITTLE PLEASURE."

—KING CHARLES II

The tiny, swarthy infant that Charles I's queen, Henrietta Maria, brought into the world on May 29, 1630, was something of an embarrassment. "At present he is so black that I am ashamed of him," was the queen's candid comment on her olive-skinned son, who resembled his Medici ancestors in the hue of his complexion. He was her firstborn, and was named Charles, after his father.

Baby Charles did not resemble his pale, slight, short, frail-looking father at all—he was robust and sturdy, and exceptionally large; at four months of age he looked like a year-old child. He was also precociously thoughtful, or so it seemed to the queen, who remarked that "he is so serious in all that he does that I cannot help fancying him far wiser than myself."

Whether or not he was wise, Charles proved to be tough and fearless as a boy, and when war broke out between his father's royalist troops and the forces of Parliament the Prince of Wales was at his father's side, in full battle armor, and with sword and pistol, though he had not yet reached his twelfth birthday.

Charles had been trained to ride, fence and shoot by his governor, the intelligent, sophisticated duke of Newcastle, who opened the boy's mind to a broad range of subjects including literature and chemistry. His father's military camp at Oxford provided another sort of education—an education in worldliness. The troops who swaggered and staggered through the streets of Oxford were often drunk and exemplars of "lewd behavior," quarreling, gambling and keeping company with prostitutes and camp followers.

Prince Charles was very much at home in this earthy, crude environment and found the company of the soldiers congenial. For as he grew into his teens, the prince developed into a tall, virile, lusty boy, quick-witted and attractive to women. The prince had none of his father's "imperious and lofty" manner, timorous disposition or haunting air of melancholy; he was bluff and genial, relaxed and always ready to have a good time, and people liked him and were drawn to him.

By the age of fourteen young Charles was given nominal command of a royal army, and acquitted himself well. But the royalists were losing the Civil War, and after the major defeat at the Battle of Naseby in 1645 King Charles cautioned his son to "prepare for the worst." The king told the prince that if he felt he could not avoid being captured by the parliamentary forces, he ought to go to the continent. Shortly before his sixteenth birthday, the Prince of Wales and his entire household embarked for France.

Young Charles's future, and the future of the monarchy, were uncertain. His family was scattered, his father in captivity in England, his mother in France and his younger brothers and one sister detained by Parliament. He was offered asylum at the French court, the inevitable difficulties of his exile assuaged by a series of balls and parties.

"To women you cannot be too civil," the Duke of Newcastle had instructed young Charles, "especially to great ones." He followed this teaching with enthusiasm, making himself agreeable to the great ladies of France, who in turn found the tall, black-haired young Englishman much to their liking. Dressed in the beautifully made cloaks, doublets and hats supplied by Paris merchants, and wearing his Garter star and diamond-hilted sword, Charles Stuart cut an imposing figure. His first love, the Duchesse de Chatillon, spurned him but an Englishwoman, Lucy Walters, became his mistress and bore him a child.

In an effort to rescue his captive father and shore up the failed royalist cause, Charles made preparations to sail to England—only to have the sailors mutiny. Then, early in 1649, he received the harsh news that his father had been executed, and that the monarchy was abolished.

Prince Charles, at eighteen, was now Charles II—king of a realm which formally acknowledged no king.

England had no king, but in Ulster and Edinburgh, Charles II was proclaimed the new monarch, and in July of 1650 Charles went to Scotland, where he was ultimately crowned at Scone, in a Presbyterian ritual. With the sanction of a coronation, the loyalty of at least some of the Highland Scots and very limited funds, he set about to raise an army to retake the moribund English throne.

He was all action and energy, "riding continually and being up early and late." He harangued his growing number of followers, set up war committees, visited town after town, his young and vigorous physical presence a rallying force.

But once the fledgling royalist troops crossed the border into England, they discovered that English support for the monarchical cause was sparse. Expected backing was not forthcoming. Desertions reduced the number of Charles's men, and by the time the remaining force rested in the town of Worcester, tired from weeks of marching, they were in no shape to give battle. When they were attacked by a much larger parliamentary army, Charles's soldiers retreated in panic.

In vain the king—as he was now—tried to rally his men, telling them "I had rather you would shoot me than keep me alive to see the consequences of this fatal day!" But Charles's fervor could not prevent his army from being massacred, and, surrounded by terrible carnage, he made the decision to save himself. Disguised as a laborer in green breeches, a leather doublet and a shirt of coarse cloth, he went into hiding.

For more than a month he lay low, mending hedges, staying out of sight in remote villages and farms. Though a high price was offered for his capture, none of those who sheltered Charles betrayed him as he made his way, sometimes on foot, sometimes on the back of a spavined horse, toward the seacoast. Finally, after surviving much danger, "sad and somber" in mood, he sailed to France to resume his exile.

Charles was only twenty-one, but his appearance, as recorded by others, indicated that he felt as weighed down by defeat as if he had been much older. He was a wanted man with a price on his head, he had no money and no reason to hope that his cause would ever revive. Most likely he would live out his life in exile, while his enemies thrived.

England had a new government, under Oliver Cromwell as Lord Protector of the Commonwealth. And Cromwell, "of majestic deportment and comely presence," was kingly, and successful, leading the realm to victory over the Dutch, seizing Jamaica from the Spanish, restoring England's military prestige, which had been languishing for decades. Word reached Charles that Cromwell had been offered the throne, but declined. England remained a Commonwealth.

Adrift, unwelcome anywhere, and virtually penniless, Charles and his small court moved uncomfortably from Cambrai to Mons to Liège to Spa, seeking an inexpensive refuge, borrowing, suffering harassment, trying to go on amid constant disappointment. Charles himself declined into apathy and dissipation. Complaining that he had nothing to do but "sit still and dream out his life," he sought oblivion in sexual excess, spending his time in bathhouses and brothels, seeking new mistresses, ceasing to care what anyone thought.

"The king is exceedingly fallen in reputation," wrote one of his councilors. "He is so much given to pleasure that if he stay here he will be undone." His mother urged Charles to marry a wealthy wife, and they fought over this and other issues. But he continued his life of dissolute pleasures and irregular unions, while his loyal supporters froze in dilapidated rented rooms, reduced to eating a single meal a day.

After years of penury and disillusionment the hopes of all the English exiles rose briefly when news came that Cromwell had died. But his son Richard succeeded him without opposition, and once again Charles and those around him were in despair.

Richard Cromwell's period of ascendancy proved to be brief, however. He was a weak leader, unable to hold together the warring political factions that soon developed. In the streets of London people were beginning to "talk loud of the king," and criticize the government.

Seeing his opportunity, Charles, in Brussels, wrote to the prominent politician General Monck. "I know too well the power you have to do me good or harm," he wrote candidly, asking Monck to "be his friend." Talks were begun, and Charles, who showed much political finesse, assured Monck and others in England that if offered a restored throne he would show the utmost respect for the authority of Parliament.

"We do assure you upon our royal word that none of our predecessors have had a greater esteem for Parliaments than we have," Charles wrote. Parliament was necessary to the wellbeing and contentment of the realm. He said nothing of the tragedy that Parliament had inflicted upon his family in executing his father. He gave other assurances: that enemies of the monarchy would be pardoned, that the parliamentary soldiers would be given their back wages, and that no harsh or narrow religious settlement would be imposed.

On these liberal terms, an agreement was reached, and Charles II was invited to return to England as its king.

Most Englishmen had never wanted the monarchy abolished, and when Charles, in new clothes provided by a parliamentary grant (his old ones having grown embarrassingly shabby in nine years of impoverished exile), landed on May 26, 1660, he was greeted by a large and delighted crowd amid a thunder of guns and shouts of "God Save the King!"

A beaming Charles kissed General Monck on both cheeks and Monck, humbled by the significance of the occasion, spoke for many when he said, simply, "Father."

All the pageantry of royalty was revived for the king's formal entry into the capital. Hour after hour the colorful troops of soldiers, officials, clergy and mounted escorts made its way through the narrow, flower-strewn streets toward Whitehall. At the center of all was the gilded coach bearing the king, in a dark doublet and plumed hat, "raising his eyes to the windows," the diarist John Evelyn wrote, "looking at all, raising his hat to all, and greeting all."

Many in the crowd wept at the sight, shouting out blessings on their king, whose name, the Venetian ambassador thought, was "as much loved, revered and acclaimed as in past years it was detested and abused." Not until nine at night did the last of the thousands of soldiers in the long parade reach the palace, and still the crowd stayed to watch, as if reluctant to let the glorious day end.

Seldom had a king had such an opportunity to begin anew, drawing on tradition but avoiding the mistakes his father and grandfather had made. At the outset Charles wisely chose the path of reconciliation. His government was politically inclusive, and his earliest acts were designed to set aside old grievances and restore harmony. The Militia Act gave Charles complete control of the army—which had been the principal ruling body in the country—and he faced no serious opposition.

There was no pardon for the principal regicides, however. Treason trials were held and there were many hangings—so many, in fact, that Londoners living near Charing Cross where the executions were carried out complained that the stench of burning bowels was making the air unhealthy to breathe. Cromwell's corpse, which had been buried in Westminster Abbey, was dug up and beheaded, the rotting head stuck on a pole outside Westminster Hall for all to see.

To preserve the memory of his martyred father, King Charles ordered that the day of his execution, January 30, be set aside as a day of national fasting and repentance. Preachers extolled the dead king as a saint, wrongly killed by villainous enemies. Like Christ, King Charles had given his life for the sins of the English, Scots and Irish, the clergy told their congregations. The late king's own political trespasses—his scorn for the rights of Parliament, what many had viewed, during his reign, as his tyranny—were cloaked in a shroud of veneration.

Charles took all the acclaim and disruption of his accession in stride, even when he was besieged by petitioners and others clamoring for his attention. His reception rooms were constantly filled with people on urgent business, each trying to outshout the others. They elbowed one another and abused the servants, stealing ornaments and fixtures—and even taking one of the king's beloved dogs.

"We must call upon you," went an ad that appeared in the *Mercurius Publicus* in July 1660, "for a black dog, between a greyhound and a spaniel, no white about him, only a streak, on his breast, and tail a little bobbed. It is His Majesty's own dog, and doubtless was stolen."

Though robbed, mobbed and ceaselessly importuned, King Charles kept his composure and his affability. He was always charming and gracious, self-disciplined and pleasant. His voice was gentle, his words courteous; those who came to his court in fear or awe went away comforted and reassured, for his features grew soft when he spoke, according to Samuel Tuke, who wrote a description of the king in 1660. Tuke was struck by Charles's "quick and sparkling" eyes, his thick mane of black hair, "naturally curling into great rings," his grace of movement and well formed body which showed to advantage when he danced or played tennis or rode.

Though only thirty years old, the king was careworn, with a touch of grey in his black hair and deep lines etched on his lean face. He had lived much in his thirty years, and grown cynical; beneath his affability ran deep currents of self-indulgence and a profound amorality grounded in years of observing the ignoble side of human nature. Whatever high ideals and scruples he may have once possessed had been abandoned during his long years of deprivation in exile, when he had been treated as a pariah and kindness was nowhere to be found. He had emerged from that experience jaded, and with an unquenchable appetite for pleasure.

Charles was, in many respects, a thoroughly secular man, appetitive, instinctive, rational and measured in his attitudes and with a well-developed curiosity about the natural world. He took an interest in science and inventions, and had a laboratory built at Whitehall, sending one of his gentleman ushers to the Royal Society to ask questions of the experts.

Indolence had always been among Charles's character flaws, and almost from the beginning of his reign his laziness interfered with his effectiveness as king. In particular, he neglected the most pressing problem facing the new government: insolvency.

At the time of his accession the Exchequer was virtually bare, yet the king spent freely. By the end of his first decade of rule the realm was over £1,300,000 in debt, and much more money—nearly a million pounds more—was needed to build up the navy.

Instead of addressing the problem, Charles turned it over to his Chancellor, Edward Hyde, Earl of Clarendon, as he did the equally difficult issue of England's need for alliances abroad. Warfare with the Dutch bled the exhausted treasury without resulting in any immediate benefit—except the English capture of the Dutch colony of New Amsterdam, which they renamed New York. The king's brother James was an able naval commander, but could not prevent the Dutch from sailing up the Thames and burning several ships, towing away the flagship, the *Royal Charles*, as a prize.

Complicating relations with the continental states was the lingering issue of religion. France, the leading continental power, was staunchly Catholic, and it seemed to the Protestant English, who since the reign of Bloody Mary had had an ingrained if irrational fear of Catholicism, that the French were about to force their beliefs on all of Europe, including England. They became suspicious of the king, who was surrounded by Catholics in his family and who might, they feared, be tempted to convert himself.

Londoners were distracted from these worries by a visitation of plague in the summer and fall of 1665. There was always plague in London in the summer, but this season was far worse than ever before in memory, with thousands dying every week by July. The wealthy fled the capital, the poor huddled in their slums, praying for deliverance. Every house where a plague victim lived was painted with a large red cross, until a plague of red crosses spread throughout the city and suburbs, reaching out into nearby towns and villages. Not until November did the virulent epidemic die down, and the macabre spectacle of corpses piled on carts and dumped into mass graves come to an end.

The shock and loss of the plague, which carried off some seventy thousand people, had hardly begun to recede from public consciousness when, a year later, fire spread through London. For five days the city burned,

houses, churches and monuments alike turning to ashes in a vast conflagration that left tens of thousands homeless and fleeing in panic to the open
spaces of Moorfields and Spitalfields where they collapsed in exhaustion.

The king, his clothes soot-blackened and drenched with water and
sweat, went in fearlessly among the burning buildings and urged the citizens to pull down houses that were still standing in order to create fire
breaks. But such measures were minimally effective, for the conflagration
soon became a firestorm, with structures imploding and great iron church
bells melting in the fearsome heat, and it was all Charles could do to take
his place in the long line of people passing buckets from hand to hand,
toiling "like a poor laborer" to save what was left of his capital.

It was to take a generation for London to be rebuilt; in the meantime
there was great disruption of trade, and a dispersal of population, amid
wild (and untrue) rumors that Catholics had set fire to the city, that the
king had abdicated, that the economy was in a state of collapse. Many people muttered that the plague and fire were signs of divine wrath against
the country, and in particular against the dissolute royal court.

For King Charles, true to his nature, set a tone of unbridled debauchery
for his courtiers, who eagerly followed him into the hedonistic, often sordid world of private vice. The diarist Samuel Pepys, worldly and sophisticated himself, noted that "at court things are in very ill condition."
"Swearing, drinking and whoring" were the order of the day, syphilis was
spreading, and the king's companions were so uninhibited that they
romped naked in taverns and made a spectacle of their drunkenness.

Charles's own promiscuity seemed obsessive. Sexual conquests were as
necessary to him as breathing, and his mistresses multiplied: the teenage
actress Nell Gwynn, the ambitious, avaricious Barbara Palmer, Lady
Castlemaine, Hortense Mancini, Elizabeth Killigrew, Catherine Pegge,
Louise de Kéroualle—a long roll call of bedmates that included clergy-
men's daughters, singers and dancers, maids of honor, anonymous companions by the score, paid and unpaid. By the time the king was
middle-aged, his mistresses had presented him with at least a dozen bastard children whom he acknowledged, and there were many others.

The diarist Evelyn recorded the scene in the king's apartments one Sunday evening. Amid an environment of "inexpressible luxury and profane-
ness," Charles sat fondling three of his mistresses, while a boy sang love
songs and a group of dissolute companions played cards, wagering thousands of pounds in gold coins. To the modern reader, habituated through
popular culture to far more startling scenes of sexual excess and reckless

gambling, the king's pastimes sound mild. And his debauchery seems almost predictable, for after all, England had been in the grip of excessive Puritanism for decades; there was bound to be a swing of the social pendulum in the other direction.

But Charles's contemporaries sensed something dark in his immersion in the erotic, a self-destructive quality, a pull toward the abyss. It was to this ill-defined but unmistakable quality in his hedonism that they reacted.

Still, the king's nights of pleasure did not seem to sap his vitality, and even into his fifties Charles rose at five in the morning to stride through the parks, his spaniels at his heels, or swim in his private canal or row a boat downriver. "He has a strange command of himself," Bishop Burnet wrote of Charles. "He can pass from business to pleasure and from pleasure to business in so easy a manner that all seem alike to him."

Though he had declined in popularity, and was so at odds with Parliament that there was fear of renewed civil war, Charles seemed unperturbed. One of his courtiers, who observed him at a court function in 1679, was struck by how cheerful he looked, "amongst so many troubles," adding "but it was not his nature to think much, or to perplex himself."

Unreflective, self-accepting, by his own admission "bolder and firmer" as he aged, King Charles entered the last stage of his life. He lived a more retired life, surrounded by his mistresses, his cronies and his spaniels, making improvements to Whitehall and Windsor, ordering the planting of trees in the parks and the installation of new turf. "Odds fish!" he cried out when confronted with a portrait of himself, his once handsome face puffy and lined, "I am an ugly fellow!" He knew that he was lucky to have lived as long as he had, having survived a near-fatal attack of malarial fever; he knew that he could not go on forever.

At the age of fifty-four, Charles suddenly collapsed, and went into a coma. He recovered consciousness, and had time, before he died, to say his goodbyes—to his wife Catherine of Braganza, his mistresses, his weeping brother James to whom, in the absence of any legitimate children, he left his crown. Having expressed a wish to convert to Catholicism, Charles confessed to a priest and took his first and only Catholic communion.

In the street outside the palace, Charles's subjects, who knew that he was dying, gathered at the gates in large numbers, weeping for the king and father they were soon to lose. They wept for the king they had been so glad to welcome a quarter century before, for their own loss, and for the realm, which was about to pass into uncertain hands—the hands of the vain and haughty James II.

JAMES II

(1685–1688)

"THIS GOOD PRINCE HAS ALL THE WEAKNESS OF
HIS FATHER WITHOUT HIS STRENGTH. HE LOVES,
AS HE SAITH, TO BE SERVED IN HIS OWN WAY,
AND HE IS AS VERY A PAPIST AS THE POPE HIMSELF,
WHICH WILL BE HIS RUIN."

—EARL OF LAUDERDALE

It is to be regretted that the memoirs of James II, which he wrote while in exile, were destroyed at the time of the French Revolution and irrevocably lost. Had the memoirs survived, they would have disclosed much about James's view of his own life, his perceptions and character.

For James's life story has nearly always been told by his enemies, not his advocates—of whom there are few. Most likely he would have been his own best advocate, and most revealing biographer.

Born in 1633 to Charles I and Queen Henrietta Maria, James was named for his grandfather James I. He was not expected to reign, his older brother Charles being the heir to the throne. But many thought James the abler of the brothers, with his dutiful behavior and appealing natural candor, his serious demeanor and evident desire to strive after virtue and understanding. He was also much better looking than his older brother, with noble, regular features and a broad brow.

James was an attractive boy, and grew into an attractive young man, but not a commanding one. Intelligent, analytical, even reflective, he nonetheless lacked shrewdness, and political intuition. The self-protective cunning that became second nature to Prince Charles was lacking in his brother. James was self-possessed but emotionally fragile; Charles was open and free with his emotions but tough—and always retained an air of mystery and self-concealment which kept others guessing and made them wary of him. There was no mystery about James, he was straightforward, easy to understand—and therefore vulnerable.

James was hardly out of childhood when he and his family were swept up in the turmoil of the Civil War. He was taken prisoner by the parliamentary army and kept in St. James's Palace while his father fought a losing war to keep his crown. At the age of fourteen Prince James managed to escape his captors by dressing as a girl and slipping past the guards; he made his way to Holland.

Commissioned as an officer in the French army, James came quickly to prominence for his outstanding bravery. The brilliant French general Turenne made him a protege of sorts, and after several rapid promotions James was made lieutenant-general at the age of twenty-one. More years of fighting in the army of Spain increased his repute. James's promise was evident to all, indeed he won more praise and admiration than Prince Charles.

And unlike Charles, James made a genuine effort to understand his times, keeping a journal, talking with prominent men in the army and at the European courts, staying abreast of events. In this effort he had only limited success, for though he was able to attain a grasp of detail, the whole invariably eluded him; he only caught fitful glimpses of the broad canvas of European affairs, and was to remain politically myopic all his life.

Like his brother, while in exile from England James indulged his robust libido, though he avoided acquiring a reputation for dissoluteness. "He was perpetually in one amour or other," wrote Bishop Burnet, who knew James well, "without being very nice [i.e. discriminating] in his choice." When his choice fell on Anne Hyde, and she became pregnant, James married her, and they had two daughters together, Mary and Anne.

When Charles came to the throne in 1660, James was prominent at his court, appointed to Lord High Admiral and given a variety of lesser posts, including governor of the Hudson's Bay Company. The prince's tall, dignified figure was highly visible, if slightly farcical, his stiff, correct manner and evident vanity and hauteur a contrast to Charles's easy informality. That James loved his brother, and was loyal to him, was touchingly obvious, but Charles, wary of James's political obtuseness, held back from giving him any weighty responsibility.

When James secretly converted to Catholicism in 1668, Charles was enraged, for given the extreme anti-Catholic sentiments of the majority of his subjects, the prince's conversion, should it become known, was bound to damage the popularity of the throne. James was heir presumptive, and it was essential that he maintain the illusion of outward conformity to the Anglican Church. Charles insisted that James hide his Catholicism, and that he raise his daughters as Anglicans.

When James's first wife died he chose his second bride from an ultra-Catholic family. Mary of Modena, fifteen years old, had been about to enter a convent when her marriage was arranged. Predictably, it was an unpopular marriage, and an unhappy one; all of Mary's babies died at birth, or were stillborn—a calamity attributed to James's enthusiastic promiscuity which, people said, resulted in venereal disease.

Despite his military gallantry and relative success as commander of the navy against the Dutch, in the 1670s James became a target of the growing opposition party in Parliament. When the Test Act was passed, forcing all office holders to take the Anglican communion—a measure expressly designed to identify and purge Catholics from the government—James resigned his naval command. Because King Charles had no legitimate children, James continued to be heir to the throne; there was a movement to exclude him from the succession. To avoid an outright confrontation, Charles sent James away from court, first to Brussels and then to Edinburgh. Not until 1682 was James able to return, still under a cloud. Parliament had never been reconciled to his Catholic marriage, and hysterical fears of a Catholic plot to kill the king and take over the government brought renewed suspicion on James.

An incident in 1682 added to the disapprobation in which James was held.

While still living in Scotland, James traveled to England to meet Charles, to discuss his permanent return. The talks went well, and plans were made to bring his entire entourage to live at his brother's court. But on his way back to Scotland, to get his wife and his household, the ship in which he sailed was wrecked off the coast of Yorkshire. It was a terrible accident, many of the crew drowned and James himself was lucky to survive. But gossip said that, as the ship was going down, the prince had no concern for the dying men, only for his retinue of priests, his dogs and his chests of coins. His reputation worsened.

In Charles's last years, James became more prominent than ever. The queen being childless, there was no longer any doubt that James would inherit the throne assuming he outlived his brother. But should James become king, his reign was expected to be short, for by the standards of the era, both he and Charles were elderly, and both had abused their health all their lives. It was a comfort to the English that James's daughters were Protestant. The older daughter, Mary, had married the Protestant hero William of Orange, Stadtholder of the Netherlands. In time, it was thought, Mary would become queen, for James's wife Mary of Modena seemed unable to bear a living child.

When Charles II died in February of 1685, sincerely mourned by James, the transfer of power took place without incident. The new king was crowned as James II, the coronation festivities marred by a freak accident which caused much loss of life. Crowds collected along the banks of the Thames to watch a display of fireworks. A wayward spark caused an immense explosion, and many in the crowd were burned, some jumping into the river and drowning.

It was an ill omen, but the king seemed unfazed by it as he went about his duties competently. Conscientious, experienced, much more dedicated to governing than King Charles had been, King James seemed at first a boon to the realm, despite his stiff manner and overt Catholicism.

"I have often heretofore ventured my life in defence of this nation," he told the privy council, "and I shall go as far as any man in preserving it in all its just rights and liberties." He gave assurances that the Anglican settlement would not be changed, which was reassuring, and he got on well with his first Parliament.

But James was fifty-two on his accession, and his mind and personality were increasingly rigid, indeed on the threshold of obsession. "He had to be served in his own way," wrote one who knew him well. He was impatient, unapproachable, demanding of regal homage. His aloofness made him disliked, his hauteur gave offense. Instead of receiving foreign diplomats informally, as his brother had, while standing in his bedchamber, James waited for them in a special room, seated in a chair and dressed in his royal robes and hat. His vanity was insatiable. He commissioned Grinling Gibbons to carve a statue of him in bronze, dressed in Roman costume, standing in a Caesarian pose. The statue dominated the courtyard of Whitehall Palace, where all could see it and be reminded of the king's noble greatness.

The hauteur and vanity, the attention given to exaggerated marks of respect were evidence of the king's fragile sense of self, and of his alienation from those around him. James was inordinately defensive toward those he distrusted, and overly trusting of those with whom he felt safe, with the consequence that he rejected much sound advice and was too quick to accept the counsel of a few intimates.

Among those intimates was his principal mistress Catherine Sedley, whom he made Countess of Dorchester. Despite the queen's protests Catherine was installed in apartments at Whitehall, and became the focus of intense conflict in the royal marriage. From the day of James's coronation on, Catherine upstaged the queen—and at times even the king. On coronation day, Catherine's infant son by James died, causing the king much grief. His spiritual advisers urged him to send Catherine away, and he did for a time, but she soon returned.

At length the weeping queen summoned a phalanx of supporters, including her confessor and the king's, plus other clergy and Catholic peers. She then requested that James meet her for a talk.

Before her array of witnesses Mary took her strong stand. Either her husband must give up Catherine Sedley, she said, or she would leave the court and the marriage and take up residence in a convent.

It was a powerful threat, for divorce was not possible—the Roman church forbade it—and if the queen withdrew to a convent there could never be a Catholic heir to James's throne. Others added their voices to Mary's, and at length James gave in. Unwillingly, Catherine Sedley moved out of the palace—but she took a house in St. James's Square, and the king continued to visit her there, making an effort to keep his visits a secret.

Within months of his accession James had to face the threat of rebellion when the Duke of Monmouth, Charles II's natural son, landed on the Dorset coast and claimed the throne. Gathering supporters from among the men of the West Country, Monmouth marched to Bristol. The king had a large standing army, but felt insecure; in order to release regiments from London to send against Monmouth and his men, James had to borrow two English regiments from the Dutch army. The rebels were crushed, and Monmouth himself captured and executed. But James continued to feel unsafe and to pray for divine aid against his enemies.

Although he had promised not to disturb the Anglican settlement, the king began to undermine it by favoring Catholics in every way he could. He appointed Catholics to important posts in the army and navy, invited priests and nuns to return to England from the continent, set up a Catholic press to publish tracts, and even established a Jesuit school in London which, because of the high quality education it provided, attracted Prot-

estant students. When in 1687 a papal nuncio—a formal diplomatic representative from the Vatican—was received at court there was an outcry.
Clearly the king had gone too far.

By this time court observers could not fail to notice that the king was
deteriorating mentally, becoming irascible and cantankerous, sometimes
lashing out with verbal or even physical violence. His campaign to advance
Catholicism reached new heights when he attempted to force Parliament
to abolish the laws which in effect barred Catholics from holding office.
Frustrated in this effort, the king issued a Declaration of Indulgence establishing religious toleration—and when seven Anglican clergy asked
him to withdraw the Declaration, he ordered them imprisoned to await
trial for seditious libel.

By the summer of 1688 the battle lines were clearly drawn, with King
James, the Catholic minority, many army officers and some Tory gentlemen on one side and Parliament, the Anglican clergy and the majority of
the king's English and Scottish subjects on the other.

Greatly increasing the tension was the fact that all Europe was braced
for war. The French King Louis XIV was poised to invade Germany, Emperor Leopold I was mobilizing his forces to attack the continental Protestant states and England and Holland were on the verge of another clash.

And there was another source of uncertainty. The childless queen,
Mary of Modena, was pregnant and if she gave birth to a healthy boy, the
succession would be altered. The king's Protestant daughter Mary would
be superseded by a Catholic prince, and England would be permanently
returned to the church of Rome.

On the evening of June 9, 1688, the heavily pregnant queen was carried
in her sedan chair to St. James's Palace, where she wanted to give birth.
The baby was not due for another month, but Mary's labor had begun, and
she insisted on being taken to the old Tudor palace for her confinement.
The king walked beside her, offering what support and encouragement he
could. The twenty-nine courtiers who crowded into the labor room talked
of nothing but the odds that a boy would be born—and that he would
survive. Of Mary's ten previous children, most had been stillborn and the
others too feeble and sickly to live. If this baby survived it would be a
miracle—or a hoax.

When to the surprise of all Mary did produce a living son, there was
great consternation. Cannon were fired, church bells rang by order of the
jubilant king. But his subjects, by now intolerant both of the king and of

the prospect of a Catholic dynasty, began to hope for liberation.

The starting point of their hopes was a rumor, widely spread and widely believed, that Queen Mary's alleged pregnancy had never happened. There had been no royal birth, it was said. Some other woman's baby had been smuggled into the birth chamber, perhaps in the "warming pan" (a closed metal container for hot coals) used to warm the bed. It was recalled that at the time of the putative birth no one had heard the newborn cry—surely a sign of deception, since newborn babies always wailed lustily.

Accusations and counter-accusations flew, and the court was in turmoil, with the angry, obstreperous king making himself more disliked than ever. Amid the confusion the Bishop of London and six prominent nobles secretly invited William of Orange to come to England. The meaning of the invitation was clear; it was hoped that William would take the throne in his wife's name.

James began to receive information that his son-in-law William was amassing ships and soldiers in the harbors of Holland, but he preferred to believe that William was preparing to attack the French, not to invade England. By the time he realized that an invasion was in fact coming, James attempted to prepare a defense—and to conciliate his subjects. But it was too late. On November 5, 1688, the Dutch armada sailed into Torbay, having managed to avoid the British fleet, and William came ashore with his thousands of troops to Exeter, meeting no resistance.

Some historians have maintained that James, in London, suffered a nervous breakdown when he heard that the Dutch forces had landed, and that many of his army officers were deserting to join William of Orange. Certainly the formidable courage the king had shown earlier in his life deserted him, and once his subjects began to perceive that he did not intend to put up any resistance, they threw their support behind the invader. Frightened and defeated, and suffering from a prolonged severe nosebleed, James fled to a small harbor on the Kentish coast where a yacht was waiting to take him across the Channel to safety in France.

But at this point tragedy turned to farce. King James's yacht, stranded on a sandbar, was commandeered by patriotic English fishermen who took James prisoner, suspecting that he was a Jesuit spy. For nearly a week they held him in a small customs building, not realizing who he was, until by chance his true identity was discovered. He was taken to London, then allowed to leave for France just before the victorious William arrived in the capital.

That King James surrendered his kingdom without a battle—indeed without even a blow—is perhaps the best argument for his disturbed state of mind. Once in France, he bored and annoyed the French courtiers of Louis XIV by his rambling, sometimes incoherent conversation. "When one listens to him," they said, "one understands why he is here."

In the spring of 1689 the king interrupted his exile at St.-Germain to attempt a reconquest of his lost kingdom. With French financial support and accompanied by French troops, he sailed to Ireland, only to be defeated by William of Orange at the Battle of the Boyne.

"I do now resolve to shift for myself," he announced after the defeat, and for the next twelve years, until his death in 1701, the deposed James II lived quietly in France, occupying himself with hunting, writing his memoirs, and watching his son, James Stuart, grow up. Young James, many years later, would invade England as the Old Pretender; his son Charles, "Bonnie Prince Charlie," would make a final futile bid for the throne in the name of the Catholic Stuarts in 1745.

When James II died, his body was buried in the church of the English Benedictines in Paris. But the church was desecrated and its graves opened during the anticlerical destruction of the French Revolution, and what became of James's remains is unknown. His former subjects did not mourn him, nor was he much respected in the country of his exile. And with the loss of his memoirs, the most intimate witness to his life was gone.

The man who had seen himself as a worthy successor to the emperors of Rome ended his life among strangers, dependent on the charity of a foreign king, convinced to the end that his deposition had been God's punishment for his persistent adultery.

WILLIAM III AND MARY II

(1689–1702)

—◆◆◆◆◆◆◆—

**"I COME TO DO YOU GOOD; I AM HERE FOR
ALL YOUR GOODS."**

—WILLIAM III

When in 1677 James, Duke of York, told his daughter Mary Clorine that she was going to marry her cousin William, Stadtholder of the Netherlands, she burst into tears and would not be comforted.

Mary was only fifteen, excitable and inclined to be overemotional, and she immediately foresaw disaster. She was attractive but very tall for a young woman, while William, whom she had never met but about whom she had heard a good deal, was exceptionally short, with a deformed, stunted body, a chronic cough and an ugly face.

That William was very wealthy, with extensive lands in many parts of Europe and an income in excess of a million guilders a year—which made him much richer than Mary's uncle King Charles II—did not make him any more attractive to her as a husband. Nor did his intelligence and cunning, nor his reputation as a Protestant hero, leader of the tiny United Netherlands against the might of engorging, aggressive France.

Mary was miserable. She cried while saying her marriage vows, went on crying while traveling to Holland with her new husband, and continued crying while adjusting, slowly, to her life as the Stadtholder's wife. William dominated her; he was twelve years her senior, decisive and accustomed to giving orders, and he expected her to do as she was told.

"He comes to my chamber about supper time," Mary wrote, "upon this condition, that I should not tire him more with multiplicity of questions, but rather strive to recreate him, over-toil'd and almost spent, with pleasing jests, that might revive him with innocent mirth."

Mary was meant to be a sort of jester to lighten the spirits of her over-worked husband. Obedient by nature, she did her best, but she was neither clever nor amusing, and before long William was seeking more sophisticated companionship. Mary protested in vain against her husband's infidelities. Eventually she accepted her lot, tolerated the mistresses, and became fond of her physically unappealing husband, as he did of her.

While Mary's uncle Charles was king, she was second in line for the throne, for Charles had no legitimate children and Mary's father James was heir apparent. Mary and her younger sister Anne were James's daughters by his first wife, Anne Hyde; they were raised in the Anglican church but James, in 1682, became a Catholic and married a Catholic princess, Mary of Modena. For many years it was assumed that James and Mary of Modena would have children, but all of Mary's many babies were stillborn or died very young. Consequently James's daughter Mary retained her place in the line of succession.

By the time James became king, succeeding Charles II in 1685, no one imagined that Mary of Modena would have more children, or that if she did, they would survive. Mary expected to become queen after her father's death, and William, looking forward to her accession, traveled to England to meet the peers of the realm and consolidate his and his wife's position.

William too was in the line of succession, though far below his wife in precedence; he was James's nephew as well as his son-in-law. The political opposition in England, which became large and formidable early in James's reign, were well disposed toward William. They distrusted the Catholic James, and suspected him of attempting to subvert the Anglican church settlement. William, the Protestant peers and clergy felt, would uphold Anglicanism—though he was a Presbyterian himself—and had shown himself to be a resolute opponent of Catholic France.

During her father's reign Mary contented herself at her husband's court in Holland, sending affectionate letters to her sister Anne in England. To pass the time she made embroidered hangings and chair seats, and took up the hobby, fashionable among highborn women, of knotting fringe. She also overindulged in food, and by her early twenties, had put on a good deal of weight.

To Mary's sorrow, she and William had no children, and her two pregnancies had led to miscarriages. "I know the Lord might still give me [children], if it seemed good to Him," she wrote in her journal. But no children arrived.

William, during his father-in-law's reign, was preoccupied as always with planning the downfall of his nemesis Louis XIV. William had been barely out of his teens when the Dutch had called upon him to take on the posts of Captain-General and Admiral General in the war against the invading King Louis in 1672. For six years he had managed to hold off the overwhelming might of French arms, saving the United Netherlands and winning a great reputation for himself.

Now in the mid-1680s, William looked forward to more military triumphs. For it seemed likely that Mary would inherit her father's kingdom, and William, as Mary's consort, would lead the English and Dutch together against the might of the French—and defeat them at last.

Both William and Mary were aware that the political situation in England had become divisive. A rebel army under the Duke of Monmouth, the late Charles II's natural son, had made some headway in the West Country before being subdued, and other conspirators were said to be plotting King James's overthrow. William was well aware of how insecure his father-in-law was militarily, for James had had to borrow regiments from the Dutch army to keep London safe while the rebels were pursued and defeated.

Opposition to James was growing stronger as the king undermined the Anglican settlement by favoring his Catholics coreligionists; he brought priests and nuns to England, established a Jesuit school in London and even received a formal diplomatic representative from the Vatican, a papal nuncio. Few were in doubt that James's goal was to facilitate the conversion of the English, Scots and Protestant Irish to the church of Rome and eventually to abolish Anglicanism entirely, as Mary Tudor had tried to do in the previous century.

And if this were not enough to cause disenchantment among James's subjects, there was the additional provocation of his deteriorating mental state. James was becoming wrathful and vengeful, quick to punish those who did not follow his often ill-chosen policies, and suspicious of all but a few trusted intimates. Defensive, haughty and vain, he alienated his servants and officials, who muttered together and increasingly looked across the Channel to Holland in hopes that James would die and Mary would become queen.

By 1687 the undercurrent of conflict between King James and his subjects was stronger than ever. But then came the stunning announcement that the queen, Mary of Modena, was once again pregnant. If she gave birth to a healthy child, and the child survived, James would have a Catholic heir, and all the hopes for Mary's succession would be crushed.

As Queen Mary's pregnancy proceeded, in the winter and spring of 1688, the French were once more threatening war and William yearned to lead England into a grand coalition against Louis XIV. Thus when a group of English statesmen invited William to come to England to "rescue the nation and the religion," he made his preparations for an invasion.

Mary of Modena's child, a healthy prince, was born in June 1688 and immediately there was consternation among James's subjects—and controversy. Despite the presence of numerous witnesses at the time of the birth, a strong rumor spread that the entire event had been a hoax. The queen, it was said, had never been pregnant at all. Some other woman's baby had been smuggled into the birth chamber, perhaps in the warming pan—a metal container for hot coals, used to warm the bed. Prince James was called the "warming pan baby," and dismissed as having no royal blood.

Amid the confusion over the succession, William's plans went forward, though not without difficulties. The undertaking was perilous, for no large invading force since the time of William the Conqueror in the eleventh century had successfully landed on English soil. The Spanish king Philip II had amassed a great armada a century earlier, and sailed from Corunna, but the ships had foundered on the Irish coast.

The logistics alone were daunting. William was attempting to bring together twenty thousand soldiers and eight thousand horses, and to supervise the building of over two hundred transport ships to carry them to England. Arms and cannon, tents and equipment, huge quantities of food and drink and hundreds of cases of ammunition all had to be amassed, and made ready for the sea journey.

William was courageous, and, in his thirty-eighth year, relatively youthful and vigorous. But he suffered severely from asthma, which became much worse under the strain of the military preparations and continued to worsen throughout the summer of 1688. In August, worried over the state of politics in the United Netherlands where his own position as Stadtholder had become none too secure, and concerned lest the French might attack his country once he left for England, William nearly gave up the entire enterprise. Though he attempted to keep his destination secret, there were French spies everywhere, and James too was suspicious.

Even if the Dutch armada was launched, there was every chance it would never arrive at its intended destination. For the ships would not be ready to leave until the fall, and fall was the season of freak storms and huge waves in the Channel.

Despite these daunting considerations, William finally made the decision to proceed, though he was running short of money and many of the soldiers and sailors were deserting, fearful of the storm season. The boats were undermanned, the soldiers underequipped.

William's leavetaking from Mary was tender. Before embarking he told her that, if he died, she should marry again—but not a Catholic husband. No doubt she prayed for his good fortune, not because she was ambitious to become queen, but out of loyalty and affection.

The Dutch armada set sail, the transports lumbering clumsily through the high waves, tilting dangerously under the weight of their heavy cargo, which included a portable bridge, an iron smithy, a printing press, eighty chests of gold coins and even William's coach. A storm swept up with such violence that the ships were scattered, and they were forced to return to Dutch ports. Several weeks later, reassembled, the flotilla set sail once again, fifty warships, two hundred and twenty-five transports. William was in his flagship, *The Brill*.

Under lowering skies, passing through occasional squalls, the long line of ships made the crossing in the first days of November 1688. From their masts flew banners proclaiming, in Latin "The Liberty of England and the Protestant Religion," "For the Protestant Faith," and "For Liberty and a Free Parliament." William's banner carried his motto, "I Will Maintain."

Though the British navy, alerted to the danger, was watching for the Dutch invaders, weather conditions protected William and his fleet. An eastern gale arose, blackening the horizon with sweeping rains and blinding the British lookouts; the Dutch sailed on past them, remaining invisible. On November 5 William sailed into Torbay, unopposed, having lost not a single ship.

He immediately disembarked and led his troops to Exeter, where he was soon heartened to learn that some of King James's army officers were abandoning their royal master and joining the invading force. James, prostrated by a severe nosebleed which lasted several days and apparently numbed into inaction by the shock of William's landing, lost heart. For weeks James did nothing, then sent his wife and infant son to France, where after several further weeks of delays, he joined them.

Now chaos was loosed. With the king gone and the invader reluctant to restore order by force—he was after all an invited guest in England—mobs rampaged through the capital, setting fire to mansions, looting shops, befouling Catholic churches. Members of James's royal council tried to get word to William to come to London, but the courier carrying the message got lost, the victim of a drunken guide, and for days the pillaging continued.

Not until February of 1689 were the legal arrangements for the new monarchy worked out, though in fact William began to exercise authority as monarch the month after he arrived in England. A Convention Parliament gathered to proclaim that James had, in effect, abandoned the throne. They offered it to William and Mary jointly (Mary having refused to rule without her husband as co-sovereign), with the understanding that although both king and queen would reign, William would govern—with Mary acting in his place when he was out of the kingdom.

The constitutional arrangements were unprecedented, and innovative. The new monarchs signed a Declaration of Rights which forbade them to act in defiance of the law (as James had done repeatedly), asserted that parliaments ought to be summoned often, and established Mary's sister Anne as her successor in the event she had no children.

Mary, who had returned to her homeland on February 12, was delighted to be back in England, indeed some critics murmured that she showed an unseemly delight at her father's overthrow. On her arrival, she embraced her sister warmly, then ran happily through the palace of Whitehall with the excitement of a girl, dashing from room to room, "looking into every closet and conveniency," wrote Anne's friend and lady-in-waiting Lady Churchill, "and turning up the quilts of the beds just as people do at an inn." The palace was fully furnished; James had departed in such haste that he had taken nothing with him. Everything was to Mary's satisfaction, and she seemed to observers "quite transported" with pleasure, as "laughing and jolly" as if she were going to a wedding.

In her memoir, Mary confessed that her extravagant demonstrations of joy were an act ("I was fain to force myself to more mirth than became me"), put on in order to convince skeptics that she was truly pleased at her accession. In fact, she overdid it, and was accused of pride and lack of decorum. The truth was, Mary wrote, that she had wanted nothing more than a regency, but that for the good of the public, had accepted the dual monarchy.

"I have had more trouble to bring my self to bear this so envied estate [the status of sovereign] than I should have had to have been reduced to the lowest condition in the world," the queen admitted. But having accepted the crown jointly with her husband, she did her best to carry out her responsibilities, and was often called upon to rule for months at a time while William was out of the country.

April 11, 1689, was the date fixed for the coronation of the king and queen. On that morning, disturbing news arrived. James was attempting to reconquer his abandoned kingdom. He had landed in Ireland with a French army and was having much success. A letter arrived for Mary from her father, accusing her of betraying him and condemning her in the strongest possible language for presuming to take his throne.

The news spread through the court, and anxiety replaced the celebratory mood of the coronation preparations. What if James should reconquer all three of his kingdoms? What revenge might he take on those who had supported William and Mary?

The new sovereigns themselves, upset by the news, were unable to proceed with the ceremony. For nearly three hours they delayed, quarreling with each other, consulting with advisers, worrying about their future. Finally, after much delay, they were crowned. But all did not go smoothly. The ritual was interrupted several times by mistakes, and at the banquet in Westminster Hall there were further irregularities. By tradition an armor-clad champion was to enter the hall on horseback to challenge any who might oppose the new monarch—in this case, the new monarchs. The champion was late, and by the time he appeared, it was too dark for him to be seen clearly. The challenge was botched.

It was an omen, for the reign of William and Mary began badly and, year by year, got worse. Though William had spent much energy and money—his own money—in the effort to save the realm from James's misgovernment, and though he went to Ireland and defeated James in his bid to reestablish himself, William was unappreciated. Political sentiment, which had run strongly against James, turned slowly back toward him as the English and Scots came to resent William and his Dutch advisers and friends. There were Jacobite plots, secret messages to St.-Germain where James was living, and nostalgic toasts to "the king over the water."

Intrigue swirled around the double throne as William grew more and more unpopular. Disparaged and verbally abused, constantly reminded of the supremacy of Parliament, William thought of giving up his crown and returning to Holland. He stayed on, embittered and angry, the strain worsening his health.

The dull and hardworking William had no time to spare for social life, and the court he established with Mary was dull in the extreme. Though

Mary was gracious and approachable, William was not; he discouraged audiences, kept conversations short and disliked crowds. "He neither loved shows nor shoutings," wrote Bishop Burnet. Living at Hampton Court— Whitehall being bad for the king's asthma—William was withdrawn. Mary occupied herself with embroidery and collecting blue and white delftware, filling room after room with china pieces and starting a fad among her subjects.

Mary's personal stature rose in the eyes of her councilors as she showed herself to be a capable ruler in William's absence. Initially shy, she gradually became commanding and decisive, showing a sense of fairness—and a well developed instinct for ferreting out corruption among the members of her retinue. Dishonest officials were dismissed, duplicitous servants sent away. Mary's diligence in working long hours at her desk won her much admiration, while her sociability helped to blunt the edge of her husband's asocial tendencies.

When William was away Mary missed him. "My impatience for another [letter] from you is as great as my love," she wrote him, "which will not end but with my life." On the whole they enjoyed marital harmony, marred only by their lack of an heir. Anne was the presumed heir, though the assumption was that, if Mary remained childless, Anne's only child William, Duke of Gloucester, would eventually become king when his aunt and uncle died.

Within months of William and Mary's accession Mary and Anne were at odds, and ultimately became estranged. The focus of their conflict were the ambitious courtiers John and Sarah Churchill, Anne's intimates. Mary thought them grasping and opportunistic, while Anne, loyal by nature, clung stubbornly to them and refused to dismiss Sarah Churchill from her household when ordered to by her sister. From 1692 on Mary and Anne did not meet.

Anne became reconciled to her father in France, but Mary never did. When James, defeated and no longer a threat to the security of Britain, sent Mary a message asking her to please send him his clothes and possessions, she neglected it. He had denounced and insulted her, and she did not forgive him.

When Mary died of smallpox at the end of December 1694, William mourned. "You can imagine what a state I am in, loving her as I do," he wrote to a friend. "You know what it is to have a good wife." An unfaithful, gruff and domineering husband, William had nonetheless loved Mary, and for the rest of his life he wore a lock of her hair next to his skin.

With Mary's death William became more unpopular than ever, and several assassination plots were uncovered. But though he thought from time to time of abdicating, and actually drafted an abdication speech at one point, William wanted above all to pursue his dream of arresting French aggression, and for this he needed his British kingdoms. Holland, England and the Holy Roman Emperor were engaged in hostilities against France throughout the 1690s, with neither side achieving lasting dominance. England's fleet dominated the Mediterranean, but French land victories were a counterweight to this preeminence. In 1697 the Peace of Ryswick ended the conflict, and Louis XIV was forced to give up many of his conquests, much to William's satisfaction.

But in the aftermath of the treaty, Parliament forced the king to reduce the size of his army and send away not only his trusted foreign mercenaries but his Dutch Blue Guards, who had been with him since 1688. "I am so upset . . . about the troops that I cannot think of anything else," William said sadly. Once again he considered abdicating, but did not; instead he turned more and more to overindulgence in drink, carousing with his cronies in a fashion reminiscent of James I. "The king," wrote Bishop Burnet with tactful circumlocution, "was now falling under an ill habit of body."

In actuality William's health was failing. Asthma, swollen legs, acutely painful hemorrhoids and his everpresent cough weakened William's misshapen body, which grew more and more thin. His eyes, once fierce with determination, became dull and he mourned for the nephew of whom he had been fond, Anne's son, who died in 1700 of hydrocephalic disease.

One day while riding at Hampton Court William's horse stumbled and fell, throwing him. He broke his collarbone, which did not heal and quickly progressed to a severe infection. On March 8, 1702, William died at the age of fifty-one and his sister-in-law Anne became queen.

With indecent haste and inadequate dignity King William III was laid to rest in Westminster Abbey, after a private midnight funeral. The man who had saved Protestantism in England was unmourned, his tomb all but unmarked. William's rites and commemorations were in contrast to the magnificent funeral he had given Mary on her death.

The only lasting monument William had ever sought for himself was the defeat of Louis XIV. But when William died, Louis continued to flourish, while at St.-Germain, an aging James Stuart waited confidently for his people to recall him to the throne of his ancestors.

ANNE

(1702–1714)

———— ✦❧✠❧✦ ————

"I AM ENTIRELY ENGLISH."

—QUEEN ANNE

Princess Anne of York was born in 1665, five years after her uncle, King Charles II, came to the throne. She was a plain, heavy-featured little girl, hefty and shy, quite overshadowed by her pretty older sister Mary. When Anne was six years old her mother Anne Hyde died, and her father, the king's younger brother James, soon remarried, taking as his bride the Italian Mary of Modena.

Disliking her stepmother, and having only a formal bond with her father, Anne was emotionally unattached; in her isolation she turned to her older sister and to another older girl, Sarah Jennings, for companionship and affection.

These bonds were to prove enduring. Even after Anne's sister Mary left England to live with her husband William of Orange, Stadtholder of the Netherlands, the two sisters corresponded, commiserated with each other, and exchanged court gossip. With Sarah Jennings Anne developed an even closer relationship, almost a symbiotic one. Sarah was five years Anne's senior, lively and attractive and quick-witted. She took the lead, Anne followed. The two girls were very different in temperament, Sarah confident and assertive, Anne self-doubting and eager to please, though with a stubborn streak and a tendency to rigidity on moral issues.

An earnest attachment to the Church of England, her mother's church, was characteristic of Anne from childhood on. Henry Compton, Bishop of London, taught her her catechism and she adhered to the Protestant tenets of the church with an unquestioned devotion—albeit a devotion nourished by fear.

For Anne's childhood was overshadowed by widespread terror of Catholics. In 1678, when she was thirteen, rumors swept London that Jesuit conspirators were plotting to murder King Charles and rule the realm in the name of the pope. Panic spread, suspicions were raised. In the aftermath of the episode, Anne's father James, a Catholic convert, was hounded and threatened with removal from the line of succession.

Anne professed herself faithful to her Protestant creed. "I abhor the principles of the church of Rome as much as it is possible for anyone to do," she wrote to her sister Mary in Holland. "I am resolved to undergo anything rather than change my religion."

Her uncle the king having no legitimate heir, Anne was third in line for the throne, after her father (unless Parliament succeeded in excluding him) and her sister. But no one expected James's younger daughter to reign. As a consequence her marriage, to the retiring, colorless Prince George of Denmark, was only a minor occasion in the court calendar and Anne and her prince went to live quietly at Kensington Palace.

Anne embarked on married life a large, fleshy woman with dark hair and eyes, a pronounced squint (she was very nearsighted) and, observers noted, an exceptionally melodious voice. She was not handsome but had a certain presence. However, she remained uncomfortable in groups or among strangers, and clung to those she knew well. She could not hold her own in witty conversation, clever people intimidated her. Anne was capable of animation but was on the whole phlegmatic, inclined to overeat and overindulge in drink. Her tastes were simple, her views largely uninformed.

Marriage suited Anne, and she was a devoted wife to Prince George. But motherhood was a severe trial to her. Again and again she became pregnant, only to miscarry or deliver a stillborn child. Eventually there were many small graves, each with a tiny coffin. One child, a boy, survived. Prince William, chatty and outgoing, was Anne's contribution to the Stuart line. But the prince was delicate, with a head too large for his body, and it was by no means certain he would reach adulthood.

Meanwhile the question of the succession had moved to center stage. In 1685, when Anne was twenty, her uncle Charles died and her father became king as James II. That there was no widespread public protest was remarkable, given James's continued adherence to the church of Rome and the British public's dread of Catholicism. By the time James had been on the throne for three years, however, his subjects were rebellious. The turning point came in summer 1688, when the previously childless Mary of Modena gave birth to a son. Suddenly the new baby, who was certain to be raised in his father's faith, replaced the Protestant Mary, Anne's sister, as heir apparent.

Anne was as alarmed and dissatisfied as anyone. She had never liked her stepmother, calling her a "great bigot" who hated all Protestants. People were saying that the birth of Mary of Modena's child was a hoax, that a commoner's infant had been smuggled into the royal bedchamber and passed off as the queen's son. Anne encouraged and spread this story, which revived the fears of the 1670s about Jesuit conspiracies. Meanwhile Mary languished in Holland, displaced by the king's new son.

Invited by a group of aristocrats, William of Orange invaded England in November of 1688 and, meeting no resistance from King James, marched his men toward the capital. Anne had left for Yorkshire, where a regional revolt against her father was under way. She seems to have been resolute in her support of her sister's claim to the throne, and in her opposition to James, who fled to France and the protection of Louis XIV.

In supporting Mary and her husband William, Anne advanced her own interests, for as Mary and William had no children, Anne became the next heir. However, the issues involved were complex. Parliament met early in 1689 and decided that, though the crown was Mary's (James having abdicated the throne by his flight abroad), William had to be made joint ruler, so that if Mary predeceased him he would retain his authority. Anne was deemed to be the next in line after both joint sovereigns died.

In agreeing to this settlement, Anne was in effect giving up the crown, or so it was generally believed. The chances that Anne would survive both her sister and brother-in-law seemed slim. And of course, Mary might still give birth to an heir.

When Mary arrived at Greenwich from Holland, ready to take her place as Queen Mary II, Anne was waiting to meet her. The sisters greeted one another "with transports of affection," Sarah Jennings, now Sarah Churchill, wrote somewhat acidly, "which soon fell off, and coldness ensued." Sarah, who had married the military commander John Churchill, was ever at Anne's side, her closest friend and confidante, her staunchest supporter.

In fact the coldness between the sisters had much to do with Sarah, for both Queen Mary and her husband distrusted the Churchills as ambitious and grasping and resented Anne's reliance on Sarah. When Mary ordered Anne to dismiss Sarah, Anne balked, and refused. Ultimately Anne left her sister and brother-in-law's court, finding no way to resolve the hostility that had arisen between them.

Anne had risen in importance, with a parliamentary grant of fifty thousand pounds a year and a palace of her own, The Cockpit. Yet she continued to seek a comforting simplicity of life. With the Churchills, she played at being an ordinary housewife, calling herself "Mrs. Morley." Sarah was "Mrs. Freeman."

"Dear Mrs. Freeman," Anne began one letter in 1692, when William and Mary were attempting to force her to dismiss Sarah from her household, "Never believe your faithful Mrs. Morley will ever submit, she can wait with patience for a Sunshine Day, and if she does not live to see it, yet she hopes England will flourish again."

It was typical of Anne to see her relations with her sister's court in personal terms, and to respond with stubborn loyalty to her friends. That John Churchill had in fact been involved in political intrigue against the crown mattered less to Anne than that he, and especially his wife, should remain her intimates. Even when King William took away Churchill's appointment as commander-in-chief in the Netherlands and had him imprisoned in the Tower of London, Anne did not disassociate herself from him or his wife.

For a few years Anne was left in a sort of limbo, no longer attached to the court, taking no part in political life—except to write to her father in exile, healing the breach caused by her failure to stand by him in 1688. She occupied herself overseeing renovations to the gardens at Kensington Palace, and commissioned the aging Christopher Wren to design an orangery, which she called her "summer supper house." She bought a cottage on the edge of Windsor Great Park, comfortably fitted out with damask furniture and marble chimneypieces, to which she and Prince George could go from time to time for a few days of complete peace.

In 1694 Queen Mary died, at only thirty-two, leaving Anne one step closer to the throne. Mary's death weakened William's position; he found himself at a disadvantage and set about restoring relations with Anne, and with her supporters the Churchills. But tensions remained. In particular, Anne was offended that William overlooked her husband's modest talents and would not give him a court appointment. Privately, "Mrs. Morley" and

"Mrs. Freeman" sneered at William and referred to him as "Caliban" or "the Dutch monster."

Anne was nearer the throne, but afflicted in health. Years of overeating and excessive drinking ("they say that she drinks too much wine and likes too strong wine" wrote one observer), numerous pregnancies and the stress of her uncomfortable position had left Anne prey to disease. Her physicians diagnosed gout, recognizing the painful symptoms: swelling and intense pain in the joints, fever and chills and overall weakness.

A change of diet might have helped alleviate the princess's condition, but no such change was made. Instead Anne grew worse year after year, her feet and ankles so deformed and tender that walking was impossible. She was carried in a chair from room to room, but when the prolonged attacks of gout were at their worst, she simply lay in bed for many hours, gasping with pain, unable even to tolerate the weight of a bed sheet covering her swollen red limbs.

In 1700 Anne's son William died. With him died her hopes, for after so many stillbirths and miscarriages, and given the severity of her illness, Anne could not expect to have more children. King William had not remarried and seemed unlikely to. So the succession was uncertain. A granddaughter of James I, Electress Sophia of Hanover, was the nearest heir after Anne herself. But there was also Anne's half-brother James (the baby Anne had once believed to be the product of a hoax), and a number of William's subjects, especially Irish Catholics and Scots, wanted James to succeed, as in their view he represented the true Stuart line. Ministers and sovereign alike remained vigilant against the threat of a Jacobite rebellion. By the Act of Settlement, passed in 1701, Catholics were barred from the throne.

King William died in March of 1702, and in April, Anne was crowned queen in Westminster Abbey. The solemnity of the ritual was marred by Anne's pitiable condition. Because of a sharp attack of gout, she was unable to stand or walk unaided, and had to perform her ceremonial functions while being carried in a special chair upholstered in crimson velvet. The effect produced was vaguely comical, for the fat, shy, squinting queen was unregal, and did not inspire awe. In an ignominious aftermath to the coronation, thieves took advantage of the celebratory pandemonium to break into Westminster Hall and steal all the queen's silver and gold plate, even taking the linen tablecloths.

Anne's penchant for informality diminished her majesty further. Unlike previous monarchs, who dined in state at long tables, on display before members of the court and public, Anne chose to dine in private, except on Sundays. Her infrequent appearances discouraged court attendance, as did her social awkwardness and dull conversation. Few people came to her royal levees, and those who did were bored. Jonathan Swift wrote of one such tedious gathering, held in the royal bedchamber, at which the guests stood around the room while the queen looked at them "with her fan in her mouth, and once a minute said about three words to some that were nearest her." She was rescued by a footman who announced that dinner was ready, and she immediately left the room.

"Her court is as it were abandoned," Swift thought, and in truth, both socially and politically the monarchy had lost prestige. In part this was the result of Parliament's pivotal role in the events of 1688/9. But it also had to do with Anne herself, for there clung to her, despite her general good humor, an air of mournful abandon. Shrewder, harder people would always take advantage of Anne; she could not seem to learn wariness or self-protectiveness.

And while the court remained the center of executive government and the source of all offices, honors and pensions, its political role was rapidly shifting. Party affiliations, party loyalties were becoming established, with one group, known as Whigs, coalescing around the right of resistance to the crown and the theory of limited, constitutional monarchy and the other, the Tories, identified with a strong monarchy and its prerogatives and the church.

"All I desire is my liberty in encouraging and employing all those that concur faithfully in my service," Anne wrote, "whether they are called Whigs or Tories." She herself had strong Tory leanings, given her lifelong advocacy of the interests of the church. But as sovereign, she knew she had to attempt neutrality, "not to be tied to one, or the other." In an effort to avoid becoming what she called a "slave" to party, Anne relied heavily on John Churchill, who took command of the English and Dutch armies after the outbreak of war in the month following Anne's coronation, and Churchill's son-in-law Sidney Godolphin, whom she named Lord Treasurer. These two, together with Robert Harley, Speaker of the House of Commons, guided Britain through the difficult early years of Anne's reign.

When she appeared before Parliament to read her first speech from the throne, Anne made an unexpectedly moving impression. Her soft, sweet voice mesmerized her listeners, and when she told them, proudly, "I am entirely English," they responded with enthusiasm. They were tired of Dutch William and his coterie of foreign friends.

Anne was dutiful and hard-working, acquiring a reputation for conscientiousness and approachability. But there was general agreement, among those who had dealings with her, that her understanding was limited. Her grasp of affairs was at best rudimentary. The replies she made to queries or requests were invariably vague, and disconcertingly indecisive. Clearly Anne needed stronger personalities around her to support and inform her own judgments.

Anne herself felt misjudged. "Everything I say," she told Sarah Churchill, "is imputed either to partiality or being imposed upon by knaves and fools." In truth her opinions were her own, she insisted. "All I say proceeds purely from my own poor judgment," she told Sarah, "which, though it may not be so good as other people's, I'm sure is a very honest one."

More than any other reign in English history, the reign of Queen Anne was overshadowed by continental war. A powerful France, her territory enlarged by the bequest of the Spanish kingdom and Spain's colonial empire, bestrode Europe like the colossus she had become. Britain, together with her allies Austria, the Netherlands and other small states, opposed King Louis XIV and his mighty armies. Britain had never before had a large army; now, under John Churchill's masterly leadership, a vast and formidable fighting force took shape.

So formidable, and so well led, were British arms that in 1704 at Blenheim on the Danube the French were handed a staggering defeat. Twenty-eight French regiments surrendered to the British, along with the commander-in-chief and several of his generals. "Within the memory of man," Churchill wrote to Queen Anne after the battle, "there has been no victory as great as this."

Anne rewarded Churchill by creating him Duke of Marlborough and giving him a royal estate where she promised to build a grand mansion at her expense. Blenheim Palace, a house of unparalleled magnificence, rose in splendor near Oxford, though Sarah Churchill called it a "wild, unmerciful house" and was not contented there.

Through the early years of her reign Anne presided over a realm triumphant with military victory, and her own popularity reflected the nation's triumph. Marlborough brought the French to their knees, Britain's prestige soared, and the crowns of England and Scotland became more firmly wedded when in 1707 the Act of Union established a single government, in London, for both realms.

Anne's "Sunshine Day" had come, but there was dissension within her tight-knit circle. The Duke and Duchess of Marlborough, dissatisfied with the dozens of honors and offices Anne gave them, demanded more—and threatened to resign and abandon the queen unless she gave them more. (Anne, in her turn, threatened to abdicate.) Anne had once vowed never to part with her friends "until death mows us down with his impartial hand." But she was beginning to rethink that vow.

Sarah Churchill became strident, confronting Anne and shouting at her, accusing her of ingratitude, and the poor queen, unwieldy and immobile, was at Sarah's mercy. The pattern of domination and submission that had prevailed between the two women since childhood continued—until Anne, managing to summon the courage to resist, began to look around for a different set of supporters.

Anne's quick-witted secretary, a modest, plain woman who was a poor relation of the Churchills, moved gradually into the role of principal confidante to the queen. Abigail Masham eventually displaced Sarah Churchill, but not before much wrangling took place and many angry scenes between Sarah and the queen.

Anne was sinking physically, weakened by continued overeating and overdrinking, her body extremely heavy and her mind under constant strain. Though she still took pleasure in attending race meetings, and managed to follow the hunt in Windsor Great Park in a small carriage which she drove herself, she went more often to Bath, to take the waters in an effort to relieve her worsening gout.

The attacks came more frequently, and were more painful, after Anne reached the age of forty. Stabbing pain in her joints sent her into prolonged agony. Because of her huge bulk and immobility she had to be moved from bed to chair, and from room to room, with hoists and pulleys—an uncomfortable and awkward procedure.

Her tortured feet swathed in bandages, her red face distorted with pain, her dress neglected and her hair in disorder, Anne was the picture of misery. One who saw her at her worst, over a period of many months in 1706 and 1707, was struck by her suffering, and called her the most wretched mortal he had ever seen.

Anne's husband George died in 1708, leaving her widowed and alone. Her last years were clouded by incessant quarrels among her ministers, and by a reaction, among her subjects, against all the costly years of war.

A serious illness in 1713 gave Anne warning that she was not likely to live much longer. But the thought that after her death her throne would go to the elderly Electress of Hanover disturbed her. She refused to allow either Electress Sophia or her son George to come to England even for a visit. In vain Anne wrote to her half-brother James, asking him to renounce his Catholicism so that he could succeed her.

While enduring a stormy meeting of her council in the summer of 1714, Anne clutched her head and fainted. She rallied, then collapsed again. On August 1 she died.

Anne's legacy was a Britain greatly strengthened militarily, and politically more self-aware, albeit more divided. Her colonial territories had increased, her trade was rapidly expanding. All this had come about largely without the queen's direct influence, but her benign if forlorn presence had steadied the realm during wartime. Anne's staunch and forthright Englishness, her concern for the church, her devotion to her husband endeared her to her subjects.

Sarah Churchill wrote sneeringly of Anne that she was "ignorant in everything but what the parsons had taught her as a child," and to an extent she was right. But there was gallantry in the queen's long-suffering efforts to do her duty as sovereign, and an appealing innocence in her wholesome values and well intentioned treatment of those around her. Even when her kind, ingenuous nature had all but broken under the burden of illness, Anne continued to face her challenges with the bravery of a good soldier, undefeated to the end.

GEORGE I

(1714–1727)

━━◆━▷◎◀◆◎▶◎◀◆━━

"IN PRIVATE LIFE, HE WOULD HAVE BEEN CALLED AN
HONEST BLOCKHEAD. . . . HE WAS MORE PROPERLY
DULL THAN LAZY, AND WOULD HAVE BEEN SO WELL
CONTENTED TO HAVE REMAINED IN HIS LITTLE TOWN
OF HANOVER THAT IF THE AMBITION OF THOSE
ABOUT HIM HAD NOT BEEN GREATER THAN HIS OWN,
WE SHOULD NEVER HAVE SEEN HIM IN ENGLAND."

—LADY MARY WORTLEY MONTAGU

Trumpeters blared a fanfare and drums beat out a solemn tattoo as the elderly, pale King George I was crowned in Westminster Abbey on October 20, 1714. He was not an impressive figure, despite his crimson robes and flashing diamonds, his posture less than regally straight and his gait clumsy. But the crowd in the abbey acclaimed him, and there was a sigh of relief that the new reign was beginning without hindrance or opposition, the Stuarts giving way to the Hanoverians, the Protestant succession assured.

There was much public curiosity about the new king, and large crowds had come out to watch his coach pass through the streets on the way to the coronation ceremony. All that was known about him was that he was Elector of Hanover, that he was a brave and successful military commander, who had cooperated with the great Duke of Marlborough on several of his campaigns, and that he was a heartless domestic tyrant who had kept his beautiful wife shut away in a castle for twenty years, after he murdered her lover.

Not everyone welcomed the new king. In London all was calm and order but in several provincial cities there were riots, and clamor for King James, the Stuart Pretender to the throne, who was in exile in France.

James had tried to seize the realm from Queen Anne six years earlier, sailing across the Channel with an invading force but encountering difficulties and ultimately giving up. Nearly everyone thought he might try again, although the Jacobite leaders who attended the coronation looked peaceable enough, if a bit peevish.

King George I was crowned, the sun shone, and the coronation banquet, held in Westminster Hall, was abundant and well attended. It was noticed that the king did not smile, and that he spoke almost no English. Apart from that he seemed satisfactory, though to judge from his age, his would not likely be a long reign.

George settled into two rooms in St. James's Palace, a bedchamber and a room for giving audiences. His needs were modest, his tastes plain. At fifty-four, he was an old man, though far from decrepit, set in his ways and with a dislike of novelty and disturbance. He had not wanted to become King of England, though he had known for many years that the throne would one day be his and had kept a personal representative in London since 1710 to look after his interests. He may have hoped that either his mother, who was Queen Anne's designated heir, or the queen herself would outlive him, enabling him to live out his life in peace in his palace of Herrenhausen, ruling his placid, obedient German subjects and protecting Hanover from continental enemies.

But both his mother and Queen Anne had died in 1714, and George, who was practical if not ambitious, saw that it was to Hanover's advantage for him to ascend the British throne. So he left his comfortable palace and made the journey to England, intending to return to his German subjects as often as possible.

England was not unknown to George. He had visited the country as a young man, in the reign of Charles II, staying for four months and pursuing Princess Anne (as she then was) as a potential wife. He knew something of the English, he had fought alongside them and was familiar enough with their history to know that they had very strong representative institutions. Parliament had decreed the death of one king and installed another married pair as joint sovereigns. George was only too aware that he owed his crown to an accident of birth and his Protestant faith, and to nothing else. Parliament, if it chose, could send him back to Hanover. Or James Stuart, with French aid, could prepare another invasion which might succeed.

It was no wonder King George lived in only two rooms; he anticipated a short stay in his new realm.

When George first arrived in England in 1714, rowed upriver in a barge to the old palace of Greenwich, he was not recognized; his son George Augustus, who arrived earlier, had been mistaken for his father and received by shouting crowds and a cluster of dignitaries. It was the first of many embarrassments. George's very limited English (he preferred speaking French, if his interlocutor spoke no German) led to misunderstandings and irritations. He was by nature neither warm nor congenial ("The Elector is so cold that he freezes everything into ice," his cousin remarked), and those who had to deal with him soon discovered that beneath his shy, benign reserve there lurked a deeply suspicious, even vindictive nature. Accustomed to unquestioning obedience, George was selfish and easily offended. And once offense was given, the wrong could never be made right.

The king's unforgiving nature was evident in his treatment of his divorced wife Sophia Dorothea. He had married her when she was barely sixteen, charming and full of fun. Her insouciance galled him, and her sparkle and jokey manner made his own blunt, coarse ways seem barbaric. George resented her, mistreated her and, when she fell in love with a Swedish officer, had the officer killed and Sophia imprisoned. She was not allowed to see their two children, or to leave her palace jail.

George had not remarried, but for twenty-three years he had lived with his mistress, Ehrengard Melusina von Schulenberg, whom he treated as a wife and by whom he had three children. Like the king, Madame von Schulenberg was aging. A contemporary described her as "a very tall, lean, ill-favored old lady." She sat with George in the evenings, playing cards or listening to music. Their domesticity was shared by another aging lady, Charlotte Kielmansegge (anglicized to "Kelmanns"), who was George's half-sister but whom everyone at court presumed was his mistress as well.

Because Ehrengard was very thin and Charlotte extremely fat, court wits christened the two women "the Elephant" and "the Maypole." (Germans had called Ehrengard "the Scarecrow".) The king kept both women near him, and gave them Queen Anne's jewels; he ignored the gross jokes and jibes made about them though he did, after a few years, acquire a younger English mistress, Anne Brett, who did not give rise to ridicule.

In the fall and winter of 1715 George faced his first major crisis when the Pretender challenged his throne, landing in Scotland and raising his standard against the king. Many Scottish towns declared themselves for James. In England, some local magistrates and government officials were mobbed and the royal ministers panicked. King George was calm; he had faced the Turks and the French in battle, he could face the Stuart rebels. In the end, there was no need. James left again for France after a little over a month, discouraged by the lack of support he received. The British punished the rebels severely, seized their weapons, and hanged their leaders. In an ugly coda to the rising, King George brutalized the wife of one of the condemned Scottish lords when she came to him to beg for her husband's life. Instead of replying to her pleas he grasped her and threw her roughly to the floor—giving his enemies another reason to condemn him for misogyny.

No sooner had the Jacobite threat receded than King George embarked for Hanover—the first of five trips he would make in the course of his reign. Hanover was at war with Sweden, and George had allied his electorate with the Russian tsar Peter the Great in hopes of acquiring territory controlled by the tottering Swedish king. The Great Northern War required his vigilance. But with King George away on the continent, his government degenerated into squabbles among his quarrelsome ministers, forcing his return.

In the previous reign, two clearly defined political parties had emerged: the Tories, advocates of strong monarchy, and the Whigs, who advocated limited monarchy and the supremacy of Parliament. The sovereign's natural affinity was with the Tories, but King George mistrusted them; he knew many Tories wanted to see James Stuart on the throne. The Whigs were in power, and though King George distrusted them as well, he was content to let them govern for the time being, unruly and full of intrigue though they were.

A short, unimposing figure, a pale elderly man in a dark tie wig wearing a plain coat and breeches, the king shunned the public, avoiding appearing before crowds and doing away with royal levees, those tedious occasions on which the monarchs received visitors while dressing. When he went to the opera, he did not sit at the center of the royal box but in some less conspicuous place, hidden behind the tall Ehrengard.

The only exception to George's social reclusiveness came when on warm nights he boarded his open barge at Whitehall with a small party of friends and went upriver toward Chelsea. Many other barges surrounded the royal vessel, so many that it appeared the whole river was covered, and one barge held fifty musicians, the sound of their music floating on the night air. George Frideric Handel had been Kapellmeister at King

George's Hanover palace, and the king brought him to London. George was so delighted with the music Handel wrote expressly to be played at these barge excursions that he asked for it to be repeated several times.

The era of Handel was also the era of Addison and Congreve, Pope and Chesterfield, a time of effervescent wit and verbal display. The royal court, by contrast, was leaden, presided over by the taciturn monarch with his few words of heavily accented English. Insulated in his small apartment, George played cards with his German favorites, Baron Bothmar, Baron von Bernstorff, the Prime Minister of Hanover and Jean de Robethon, an experienced courtier who had served William III and who was a target of much English criticism for his prying and intrigue. Ehrengard and Charlotte were on hand to receive visitors and petitioners; if a courtier hoped to advance himself or to obtain a valuable position from the king, a gift of money to either of these ladies was sure to secure it.

There were two other guardians of the king's privacy, his Turkish attendants Mahomet and Mustapha. These two exotic turbanned gentlemen, whom the king had taken prisoner many years earlier when he was an officer in the imperial army, had been his servants for decades. George told them everything, and they, in turn, were fanatically loyal—and armed with wicked-looking curved scimitars that could decapitate a man with a single blow. Mahomet and Mustapha were officially Pages of the Backstairs, and as such occupied an important office in the monarch's personal household. Unofficially, they were the repositories of the king's secrets, and a rich source of gossip. Ministers, courtiers, visitors from abroad sought out the Turkish pages whenever they needed to know what King George thought or what he planned to do.

Because it was assumed that the elderly King George would not live much longer, his outgoing, personable son George Augustus was sought out as the rising sun, the hope of the coming reign. George Augustus was warm where King George was icy and remote. George Augustus had a witty, well-read wife, Princess Caroline, while King George had risible female companions. George Augustus was "civil and kind to everybody," as one court observer put it, full of compliments about English culture and pleased when anyone mistook him for an Englishman. King George, on the other hand, was sour and irritable, full of dispraise for his English subjects and frequently off in Hanover where he clearly preferred to be.

Father and son were bitterly at odds. George Augustus had never forgiven his father for imprisoning his mother, and did not care who knew it. He was impatient for the king to die, not so that he could succeed him, but so that he could free his mother from her long captivity. As for King George, he despised his son passionately, considering him unfit to rule, unfit to serve as regent during the king's absences in Hanover, unfit even to mingle with the officials of the court.

"The father treats the son with excessive rigor," was the comment of one who saw them both at their worst. "On the other hand, the son behaves in such a manner that the king has good reason to complain." Mutual provocations were bitter and constant.

When George Augustus's fifth child was born, the christening was held in the Princess of Wales's bedchamber at St. James's. The king insisted on choosing the infant's sponsors, and deliberately included among them one of George Augustus's enemies, the Duke of Newcastle. At the ceremony a violent quarrel erupted, the prince assaulted the duke and threatened to kill him. King George, who had most likely anticipated the fight, used it as an excuse to order his son's arrest. That night George Augustus, Caroline and the tiny child moved out of the palace, though the king did not permit them to take their three daughters with them; he kept his granddaughters as hostages. In a sad coda to the entire squalid drama, the baby soon died.

The breach was permanent. George Augustus and Caroline set up a household of their own, one marked by glittering receptions, gatherings of politicians, artists and cosmopolites, and splendid entertainments. The prince's mansion became a rival court, to which opponents of the government were drawn. King George issued an ultimatum: no one who visited the Prince and Princess of Wales would be received at the royal palace.

It was left to the skillful, politically astute Prime Minister, Robert Walpole, to bring about a chilly reconciliation. Walpole got on well with King George—one of the few, outside George's circle of German favorites, who did—and persuaded him to allow George Augustus to return to live at St. James's. A brief meeting between father and son, the first in years, was arranged. An emotional explosion was expected, but in fact the meeting was anticlimactic. Courtiers and servants who listened outside the closed doors reported hearing the king's voice muttering "Votre conduite! Votre conduite!" ("Your behavior! Your behavior!") What the prince may have muttered in reply is not recorded.

Conflict in the royal family interested King George's subjects far less than the financial corruption that emanated from the court—corruption they blamed squarely on King George himself.

For the king was governor of the most notorious financial enterprise in

England, the South Sea Company, and because of the Company, thousands of people were ruined.

The South Sea Company (the exotic tropical name was misleading) was a finance firm which obtained an extremely lucrative contract to refinance thirty thousand pounds of the national debt—an unimaginably vast sum in the early eighteenth century—by converting the debt to shares of the company's stock. Greedy for the profits they believed would inevitably be theirs, investors rushed in to buy the shares, which sold at ever more inflated prices. The king invested heavily, as did his Whig ministers, his friends, his courtiers, indeed virtually everyone of influence. Confidence in the company rose as it appeared the court and government, even the throne itself, were backing the venture.

South Sea shares rose higher and higher, more and more investors poured money in, and soon other companies too began to benefit as their shares grew at an inflated rate. Speculation grew frenzied, there was no stopping the upward spiral; for every share that was sold, always at a large profit, there were dozens of eager buyers outbidding one another.

In 1720 the price of South Sea stock rose fantastically, increasing more than sevenfold from April to July. Then in autumn panic selling began. Suddenly the crowds of once-eager buyers melted away. The shares plummeted in value, becoming worthless. Bewildered, then angry, the disillusioned shareholders blamed the king and his government for their huge losses. British credit abroad was severely damaged.

Now the Jacobites clamored once again for a Stuart restoration. The Hanoverian king had swindled the entire nation, they insisted. Let him go back to Hanover where he belonged, and let the rightful king be restored. In 1722 a conspiracy was uncovered in which the plotters intended to murder King George. Fortunately for him, the conspirators were discovered and their plan interrupted.

Of King George's own reaction to the South Sea Bubble, as it came to be called, little is known. Like so many of his subjects, he lost money, and also lost political servants, as the investigations which followed the collapse of the infamous Company led to suicides and resignations. But he was sixty years old, and weary of responsibility. He clung to his few pleasures, the companionship of his children with Ehrengard, listening to music, playing cards with his comfortable familiars, spending time with Anne Brett. Walpole ran the government, and ran it very skillfully. The succession was assured. (King George encountered the Prince of Wales once a week, at his formal receptions. The two exchanged the frostiest of civilities.)

Tottering but not doddering, King George sank into very old age, and in his last year, 1727, grew eager to return once again to Hanover. His wife Sophia Dorothea had died the year before, but the lean, elderly Ehrengard lived on, and never left his side. She rode beside George when, in the spring of 1727, he set out on his final cross-Channel journey.

The king was agitated and anxious—and more ill than he realized. As his coach rattled over the muddy roads of Holland, he clutched his head in pain. A stroke all but incapacitated him, but he managed to indicate to his servants that he wanted to go on, to reach his destination of Osnabrück, the ancient episcopal town where he had been born sixty-seven years before. He died at Osnabrück in June, and was buried in a nearby church.

When the news of King George's death reached England, there was general relief—even glee. "The devil has caught him by the throat at last!" proclaimed one meanspirited broadsheet. The Prince of Wales ascended the throne as George II, and seldom mentioned his hated father again.

GEORGE II

(1727–1760)

❦ ✦ ❦

"I AM SICK TO DEATH OF ALL THIS FOOLISH STUFF
AND WISH WITH ALL MY HEART THAT THE DEVIL MAY
TAKE ALL YOUR BISHOPS, AND THE DEVIL TAKE YOUR
MINISTERS, AND THE DEVIL TAKE YOUR PARLIAMENT
AND THE DEVIL TAKE THE WHOLE ISLAND, PROVIDED
I CAN GET OUT OF IT AND GO TO HANOVER."

—KING GEORGE II

George II was forty-four years old on his accession, an intense, aggressive, dynamic man with exophthalmic blue eyes, a reddish
complexion and a large and prominent nose. As Prince of Wales
he had begun by being a model of courtesy, but by the time his father
George I died he had become irascible in the extreme, with a bluntness of
speech and a rudeness of manner that invariably gave offense.

The new king seemed to spend his energies criticizing people. He could
not walk through a room without passing judgment and chiding its occu-
pants. A contemporary once watched him and recorded how he "stayed
about five minutes in the gallery; snubbed the queen, who was drinking
chocolate, for being always stuffing, the Princess Emily for not hearing
him, the Princess Caroline for being grown fat," and so on. One courtier
was rebuked for "standing awkwardly," another for "not knowing what
relation the Prince of Sultzbach was to the Elector Palatine." Having delivered himself of these sharp corrections, the king offered the queen his
arm and led her off to the garden, where no doubt he continued his critical
remarks.

Such a flow of blunt rudeness inevitably made George unpopular; according to the acerb chronicler of his reign, Lord Hervey, "the disregard

with which everybody spoke of him, and the open manner in which they expressed their contempt and dislike, is hardly to be credited."

The English, it seemed had had their fill of kings from Hanover, especially kings who spent large stretches of time, as George II did, in their continental dominions. The king, for his part, had developed a hearty hatred for his English subjects. As Prince of Wales he had praised them, but as king he announced his contempt for the English as regicides and enemies of monarchy. The Tories were all secret Jacobites, he complained, while the Whigs were so corrupt and venal that he had to bribe them to prevent them from cutting his throat.

King George was forever singing the praises of Hanover, his preferred realm, where "the men were patterns of politeness, bravery and gallantry, the women of beauty, wit and entertainment," the troops the bravest in the world, the counselors the wisest, the subjects the happiest. "At Hanover," he insisted with characteristic vehemence, "plenty reigned, magnificence resided, arts flourished, diversions abounded, riches flowed, and everything was in the utmost perfection that contributes to make a prince great or a people blessed."

The more the monarch extolled the virtues of Hanover, the more his English subjects despised him, in a vicious cycle that seemed to worsen in the early years of his reign. Every time George left for his electorate, the English rejoiced. On his return, they grew glum, for each time he returned he was furious, "trembling with passion." Traveling was painful—the king was in agony from hemorrhoids—and journeys invariably worsened his temper.

After one such return, when George was beside himself with fury, Queen Caroline bluntly remarked that since coming to England made him so angry, and since there was no pressing reason for his return (for the capable Whig Prime Minister Robert Walpole was in deft control of the government), he ought to have stayed in Hanover. The remark set off a fresh spasm of choler in the king, but he did not explode into a tirade; he simply left the room "in a great huff."

The intelligent, strong-minded Queen Caroline knew how to blunt the edge of her husband's wrath, and in fact, despite George's energetic pursuit of other women, the king and queen got on well. When he was away in Hanover, George sent his wife long letters full of endearments; beneath his harsh and caustic veneer there lurked a sentimental heart.

Sentiment was one thing, sex was another. King George had a vigorous if not quite insatiable sexual appetite and spent a good deal of time with his various mistresses, Madame Walmoden in Hanover and a series of court ladies in England, including Queen Caroline's Mistress of the Robes, Lady Suffolk. For Lady Suffolk, who (like the queen) was cultivated and well-read, George built a mansion, Marble Hill, at Twickenham. There she entertained Pope, Swift and lesser literary figures. In time the king tired of Lady Suffolk, but Queen Caroline, who tolerated the liaison because she knew her Robes Mistress to be no threat to her own influence over the king, contrived to perpetuate it.

A power struggle developed. The king wanted Lady Suffolk removed from her court post—and from his life. The queen kept her on. George objected strongly. "What the devil do you mean by trying to make an old, dull, deaf, peevish beast stay and plague me when I had so good an opportunity of getting rid of her!" he snapped. Caroline was stubborn, Lady Suffolk stayed—but was replaced, as the object of the king's lust, by his daughters' governess Lady Deloraine.

The king spent many long, dull evenings with Lady Deloraine and his daughters, playing cribbage, basset and other card games. Tedious public gatherings were occasionally held, where an orchestra played while the guests yawned behind their fans and lace-trimmed sleeves. On summer Saturdays King George took his family, the queen's ladies and the officers of his household on an outing to Richmond, where they dined and promenaded in the garden. The itinerary never varied; the procession of coaches departed at midday, "with the heavy horseguards kicking up the dust before them." After the meal and the walk, the king and his guests returned to the coaches at precisely the same hour each week, the horses stirring up dust once again as they retraced their route.

During the first decade of George II's reign, private matters were predominant. One was the queen's illness, known only to her husband, her German nurse and one of her ladies-in-waiting. Alternately impatient and sympathetic, George stood by as Caroline, once robust and handsome, grew fragile and haggard, enduring great pain. The other was the problem of "the Nauseous Beast," as the Prince of Wales, Frederick Lewis, was known in the family.

Princess Caroline, George II's favorite daughter, once said of her brother that "the Nauseous Beast cares for nobody but his own nauseous self." Self-absorbed Frederick was, and also sensitive, artistic (he played the cello fairly well and collected Van Dycks and Holbeins), mildly extravagant and, to judge from others' opinions, false and deceitful. In a loud, coarse family Frederick stood out as timid and sickly, a physical weakling and a moral equivocator. His father the king, who was always brutally honest himself, despised Frederick for his falsity and lack of manly strength; he preferred his stolid, unimaginative son William, and tried, unsuccessfully, to remove Frederick from the succession so that William would become the next king.

George II's preoccupation with despising his heir was excessive, and was connected to that older feud between George and his own father, George I. For Frederick had been his grandfather's favorite; George I had supervised Frederick's upbringing and had even chosen a bride for him, though the marriage did not take place. Resentments rankled across the generations.

In 1736 Frederick married the bride his father chose for him, the rather immature Augusta of Saxe-Coburg, and in due course Augusta became pregnant. Queen Caroline, whose loathing for Frederick was if possible even greater than her husband's ("I wish the ground would open this moment and sink the monster to the lowest hope in hell," was how she expressed her sentiments), suspected that there was no pregnancy, that Frederick was plotting to pass off a commoner's infant as Augusta's, simply in order to remove his brother William as heir apparent. Frederick was eager to prove his mother wrong. Thus when Augusta's labor pains began, two months early, he brought her to St. James's Palace where she hastily gave birth "between two tablecloths."

It was an undignified, thoroughly upsetting scene: the uninvited arrival, the unprepared, improvised birth chamber, and worst of all, the baby itself, a tiny, squalling "rat of a girl," a disappointment unworthy of all the fuss, especially since the palace was in a state of near-mourning with Queen Caroline gravely ill.

King George banished Frederick, Augusta and the baby, and when, a few months later, the queen was on her deathbed, she refused to see Frederick and died unreconciled to him.

All this family Stürm und Drang set King George's teeth on edge and roused his everpresent ire. He had had enough of quarrels, domestic and political, he was fed up with contending ministers and fractious Members of Parliament, he felt his authority eroding as his unpopularity increased.

"I am sick to death of all this foolish stuff," he declared, "and wish with all my heart that the devil may take all your bishops, and the devil take your ministers, and the devil take your Parliament and the devil take the whole island, provided I can get out of it and go to Hanover."

Despite this sweeping indictment the king stayed on, full of bluster but not deserting his post. He brought his Hanoverian mistress Madame Walmoden to England, gave her a title and a generous income and made her his constant companion. Together they turned their back on the courtiers, creating an oasis of German culture and German language and becoming the subject of countless jokes—although Madame Walmoden was not as easy to caricature as George I's companions had been.

From 1739 on, England had been at war, first with Spain and then, from 1742, on the side of Austria, defending the rights of Empress Maria Theresa, in the War of the Austrian Succession. George was at his fierce, bustling best in wartime, and despite his advanced age, was eager to lead his troops into battle. When the coalition army, composed of Hanoverians, Hessians, Austrians and Dutch, was arrayed against the formidable French troops at Dettingen in Bavaria, intent on driving the French out of Germany, George was in command, in a state of high excitement.

"I have slept three nights upon the ground, rolled up in my cloak without any covering except the sky, and my skin, or rather my hide—which is well tanned, has been wet with the dew of heaven, yet am I as well as ever I was." So George wrote from the camp as he waited to engage the French. When the allied forces attacked, the king was in the thick of the fighting, waving the men on with his sword, his warhorse rearing under him. Cannonballs whizzed by, narrowly missing him, but he would not heed the warning of his officers to retreat to a safer location.

"Don't tell me of danger!" he shouted. "I'll be even with them!"

According to an English officer who was present, King George "rode about like a lion, drawing up his men, standing by the artillery as the cannon were fired" even though the French shot was "as thick as hail" around him.

"Now, boys," the officer heard George shout, "for the honor of England, fire, and behave bravely and the French will soon run." The king was wounded, but the French were beaten, and all were agreed that King George "behaved as bravely as a man could."

He returned to England a hero. Overnight his years of unpopularity were forgotten and Londoners poured into the streets to welcome him. There were parades, fanfares, bonfires and fireworks. Crowds rioted in pleasure long into the night. "Long live King George!" they cried. "Long live Hanover!"

In England, the popularity of the monarchy had never been higher. But in parts of Scotland, where the Jacobites were once more making preparations for a Stuart takeover, King George's name was anathema. In June

1745 Prince Charles Edward Stuart, the charismatic twenty-four-year-old son of the Old Pretender, raised an army from among the highland clans and marched on Perth and Edinburgh, capturing both. Thousands came to fight for "Bonnie Prince Charlie," and the Jacobite army defeated an English force at Prestonpans. Charles Edward led his men across the border into England but soon found that few of the English were ready to desert their anointed king. The Stuart army retreated, and in April 1746 Prince William, King George's favorite son, defeated the rebel forces at Culloden. A severe and merciless harrying of the highlands followed.

King George had wanted to lead an army against Charles Edward, but old age, combined with the rigors of campaigning in Bavaria, had finally caught up with him. He had to content himself with dressing in his old uniforms and reminiscing about his exploits. He still grumbled about his constitutional role ("Ministers are the kings in this country. . . . I am nothing") and swore at "that damned House of Commons," but on one issue at least his mind was eased. His hated son Frederick died in 1751, and the succession passed to Frederick's son George (later George III), a humorless, dutiful boy who promised to be nothing like his father. The king rejoiced.

"I am old and want rest," George complained in 1755, when he was seventy-two. He was growing blind and deaf, he felt ineffectual. Yet his years of glory were still ahead of him.

During George's reign Britain expanded geographically and in terms of wealth and power. Robert Clive established British influence in Bengal, British arms won Canada from the French. By the end of the Seven Years War, in 1763, Britain was the preeminent global power, with colonies and territories in the West Indies, North America, Asia and even Africa. British sea power was unmatched. French hegemony had been broken.

The expansion of Britain's empire was matched by the expansion of London, which became, by the end of George II's reign, a city of seven hundred thousand people—and growing. Sprawling, congested slums backed up against elegant new streets and squares, built in the style which took its name from the king's. Along the Thames wharves, ships from all the world's oceans brought cargoes of tea and sugar, rum and spices, cotton and hemp and ship's masts. And coal, great quantities of coal, which was burned for fuel, the thick black coal-smoke darkening the skies.

Over all this growth King George presided, exerting more influence than he knew, even as his physical powers declined. Robert Walpole was long gone, but William Pitt, who led the government during the Seven

Years War, attested to the force of the monarch's will and especially the crushing weight of his displeasure. Yet Pitt, like his predecessors, learned to appreciate King George's basic common sense and honesty, and endured his quarrelsome nature, even developing a grudging fondness for him.

They were more than a little ashamed, however, of his lingering libido. The elderly king liked to prowl the darker alleys of Ranelagh, London's somewhat tawdry pleasure garden, looking for young women to seduce. He went disguised (fooling no one) to masquerades and balls, and pursued actresses at the theater. He was particularly drawn to one actress, Miss Chudleigh, who portrayed Iphigenia in a scanty costume, and made a fool of himself over her.

Toward the end of George II's life the church bells rang again and again to celebrate victories of the British and their allies. The king's popularity, which had remained high since Dettingen, rose even higher. He was content about the succession, he had made his peace with Pitt and the realm was in good order and prosperous. On October 25, 1760, George collapsed and died—a sudden, quick end to an exceptionally long life. At his funeral many wept and even his ministers were inconsolable.

GEORGE III

(1760–1820)

❖ ⋙❖⋘ ❖

"MY FATHER WAS THE FINEST, PUREST, AND MOST
PERFECT OF ALL CHARACTERS. HE WAS A MAN
AFTER GOD'S OWN HEART."

—PRINCESS ELIZABETH,
DAUGHTER OF GEORGE III

A quiet, self-effacing and shy boy, Prince George—the future George III—resembled his grandfather and predecessor George II only in his protuberant blue eyes and his tendency to criticize others. He had lost his father, Prince Frederick, at the age of twelve, and having an affectionate, sentimental nature, Prince George attached himself to his younger brother Edward and to Lord Bute, his rather pedestrian tutor. He clung to these attachments long after he might reasonably have been expected to outgrow them.

Young George had a strong musical ear and played the harpsichord well. He also had a gift for drawing and his sketches of landscapes were pleasing. But he was lazy in his formal studies—not backward, as Walpole wrote—and his beloved brother Edward, his parents' favorite, outshone George both in his studies and in his personality. The unfortunate George, reticent and retiring, had a leaden quality while the cheerful, outgoing Edward had sparkle. George also tended to see the world as full of enemies, snares and pitfalls; most men, he seems to have believed, were immoral and corrupt and goodness was in short supply.

When his feisty, bustling grandfather George II finally died in 1760 at the age of seventy-seven, young George was at a loss. He was twenty-two, tall and physically strong, with appealing fair looks and the pink cheeks of a boy. Immature George certainly was, and utterly dependent, at first, on the handsome, socially adept but politically inexperienced Bute. George implored Bute to be his mentor in the work of kingship, fearing the burden of monarchy and privately wishing he could "retire to some uninhabited cavern" to escape it. But this was a role Bute was not equipped to play, and before long, ridiculed and savaged by his critics, he left office.

George was on his own. Unsteadily, he struck out from shore into deep political waters, full of plans but stymied by his own lack of experience in managing the House of Commons and hampered by a series of inadequate ministers with whom he felt ill at ease. For a king with a deep inherent distrust of politicians, and a world view that envisioned conspiracies everywhere, to attempt an active reign was bound to lead to disaster. George buckled under the strain.

"I can neither eat nor sleep," he wrote to Bute, "nothing pleases me but musing on my cruel situation." The realm was unsettled, the people in upheaval from food shortages that led to rioting and financial crises that led to condemnation of the crown. The king, dull of eye and devoid of wit, was denounced as an ineffectual bumbler whose only merit was his otiose dignity and whose only achievement was the raising of a superior strain of pigs.

Gradually, however, the king began to win grudging admiration for his rectitude, which stood out all the more in an era of louche morals and decadent living among the aristocracy. George's beloved brother Edward died of syphilis at twenty-eight, his brother Henry disgraced the family through sexual adventurism and his sister Caroline, Queen of Denmark, was arrested for adultery and imprisoned in Kronborg. In contrast, King George married the plain, stolid, unimaginative Charlotte of Mecklenburg-Strelitz—a choice made from duty rather than romantic inclination—and devoted himself to her with unswerving loyalty. The marriage proved to be a satisfying partnership. Looking back after two decades of wedded life, George was to declare "with truth that . . . I could not bear up did I not find in her a feeling friend to whom I can unbosom my griefs."

Griefs there were, and in abundance.

In the 1760s the Grenville ministry managed to alienate the British colonists in America through a series of ill-advised measures requiring them to provide quarters and supplies for troops and pay taxes on molasses, and putting restrictions on trade and imposing port duties. King

George was denounced as tyrannical, his reign condemned by the Americans as "a history of repeated injuries and usurpations." An image of George as a monster, unfit to govern, spread outward from America across Europe as conflict between the colonies and the mother country loomed.

King George reacted to his rebellious American subjects as he did to his own wayward children: with an uncompromising insistence on obedience. As he grew older he was becoming more and more obstinate, more inflexible in his views. Having struggled for years to find a minister with whom he was personally compatible, he found one in Lord North, who took over the government in the spring of 1770 with the American colonists in open defiance of their British master. The situation rapidly deteriorated, and King George, continually execrated as a tyrant, raised troops to subdue the Americans. Warfare went badly for the British but the king would not admit defeat, nor would he allow the hapless North to resign.

The crisis in America brought out King George's obstinacy and obtuse wrongheadedness; having taken a stand to prevent the colonists from attaining their autonomy, he would not retreat from his position, no matter how futile and damaging that position became. Hated, reviled and ultimately humiliated by the loss of the American colonies—and by the fall of Lord North—the king thought seriously of abdicating, but stopped short of taking that radical step.

The loss of the colonies was widely perceived as a harbinger of destruction for the British Empire, and a symbol of decline for both the monarchy and the realm. As it proved, Britain not only survived her humiliation but went on to enjoy unprecedented might and prosperity. But for a time King George knew in full the pain of having brought disaster on his kingdom.

George III in his forties had become a stern paterfamilias with thirteen handsome but wayward children. His six daughters were attractive, his seven surviving sons (two died in early childhood) tall, thin and aristocratic. The favorite son, Adolphus ("Dolly"), was musical like his father, well behaved and dutiful. But the others, especially the high-strung, vain George, Prince of Wales, were troublesome in various ways, William deeply in debt, Edward explosively violent with a tendency to smash furniture, Augustus asthmatic and Frederick—the best of the lot—overly eager to enrich himself. The Prince of Wales, extravagant and over-emotional, embarrassed the monarchy with his excesses, and had the bad judgment and ill grace to marry a Roman Catholic, Maria Fitzherbert, contrary to the Royal Marriages Act.

It was as if the royal children, goaded into rebellion by their father's severely high morals and pure living, were determined to choose darker and more labyrinthine paths. And the more they strayed from virtue, the more their father was confirmed in his often repeated observation that "we live in unprincipled days." Prayerful, abstemious in food and drink, honest and hard-working, King George plodded on, presiding with dignity over a dull court where any breach of etiquette resulted in censorious looks from the monarch.

The novelist Fanny Burney, who endured the discomforts of that court for five uncomfortable years as a member of Queen Charlotte's household, recorded its repressive rules.

"If you find a cough tickling your throat, you must arrest it from making any sound," she wrote. "If you find yourself choking with forbearance, you must choke, but not cough." Sneezing was forbidden, even to those with heavy colds. "You must not, upon any account, stir either hand or foot. If, by chance, a black pin runs into your head, you must not take it out."

In 1788, when he was in his fiftieth year, King George became seriously ill. What brought the illness on can never be known for certain. He was under strain, made anxious by political and social turmoil and by the increasingly flagrant misconduct of his children. He had been ill before, suffering from insomnia and weight loss, fever and overly rapid pulse, and had been treated with large doses of asses' milk. But the malady that descended on the king in 1788 was of a different order, alarming and baffling to the doctors, and it was to determine the entire future course of the reign.

It began with a terrible nightmare. When George awoke from his awful dream, full of fear, he was violently agitated, trembling with a nervous excitement that made him talk incessantly.

"He is all agitation, all emotion," Fanny Burney said after the king talked to her, feverishly. He broke out in a rash and had severe stomach pains and leg cramps. He sent for the Prince of Wales and, when the prince burst into tears at the sight of his disturbed father, attacked him, seizing him by his collar and throwing him against the wall.

"I am nervous," the king repeated again and again. "I am not ill, but I am nervous."

Doctors were summoned, and they forced castor oil down the royal patient's throat and, when this failed to calm him, administered laudanum. But nothing could dampen the king's dreadful "hurry of spirits" and flow of jabbering, all but incoherent talk. The veins stood out in his empurpled face, and his eyes—the eyes of a madman, observers thought—bulged in his head as the words poured forth, a torrent of delirious imaginings. The queen had been kidnapped, George announced shrilly. A great flood was coming that would destroy London. The king of Prussia had arrived and was waiting for an interview. Hoarse from shouting, his voice rising to an anguished thin wail, the king rushed here and there, talking to trees in the garden, calling for his horse and riding it into church, raving on until he "foamed with rage."

More treatments were tried: scalding hot baths, swaddling, burning plasters applied to the king's feet, leeches applied to his temples. The courtiers, horrified at the violent change in their master, at first expected him to die. When he continued to live on in his appalling state, they decided that he was simply mad, and summoned a doctor who specialized in the treatment of lunatics. Now the king was restrained with ropes and wrapped in a sort of straitjacket, dosed with an emetic which made him agonizingly nauseous, and threatened with worse punishments—on the theory that if he were made to suffer sufficiently, he would change his behavior.

Four months after the onset of the king's affliction his ravings began to subside, and his restraints were loosened, then removed. He gradually recovered. Soon he was performing all his old duties, and touring farms in pursuit of his agricultural interests.

The king was himself again—or was he? Everyone at court, especially the Prince of Wales, was watchful, waiting for a relapse. Care was taken to prevent undue pressure on the monarch, who seemed fragile, unable to apply himself to matters of state for long periods of time. The terrible episode had clearly aged him; no one could say how long he would live, or how lasting his apparent recovery of health would prove.

No one in King George's lifetime was able to explain his illness. But modern doctors have identified it as porphyria, a blood disorder in which the nervous system is compromised and the brain affected—hence the king's delusions and delirium. A key diagnostic clue is dark purplish urine, which King George produced—and which gives the disease its name, from the Greek word for purple.

In the year of King George's recovery, 1789, the French Revolution began, inaugurating a new political era and ultimately leading to war between Britain and France. King George was presiding over an age of rapid and fundamental change—a time of political ferment, in which democratic ideals were challenging monarchical tradition; of a broad cultural shift from classicism to romanticism; above all of a vast increase in Britain's wealth through increased trade and the swift spread of industry. The Britain of farms, villages and shopkeepers was giving way to a new Britain of factories, expanding towns and burgeoning seaports and prosperous industrialists. British naval and military forces were amassed to fight Napoleon, and fight him they did, with valor and, often, a surprising degree of success.

King George, who entered his sixties in the last years of the eighteenth century, inspired and encouraged the troops and the seamen and put heart into his people during the long years of war. He was still vigorous, still able to ride for hours with his sons and daughters in Windsor Great Park. When Napoleon prepared a large invasion fleet to carry his soldiers across the Channel to England, King George declared himself ready, old as he was, to lead England's defense—and made plans to carry his proposal into effect.

For this, and for his steady, old-fashioned courage, George III's subjects admired him. Once they had thought him inept and obtuse, and had ridiculed his saurian manner and stolid personality. But now, when Britain was under threat, the king's time-honored virtues shone forth as beacons of stability and decency in a time of chaos. The paterfamilias had become the Father of his Country, much valued and even loved.

In 1800, King George's personal courage was put to the test. A would-be assassin shot at him at close range as he entered his box at the Drury Lane Theater. The shots narrowly missed George, who "on hearing the report of the pistol, retired a pace or two, stopped, and stood firmly for an instant: then came forward to the front of the box, put his opera-glass to his eye, and looked round the house without the smallest appearance of alarm or discomposure."

His failure to panic, and his brave refusal to duck (which was, at the very least, imprudent, at most foolish; the king was lucky he wasn't killed), set Londoners to cheering. With the theater in an uproar, the assassin was surrounded and disarmed, and the danger passed. But the audience insisted on singing the national anthem three times in honor of their courageous monarch, and King George, pleased to be lionized, nodded and bowed with pleasure.

Not long after his escape from his would-be assailant, the king experienced another attack of his mysterious illness. It passed relatively quickly, but recurred in 1804, with the same fearsome agitation, incoherent talking, racing pulse and delirium. Each attack, observers thought, would be his last—yet he recovered, and resumed his obligations.

Portrait of King Charles II, circa 1675.
Private collection/Bridgeman Art Library

King William III by Sir Godfrey Kneller.
The Crown Estate/Bridgeman Art Library

Portrait of Queen Anne by William Wissing and Jan van der Vaardt.
Scottish National Portrait Gallery, Edinburgh/Bridgeman Art Library

Portrait of George III in
his coronation robes by
Allan Ramsay, circa 1760.
*Private collection/Bridgeman
Art Library*

Portrait of George IV
by Sir Thomas Lawrence.
*Vatican Museums and Galleries,
Vatican City/Bridgeman Art Library*

Portrait of the young Queen Victoria.

Portrait of George V in robes of state, 1910.
Hulton/Archive by Getty Images

The Duke and Duchess of Windsor with their prize-winning dogs at the International Canine Exhibition, Paris, 1956.
Hulton/Archive by Getty Images

George VI and Queen Elizabeth inspect the aftermath of an air attack at Buckingham Palace, 1940.
Hulton/Archive by Getty Images

Princess Elizabeth (later Queen Elizabeth II) marries
Philip Mountbatten, November 20, 1947.
Hulton/Archive by Getty Images

Nothing, it seemed, could kill King George—not an assassin's bullets, not Napoleon or his menaces, not the king's terrible disease, nor the grave strain of family tensions, which were increasing. King George's most distinguished son Frederick, Commander in Chief of the army, was the subject of investigations in the House of Commons, accused, along with his mistress, of profiting from the sale of army promotions. Frederick was judged guilty—and lost his post when it was discovered that he had disclosed military secrets to his mistress.

It was a blow to the king, who had been proud of the manly, physical Frederick and liked to lay his tired old head on his son's strong shoulder. If even Frederick was corrupt, what hope was there for the other sons—the blubbering, babyish, disgustingly obese George, Prince of Wales, the sadistic Edward, who took perverse pleasure in viciously flogging the soldiers under his command, the foolish William, with his embarrassing brood of bastard children, or the sinister Ernest, who spread lies within the family and was reputed to have seduced his valet and then killed him?

Of the most shameful family scandal the king knew nothing. His daughter Sophia, having grown into a moody and mercurial woman, had rebelled against what she and her unhappy sisters called the "nunnery" of their father's court and had an affair with an ugly man nearly old enough to be her grandfather; the result was a bastard child. (Malicious gossip said that Sophia's brother Ernest was the child's father.) The king, in his ignorance, praised his daughters as "all Cordelias," Cordelia being King Lear's faithful and unselfish child, and would have been injured terribly to learn of Sophia's moral lapse.

By 1810 King George was barely able to see his children, for he was nearly blind. He still shouted at them—indeed he shouted at everyone, for he was going deaf—and shouted at Queen Charlotte too, though they no longer lived together as man and wife, Charlotte having had her fill of her husband's violent and frenzied episodes of madness and forbidden the king access to her apartments for some years. He walked jerkily along, still capable of bursts of vigor, though he occasionally held onto the arm of a servant, or leaned against Frederick, or against his kind, warmhearted daughter Mary. The king's attentiveness to the business of governing was still keen, though it quickly faded; in practice he left the running of affairs to his ministers.

The year 1810 was King George's Royal Jubilee, the fiftieth anniversary of his accession, and to commemorate the occasion Londoners staged elaborate pageantry. Buildings were festooned with greenery and outlined in colored lights. Fireworks exploded in the night sky. Choirs sang and bands played, troops paraded in honor of the king. The crowds in the streets were immense, cheering for their beloved ruler, the only king most of them could remember, for by 1810 George III had reigned longer than any earlier British monarch.

But George, amid the din of celebration, was in a somber mood, grieving for his daughter Amelia, who was dying, and beginning to suffer, yet again, from his chronic disease. The dreaded nightmare that always signaled its onset came to him once more, and soon he was in the grip of nervous excitement, body pains, and agitated, talkative delirium once more.

This time the lapse into illness proved to be permanent.

On February 6, 1811, Parliament passed a Regency Bill putting the government into the hands of the Prince of Wales, or the Prince Regent, as he was henceforth to be known. While the Regent struggled to master his anxieties, dosing himself liberally with brandy and laudanum, the realm at first drifted, then found its course. Napoleon reached the zenith of his power, then began to falter, failing to conquer Russia in 1812 and being defeated by a coalition army at Waterloo in 1815. Through these and other climactic events King George lived on in troubled oblivion, now restlessly pacing his apartments at Windsor, now sitting for hours, unmoving, remarking, when approached, that he was "looking into hell."

"To deal plainly," the king said, "I am not in my perfect mind." The extreme understatement would have been amusing had it not been so sad, for George, who sometimes referred to himself as "the late king," was degenerating pitiably. Gaunt, bent and feeble, his uncut white hair flowing down his back, confined to his drafty rooms, he talked by the hour in his hoarse voice, addressing the empty air. He ate his frugal meals alone, and spent his long waking hours sitting at his harpsichord, an instrument that had belonged to Queen Anne, playing and singing, his voice still "strong and firm," as Frederick thought when he heard him.

"He appears to be living in another world," the doctors said, and the *Morning Chronicle* reported that the king was happy—which was what Britishers wanted to hear. But the truth was probably much harsher. For the last ten years of his life King George suffered mentally and physically, shivering and neglected, while the world forgot him.

In the bitterly cold January of 1820, King George lay on his bed, unable to get up or walk, unable to eat or drink anything but milk. The doctors had announced that the king's life was ending, and Frederick had come to sit beside him. The Prince Regent, overcome and very likely prostrate himself at the prospect of inheriting the throne, stayed away. Later Frederick would say that his father enjoyed a brief return of lucidity before he fell asleep for the last time, and was pronounced dead on the evening of January 29.

GEORGE IV

(1820–1830)

❖═✴═❖

**"I AM A DIFFERENT ANIMAL A DIFFERENT BEING FROM
ANY OTHER IN THE WHOLE CREATION."**

—GEORGE IV

The eldest son of King George III and Queen Charlotte was a lively, energetic child with a round face and a good deal of intelligence. He was called George after his father, and as Prince of Wales he occupied the honored position among the thirteen surviving royal children.

But unlike his brothers, whose personalities were easily comprehended, George was an anomaly. As a boy he was oversensitive, often in tears, running away from conflict instead of defending himself. He lacked self-control, and displayed a vanity and a love of finery and possessions that disgusted his self-sacrificing, stalwartly plain father. As Prince George grew toward manhood he seemed to embody everything his father despised. He was effeminate in manner, a dandy, and often overindulged in drink. The prince ran up huge debts, took an inordinate interest in fine art (instead of the manly pursuits of hunting or the military), and, worst of all, showed an alarming tendency to abandon himself to the heights and depths of romance.

He wallowed in love, lived for it, swore by it, not infrequently threatened to kill himself over it. He was in love drunk, and in love sober. To say that he went overboard in his romantic life would be a gross understatement; Prince George was constantly overboard, head over heels and drowning.

And he did not choose his lovers wisely. Indeed he seemed to choose those with the greatest potential for causing embarrassment to his father the king. Prince George's youthful affair with the actress Perdita Robinson cost King George III the very large sum of five thousand pounds—the amount the actress demanded for the return of the prince's letters to her, letters full of erotic effusions. In addition, the king was forced to arrange for Perdita and her daughter to receive income for life. It was not so much the money that was galling to the monarch—though the frugal King George III was angered at the outlay—but the immorality, and the scandal. Prince George's liaison with Perdita gave fodder to the London gossips for many months, and the gossip threatened to undermine the high moral tone the king had always attempted to maintain.

But the Perdita Robinson scandal was only one of many. Prince George could not seem to prevent himself from becoming the object of gossip. The prominent older women he seduced were not discreet. One of them, Lady Bessborough, described to her many friends how the clumsy, overweight, near-hysterical prince threw himself at her, "sobbing and crying," making vows of eternal love. At first she was revolted and disgusted, but gradually she began to find the situation amusing, because of what she called "that immense, grotesque figure flouncing about half on the couch, half on the ground." The story was told and retold in fashionable drawing rooms.

When he was twenty-two, Prince George met the woman he would always consider the love of his life, Maria Fitzherbert. Maria was twenty-eight, a widow twice over, and George was so utterly captivated by her that he swore no obstacle would ever come between them. There were obstacles in abundance; the prince could not marry without his father's permission, and King George was unlikely to permit him to take as his wife a Roman Catholic six years his senior who had already buried two husbands.

But the prince, willful and determined to have his way, found a minister who could be bribed—George promised to make him a bishop once he inherited the throne—and married Maria in a secret ceremony. The liaison lasted many years, and although George was not faithful to Maria she remained his romantic ideal.

In his twenties and thirties George became increasingly convinced that no one, except possibly Maria Fitzherbert, understood him. "I am a different animal a different being from any other in the whole creation," he said, and he might have added that his uniqueness condemned him to a life of alienation, as a victim of the scorn and persecution of less sensitive mortals. Among these less sensitive persecutors he counted his parents, who wished fervently that one of their other sons, preferably Adolphus or Frederick, had been the firstborn. The king lectured the Prince of Wales, chastised him for his profligate living and his high debts. The queen too had words with him.

"I am sorry to tell you," Prince George wrote to his brother Frederick, "that the unkind behavior of both their Majesties, but in particular of the queen, is such that it is hardly bearable." Queen Charlotte accused him of a long list of improprieties and misbehaviors, George said, "all which I answered, and in the vulgar English phrase gave her as good as she brought." But the conflict left him bruised, as all conflict did, and he retired to lick his wounds and complain.

An idealist whose imaginings were filled with visions of romantic bliss and family harmony, Prince George was perpetually shocked by collisions with the imperfect world. He retreated from the harshness of reality into a rich fantasy life, enhanced by drink and by the laudanum (an opium derivative) he took to help him sleep. Nowhere was this fantasy life lived more opulently than at Brighton, his favorite town, where he built a famous pleasure palace.

Ever since the 1780s Brighton had been Prince George's special retreat, a seaside village where a relaxed moral code prevailed and civilized vice was tolerated. Thanks to the prince's frequent presence, Brighton became fashionable, grew and prospered; the citizens of the burgeoning town put up a plaster statue of the Prince of Wales and made his birthday, August 12, a holiday, celebrated with military reviews, brass bands and a town fete.

The prince's mansion, a neoclassical villa called the Marine Pavilion, was the social center of the town. In its spacious, overheated salons Prince George entertained his friends—and indulged his taste for extravagant interior decoration. Reviving a style which had long been dormant, chinoiserie, the prince adorned his pavilion with Chinese wallpaper, Chinese lanterns, dragons, pagodas, lotus leaves and serpents. Models of Chinese junks cluttered the corridors, along with lifesize carvings of emperors, imitation palm trees and bamboo chairs and couches.

At Brighton Prince George was at his most comfortable, presiding over sumptuous banquets, lolling voluptuously on silken sofas, attending race-meetings and balls with his disreputable friends from the racing and sport-

ing worlds, along with writers, painters, and, after 1789, aristocratic emi-
gres from France. He could have gone on this way forever, oblivious to the
claims of his position—and oblivious to the demands of his unpaid credi-
tors. But reality intruded. In 1788 King George III fell ill and for a time he
was expected to die. Prince George, summoned to court, waited in dread
for the announcement of his father's death, and for his own accession. After four months King George was restored to lucidity and competence,
and the crisis passed, but the disturbing possibility of a relapse remained,
and the prince was uneasy.

In 1795, when the Prince of Wales was thirty-three, he succumbed to
parental coercion and agreed to marry. Only if he married would Parliament pay his debts, which had risen to an intolerably high amount.
George's marriage to Maria Fitzherbert was held to be without legal validity, as it was contracted contrary to law and without the king's approval.
Consequently the prince was available to marry the bride his father chose
for him, his first cousin Caroline of Brunswick.

Caroline proved to be the worst possible choice. Plump, plain and gross
in her manners, with a hearty, noisy joie de vivre and a strong sexual appetite, the new Princess of Wales made her horrified husband shudder
with fastidious distaste and gave him palpitations. He managed to tolerate
her in his bed for one night only—but that night was sufficient for the ill-
matched pair to perpetuate the royal line. Caroline gave birth in due
course to a daughter, Princess Charlotte, but Prince George refused to
have anything further to do with his wife and she continued to be an irritant on the margins of his life.

Prince George was forty-eight in 1810 when his father suffered the
worst attack of his alarming illness. The king paced excitedly from room
to room, raving incoherently, the look of a madman on his thin face. As in
his previous attacks, King George was turned over to doctors who restrained him and subjected him to barbarous treatments—scalding baths,
smothering in hot blankets, purging with harsh emetics—but he got no
better. Meanwhile the ordinary business of government came to a halt,
Parliament was adjourned and there was much worried speculation about
what the political outcome of the king's incapacity would be.

Prince George, anxious and unnerved by the uncertain situation, collapsed and took to his bed, his pulse racing wildly at the prospect of being
appointed regent. Tense and fearful, he drank quantities of cherry brandy
and dosed himself with laudanum while he waited for the outcome to
grow clear.

Though he had grown grotesquely fat, Prince George had not entirely lost his boyish good looks, and his round, cherubic face could still appear puckish at times, though more often it held a petulant expression, or a look of sorrow, for he was grieving for his beloved sister Amelia whose premature death coincided with George III's incapacity. Torn, as he often was, by a variety of strong emotions, the prince struggled to overcome his fears and his sorrows, weighed down by self-pity as well for he felt very much alone. His long liaison with Maria Fitzherbert had cooled, and his latest mistress, Lady Hertford, was proving incapable of taking Maria's place.

George was well aware that the British public despised him. For years he had been caricatured in the newspapers as a shallow, worthless hedonist who gorged himself while the underpaid workers of Britain starved. Critics had heightened the contrast between the sober, dutiful, faintly pathetic King George III and his wastrel eldest son, who along with his wayward brothers had little to offer the nation in its time of crisis.

For Britain, in 1810, had reached a dangerous impasse. The war with the French threatened to spiral out of control, Napoleon was reaching the apex of his power and the British treasury was depleted. A trade crisis had forced many British firms into bankruptcy, and many workers into worsening poverty. At a time when patriotic feeling was most needed, resentment of the government was mounting and republican sentiment was on the rise. It was not inconceivable that, with a deeply detested regent exercising power, the monarchy itself might topple.

Hence the reluctance of the ministers to take action to make the Prince of Wales regent for his father.

The unsettled situation dragged on until early February 1811, when Prince George was officially named Regent, inaugurating a decade of social turbulence and reducing the prestige and political force of the monarchy to a low ebb.

Almost from the beginning of his regency the Prince Regent was at a disadvantage. He became ill within months of assuming authority and it was rumored that he had the same disease as George III. Inflammation and swelling spread throughout his elephantine body, producing, according to official announcements, "a degree of irritation on his nerves nearly approaching delirium." When he lost feeling in his fingers he panicked, thinking that he was paralyzed; in fact it was only that his chubby hands were cumbered with so many rings and bracelets that they cut off his circulation.

While the Regent suffered, the realm convulsed. Luddites rioted, protesting mechanization. There were food riots and the Prime Minister, Spencer Perceval, was assassinated. And when Prince George recovered, his first thought was not of restoring order or alleviating the widespread distress but of giving a party—and not just any party, but the grandest and most lavish entertainment London had seen in a generation.

The Regent's great ball at his London residence, Carlton House, in June of 1812 overawed the thousands of guests who attended and the greater number of Londoners who were permitted to view the house in the following days. Some said the splendor of the Regent's mansion was enough to rival Versailles, with the fine paintings, rich carpets, costly tapestries and expensive furnishings blending into a resplendent whole. And as a reminder of Versailles, the claimant to the French throne was among the guests, the future Louis XVIII. Gracious and regal, the regent presided over all, wearing a scarlet uniform, a saber at his waist.

As the Regency went on, Britain's military situation improved until at last, in 1815, Napoleon was defeated and exiled to St. Helena. But with the long war at an end, the Prince Regent was no more popular, and criticism of the monarchy continued. It was clear that the aged King George III, confined to his apartments in Windsor Castle, would never recover and that before long the Regent would succeed him as king. His accession was dreaded, not only because he was widely detested but because, once he became king, his estranged wife Caroline would become queen, and no one, except possibly Caroline herself, wanted that.

For the Princess of Wales, loud, vulgar, dumpy and cheerfully blowsy, had become notorious. Her promiscuity was common knowledge, and it was said that she had had an illegitimate son. Bizarre in her appearance and her behavior, Caroline had visited a number of European courts, ending up in Italy where she lived with a handsome ne'er-do-well named Bergami. It was not Caroline's lack of morals that caused discomfort in the Regent's advisers; it was her indiscretion. She courted publicity. And more negative publicity was the last thing the monarchy needed.

In January of 1820 the old king died at last and his son was proclaimed as his successor. At fifty-eight, George IV was an old man himself, weaving from side to side as he walked, his ungainly, overscented body bulging from his tight waistcoats and wide trousers, an oily brown wig covering his sparse grey hair. Beneath his rouged cheeks his skin was sallow, and his face in repose was deeply lined and sad. He was often ill, and more often intoxicated.

When Queen Caroline landed at Dover the full extent of the public's loathing for their king became evident. King George demanded that the Prime Minister, Liverpool, introduce a bill in the House of Lords to declare his marriage at an end, denying Caroline her royal status on grounds of adultery. But the king's enemies championed Caroline and her rights, not because they genuinely pitied her, or believed her to be innocent, but because by taking her part they were able to protest against her husband.

"The aversion to the king," Lord Liverpool commented, had "risen to the greatest possible height." Shouting crowds professed themselves loyal to Queen Caroline, the Guards drank to her health and in the House of Lords, the bill to dissolve the marriage failed to pass.

But in the end King George had his way. At his magnificent coronation, in July of 1821, there was no place for the queen. When coronation day came, she insisted on being admitted to the ceremony, but was kept out, on the king's orders. Splenetic, her health overtaxed by all the strain, Caroline took too much opium and was stricken with severe abdominal pains. She died within weeks.

Now the king was free at last, but the contempt of his English subjects had deepened. In Scotland and Ireland, which he visited to considerable acclaim, King George IV was more popular. But in London he met with nothing but derision and scorn, and soon discovered that he had no influence whatsoever with his ministers. His political impotence was irksome, but in truth King George had never possessed any political ambition, only vanity. He made life difficult for the government in petty ways—refusing, for example, to deliver speeches the ministers had prepared for him, claiming that he had lost his false teeth—but was not a serious obstacle. When he proposed candidates for positions in the government or in his household, they were routinely ignored; when he objected to policies or bills, his objections were disregarded.

More conscious than ever that he was "a different animal," unregarded and misunderstood, the king withdrew from public life and devoted his gradually failing energies to the renovation of Windsor Castle, and to patronage of the arts. The most cultivated of the Hanoverian sovereigns, George IV was an art connoisseur who not only collected Rembrandts and Titians but commissioned paintings from Gainsborough and Lawrence and was a donor to the National Gallery. Writers, chemists, astronomers and inventors also enjoyed his patronage.

Generous and gifted with discrimination when it came to the arts, George remained myopic where personal relationships were concerned, and restricted himself socially to a dwindling group of companions, who, as he aged, enjoyed his company less and less.

The diarist Charles Greville, who was a member of this uneasy little circle, recorded his impressions of an evening at the Marine Pavilion. "The gaudy splendor of the place amused one for a little," Greville wrote, "and then bored me. The dinner was cold and the evening dull beyond all dullness." "The king was in good looks and good spirits," he added, "and after dinner cut his jokes with all the coarse merriment which is his characteristic."

In old age the pavilion became George's stage, his fortress, his refuge against the incomprehending world. Safe within its fantastic walls—the pavilion had been redesigned in a whimsical Indian style—he could dress up as Henry V, or boast about having led troops in Spain, or even recall the glories of his (imagined) Waterloo command, all without fear of contradiction. He could tell his favorite off-color jokes, or quote Homer in Greek, or stumble drunkenly around the room, trying to dance. On one memorable evening the king forced his guests to try their hand at target practice, shooting with loaded guns, with the result that one of the musicians in the royal band was wounded.

The king spent his final years in sybaritic excess, soaking in his white marble bath sixteen feet long, sleeping under four paper-thin swansdown blankets, anointing his elephantine body in jasmine oil and milk of roses, with the opulently fleshed Lady Conyngham, his last mistress, always on call when he required companionship.

But he was chronically ill, and with each passing year his body succumbed more and more to stomach pain, pulmonary failure and a weakening heart and circulatory system. He cradled his sore gouty feet in satin, his sore head was treated by an Arab "shampooing surgeon," who ran Brighton's Indian Baths. Doctors had to puncture his painfully swollen legs. To dull the endless, mounting pain King George drank quantities of eau de cologne along with his usual brandy and water. Yet no alcohol or opiates could alleviate his suffering, and toward the end of his life his terrible cries and moans could be heard in the gardens outside his bedroom.

By the summer of 1830 King George was weary of his struggle and ready to die. "God's will be done," he said to his doctors, his voice so faint it was nearly inaudible. With the members of his household nearby, but without the comfort of family, George IV died on June 26, and the throne passed to his brother William.

When his executors went through the late king's possessions, they found the detritus of an empassioned, profligate, yet sadly wasted, life: hundreds of locks of women's hair, trophies of his love affairs, stacks of women's gloves, love notes, "trinkets and trash," and, in hundreds of wallets, purses and boxes, the sum of ten thousand pounds in cash. Enough, the late king's critics said, to alleviate much poverty among his subjects.

"Never was an individual less regretted by his fellow creatures than this deceased king," wrote *The Times* after George IV's death. He would not be missed, "that Leviathan of the *haut ton*," whom the Duke of Wellington had called "the most extraordinary compound of talent, wit, buffoonery, obstinacy and good feeling . . . that I ever saw in any character in my life."

King George would not be missed, for in attracting ridicule he had trivialized the throne. His had been a monarchy of the absurd, he himself had been the apotheosis of scandal.

When his body lay in state under its purple canopy, in the last hot days of June 1830, King George's former subjects were permitted to pay their last respects. They came in their thousands, laborers, clerks, street sweepers, seamstresses, mudlarks, the crowd flowing past the gilded coffin in a smirking, guffawing stream. Women screamed at the late king, men made gross jokes. No one bothered to wear black. For the man who had been the most sartorially correct of monarchs, it was a ragged, shabby farewell.

WILLIAM IV

(1830–1837)

"ALTOGETHER HE SEEMS A KIND-HEARTED,
WELL-MEANING, NOT STUPID, BURLESQUE, BUSTLING
OLD FELLOW, AND IF HE DOESN'T GO MAD MAY MAKE A
VERY DECENT KING, BUT HE EXHIBITS ODDITIES."

—CHARLES GREVILLE

T he third son of George III and Queen Charlotte, Prince
William, was born on August 21, 1765, and until he reached
middle age, he was largely viewed as a nonentity. His oldest
brother George was heir to the throne, his next brother Frederick was
available to become king if needed; William, it was thought, would very
likely not be needed, and besides, George III had four other surviving
sons, and many daughters.

A good-looking, high-spirited boy, William at the age of thirteen gave
early evidence of possessing the robust sexual energy of the Hanoverians
by seducing one of the queen's maids of honor, much to the dismay of his
highly moral father. In vain George III lectured William on the need to
correct his faults and restrain his impulses, reminding him that he was a
poor scholar and a lax and inattentive churchgoer and deploring his precocious "love of dissipation." The best thing for William, his father thought,
was the discipline of the navy. Accordingly, in the summer of his fourteenth year, the prince was taken to Spithead and put aboard Admiral
Robert Digby's ship the *Prince George*, where he was enrolled as a midshipman.

The year was 1779, and Britain was at war. Midshipman William saw a good deal of combat, and was nearly drowned when the *Prince George* almost collided with another British warship during a storm off Cape Finisterre. In action against the Spanish fleet, a number of enemy vessels were seized, and one of the captured Spanish men-of-war was rechristened the *Prince William*.

The fighting stimulated William's "volatile turn of mind and great flow of spirits," exciting him and bringing out all his aggression.

"Won't we give these haughty dons a thrashing!" the prince yelled out to one of the officers as the action against the Spanish vessels began. He seemed "almost in a state of insanity," overcome with zest for the conflict. And when, after a year and more at sea, he returned home to his father's court he brought with him a trophy: the captured flag of the Spanish admiral.

Prince William was not only a success as a midshipman, he was popular with his shipmates, telling the seamen "I am nothing more than a sailor like yourselves" and calling himself "Midshipman Guelph." He was given no special treatment and shared the foul-smelling, cramped quarters, weevil-infested food and strict discipline of the other young men. Only the presence of his tutor, and the occasional hospitality of the admiral, who invited William to dine with him, marked Midshipman Guelph as a person of exceptionally high social standing.

Soon William had adopted the swagger, crude language and rough manners of his companions. He fought, he drank, he visited brothels and sometimes, with his fellow midshipmen, wrecked them, as he did at Barbados where a bill for seven hundred pounds was sent to King George to pay for the damage. When he was sent to New York—a loyalist British stronghold during the colonial war—the prince was nearly kidnapped by rebels. By the time he was sixteen, William had been toughened by war and hardened by life. To complete his education his father sent him to Hanover so that he could be turned into a skilled military officer and a gentleman.

But if King George thought that his swearing, swaggering son could be made to learn German and buckle down to mastering engineering, artillery and military tactics he was wrong. The volatile, energetic William pursued women, played whist and gambled, losing a good deal of his father's money. Hanover bored him. His tutor complained to the king that the prince was "so excessively rough and rude that there was no bearing it," and suggested that he be sent somewhere else.

William was sent back to England, but was no more content there, especially after he fell in love and King George objected to the lady of his choice. "I am really unhappy," the prince wrote to his brother the Prince of Wales in February of 1786. "Everything goes against me. I have been obliged to leave the girl I adore . . . my father . . . does not even show me common justice." Given his own command of a frigate, William continued his naval career, but was not promoted further. Denied the chance to distinguish himself in Britain's war against revolutionary France, he continued his career of dissipation, and at twenty-six began a long liaison with Dorothy Jordan, a celebrated comic actress.

For years the British public had taken an increasingly dim view of all George III's sons, whom they regarded as reprobates and scoundrels. With the sudden incapacity of the elderly king in 1811, and the appointment of the Prince of Wales as Regent, the disapproval of the public deepened. William too was held in contempt—when he was thought of at all, which was seldom—but he was less despised than ridiculed. He was not regarded as a gluttonous voluptuary like the Regent or a taker of bribes like Prince Frederick or a presumed murderer like Prince Ernest: in the view of the public, William was merely Mrs. Jordan's lover, whom she supported with her acting income and who was the father of ten of her illegitimate children.

When the Prince Regent's only child, Princess Charlotte, died in 1817, a dynastic crisis threatened, for Charlotte had been King George III's only grandchild; there was no heir to the throne in the next generation. Prince William had been looking for a wife for several years, having parted from Dorothy Jordan. He proposed to several women, a princess of Denmark (too young), an English heiress (too unstable) and the sister of the Russian tsar (who rejected him as "awkward, not without wit, but definitely unpleasant").

Finally he settled on the kindhearted, affectionate Adelaide of Saxe-Meiningen, homely and domestic and half his age (William was nearly fifty-three when he married her, Adelaide twenty-six or twenty-seven), whose decency and goodness made her suspect at the Regent's sophisticated court but whose wholesome influence improved her husband's manners. After a few years of marriage, William seemed to change. The rough, foulmouthed former midshipman became "gentlemanly in character," an observer thought, "and did not say a single indecent or improper thing."

But his underlying excitability and wildness of manner remained, and even became more pronounced as William grew older. The shadow of George III's illness, now known to have been porphyria, a nervous disorder, but at the time presumed to be insanity, hung over all George's sons.

William's "general wildness" was believed by many of his contemporaries to "indicate incipient insanity," as one of them wrote. It was not thought to be an entirely bad thing that the direct Hanoverian line was dying out.

Adelaide became pregnant several times but, much to her sorrow, none of her babies survived. William, who grew to love his wife, was full of sympathy for her.

"I want words to express my feelings at these repeated misfortunes to this beloved and superior woman," he said. "I am quite broken hearted."

During the ten years of George IV's reign, William lived contentedly at Bushy Park, and at his newly built London mansion, Clarence House. He and Adelaide visited the king at Brighton, but were quite out of their element there; the overheated, overscented rooms with their exotic furnishings, the Regent's oily narcissism, the rich food and drink upset Adelaide's tender stomach and gave William gout. William loved his brother George and was unfailingly loyal to him, but the two could not have been farther apart in sensibility.

In 1827, William's brother Frederick died, leaving William, quite unexpectedly, heir to the throne. Suddenly he went from obscurity and neglect to prominence and popularity. Politicians and socialites who had never taken the slightest notice of him became fawningly deferential, and he was invited everywhere. Most important, to William, was his appointment, by the new Prime Minister Canning, as Lord High Admiral.

All was now changed. At sixty-two, Prince William was important, watched, listened to. He sailed in his flagship, held receptions, investigated naval practices and proposed reforms. Taking as his motto, "The Eye of the Lord High Admiral Does Infinite Good," William made a beginning at transforming the navy, suggesting much-needed improvements in gunnery, outlawing excessive flogging, and altering the way promotions were decided upon. William's ideas were progressive, but he lacked tact and above all self-restraint in putting them into effect. He alienated the admiralty by encouraging commanders to go against their orders. And in one memorable episode, he led an entire squadron of vessels out to sea, keeping them there for weeks, while the admiral who was supposed to be in command fumed and complained. William had gone too far; King George reprimanded him, and William resigned.

When George IV was on his deathbed no one was more attentive to him than William, who "cried like a child" to see his brother in such agony. But his sorrow was tempered with thrilling anticipation of his own accession, and when on June 26, 1830, messengers came to Bushy Park to tell William that he was now king, his delight was immeasurable. Within hours he was on his way to Windsor, bowing and waving to startled bystanders who happened to see the royal coach pass.

In the first month of his reign King William IV went out of his way to be seen by his subjects, and to court popularity. He had himself driven very slowly through Windsor Great Park with his head out the window, "bowing right and left," and walked along the terrace every Sunday in full view of the crowd that gathered. He liked drawing crowds, he sought an audience. He even strolled along St. James's Street, much to the amazement of passersby, who recognized him and gathered around, making further progress impossible. A streetwalker came up and kissed him on the cheek. Nothing fazed, the king would have remained as he was, surrounded by a growing mob of Londoners, but was rescued by a group of men from White's Club who broke through the crowd, gathered up William and escorted him back to the palace.

"Oh, never mind all this," William said dismissively when he was safely back in his royal apartments. "When I have walked about a few times they will get used to it, and will take no notice."

The king's familiarity with the public, and his unpretentious folksiness were appealing. He cared nothing for etiquette—indeed he seemed unable to understand it, much less follow its exacting protocols. He disdained luxury and magnificence in all forms, and dismissed his brother's excellent French chefs from the royal kitchens saying he preferred plain British fare. He chose a hard cot over the late king's featherbeds and swansdown blankets. As for his dignity as king, William had none, and wanted none. When a group of Quakers, famous for refusing to show deference to royalty, came to visit the king he made it clear that they need not bow or kiss his hands.

"Oh, just as they like," William told his ministers. "They needn't if they don't like; it's all one."

William's simplicity, friendliness and good nature were very welcome, especially after the reclusiveness and preposterous vanity of King George IV. "Altogether he seems a kind-hearted, well-meaning, not stupid, burlesque, bustling old fellow," wrote the diarist Charles Greville, "and if he doesn't go mad may make a very decent king, but he exhibits oddities."

The "oddities" soon began to show themselves. At George IV's funeral King William "talked incessantly and loudly to all about him so that the most frivolous things were overheard." He left before the service ended, tottering in an undignified hurry toward the exit in his long purple cloak. He was overly excitable, his flow of talk excessive and his gestures extravagant. "I tremble for him," Greville wrote soon after William's accession. "At present he is only a mountebank, but he bids fair to be a maniac."

With his ministers, and especially with the new Prime Minister Wellington, William was cooperative and conscientious in his duties. Addressing the enormous backlog of work that had accumulated during the late king's final months, King William sat down day after day and signed documents, tens of thousands of them, while Queen Adelaide sat beside him with a bowl of warm water in which he soaked his stiffening fingers from time to time to ease them.

William was genuinely, if a trifle obsessively, interested in issues and policies, and did his best to understand them. He asked many questions, and was not afraid to reveal his wide ignorance; patiently Wellington and the others explained and discussed what the government was attempting to do. There was no question, with William, of his finding contradiction distasteful. On the contrary, he welcomed debate, and saw it, overoptimistically, as leading to consensus.

On the whole William was a great improvement over George IV, but he had drawbacks. His opinions were often shallow and eccentric, he had an obstinate streak and he tended to confuse one councilor with another. ("D'ye know," he confided as he peered at the privy council, "I am grown so near sighted that I can't make out who you are.") He also had a tendency to fall asleep in the middle of a conference.

The worst fear of King William's ministers was that the sovereign would bring ridicule on himself and the government by ill-advised remarks. He tended to make long, wearisome, intemperate speeches, punctuated by indiscreet accusations and embarrassing vulgarity (when it came to speeches, Adelaide's wholesome influence was limited). He insulted important people. He offended the opposition, the Whigs, who had long been out of office but were beginning to gather strength. He seemed not to realize the harm that he did, not only by saying too much, but by making himself too visible, a target of caricature.

The more he speechified, the more William was laughed at. The diarist Greville noted that the king's after-dinner speeches at the Jockey Club were "so ridiculous and nonsensical, beyond all belief but to those who heard them, rambling from one subject to another, repeating the same thing over and over again, and altogether such a mass of confusion, trash, and imbecility, as made one laugh and blush at the same time."

"What can you expect," one court wag remarked, "from a man with a head like a pineapple?"

Everything about King William, from his pineapple-shaped head to his dislike of opera, literature and fine art to his embarrassing pro-slavery views, began to come under attack. "I know no person so perfectly disagreeable and dangerous as an author," the king opined—surely a thoughtless remark to make in the literary capital of Europe.

Before long the monarch was being pilloried as a foolish old man, worthy of no one's attention. The throne itself, already badly tarnished under George IV, lost more of its gilt. "The regal authority has fallen into contempt," Greville thought, and just at a time when Britain was about to undergo a major political convulsion.

By the early 1830s pressure for electoral reform was extreme, and growing. A major redistribution of population was under way, with the heavily industrialized cities of Birmingham, Manchester and Leeds growing rapidly yet unrepresented in Parliament. Seats in the House of Commons were distributed under archaic, and often corrupt, rules. In many places only a small minority of the inhabitants could vote, and balloting was not secret—which meant that bribery was all but inevitable.

King William agreed with the Whig leader Lord Grey that reform was needed, but achieving it took time, and led to much political and social turmoil. William rose to the occasion, intervening when the conservative House of Lords rejected the reform bill and threatening to create enough new liberal peers to make passage certain. His intervention was decisive. In June of 1832 the reform bill passed and the king, "like a boy in spirits and delight," rejoiced.

But his pleasure was short-lived. Before long the king had descended into a state of more or less constant depression, and was irritable and forgetful. In 1832 he was sixty-seven, and appeared even older. "Looking at him," Greville wrote, "one sees how soon this act will be finished." His prejudices came to the fore—his distrust of the Whigs, his dislike of all foreigners, his irrational eagerness to go to war. The ministers murmured to one another that King William was "exhibiting some symptoms of a disordered mind," continually calling everyone by the wrong name, giving absurd advice, urging Wellington to buy the island of St. Bartholomew lest the Russians, of whom he was morbidly fearful, buy it first.

"His Majesty begs to call the attention of the Duke to the THEORET-ICAL state of Persia," went one of the king's enigmatic messages. Wellington, diplomatically, wrote back that for the moment, the state of Persia was not of urgent importance.

By the time the Melbourne ministry began in 1835, William had become recalcitrant and difficult, cursing the ministers and actively seeking to thwart them, albeit to no effect. His closest confidants reported that the king was in near-constant misery, frequently in tears, repeating that "he felt his crown tottering on his head." His doctors had been saying for some time that the king was in poor health, and would soon "go the way of both his brothers" George and Frederick, who had died in their sixties.

The king's distress was genuine; he feared for the future of the realm, and did not trust the elected leaders to protect Britain against what he dreaded most: a Russian invasion. That his fears were groundless did not make his anguish any less. He fought with the cabinet, threatening to have the members impeached. He lashed out at his servants, at the press for publishing what he termed "damned lies," at his sons, who hounded him for more titles, offices and money.

When his grandchildren were brought to Windsor for their dancing lessons, William was seen to smile. His daughters too gave him comfort, especially the eldest, Sophia, who went driving with him in the afternoons and remained loyal. But his world had permanently darkened, and he had little to live for. His heir, Princess Victoria, was being kept away from his court by her haughty, ambitious mother, the Duchess of Kent. William lived long enough to take some satisfaction from Victoria's legal emancipation, when she became eighteen in May 1837. On the question of the succession, at least, he had no worries.

By the spring of 1837 it was evident that the king could not live much longer. His health had broken. Exhausted, asthmatic, unable to sleep, William grew steadily weaker and on June 15, Melbourne asked that prayers be offered in the churches for the sovereign's recovery.

The one wish of the dying king was to survive until June 18, the anniversary of the Battle of Waterloo. He got his wish; lying in bed, with his wife and children around him, William grasped a small flag captured at Waterloo and sent a message of congratulations to Wellington, victor of the great battle and in the view of many, savior of Britain.

When Britons learned, on June 20, that their king had died early that morning they were saddened. "Party is forgotten and all mourn," wrote one Londoner. The king had been undignified, often foolish and unregal, but unlike his brother he had been one of them, and they had been fond of him. With William's passing the Georgian era departed and a new and unpredictable age was ushered in.

VICTORIA

(1837–1901)

————◆◦◈◦◆————

"SHE FILLED THE ROOM."

—THE DUKE OF WELLINGTON

I n the late 1820s the only surviving grandchild of George III was a plain, plump, ringletted little girl called Drina, who lived with her imperious, self-important mother in a few shabby rooms in Kensington Palace. The king, Drina's uncle George IV, whose own daughter had died, thought seriously of bringing Drina to live with him, but was persuaded not to. When King George died and his brother William succeeded him as William IV, Drina once again became an object of attention, for Uncle William had no legitimate children and Drina was almost certain to be his heir.

Alexandrina Victoria, daughter of the late Edward, Duke of Kent, was eleven years old when her Uncle William came to the throne and was miserable.

"I led a very unhappy life as a child," she wrote later. "I had no scope for my very violent feelings of affection—had no brothers and sisters to live with—never had a father—from my unfortunate circumstances was not on comfortable or at all intimate or confidential footing with my mother . . . and did not know what a happy domestic life was!"

Despite her high birth, Drina was trapped in a tense domestic triangle from which she could see no escape. Her mother Victoire, Duchess of

Kent, had foolishly chosen to ally herself with an unscrupulous servant—her late husband's equerry John Conroy—who managed her very limited funds and drew her into his plans to enrich himself at Drina's expense. The duchess was indebted to Conroy, and quite probably they were lovers; together they waited for the elderly King William to die, and for Drina to become queen, so that they could help themselves to Drina's very large inheritance.

In the meantime, however, the duchess and Conroy quarreled, nervous strain filled the Kensington household, and the little girl who was the focus of all hopes was controlled, stifled and guarded, kept away from other children and subjected to constant surveillance. She was not allowed to see Uncle William or Aunt Adelaide, or any of their courtiers. She was punished for the slightest infraction of Conroy's harsh and overprotective rules. When she rebelled, as she often did, she was put out on the landing with her hands tied behind her back and left there until she became contrite.

"I was extremely crushed," she remembered, "and kept under and hardly dared say a word."

Predictably, Drina's hatred of Conroy—and deep resentment of her mother—expressed themselves in tantrums. She screamed, pounded with her small fists and shouted herself hoarse. She threw scissors at her governess, Louise Lehzen, refused to learn her lessons, and burst into angry tears when forced to wash, or to dress or have her hair brushed. Put out on the landing for her daily punishment, she stood silent, inwardly embattled against the world.

"I was always taught to consider myself a soldier's child," said Drina years later. She knew that her father had been an officer, and that British officers—and their children—were tough and courageous. She toughened herself, inwardly, against the blows of fate.

Drina's unhealthy domestic situation ended when she reached the age of eighteen, and was legally emancipated from her mother's guardianship. Uncle William, who had looked forward to this day, was near death, and when he died on June 20, 1837, Drina—now called Victoria—became queen.

Though she relished her freedom, Victoria had not wanted the burden of rule. She had cried when learning that she was next in line for the throne, and had hoped that Queen Adelaide would have a child so that she would escape the unwanted obligation. But when it came, Victoria rose to the challenge, indeed she exceeded all expectations.

"Never was anything like the first impression she produced," wrote the diarist Charles Greville of young Queen Victoria's first meeting with her council, "or the chorus of praise and admiration which is raised about her manner and behavior."

She entered the council room escorted only by her elderly uncles, bowed to the Lords, took her seat, and then read her speech "in a clear, distinct, and audible voice, and without any appearance of fear or embarrassment." She was poised throughout, perfectly calm and self-possessed, firm, yet without the slightest touch of self-importance. Her flawless performance left the experienced politicians open-mouthed with astonishment. Wellington expressed their overall impression when he said simply, "she filled the room."

The queen wrote in her journal that she had been "not at all nervous," adding, with typical modesty, that she was glad to have satisfied expectations. Her opinion of herself was excessively modest; she referred to "poor stupid me" and chided herself for being "far from what I should be."

Hot-tempered, obstinate, self-willed, Victoria was a true Hanoverian, though she had counterbalancing virtues. And after years of being controlled and repressed, she was eager for fun and frivolity—and found it in dances and parties. Her tiresome mother and the despicable Conroy (who had tried to coerce Victoria into letting him manage all her affairs) were pushed to the margins of the young queen's life, while she concentrated on fulfilling her royal duties and enjoying herself.

With the urbane advice of her first Prime Minister Lord Melbourne, and the help of the worldly Baron Stockmar, sent by Uncle Leopold, King of the Belgians, to be her mentor, Victoria managed affairs capably—though she became overly dependent on Melbourne and when his government fell, she was inconsolable. ("All, ALL my happiness gone . . .")

Fearing to be controlled, as she had been by her mother and Conroy, Victoria announced that she did not mean to marry. She valued her independence—and besides, she had a fear of the pain and danger of childbirth, which in the 1830s often led to the death of the mother.

Yet in an age when women were considered childlike themselves and in need of male guidance, and were encouraged to be helpless, it was inconceivable that a queen of England would not marry, and in fact a likely husband had been found, Victoria's first cousin Albert of Saxe-Coburg. When she first met her German cousin, she resisted him, but on second meeting, fell helplessly in love with the extremely handsome, highly intelligent, self-sacrificing Albert, and soon proposed to him. (It would have been against protocol for him to propose to her.)

Utterly carried away by her feelings, the queen told her husband-to-be that she was "quite unworthy of him" and acknowledged that he would be giving up a great deal in becoming her husband. Kind and fatherly, fond of his charming, ingenuous cousin, and sincerely believing that he could be of use to his wife's subjects, Albert agreed to marry Victoria.

"Oh! To feel I was, and am, loved by such an Angel as Albert was too great to describe!" Beside herself with delight, the queen married her paragon, and they eventually had a large family, nine children in all.

Albert changed Victoria's life profoundly. He was her mentor, her protector, her guide and adviser. He read Goethe to her, he served as her private secretary, he read her state papers for her when she was indisposed. Though never giving up any of her sovereign authority, Victoria relied on Albert as her principal adviser, and they worked side by side, at adjoining desks, fortunately sharing common views on most issues. In the beginning of their marriage, Victoria learned from her well-read, thoughtful husband; as the years went by and she gained experience, she needed his counsel less, but became more and more emotionally dependent on him.

Victoria's reign coincided with Britain's remarkable surgency in wealth, colonial expansion and global influence. The population of the United Kingdom had risen to twenty-five million, and the capital had doubled in size in a single generation, with the major industrial cities growing at an even faster pace. The volume and complexity of government business was at an all-time high; matters of urgent social concern, such as the deadly Irish famine of the 1840s and the worsening condition of Britain's impoverished laboring classes, combined with pressing geopolitical issues and intermittent war to make the task of monarchy vast indeed.

Victoria faced her responsibilities without shirking or flinching, though the sheer volume of work involved—papers to be read and signed, questions to be addressed, policy matters to be grasped—was staggering. By the time her reign began, the powers of the monarchy had shrunk considerably. Victoria was a constitutional monarch, but within the range of her limited powers she wielded considerable influence. Her nemesis, Prime Minister William Gladstone, remarked that "the queen alone is enough to kill any man," and Gladstone's foreign secretary conceded that Victoria "had the aperçus of a great statesman in some things."

The political rights of the sovereign had eroded, but the influence of the crown—something Victoria's gradually accumulating experience, her integrity and her good sense greatly enhanced—remained strong. When it came to a confrontation with her Prime Ministers, the queen not only made her views known ("The queen will not be dictated to") but used every tactic at her command to delay and obstruct unwanted political outcomes.

Still, Victoria let it be known that she "hated politics and turmoil" and preferred to leave both to Albert.

"We women are not made for governing," she remarked, "and if we are good women, we must dislike these masculine occupations." She was happiest when at Osborne, the mansion Albert designed and built for her and their growing family on the Isle of Wight, sitting under a tree and sketching, or at Balmoral, her highlands retreat, far from the toils and strife of Parliament and the ministries.

Victoria's eighth child, Leopold, had hemophilia and his arrival caused great strain in the royal household. The queen called Leopold her "child of anxiety," for with every move he made he risked the onset of a fatal internal hemorrhage. Apprehensive for him, and burdened by worries over her other children, Victoria became querulous and accusatory, her hot temper flaring for no reason and her outbursts of anger leading to violence.

She attacked the ever patient Albert for "want of feeling, hard heartedness, injustice, hatred, jealousy, distrust" and a dozen other faults—and Albert, retiring from confrontation, enraged her further by turning his back on her and leaving the room. The quarrels escalated and became more and more frequent; Victoria followed Albert from room to room, shouting insults, her tirades lasting an hour or more and leading to bitter silences for days afterwards.

"I am very often sadly dissatisfied with myself," Victoria wrote in her journal, "and with the little self-control I have." Yet though she was not without self-awareness, the queen could not seem to avoid making harsh scenes, and her marriage, which she had considered idyllic, turned corrosive.

Meanwhile Albert, overburdened by endless hours of work, was rapidly aging, and suffering. "You hurt me desperately," he wrote to his imperious wife—and it was not only Victoria who hurt him, but his stomach, his rheumatism, his aching head. The British public, generally accepting of Albert, had become hostile; feeling unappreciated, and worried about the condition of Europe, especially his beloved German homeland, the Prince Consort fretted and grew physically weaker.

Both Victoria and Albert were deeply concerned about their eldest son, Albert Edward ("Bertie"), who bullied and mistreated his siblings, threw stones in his tutor's face, and, like his mother, often became violent. As he grew into young manhood he was not only idle, weak and dull-witted, but pleasure-loving and prone to vice. The thought that such a wastrel would inherit the realm was all but intolerable to both parents.

In vain Albert lectured Bertie. "Life is composed of duties," he told the wayward prince, "and in the due, punctual and cheerful performance of them a true Christian, true soldier and true gentleman is recognized." The words summed up Albert's own creed—and Victoria's. But Bertie saw life, not as a series of duties, but as a series of opportunities for enjoyment, and when, at the age of twenty, opportunity beckoned, he responded. He had been sent to Ireland, for ten weeks of training with the Grenadier Guards. With the encouragement and complicity of the guardsmen, Bertie acquired a mistress, whose indiscreet boasts ensured that the prince's sexual initiation became widely known.

Heartbroken to learn of Bertie's behavior, and seriously ill, Albert succumbed to typhoid and died in December of 1861, leaving Victoria a widow at forty-two.

It was the supreme sorrow of her life. Wrung out by exhaustion and despair, too shattered to do more than weep, Victoria wanted to die herself, so wrenching was her pain. She renounced all pleasures, vowed to wear black for the rest of her life as a token of mourning, and spent many of her waking hours kneeling in Albert's carefully preserved bedroom, pouring out her heart.

"How fervently do I implore his aid, and how I wring my hands towards heaven and cry aloud: 'Oh God have pity, let me go soon! Albert, Albert, where art thou?'"

That the queen's effusions were melodramatic did not make them any less sincere, and her grief was cankered by a stubborn wrath against Bertie, whom she hated and blamed for bringing on her cherished husband's final illness.

Victoria's loathing and contempt for her son was among the themes of her ongoing reign, along with her increasing conservatism and her eccentric reclusiveness. In the years immediately after Albert's death, Victoria was so withdrawn that there were rumors that she had died—and other rumors, salacious and wounding to her, that she had an ongoing sexual relationship with her highland servant John Brown. ("Lees, all lees!" said Brown in his thick Scots accent.)

Some grumbled against the monarchy, and called for its abolition. But in the main the British public remained loyal to Victoria, especially after she endeared herself to them by publishing a modest little book, *Leaves from the Journal of My Life in the Highlands*, which revealed just how ingenuous, sentimental and pure-minded she really was. The book was a great success and the queen's subjects, taking her to their hearts, clamored for another. Before long she wrote a second volume.

By the time Victoria reached her early fifties she had grown "very large, ruddy and fat," her cheeks bulging, her chins multiplying. She stuffed herself with pralines and fondant cookies and chocolate sponge cake, and she often felt sad, "like a poor hunted hare, like a child that has lost its mother, and so lost, so frightened and helpless," as she confided to Uncle Leopold. Yet the set of her small mouth bespoke determination, and her faded blue eyes held a look of steady resolve. The poet Tennyson, who met the queen in 1870, was struck by her self possession, her sad, sweet voice and her unique quality of "stately innocence."

The world had moved on, mores and values were changing but the commonsensical, stalwart little queen went on, a comfortingly familiar figure amid the swirling currents of change. Convinced, despite all, that the world was steadily becoming a better place, Victoria denounced the increasing laxity of morals (epitomized by the behavior of her playboy son) and was outraged by the campaign for women's rights ("dangerous, unchristian and unnatural"). Having been so long on the throne, she declared, she "therefore ought to know what should be." And often her instincts were sound, though she was increasingly out of touch with both technological changes and prevailing attitudes.

In her fifties, Victoria had managed to undergo a profound inward alteration. She came to appreciate her own vitality and force of will, her power to endure. In the past she had always looked up to Albert as having been wiser, finer and stronger than herself; the longer she lived, the more she was forced to acknowledge that, of the two of them, she had been the stronger, and this recognition helped her to go on. She continued to grieve for Albert, indeed almost to deify him, building monument after monument to his memory. When at Windsor, she went every evening to visit Albert's "dear holy chamber," the mausoleum she had built to house his body at Frogmore. But she knew, deep down, that she was better able to cope with the harsh realities of life than he had been, and the knowledge gave her satisfaction.

By the time she reached seventy, in 1889, Victoria was still soldiering on, meeting with her ministers, reading documents and signing them, proofreading the court circular and correcting every detail. Four enormous bags of papers arrived at the palace each day and, with the help of her secretary Fritz Ponsonby and her youngest daughter Beatrice, her "dove and angel of peace," the queen managed to go through them all. Reluctantly, she allowed Bertie—now middle-aged, married and a father, but still creating scandal—to be trained as her successor.

The number of her subjects had increased greatly, for she had become Empress of India, with its two hundred and fifty million people, as well as reigning over her millions of subjects in Canada, Australia, New Zealand and South Africa. On her severe black mourning gowns she liked to wear blazing jewels in the manner of an Indian maharani, and she collected Indian furnishings and paintings and ordered a vast new wing built at Osborne to house them. Abdul Karim, her Personal Indian Clerk, was a conspicuously honored member of her retinue—until it was pointed out to her that Karim and his friends were stealing from her, taking advantage of the fact that her eyes were dimmed by cataracts and she could no longer see clearly.

Victoria had plenty of cause for disillusionment, and for sadness. Two of her children, Alice and Leopold, had died young, and those that survived occasionally quarreled with one another. "Children are a terrible anxiety," Victoria remarked to her oldest daughter Vicky, whose own son, Kaiser Wilhelm, gave Vicky much grief, "and the sorrow they cause is far greater than the pleasure they give." She thought the same of her dozens of grandchildren, each of whom she remembered and took careful note of, sewing quilts and knitting baby blankets and sending birthday remembrances to each one from "Gangan." In 1894 the queen's great-grandson Edward, the future Edward VIII, was born, and she proudly had her photograph taken with the three generations of her descendants.

In June of 1897 Londoners turned out by the tens of thousands to celebrate Queen Victoria's Diamond Jubilee. They cheered lustily at the sight of her small, shrunken figure as she passed in her coach on the way to Westminster Abbey, and sang "God Save the Queen" over and over again. Most of them could remember no other ruler; from time immemorial, it seemed, Victoria had been the crown, the empire, the royal family— indeed Victoria had been Britain itself, her glory Britain's glory, her endurance Britain's triumphant durability in a world of change.

Clutching her black lace parasol, feeling "a good deal agitated," the queen, in her late seventies, did her best to bask in the adulation of her subjects, but all the excitement overtaxed her and she was not able to get down from her carriage. When she heard a hymn sung within the cathedral, she broke down and wept.

The advent of the Boer War brought Victoria fresh grief, for she had relatives among the casualties, but even in her extreme old age the queen found pleasure in many things—good food, trips to the continent, Beatrice's young children—and laughed heartily at risque jokes. She joked about her age and insisted that she "felt quite young."

When she finally died in January of 1901, surrounded by family and supported by her grandson Kaiser Wilhelm, Victoria's body was laid out according to her written instructions. Dressed in her wedding veil, the sash of the Garter across her frail corpse, she was placed in her casket along with Albert's dressing gown and cloak, shawls and photographs from loved family members, a model of Albert's hand and the wedding ring John Brown's mother had once worn.

Victoria bestrode her times, and gave her name to her era. Millions of people all over the world felt the loss when she died, for she had succeeded, as Lady Balfour remarked, in making the throne a "vibrant living center," a symbol, to the majority of her subjects, of all that was noble and elevated. Her image had become familiar around the globe, a matriarchal, benevolent image; with her passing, Victorian rectitude gave way to Edwardian worldliness, and a new and less elevated image of monarchy, that of the rotund, cigar-smoking Edward VII, came to the fore.

EDWARD VII

(1901–1910)

❖❖❖❖❖❖

"HE HAD A MOST CURIOUS BRAIN, AND AT ONE TIME
ONE WOULD FIND HIM A BIG, STRONG, FAR-SEEING
MAN, GRASPING THE SITUATION AT A GLANCE AND
TAKING A BROADMINDED VIEW OF IT; AT ANOTHER
ONE WOULD BE ALMOST SURPRISED AT THE
SMALLNESS OF HIS MIND."

—FREDERICK PONSONBY

I never in my life met with such a thorough and cunning lazybones," wrote Albert, the Prince Consort, in a letter to his eldest daughter Vicky. "It does grieve me when it is my own son, and when one considers that he might be called upon at any moment to take over the reins of government in a country where the sun never sets."

The lazybones was the crown prince, Albert Edward ("Bertie"), oldest son of Queen Victoria and Prince Albert and his parents' principal source of grief. Bertie was the worst of schoolboys, impossible to teach, stubborn and truculent, spitting and biting and making faces, stamping his feet and throwing his books against the wall.

"I won't learn, and I won't stand in the corner," he announced to his governess when he was eleven years old, "for I am the Prince of Wales." To emphasize his words Bertie kicked at a windowpane, shattering the glass. The governess could do nothing with him. Albert was summoned. Albert read to his son from the Bible: "He that spareth the rod hateth his son; but he that loveth him chasteneth him." Albert proceeded to beat Bertie with a switch.

The cycle of tantrums, punishment and escalating disapproval seemed to have no end. That the responsible, dutiful Queen Victoria and her high-minded, self-sacrificing husband Albert should produce such an indolent and willful son seemed almost unnatural—until it was recalled that Victoria too, as a child (and her father Edward before her), had had tantrums and had stubbornly insisted on having her own way. Still, much was expected of Bertie, and he seemed destined to be a disappointment, not only to his parents but to the nation.

Born in 1841, the second child in the family, Bertie suffered by constantly being compared with his older sister, Vicky, who was their father's favorite. Vicky was clever and precocious, babbling away in both French and English by the time she was three. Bertie, by contrast, was mentally slow and inarticulate; he could barely stammer out English words. Vicky was quick to learn, and full of imagination and ideas like her father. Bertie liked to crawl under his desk and tip it over, and could barely read.

It was Bertie's misfortune to be born in an era that exalted dedicated endeavor, while he, as he grew older, appeared to incarnate an easy hedonism that made most Victorians shudder. He liked playing silly pranks, throwing water on his tutors and pouring wax on the footmen's uniforms. He gorged on sweets. When his parents took him to France as a boy, he loved every minute of the experience, responding with unaccustomed energy to the vivacity and style, the unbuttoned gaiety of Paris. The brisk, dapper Napoleon III appealed to Bertie much more than his own severe father, and the beautiful, elegant and warm Empress Eugénie seemed infinitely preferable to his stout, dowdy, disapproving mother.

"You have a nice country," Bertie told the emperor. "I would like to be your son."

Bertie reached his teens without improving either intellectually or physically. Short, puny, listless and glassy-eyed (when not throwing stones at his long-suffering tutor or attacking his brother Affie, who shared his schoolroom, with a knife), he ate too much and had to be closely watched, his mail intercepted and read, his companions limited to young men of stern moral character whose official task it was to train the future king in "Manners and Conduct" and "Appearance, Deportment and Dress." He attended discussions at the Oxford Union, but only because it gave him an excuse to escape from his designated companions and spend time with new friends who liked to drink and play cards and carouse.

"He is so idle and weak," Queen Victoria exclaimed when Bertie was seventeen—though she was forced to admit that despite his shortcomings, her son had a "good, warm and affectionate" heart.

In fact, he had more than that: he had charisma. When sent on a tour of Canada at eighteen, the Prince of Wales was an unexpectedly great success. He loved the limelight, knew how to please a crowd and enjoyed the parties and balls given in his honor—something his stiff, correct father and rather dull mother never had. Bertie danced well, was popular with the ladies, and was accepted as a good fellow by the men. He became an instant celebrity in Canada, and even more of one in the United States where, amid the turmoil of an election campaign, he traveled widely and encountered legions of fans.

To Bertie, accustomed to being criticized, punished and generally found wanting, the newfound popularity came as a revelation. "This is for me! All for me!" he shouted when huge crowds cheered as he rode up Broadway in an open barouche, flowers strewn in his path. American women snatched at his clothing, stole his gloves and cravats as souvenirs, even paid for locks of his hair sold by an enterprising barber.

But on his return to England the Prince of Wales found his situation unaltered. His father continued to lecture him on doing his duty, and his mother sighed over his weak chin, long nose and poor profile. The family doctor put him on a strict diet, to no avail. In an effort to make a man of him, the decision was made to send Bertie to Ireland, for ten weeks of training with the Grenadier Guards. In the summer of 1861 he left for Kildare.

It turned out to be a fateful decision. In the company of the worldly, hard-living guardsmen, Bertie was initiated, no doubt all too willingly, into the pleasures of sex by an experienced camp follower, Nellie Clifden. His liaison with Nellie continued on into the fall, after he returned from the military camp, in fact he even brought Nellie secretly into the palace to share his bed. Nellie was proud of her association with the prince and grew boastful; before long gossip about the prince and his mistress reached the gentlemen's clubs, and the embassies on the continent. Word was soon brought to Albert.

Bertie was twenty years old in the fall of 1861, approaching his majority. To expect him to remain sexually innocent would have been unrealistic. Still, Albert was filled with dismay when he heard of his son's behavior, and Victoria even more so. Both foresaw disaster. All their efforts to raise the moral tone of the monarchy, to create a wholesome family life were threatened by the prince's fall from grace. Albert, weak, overworked and demoralized, became seriously ill and did not rally. Bertie was at his bedside when he died in December of 1861.

Though the relationship between father and son had always been a formal and, for Bertie, an emotionally unsatisfying one, he mourned his father's passing and suffered in the knowledge that his mother blamed him for causing Albert's death. At Albert's funeral Bertie walked behind the coffin, carrying out his ceremonial role with correctness, but almost immediately afterward the queen sent him away—as far away as possible—on a long foreign journey to Greece, Egypt, the Holy Land and Turkey. On his return she saw to it that Bertie became engaged, hoping that marriage would curb his unruly lust and force him into maturity and responsibility.

Fortunately, Bertie did not rebel against this plan for his future, and in 1863 he married the Danish princess Alexandra, a sweet-natured, beautiful young woman who was to stand affectionately beside him for the rest of his life. Alexandra produced royal children in rapid succession; to all outward appearances, the marriage was a success.

But as Bertie reached his mid-twenties it was becoming clear that he had an eccentric, dark side, and that his bonhomie and restless pursuit of merrymaking and pleasure were meant to mask a deeply troubled persona.

"He had a most curious brain," the royal secretary Frederick Ponsonby wrote of the Prince of Wales, "and at one time one would find him a big, strong, far-seeing man, grasping the situation at a glance and taking a broad-minded view of it; at another one would be almost surprised at the smallness of his mind." Ponsonby found Bertie to be "almost childish in his views," regressing and becoming obstinate and refusing to understand what he was told, just as he had refused to learn as a child.

He was erratic, unpredictable, changeable in his moods and alarmingly hostile at times. "There can be no doubt that even his most intimate friends were all terrified of him," Ponsonby wrote. Always avid for company, and with a dread of being alone, Bertie was so mercurial that a companion could be welcomed and cherished one moment and insulted and thrown out of the palace the next. A single ill-judged remark from a friend could make the prince turn cold, especially if the remark had to do with Bertie's status or dignity as Prince of Wales.

Bertie's incessant talkativeness, his compulsive need for noise and company, his boisterous silliness all bespoke more than mere immaturity. It was no wonder his friends were afraid of him, when at any moment his teasing could develop an edge of meanness. He stubbed out lit cigars in people's hands. He inflicted injury—and enjoyed it. And the older he grew, the greater became his excesses, until excessive indulgence became the core of his life.

He ate to excess, sitting down to gargantuan meals of turtle soup and stuffed pheasant, platters heaped with meat and fish and fowl, cream pastries and brandied cherries, all washed down with champagne and followed by port and liqueurs. Ten courses were not enough to satisfy him, and he ate five meals a day. Between meals he smoked cigars, twelve a day, and between cigars he smoked strong cigarettes. He gambled excessively, playing cards for high stakes, betting on horses, prizefighters, wagering with friends on anything and everything. He stayed up too late and drank too much, spent more than he had (though his income as Prince of Wales was very high) and, increasingly, indulged his obsessive craving for sex.

The prince's women were many and varied, from the curvaceous Hortense Schneider, a musical comedy soprano and cancan dancer, to the aristocratic Princesse de Sagan to a series of highborn married Englishwomen. Society tolerated discreet adulterous liaisons, as long as they remained private, but Bertie did not follow the rules. He was imprudent, and made himself vulnerable to blackmail—and the throne vulnerable to scandal. He often relied on an abortionist, Dr. Clayton, to rescue him, and his paramours, from awkward situations.

By the time he was twenty-five the prince was said to be "ruining his health as fast as he can," gorging himself, staying up all night gambling, drunk on brandy and perpetually encircled by a thick cloud of smoke. Night after night he was seen in disreputable music halls and gambling clubs, with an entourage of high-living friends, dashing from one sordid venue to another in cabs, not coming home until dawn. Even when his wife was ill, he was seen "haunting the theater," eyeing the prostitutes who were to be found there, heedless of his worsening reputation and the damage he was doing to the monarchy.

For the timing of the prince's headlong rush into debauchery could hardly have been more ill-judged. The queen, withdrawn in her prolonged mourning, was losing popularity and a clamorous movement to abolish the monarchy was gaining force. The Prince of Wales's escapades were lowering the monarchy further in public esteem—and had the full story of his extramarital activities been known, the popular reaction would have been much stronger. As it was, the prince was called upon to be a witness in an unsavory divorce case, and the public was left to draw its own conclusions about his role in the whole highly improper affair.

But the political attacks being made on Bertie ceased when, late in 1871, at the age of twenty-nine, he became severely ill with typhoid.

His much abused body had little resistance to the disease. He grew worse and worse, and was not expected to live. He lay in his sickbed at

Sandringham, his Norfolk estate, with his wife and six young children waiting for the end to come. The queen, in tears, came to say her goodbyes and the nation, forgetting Bertie's flagrant transgressions, mourned its prince.

To general amazement, the prince recovered, and there was much official and unofficial rejoicing. His value to his future subjects was underscored when, soon after his recovery, the queen was shot at by a young would-be assassin. Had the attempt succeeded, Bertie would have become king.

He would have become king—yet he was entirely unprepared to carry out the duties of a monarch. Queen Victoria did not trust him, knew that he was too indiscreet to be told state secrets and disliked having him near her, as he reminded her of Albert's death. She refused to allow Bertie access to state papers or important documents. She did not let him confer with ministers or sit in on meetings at which government policy was discussed. He was kept in ignorance, left to idle on the margins of the political world; his offers of participation were invariably rejected. All that he was allowed to do, from time to time, was to preside at the ceremonial openings of public buildings or make state visits abroad.

Even when the prince had become middle-aged, with grown children of his own, the queen denied him any opportunity to familiarize himself with the craft of rulership, a craft at which she herself had become very adept. While he waited for the throne, the prince spent his time at Sandringham or at Marlborough House in London, with frequent visits to country houses where he hunted and shot, socialized and enjoyed romantic dalliance. He liked to take the waters at foreign spas, spent much time in Paris and was often to be seen at the Moulin Rouge, Maxim's, or the "House of All Nations," an elite Left Bank bordello.

Paris suited him perfectly. "Everybody recognizes me and nobody knows me," he remarked. And indeed as he aged, the prince took on the appearance of a wealthy Parisian man of the world, bearded, expensively tailored, carefully and somewhat raffishly dressed. His increasing girth made him distinctive, as did the charm of his public manners and the heavy sensuality of his features.

By the time he reached his fifties Bertie was known throughout Europe for his array of beautiful mistresses, including Lily Langtry, Daisy Brooke, and Liane de Pougy of the Folies-Bergère. He was a connoisseur, a world-class collector of women. Evangelicals and moralists hissed him, but most Britishers had come to accept his way of life, having become accustomed to it over the decades. Mores were changing, the strict earnestness of the mid-Victorian era was being undermined by the advent of the "fast" girl, the freethinker and the iconoclastic Pre-Raphaelite. The prince was in the vanguard of changing times.

In 1890, however, he became involved in a scandal he would never quite live down. While staying at the country house of Tranby Croft during a race meet, he played baccarat, which was illegal, and again broke the law by agreeing to suppress the fact that one of the guests had been cheating. In doing so the prince had breached the code of honor among gentlemen. The press attacked him for it, and the public was alienated.

The Tranby Croft scandal was the nadir of Bertie's popularity, and it coincided with the ebbing of political power in the monarchy itself. Over the course of Queen Victoria's long reign, the broadening of the electoral franchise had made the political parties and their leaders more powerful, and the queen less so. But at the same time the monarchy had gained in popular visibility; the queen had become a celebrity, and the prince an even more notorious one. Millions followed the lives of the royals through newspapers and magazines. Royal weddings, christenings and funerals were photographed and described in detail. The lives of Victoria and Bertie were no longer their own, but at the same time, they belonged to their subjects in a new, uniquely personal way.

Scandal diminished the reservoir of good feeling the Prince of Wales had possessed, but over the course of the 1890s he began to recover it. As a yachtsman, a racing stable owner, a world traveller the prince was still admired; when his horse Persimmon won the Derby in 1896, he was lionized. There was no escaping his rotund, avuncular image, it was on cigar packets and billboards, displayed in shop windows and on magazine covers.

And another image was becoming familiar to the British public, that of Alice Keppel, Edward's latest mistress. He was fifty-six, she twenty-nine when their liaison began. Alice was tall, voluptuous, and alluring and the prince insisted that she be treated almost as if she were his wife. He took both Alice and his wife to house parties. He had Alice join the group in family photographs. Alice was his bridge partner, his companion, his nurse when he was ill. The prince's former lovers gossiped about his waning virility and said privately that the relationship between Bertie and Mrs. Keppel could not be anything other than platonic. Platonic or not, Alice was ubiquitous. Whenever the prince appeared in public without her, there were shouts of "Where's Alice?" and Bertie acknowledged them with a smile and a wave of the plump royal hand.

Finally, when the prince was in his fifties and the elderly Queen Victoria had begun to tire, she allowed him access to the state papers. And in 1901, when Bertie was nearly sixty, the old queen died and her son became King Edward VII.

At last the prince came into his own, not only dynastically but personally. He had lived long enough for upper-class British society to adopt his ways; he presided over a culture of overripe excess and self-indulgence, a fin-de-siècle mentality whose motto was, in some circles at least, "Eat, drink and be merry, for tomorrow we die!"

Obese and atherosclerotic as he was, the new king proved to be active and energetic, continuing his travels (he made state visits to Berlin, Stockholm, Athens and Tallinn), meeting foreign heads of state, using his celebrity to advance the cause of European peace. His subjects called the king "Edward the Peacemaker" and assumed, wrongly, that he had significant influence on the world stage.

In actuality Edward's influence was illusory. His ministers tended to ignore him, and did not consider his opinions worth asking. The Liberal government which came to power midway in Edward's reign was unlikely to take advice from a Tory king, especially one who had an aversion for details and tended to form his views based on personal likes and dislikes rather than on sound political principles.

Edward presided over a decade of sweeping political change, which saw the advent of national insurance, the legal empowerment of labor unions and old age pensions, not to mention wage increases and long overdue improvements in the conditions of work. But he had little to do with these developments. As king he was an amiable, accessible figurehead, reassuring to his subjects but remote from the actualities of governing.

King Edward's genial presence tended to mask the divisive character of the age, which was one of increasing hostility among the European powers, and an immense buildup of armaments. Edward's nephew, Kaiser William II, was building a formidable navy and Britain's response was prompt and costly. The king was among the staunchest proponents of enlarging the fleet, and spoke out against lowering the military budget—something the expanded social services voted in by the Liberals made all but imperative.

The tone of the era was ominous, but the monarch himself was content. As king, Edward attained that rarest of blessings, a truly gratified life. His addictions to gambling and sex had receded. He still overate and drank too much, but so did his companions. The penumbra of parental disapproval had disappeared, leaving the king free of all restraints, and he savored that freedom. Alice Keppel provided comfort, Queen Alexandra and the royal children provided respectability. The king's subjects, who looked on him (as they had on his mother) as a symbol of stability and continuity in a time of flux and uncertainty, gave him all the affection and loyalty his lonely heart required. And in all, his horses won the Derby three times.

Neither the increasing threat of European war nor the deadlock between the Conservative House of Lords and the Liberal House of Commons darkened the king's final months. His heart gave out in May of 1910, and he died much as he had lived, dressed in a frock coat as if on his way to a party, an unlit cigar in his hand.

GEORGE V

(1910–1936)

"I AM AN ORDINARY MAN."

—GEORGE V

Edward VII's small but lively younger son, Prince George Frederick Ernest Albert, was a cheerful boy, "always merry and rosy," who loved the outdoors and showed an early talent for handling small boats. Being the younger of the two princes, George was not expected to reign; that future was reserved for his brother Eddy, sixteen months older than he. Yet the sturdy, resilient George watched over the slow-moving, listless Eddy with the vigilant care of an older, not a younger, brother. It was as if Eddy, though physically taller and more developed, drew strength and life from George, who was his prop and mainstay. The boys had their lessons together, ate and played together and, at the ages of twelve and thirteen, went aboard the naval training ship *Britannia* to learn the arts of seamanship.

Born in June of 1865, when his kind but critical and outspoken grandmother Queen Victoria had been on the throne for nearly three decades, George was spared the worst moral and physical rigors of a Victorian childhood. His father Edward, Prince of Wales, was in rebellion against the overregimented, overdisciplined upbringing he himself had endured as a boy, and allowed both his sons a most un-Victorian latitude.

The queen disapproved. In her view, George and Eddy were "such ill-bred, ill-trained" children that she "couldn't fancy them at all." Her harsh judgment of the boys' manners seems to have been exaggerated, but in one respect she was right: both George and Eddy were badly educated. They couldn't spell and their grammar was full of flaws. George was unable to learn French, despite being sent to a special tutor in Switzerland, and when confronted with the complexities of German he pronounced it a "rotten language" and "beastly dull."

George's naval education too had its hardships. The *Britannia*, anchored in the River Dart in Devon, was home to a large group of boys, and the princes were given no special privileges—and no protection against the assaults of their shipmates. Fighting was common, and as George was puny, he was often picked on and bloodied. Forced to hold his own against bigger boys, sleeping in a hammock in a cold cabin, coping with homesickness George became toughened, as he was meant to. While becoming adept at navigation and advancing in mathematics, he also acquired the naval virtues of promptness, fortitude in adversity and scrupulous attention to duty.

But while George flourished, Eddy withered. He would not study, he was physically inactive and often gave in to a self-indulgent sensuality which horrified his grandmother. Eddy posed a serious problem for the family. As his father's heir, he needed to become an individual, self-reliant and independent. But in order to do anything at all, his tutor said, he required the stimulus of his brother's company.

Clearly the symbiosis between the two young princes was unhealthy, yet it seemed to be necessary for the future of the realm. What effect it had on George is unclear. He was fond of Eddy and accepted his role as his brother's "prop and mainstay." There was no detectable jealousy or rivalry between the two—in itself a sign both of George's cooperative nature and Eddy's apathy. That it was Eddy who was destined to rule aroused no resentment in George, who wanted nothing more than a naval career and a quiet life.

As a future naval officer it was time for George to take his first long voyage, and in the fall of 1879 he set sail aboard the corvette *Bacchante*. He was fourteen. ("So old and so small!!!!" Queen Victoria wrote in her diary, with characteristic overemphasis.) He did not sail alone, however. Eddy was with him as usual, and for the next three years the royal brothers roamed the oceans of the world, visiting ports in Africa, Latin America, Australia and Asia. They played "rowdy games" on the Nile, acquired dragon tattoos in Japan, and picked up a baby kangaroo as a pet in Sydney.

The voyaging broadened George's perspective and gave him an abiding regard for the British Empire and its diverse populations.

When a strong gale disabled the *Bacchante* four hundred miles from the nearest port, George joined the other officers in a dangerous three-day vigil while repairs were made. The experience matured him, and he returned from sea at seventeen, a slight, good-looking young man with a loud voice, genial and unselfish, with no royal airs and the promise of considerable skill in his chosen profession.

The princes now parted company, their symbiosis lessened by distance. George began a series of naval postings that culminated in independent commands, with further study of navigation, gunnery and seamanship at the Royal Naval College. Without George to buoy him up, Eddy was lost, his mental powers "abnormally dormant," according to his tutor, his morals in a shambles, involved in squalid escapades that embarrassed the family. Everyone, including George, who knew the truth about Eddy—a truth carefully kept from the British public—was alarmed for the future.

Efforts to bring order and respectability to Eddy's life by finding him a bride failed until in 1891, Queen Victoria intervened to all but force Eddy to propose to a young relative of hers, May of Teck. Eddy proved malleable, and May did her duty and accepted his proposal. But when Eddy died in January of 1892, a month before the wedding was to take place, George's life changed forever.

At the time Eddy died, George was recuperating from a serious attack of typhoid fever. He was weak and thin, his spirits low, and the loss of his boyhood companion, his shipmate, almost his second self must have been severe indeed—though it would have been out of character for the stolid, self-disciplined prince to reveal his distress.

George now stepped into his late brother's role as his father's heir, and the future king. In an odd homage to Eddy, prodded by his royal grandmother and others, George began, tentatively, to court May for himself. To others he appeared cool and offhand in his wooing, while May, an imperious young woman with an air of hauteur, seemed anything but swept away by romance. But these appearances were deceptive. In actuality George was happily ardent, May devoted. ("I love you more than anybody in the world," she wrote him.) They were married in July of 1893, when George was twenty-eight.

Now enjoying the title Duke of York, with a generous income and extensive property, George settled down to build a life with May. His naval career, unsuitable for one in direct line of succession to the throne, was put aside, and he lived the pleasant, unhurried life of a rich country squire, a life geared to the shooting calendar.

George became, and remained until the very end of his life, a world-class shot, the best shot in the royal family. With his twelve-bore Purdeys he pounded away at pheasants and ducks, partridges and woodcock. It was not unusual for him to bring down a thousand birds in a day. Tramping the extensive Sandringham acreage was his chief joy in life; he found the bleakness of the raw open land invigorating, the brisk marine air refreshing. Out in the country, his thoughts on nothing other than the day's shoot or the afternoon's walk, he could forget the future and his dread of it. On his return to York Cottage, the small house on the Sandringham estate where he and May lived, he could peruse his growing stamp collection and lose himself in its minutiae.

The distractions of shooting, stamps and family life could not entirely keep George's dreads at bay. On the surface an amiable, genial man, hearty and extroverted, with a sailor's foul-mouthed bluntness, underneath his bonhomie was a darker self, prey to rage and vitriolic outbursts, and the stress he was under showed itself in attacks of stomach pain and frequent indigestion.

George's bluff persona had an obsessive edge. He fussed endlessly over details of dress and the proper placement of medals and decorations on uniforms. He became "nervously excitable" when housemaids moved his possessions while cleaning. He was so fanatical about punctuality that he set all the clocks in his residences one half-hour ahead, and punished houseguests who came late to breakfast by denying them food. These eccentricities, and the unpleasantness they frequently led to, were marks of a deep-going unease, signs that beneath his dutiful exterior George was, at bottom, in rebellion.

Worst of all, George proved to be a punitive father.

Six children, five boys and one girl, were born between 1894 and 1905, and all came to fear their father's strictness, censure and shouted accusations. He criticized not only their misbehavior but their dress, their conduct, even their achievements. Times were changing, but George could not bear to let his children change with them. When they showed signs of adopting modern habits of speech or social relations he became angry and caustic. Even George's most generous biographer, Kenneth Rose, had to admit that he was rigid, exacting and highly critical of his sons and daughter, and concluded that "it cannot be by chance that every one of his children was in some degree afflicted by nervous strain."

The strain was particularly apparent in the oldest son, Edward Albert, always called David. As he grew out of childhood, David was handsome, charming, urbane—and incurably outspoken. He knew his own mind, and he expressed it, and since his opinions were invariably at odds with his father's, serious clashes between father and son were frequent.

Meanwhile George, in his thirties, became Prince of Wales when his father came to the throne as Edward VII. Though his own accession loomed, George continued to preoccupy himself with country pursuits, though he did become familiar with the routines of rulership, thanks to his father's tutelage and that of the skillful Private Secretary, Sir Arthur Bigge. A tour of India in 1905 left an enduring set of impressions on George and May both, and created in George a sentimental attachment to the subcontinent.

On May 6, 1910, Edward VII died, and George wrote in his diary that he had lost his "best friend and the best of fathers." "I am heartbroken and overwhelmed with grief," he added, "but God will help me in my responsibilities and darling May will be my comfort as she has always been. May God give me strength and guidance in the heavy task which has fallen on me."

And a heavy task it was to be, for as king George V would reign over one of the most turbulent eras in British history. He was nearly forty-five years old, seasoned in his views and set in his ways. Yet though he had seen much of the world, he had lived an insular life. He had not wielded power or influence, or struggled to obtain either; he had never had dealings with politicians. The ways of the sophisticated world were, and would remain, a closed book to him.

The new king came to the throne in the midst of a constitutional crisis. A deadlock had arisen between the very conservative House of Lords and the (then) progressive House of Commons, and until the power struggle was resolved, the government could not be funded. Two elections had been held in an effort to break the impasse, but without success. In desperation the Prime Minister came to the king and threatened that the government would resign unless King George agreed to create enough Liberal peers to outvote the Conservatives.

George complained to friends afterward that he had been "bullied for an hour and a half" and that he had felt as though a pistol was being held to his head. In the end he agreed, "very reluctantly," to what was being demanded.

It was a harsh political baptism, and a lesson in both the powers and limitations of his royal role. Hard on the heels of the parliamentary crisis came an increased threat of conflict in Ireland, where both Ulster Protestants and Nationalists were smuggling in rifles and cartridges and civil war seemed likely.

"Grieved beyond words" by the apparently irresolvable dilemma and the ugly hostilities it created, the king was able to do little but continually propose compromise. He did not dare take sides, he had to retain an image of neutrality. "He remains quite calm," one government observer wrote of King George during the Irish crisis, "is sure of his constitutional position and is being of real service in seeking a way out."

Labor unrest, strikes and agitation clouded the early years of George V's reign, and the movement for women's suffrage was reaching its peak of protest. ("Nice ladies, aren't they," the king remarked, "breaking everybody's windows. I hope they will be severely punished.") King George and thousands of others were horrified when a suffragette threw herself under the hooves of one of the king's racehorses at the Derby in 1913.

Such shocking demonstrations assaulted King George's frayed nerves and brought on attacks of indigestion. He was often overanxious and trembled when he had to open Parliament and make a brief speech. He had never relished being the center of attention, and disliked his public role, with the inevitable loss of privacy and unwelcome scrutiny it invited. The press was unkind to him, printing stories alleging that he was an alcoholic (in actuality he was only a light drinker) and a bigamist, married to both the queen and an admiral's daughter whom he had met on Malta. The latter allegation actually led to a prosecution for libel, which the king won. It was no wonder he despised the press ("those filthy rags of newspapers") and shouted and swore when he read farfetched stories about himself and his family.

Sophisticates and the fashionable scoffed at King George's plain tastes and dislike for society, and could not decide whether the king or his imposing, rather stiff queen—who had given up her familiar name "May" for the more formal "Mary"—was the more dull. They ridiculed his preference for the modest, brownstone York Cottage at Sandringham ("a glum little villa," as the diplomat Harold Nicolson called it) over Buckingham Palace, his choice of inexpensive middle-class furniture and his indifference to fine art. "They're simple, very, very ordinary people," Lloyd George wrote of the king and queen. "The king is a very jolly chap but thank God there's not much in his head."

But if some scoffed and patronized, the majority of George's subjects warmed to the sailor king, liking his unpretentious, extroverted persona. Were it not for an accident of birth, he might be one of them, so conventional were his tastes, so middlebrow his preferences. It pleased the public that their king described himself as "an ordinary man"—though his income was certainly far from ordinary—and that he deplored both opera and American jazz and liked listening to *The Song of the Volga Boatmen* on the gramophone and the music of military bands. ("Went to Covent Garden and saw *Fidelio*," the king wrote in his diary. "And how damned dull it was!!")

Guests at York Cottage were surprised at the simplicity and utter lack of grandeur in which the royal family lived, and were even more surprised when the king himself took each new arrival to his or her room to make certain the servants had prepared it properly. If necessary, he knelt by the hearth and lit a fire. At meals, George allowed his pet parrot, Charlotte, to fly freely around the small dining room, sometimes perching on the edge of a plate to steal a piece of food.

It was perhaps the king's essential humility that appealed to his subjects most. Far from putting on airs or taking pride in his rank he was self-effacing, unpretentious, approachable and friendly for the most part with those he met—when they didn't irritate him or arouse his ire. He read a chapter of the Bible every night before sleep, a habit acquired in boyhood, and took pleasure in singing hymns; his faith was sure and unquestioned. An excellent yachtsman, he never boasted of his prowess. Even his rages were not the bellowings of an inflated ego but the stentorian complaints of an easily frustrated, nervous man placed in a lonely position, conscious of his shortcomings.

When war came in 1914, King George was sympathetic with his subjects' anxieties and deprivations. "I cannot share your hardships," he announced, "but my heart is with you every hour of the day." Two of his own sons were serving officers, and as British casualties mounted George understood the anguish of worried and grieving parents. He visited hospitals, shipyards, factories and barracks, went to the bedsides of air-raid victims, and conferred thousands of medals for gallantry. On a trip to France to inspect the Royal Flying Corps on the Western Front, the king's horse fell on top of him, causing a painful pelvic fracture that never fully healed and that gave him intermittent pain for the rest of his life.

The war proved to be long and costly in lives, the ghastly suffering of the troops, enmired in stinking trenches and struggling in vain to gain a few feet of ground, almost beyond imagining. George V's beard turned white from the strain. Emotions unleashed by the tensions of the war alarmed him: the rabid hatred of the German enemy, the radical republicanism of the British, many of whom wanted to do away with the monarchy entirely, the endless grieving and the resentments over food shortages and other miseries.

When asked to provide a haven for his beleaguered Romanov cousin, the deposed Tsar Nicholas II, and his family George said no, fearful of inflaming anti-monarchical sentiment. In the summer of 1918 he learned that the Bolshevik government had executed the Romanovs—a fate for which he felt partially responsible, though he could not have foreseen the consequences of his decision to deny them asylum in England.

By 1918 George was depressed. He found temporary solace and relaxation with his stamp collection, but military losses and political conflicts dragged his spirits down. "Very often I feel in despair," he confided to Queen Mary. "If it wasn't for you I should break down." Finally, in the late summer of 1918, the enemy began to pull back, and the Allied forces to advance. Armistice came in November, and the sovereign rejoiced with his people.

During the course of the war the ruling family had changed its name from Saxe-Coburg-Gotha to Windsor. The House of Hanover, its German ancestry an embarrassment and a liability, became the House of Windsor. (That the queen spoke with a detectable German accent remained awkward.)

The postwar world brought sudden and dazzlingly rapid change: looser morals, a political shift to the left, severe unemployment by the early 1920s and with it, strikes and hunger marches. The police were ineffectual, soldiers were summoned and rioting broke out. The king, now approaching sixty, was nearly as hostile to the changes as he was bewildered by them. He belonged to another era. Everything about him, from the old-fashioned cut of his clothes to his outspoken attitudes (he privately excoriated the Labour Party in violent language) to the footmen he kept at Windsor with powdered hair and knee breeches, bespoke the past. When the General Strike broke out in 1926, bringing the country to a standstill, King George called for conciliation and compromise, and despite his detestation of Labour, when they gained a majority he was staunch in his public support. Labour ministers liked the king, and always found him to be congenial.

In the winter of 1928/9 George V was suddenly taken ill with blood poisoning and heart disease and despite the attentions of eleven specialists, continued to decline. His recuperation took five months—a reminder to the ministers that a change of reigns could not be far off. But the heir, David (Prince Edward), was unpromising. At the time of his father's illness David was thirty-five, still unmarried, a charmer and pleasure-seeker whose liaisons with married women attracted the scandal-mongering press. David alarmed the ministers, and alternately grieved and infuriated his father, who lectured him, fruitlessly, on morals and duty and self-respect.

George V's last years were overshadowed by the great worldwide depression and Europe's drift toward war. Tired and chronically ill, heartsick over the continued louche behavior of his son, whose admiration for Hitler and Fascism was well known, King George watched the course of events with an increasing sadness. He received the loud popular acclaim on the occasion of his Silver Jubilee in 1935 with pleasure, but it was a pleasure tainted by his dread of another war.

"I will not have another war," he told Lloyd George in the year of his Jubilee. "I will not. The last one was none of my doing and if there is another one and we are threatened with being brought into it, I will go to Trafalgar Square myself and wave a red flag myself rather than allow this country to be brought in."

His determination was strong, but his body was failing rapidly. In his seventieth year King George could no longer shoot or sail, and had to content himself riding a pony around the Sandringham estates, with Queen Mary walking beside him. There was little more he could do. Hitler and Mussolini were gaining strength, David was enmeshed in fresh scandal with a divorced American mistress. Anxious for the future, the old king made a last prediction about his exasperating son. "After I am dead," he said, "the boy will ruin himself in twelve months."

During the four days in which George V's body lay in state, nearly a million of his subjects came to pay their respects. They mourned not only the sovereign they had loved but the loss of the age he represented, an era of punctuality, rectitude and a forthright, albeit narrow, view of duty. Deprived of his reassuring avuncular presence, they viewed the uncertain future with dismay.

EDWARD VIII

(1936)

"WE BELONG TO EACH OTHER FOREVER....
WE LOVE EACH OTHER MORE THAN LIFE."

—EDWARD VIII TO WALLIS SIMPSON

The blond, blue-eyed, slim and dapper eldest son of King George V, Prince Edward, was as popular as a movie star and had much more class and polish. Thanks to newspapers and newsreels he was known around the world in the years following the First World War; his tours of Commonwealth countries ensured his popularity with millions of fans, to whom he was Prince Charming come to life.

Edward, called David by his family, seemed to lack nothing that would make for earthly happiness: good health, strong charisma, a large private fortune, adulation—and the ultimate promise of the throne. But those who knew him best saw that he was in distress. He often clashed with his gruff, highly critical father, he lacked the affection and approval of a loving mother (Queen Mary being a distant, unaffectionate parent), and a sense of security eluded him. He had a habit of looking down, instead of meeting the eyes of whomever he was speaking to, and he exhibited nervous tics and a tense way of endlessly adjusting his tie and collar. And the prince had a combative streak, a tendency to lash out verbally, which was provocative and which tended to keep others at arm's length.

There was much about the Prince of Wales that was private—and kept well hidden from all but those in the inner circles of the government and the royal household. His three brothers Albert ("Bertie"), George and

Henry noted a change in him at adolescence, how he seemed to lose much of his affection for them and became emotionally distant—even though he continued to joke with them and treat them as playmates. Restless, unable to concentrate (David found studying "a dreadful bore" and did poorly at the Royal Naval College at Dartmouth and later at Magdalen College, Oxford), completely lacking any spiritual or aesthetic feeling, David found an outlet in physical activity, though he was not particularly good at sports.

The Prince of Wales's biographers have suggested an explanation for his being ill at ease and emotionally disconnected. Some of those close to him said that something "went wrong" with David when he reached puberty. At sixteen or seventeen both David and his brother Bertie came down with mumps, and David may have suffered a complication called orchitis, inflammation of the testicles, which could have caused a hormonal imbalance and/or left him sterile. He was small and thin, with sparse body hair, rarely needing to shave; he could have been deficient in male hormones.

Described by one of the court officials as "backward but sweet" at sixteen, David clung to boyish pastimes long after other boys had given them up. Even as adults David and Bertie amused themselves throwing records off the terrace to see if they would break, flinging missiles at table lamps and romping like large children, roaring with laughter. David wrote of his brother that "we became more than brothers—we became close friends," but his emotional detachment remained—even as his marked taste for pleasure expanded.

During the prince's two years at Oxford, parties, drink and the company of older women were a constant distraction. However, when war broke out in 1914, the twenty-year-old David did not hesitate to abandon his pleasures and was eager to go to the Front.

Told by his father that he must accept a staff post behind the lines instead of risking his safety in the trenches, David was disappointed. Even so, he was often in harm's way and was nearly killed. His car was hit by an enemy shell, killing his driver; the prince had gotten out of the car only minutes before the accident happened.

After the war, David visited Canada, America, New Zealand and Australia, wearing his Military Cross and greeted with enthusiastic acclaim. He was heralded as an apostle of modernity, a modern man for a modern age. The rising generation, David's generation, was abnormally conscious of its distinctiveness. The war had swept away much that the prince and his contemporaries saw as outmoded—long skirts and long hair for women, social formality, a rigid sexual and moral code. Victorian ideals of duty and self-sacrifice, prudery and a confining class and political structure came under assault and new attitudes began to spread. Prince Edward's relaxed, unpretentious manner, his evident enjoyment of life and his seeming freedom from the trammels of politics made him a symbol of a welcome new age.

He became a familiar figure at London's nightclubs, where he sometimes played drums with the band. Energetic and fun-loving, the prince kidded and teased his friends, danced and sang, and threw himself enthusiastically into an active sex life with many partners, the most enduring of whom was Freda Dudley Ward, the wife of a Liberal Member of Parliament.

Sympathetic observers associated David's hedonism with the postwar mood of reckless enjoyment: eat, drink and be merry, for tomorrow we die. Clearly the prince carried deep within him the haunting, wounding scars of his war memories, it was said, for there was an unmistakable sadness in the depths of his blue eyes and an air of frailty and despondency clung to him.

But as the years passed and the prince's pursuit of pleasure became more frenzied and more obsessive, members of the royal household and government officials became apprehensive about him, and pessimistic about his future reign. He lacked character and discipline. He could not seem to persevere at anything meaningful. He was initiated into the Masonic Order and made fitful attempts to devote his time to supporting the interests of ex-servicemen and the unemployed. But these pursuits soon withered, and he yielded to the dark side of his temperament, becoming sullen and agitated, avid for amusement as an antidote to the crushing boredom that weighed him down and made him irritable.

As he reached his mid-thirties maturity continued to elude David. Though urged to marry, he resisted the pressure to settle down, perhaps knowing that he would not be able to father a child to continue the dynasty. Putting Mrs. Dudley Ward aside, he found a new companion, a beautiful, rather empty-headed American, Thelma Furness. With Thelma he retreated to his weekend mansion, Fort Belvedere, where they surrounded themselves with a tight circle of close friends. But David remained restless, going on safari in Africa (and nearly dying of malaria), flying to Paris frequently, yachting on the Riviera, dashing off in the evenings to Ciro's or the Embassy.

Thelma taught David to do needlepoint ("The hand that holds the needle cannot hold the brandy snifter," she said revealingly) and now and then they sewed together in the evening, while Thelma's father, Consul Morgan, read aloud to them from the works of Walter Scott or Charles Dickens. Such domestic interludes were fleeting, however. Before long David was roaming agitatedly from one arena of pleasure to another, in an endless search to assuage the tedium of life.

"The heir apparent, in his unbridled pursuit of wine and women, and whatever selfish whim occupied him at the moment, was rapidly going to the devil," David's assistant Private Secretary told Prime Minister Stanley Baldwin in 1927. Unless he made a serious effort to redeem himself, he would be "no fit wearer of the British Crown." He reacted badly to royal duties, becoming irritable and obstinate when forced to undertake wearisome ceremonials and to attend long meetings and dull social gatherings. He chattered on inattentively, yielded to erratic impulses, became embarrassingly capricious when confronted with the need to behave responsibly in his public role. His handlers were at their wits' end.

The exasperation with David in government circles ran deep, and the aging King George, feeble and ill, despaired of his son and announced prophetically that once he was dead, the prince would "ruin himself" in less than a year. The public, however, knew nothing of this and continued to idolize their popular prince.

Amid the political alarms of the 1930s the views of the Prince of Wales veered sharply to the right. Contemptuous of the inability of Britain's parliamentary system to cope with postwar economic crises, he developed a dangerous penchant for fascism, as did many in his aristocratic circles. By June of 1933, David's cousins in Germany were reporting that the Prince of Wales was "quite pro-Hitler," and opposed to any efforts on the part of the British government to interfere in Germany's affairs. His declarations of friendship with Germany provoked a reaction from the king and led to yet another confrontation between father and son.

But by this time something much more alarming had taken place in David's life.

He had met, befriended and ultimately become enchanted by another American woman, Wallis Warfield Simpson. Like David, Wallis was lively, energetic and outspoken—to the more sedate members of the British establishment she seemed brash—and had had a lonely childhood. Divorced from a brutal, alcoholic first husband, she married the Anglo-American businessman Ernest Simpson and came to live in London.

The attraction between the Prince of Wales and the American divorcée had become overwhelmingly strong by 1935. "I love you more and more and more and every minute and miss you so terribly here. You do too don't you my sweetheart?" David wrote to Wallis. "We belong to each other forever. . . . We love each other more than life." Wallis, who was still married, considered the prince to "have the makings of a saint." He was, she wrote, "much too good for the likes of me."

Gossipmongers at the time, and the prince's biographers since, have speculated endlessly on the exact nature of the couple's bond, many seeing Wallis as the dominant partner (David having been seeking all his life for "a woman with a strong male inclination"). David's letters to Wallis have an infantile quality, and he seemed to others happiest when "obeying her slightest wish." Winston Churchill, who was David's friend and confidant, noticed that many of the prince's nervous mannerisms disappeared when he was with her. In her presence, Churchill thought, "he was a completed being instead of a sick and harassed soul." And Stanley Baldwin remarked that when the prince spoke of Wallis, his face "wore at times such a look of beauty as might have lighted the face of a young knight who had caught a glimpse of the Holy Grail."

Clearly in Wallis, David had found what he needed. The fact that she was unable to have children, something David knew but no one else in the royal family did, was something he brushed aside mentally as of minor importance compared to the great happiness she gave him.

Many of the prince's household members believed that he intended to elope with Wallis, who would obtain a quick divorce and marry him. But before he could carry this plan into execution George V died, and David became king as Edward VIII on January 20, 1936.

Exceedingly dismayed, upset by the loss of his father and equally upset by the frustration of his plans to marry Wallis, King Edward VIII embarked on his reign. Widespread poverty and labor unrest challenged the government, and the worsening international situation, with civil war in Spain and Hitler reoccupying the demilitarized left bank of the Rhine, caused widespread apprehension for the future. Britain began to rearm in preparation for possible war.

Far from undertaking his new responsibilities in a dutiful spirit, King Edward continued to live largely as he had before his accession, refusing to keep regular working hours at Buckingham Palace, frustrating his ministers and staff by escaping to Fort Belvedere—where they were not allowed to disturb him—or closeting himself with Wallis for hours on end. The work piled up, with the king dismissing the heaps of unread, unsigned papers as "mostly full of bunk."

Looking back over his reign, David was to write later that "for a year as king I worked as hard and selflessly as I knew how." He prided himself on his attempts to demolish the "Victorian flavor" of the court—which he did by dismissing many longtime servants—and bring in a new order.

Others remembered his reign differently, noting how King Edward's overworked staff, frustrated by the king's quixotic work habits, had to resort to subterfuges to disguise his lack of accomplishment and were also concerned about protecting the secrecy of the despatches.

By the summer of 1936 Edward was falling more and more behind—and to all appearances, caring less and less. He took Wallis and others on a cruise during which members of the foreign press (the British press preserving a patriotic silence on the subject of the king and Mrs. Simpson) were given firsthand evidence of the king's infatuation with Wallis—and also of the king's indiscreet drinking. Soon after the cruise ended, Wallis began divorce proceedings against her husband.

Now, at last, the king's long-desired marriage was in sight. Late in October, 1936, the divorce decree was granted, which meant that in six months, Wallis would be free. King Edward was theoretically free to marry any woman he chose, provided she was not a Catholic. In practice, however, the cabinet had a veto power over his choice, since if they disapproved, and resigned, it might be impossible to form another administration—in which case the king would have to give up his projected marriage or give up the throne.

Gradually, over the course of November 1936, the political restrictions which hemmed him in became more and more clear. The issue was a delicate one, touching on public sentiment as well as law and politics. If he married Wallis, the Prime Minister told the king, his subjects would reject her as unsuitable. She was believed to be an adulteress; she was distrusted as an adventuress (which she evidently was not, judging from the surviving correspondence), and her status as twice divorced put her outside the bounds of acceptable royal society. The monarchy, Baldwin said, might not survive the scandal once the king's intentions became known. And the press silence, long maintained, was about to be broken.

For weeks King Edward struggled against the looming necessity of abdication. He never wavered in his determination to marry Wallis, but he explored all the possible ways to achieve this and keep the throne. ("I wished to remain king," he wrote afterwards in his memoirs.) He suggested broadcasting to the nation, asking for support against the views of the government; predictably, this was not permitted. A morganatic marriage was suggested, in which the couple would be married but Wallis would not become queen, but the cabinet refused to sanction this as well. Wallis, at the last minute, offered to break off the relationship if that would help the king do his duty.

But Edward was adamant; he had already told his brother Bertie, who trembled at the prospect of inheriting the throne, that if thwarted in his marriage plans he would certainly abdicate. As all the options ran out, the king's abdication speech was prepared—with the assistance of the eloquent Winston Churchill.

"At long last I am able to say a few words of my own," Edward began, in his famous broadcast of December 11. He had already signed the instrument of abdication, and Parliament had passed the Abdication Bill. "I have found it impossible," he told his millions of listeners, "to carry the heavy burden of responsibility and to discharge my duties as king as I would wish to do without the help and support of the woman I love."

The British public was not, on the whole, sympathetic. Up to the last moment, the king had received stacks of telegrams, not only from Britain but from Commonwealth countries, advising him "For God's sake, don't abdicate." Giving up the throne seemed shameful to many Britons, though elsewhere, especially in America, it appeared to be the ultimate romantic gesture, and made the Duke of Windsor—as he was henceforth to be called—even more of a celebrity than he was before. Wallis too was surrounded by a romantic haze, as the greatly loved woman for whom a king would give up his kingdom. *Time* magazine made Wallis its Woman of the Year for 1936.

When in April of 1937 the Duke of Windsor married his duchess, in a simple ceremony at a French chateau, none of the royal family was present—though they sent telegrams of congratulations. Bertie, who on succeeding his brother had taken the title King George VI, had become somewhat estranged from David, relations between the two strained because of David's incessant pestering phone calls and because the financial settlement arranged between the brothers was altered (though the duke had considerable private means). A further cause of bad feeling was the family's denial, to Wallis, of the title "Royal Highness."

At his wedding, David looked, to the photographer Cecil Beaton, "essentially sad." His congenital melancholy had not, it would seem, been exorcised, though whether he ever regretted his abdication will never be known. Certainly he never said so publicly, and he and Wallis remained married while other members of the royal family eventually divorced.

Six months after their wedding the duke and duchess went to Germany, and were entertained by Hitler at Berchtesgaden. Headlines in the British newspapers read, "Duke of Windsor Salutes, Cries 'Heil Hitler.'" Deeply misguided, believing himself to be an emissary of peace, the duke in fact invited speculation that he was plotting with Hitler to regain the British throne—as a German puppet ruler. When war broke out, David continued to make divisive statements predicting Britain's inevitable loss and, in the name of furthering peace, actually gave aid and comfort to the enemy. After the fall of France he was brought to England for the briefest of meetings with his brother the king, following which he was sent to the Bahamas as Governor for the duration of the war, to the relief of the British war ministry.

For the rest of his life a penumbra of glamour continued to surround the Duke of Windsor, as he and Wallis settled down in France with frequent trips to New York and Palm Beach where they were feted as if they were royalty. The city of Paris made the couple a gift of a beautiful house in the Bois de Boulogne, and the French government exempted them from income tax. Financially secure, their income increased by the duke's three bestselling ghostwritten books and the duchess's memoirs, they led a life of leisure. David played golf, dug in his garden, escorted his wife to dinner parties—and endured more scandal, for gossip clung to the couple.

In 1953, when Elizabeth II had become queen, the Windsors crossed the Channel on a luxury liner, taking with them five pug dogs, two valets and Wallis's reputed gay lover Jimmy Donohue. They were not invited to Elizabeth's coronation, but watched it on television, and afterwards the duke wrote a long article about it for an American magazine, for which he was handsomely paid.

He had long since learned the art of making himself a commodity, and he may have been content with that, and with Wallis, however her sexual tastes had evolved.

Yet there was a note of pathos in their life together. When Prince Charles went to visit the duke in Paris in 1971, the year before he died, he found a bizarre scene. Amid the costly furnishings and fine paintings were reminders of Buckingham Palace—a red despatch box labeled "The King," war medals, footmen wearing copies of the scarlet and black Buckingham Palace liveries.

When Queen Elizabeth came to say her goodbyes to her uncle in the spring of 1972 he was so wasted by lung cancer that it was difficult for him to stand, yet he rose from his wheelchair and kissed his niece, murmuring "My dear." Both knew that the visit was more diplomatic than personal, an act of formal closure meant to deflect criticism of the queen.

By this time the duke was seventy-seven, and the abdication was thirty-six years in the past, one episode among many, though arguably the most important one of his life. Something of the aura of the celebrity prince still clung to the handsome old man in his last days, his fairytale marriage still intact and the withered Wallis still by his side, his life having long since become the stuff of tabloid mythmaking.

GEORGE VI

(1936–1952)

"THIS WAS, BY ANY STANDARDS, ANYWHERE,
A GOOD MAN."

— *THE DAILY MIRROR*

Prince Albert was the ugly duckling of King George V's family. Anxious, oversensitive, self-conscious and often in tears, "Bertie" as a boy lurched from one unhappy situation to the next, always feeling far inferior to his outgoing, good-looking older brother Edward ("David" to the family) who was heir to the throne.

Deprived of maternal affection, as were all the children in the royal family, and shouted at by his brusque, critical father, Bertie suffered severe gastric pain and was forced to wear, day and night, painful splints on both legs to correct his knock-knees.

Everything was painful to Bertie—the punishing verbal assaults of his father, the harsh teasing of his brothers, his humiliating performance in the schoolroom, where he consistently failed to learn his lessons, and above all his maddening inability to talk normally because of a stammer that afflicted him from early childhood on.

Depressed and frustrated, Bertie was often reduced to bitter tears, which led his father and brothers to despise him as unmanly—which in turn led to more tears, and sometimes to outbursts of violent rage in which he attacked his brothers. Sports provided a much needed outlet for Bertie's pent-up energies, and he was a good athlete, but his bookish tutors kept him indoors. He struggled in vain with his worst subject, mathematics, and found French and German an agony because of his stammer.

When Bertie and his brothers went out shooting with their father, the mood lightened, and the anxious, unhappy prince knew something like contentment. Their father was jovial on his shooting jaunts, and liked to teach his boys the lore of wild game. Walking across the broad heathland and through the marshes, Bertie was able to relax, and was praised for being a good shot with "an eye like a hawk." But the shooting trips were all too rare, and the hours in the classroom long and arduous. Bertie was sent to the Royal Naval College at Osborne, where his tradition of poor academic performance continued.

"He is always very penitent with me, assures me that he is doing his best, and so on," wrote one of the prince's tutors. But he was continually inattentive, distracted by excitement or made apathetic by depression, and he simply could not learn. Again and again his tutors were forced to report to King George that Bertie had "come to grief" on his exams, and was at, or very near, the bottom of his class.

He went on to Dartmouth at the age of fifteen, joining brother David, and did not improve academically although his tutor wrote that Bertie was "quite unspoiled, and a nice honest, clean-minded and excellent-mannered boy." He might have added that the prince was, inwardly, a wilderness of jagged emotions, worries and fears, lacking in self-confidence and with an exaggerated sense of his inferiority to his charming, handsome older brother. Bertie might be good at cricket, golf and tennis, but David was good at so many other things, including recovering quickly from discouragement. For Bertie, discouragement was constant; each defeat compounded previous ones until a mountain of failure loomed.

With the exception of one brief and memorable episode, Prince Albert's experience in World War I increased his disappointment with himself. The stress of serving aboard a battleship led to a revival of his severe stomach pains, and ultimately to the removal of a duodenal ulcer. A series of long sick leaves made him feel that his contribution to the war effort was shamefully small, although when the Battle of Jutland came, the prince was in it, and had a chance to show his bravery.

"I am quite all right and feel very different now that I have seen a German ship filled with Germans and have seen it fired at with our guns," Bertie wrote to a friend. "It was a great experience to have gone through and one not easily forgotten."

German torpedo craft and an enemy warship fired on the prince's ship repeatedly. "How and why we were not hit beats me," Bertie wrote, evidently gratified with his own courage under fire. His father was gratified too. "I am pleased with my son," was George V's laconic but welcome announcement.

The Jutland episode was gratifying, but overall, Bertie still tended to discount his worth and to be ashamed of the medical problems that had sidelined him so often during the war years. He had learned to fly but had never actually flown solo. He had not succeeded in finding a circle of friends, or establishing his independence; he remained, not an individual in his own right, but David's brother, in David's shadow. Photographers and journalists pursued David endlessly—but avoided the self-deprecating Bertie. And although he was glad they did, since having to confront the press would have brought forth Bertie's tormenting stammer, still it rankled that he had no independent claim to attention.

Not that George V's second son avoided royal duties. On the contrary, he was exceptionally zealous to do what he could, and when he was made President of the Industrial Welfare Society, Bertie was assiduous in visiting factories and workplaces throughout the realm. He took it as his special mandate to see how the average working man and woman was faring, touring factories, descending into the blackness of coal pits, visiting construction sites and even driving trains, all in the service of gaining a greater understanding of working conditions. His evident genuine interest and concern impressed those of his father's subjects with whom he talked, and the prince took those talks to heart. So involved did he become in this work that his brothers began to call Bertie "the Foreman" and in the newspapers he was referred to as "The Industrial Prince"—a strong contrast to the Prince of Wales, who was "Prince Charming" to the press and who was associated with nightclubs, beautiful married women and glamorous parties.

In 1921 Bertie began a project that remained close to his heart for many years, the Duke of York's camp. A hundred elite public schools and a hundred industrial firms each sent two boys to Romney on the Kentish coast, where for a week they shared sparely furnished huts, ate together in a large dining hall, played sports, swam and developed a camaraderie they would never have known under other circumstances. Bertie led the hundreds of boys in campfire singing, games and play—the outdoor life he had known too little of as a boy himself—and had the satisfaction of seeing class barriers fall away, at least for a limited time.

The factory visits and the supervision of the Duke of York's camp were well within Bertie's capabilities. But he was called upon from time to time to perform other duties which were nerve-wrackingly difficult. Speaking before groups made him so nervous that, at times, his words were reduced to what one listener called "a painful, wordless mumble." When he spoke before tens of thousands of people, his amplified voice was clear, but his phrases "came awkwardly, with long, unnatural pauses. Sometimes there was an agonizing silence as he stumbled over some difficult word."

It was Bertie's great good fortune to choose as his wife a commoner of enormous charm, attractiveness and naturalness, Elizabeth Bowes-Lyon, daughter of the fourteenth Earl of Strathmore. She buoyed his spirits and gave him a new perspective on life and the world; she made him happy and self-accepting for the first time. The prince's anxieties receded somewhat under his wife's sunny, warm influence, though he still had occasional explosions of temper. He cherished his family life and was delighted with his two daughters Elizabeth and Margaret Rose.

Contributing to Bertie's contentment, as he entered his thirties, was the help he received from the speech therapist Lionel Logue. Logue's unique breathing techniques, and Bertie's own willpower and perseverance (Logue called the prince "the pluckiest and most determined patient I ever had"), combined to improve his talking and speech-making a good deal, though the stammer was never entirely overcome and Bertie continued to require help from Logue before every important speech.

Comfortably enfolded within his harmonious family circle, Bertie devoted himself to the pleasures of watching his children grow and developing his interests, which included cultivating rhododendrons, planning the design of gardens and keeping meticulous meteorological records. He played golf with his brother David, went shooting, played tennis and, in the summer, held the Duke of York's camp.

Nothing prepared Bertie for the dynastic and political crisis that came in 1936, and that ultimately brought him to the throne as George VI.

While Bertie was settling down as a family man, David, after many love affairs, found the one woman who complemented him ideally and with whom he became obsessed: the American divorcée Wallis Simpson. Even before George V died and David became king as Edward VIII in January of 1936, he had been determined to marry Wallis once she divorced her second husband. But as the new king's reign began, the urgency of the situation increased. The king's indiscreet liaison with Mrs. Simpson, and the divorce proceedings she initiated, brought on a governmental crisis. Bertie, who was heir apparent, cringed at the prospect of having to become king should David abdicate.

Throughout November and early December of 1936, Bertie watched events unfold with a mounting sense of dread. Legally, the king was free to marry whomever he liked, provided his wife was not a Catholic. Politically, however, he was hampered by the will of the ministers, and the attitudes of the Dominion leaders, and both groups were strongly opposed to accepting the divorced Mrs. Simpson as queen, or even as the king's morganatic wife.

Self-absorbed and intent on attaining his lone goal of marrying Wallis, King Edward rarely consulted with his brother during the tense weeks of political conflict and gave little consideration to his feelings. By December 9 it was apparent that Edward VIII had only two choices: to give up Mrs. Simpson or to give up the throne. Without hesitation he chose the latter course, and conveyed his decision to his brother.

Bertie went to inform his mother. "When I told her what had happened," he wrote afterward, "I broke down and sobbed like a child."

Suddenly all Bertie's fears and his ingrained sense of inadequacy rose up to assault him. On the day the king's abdication took effect, December 11, one who saw Bertie thought his face looked "deathly serious," and when he went to meet his privy councilors for the first time he was pale and drawn from strain and lack of sleep. His stammer returned with a vengeance, as it always did in times of stress, and he confided to a court official that he was worried, not only about his own ability to perform his duties, but about the future of the monarchy itself. His brother had been a popular king. With the departure of that popular figure, would the public clamor for an end to the monarchy?

Yet despite these fears, the transfer of authority went smoothly. David, now Duke of Windsor, departed to the continent where he soon married Wallis. And Bertie, who took the title George VI, prepared for his coronation.

Kingship transformed the timorous, insecure Duke of York. Within a few months of his accession, an observer noticed, "all diffidence had gone. Those hesitant gestures that had been characteristic of his personality had been replaced by a sureness of movement and an ease of manner." The ugly duckling had become, if not exactly a swan, at least an eagle, finding his wings and beginning to soar.

When skeptical reporters predicted the worst, the king scoffed. "According to the papers," he said, "I am supposed to be unable to speak without stammering, to have fits, and to die in two years. All in all, I seem to be a crock!" At his coronation King George confounded his critics; having rehearsed again and again with his faithful Lionel Logue, he was able to say the words of the difficult Accession Declaration flawlessly.

As Hitler's aggression moved Europe closer to armed conflict, George VI continued to hope and work for peace, and warmly supported the policy of his Prime Minister, Neville Chamberlain, to avert war at any cost. When it came to foreign affairs, the king was neither shrewd nor insightful, and his ministers found him to be frustratingly slow to grasp what he was told. However, he worked diligently and with earnest good will. And when war came, King George provided what many a cleverer man could not: a model of stalwart, resolute courage.

Always wearing his uniform, refusing to leave the capital even after heavy bombardment began and Buckingham Palace came under attack, the king was an inspiring example to his subjects.

"The decisive struggle is now upon us," he told his people in a broadcast after the enemy overran the Netherlands and Belgium and France collapsed. "Against our honesty is set dishonor, against our faithfulness is set treachery, against our justice, brute force." Knowing that Britain might be invaded, the king shared his subjects' alarm. "I am very worried over the general situation," he said privately, "as everything we do or try to do appears to be wrong, and gets us nowhere." It was an understatement. The danger was grave, and the king, touring bomb sites with his wife in order to put heart into the Londoners, did whatever he could to provide comfort and strength.

Working in London during the day and sleeping at Windsor, where his children were, at night, the king was constantly in harm's way. On September 10, 1940, a bomb exploded directly below King George's study, and three days later, as King George and Queen Elizabeth were in the king's sitting room overlooking the quadrangle, they heard the zoom of a plane and saw two bombs fall and explode only thirty yards away.

"The whole thing happened in a matter of seconds," George wrote in his diary. "We all wondered why we weren't dead." A shock reaction set in; the king was not himself again for several days. What upset him most was the suspicion that the attack had been an assassination attempt on the part of one of his German relatives, part of a larger plan to kill him and restore the Germanophile Duke of Windsor to the throne. No evidence was ever found to support his suspicions.

The shared experience of the bombing, and the king and queen's frequent presence at the bomb sites, with George "evidently most interested and talking to all and sundry," guaranteed a strong and enduring connection between the sovereigns and their people. When it was publicized that the royals were subjecting themselves to food rationing, and that the king had personally marked all the bathtubs in Buckingham Palace with a line for water rationing, his subjects felt a surge of loyal affection. What they did not know was that King George's frugality with rationed cloth extended to his own wardrobe. When his collars and cuffs frayed, he had new ones made from his shirttails. And in his spare time on weekends, what little there was of it, the king made parts for anti-tank guns on a lathe he had installed at Windsor.

It was no wonder that when the royal carriage appeared amid the rubble of Shoreditch and Bethnal Green, the king and queen were cheered. Shouts of "Good luck!" "God bless you!" followed them, and "Thank Your Majesties for coming to see us."

By the time the war in Europe ended, King George was gaunt, his face wizened with the lines of age, his exhaustion evident. Years of staying up too late and smoking too many cigarettes under the stress of war had worn him down. He was not quite fifty, but looked like a much older man. "I feel burnt out," he wrote—and admitted, in his diary, to mental confusion. He was well aware that Churchill, Stalin and Roosevelt were at work drawing up plans for the future, yet he could not comprehend all that was being told him about the negotiations. And when Churchill, with whom he had worked so closely throughout the war, fell from power, the king was truly at a loss.

"I shall miss your counsel to me more than I can say," he wrote to the former Prime Minister, and continued to solicit his advice for many months after he left office.

The postwar world was in many ways bewildering to King George, and he needed counsel. Economic hardship made life grim for many of his subjects, and financial crises menaced the government. The Cold War divided east and west and, in the summer of 1950, the Korean War began, with widespread fear that America might use the atomic bomb.

Personally, the postwar period brought potential embarrassment to the royal family. Captured German documents included records concerning the Duke of Windsor and his relations with the German government. At King George's request, revealing papers were destroyed—but he knew what they contained, and the extent to which his embittered brother had contemplated treason.

"The incessant worries and crises through which we have to live have got me down properly," the king told a friend. He withdrew to Sandringham, where he went out shooting as often as he could, frequently with his brother Prince Henry. Walking had become difficult because of the severe cramps in his legs caused by arteriosclerosis, yet the king forced himself to go out, his yellow Labradors at his heels, wearing tweeds of his own design. Nothing pleased him more than lying in wait for hours on a cold winter morning, watching for a flight of wild duck or wild pigeon.

King George was not told how very ill he was. Beyond his severe circulatory problems he had lung cancer—he was told it was only a bronchial blockage—and his left lung was removed in September of 1951. Despite his evident decline the king encouraged his daughter Elizabeth to begin a tour of Africa, Australia and New Zealand early in 1952. When she left on January 31, he seemed to be in good spirits, and drank a glass of champagne. Five days later he was at Sandringham, shooting rabbits. That night he died, peacefully, in his sleep.

Londoners, hearing the news of the king's death, got out of their cars and stood silently in the street, out of respect. Many wept. King George had been one of them, they felt, and his loss was not only a national loss but a personal one.

"This was, by any standards, anywhere, a good man," the king's obituary in *The Daily Mirror* proclaimed. And if, as the French ambassador in London remarked, the measure of a king is determined by how well he fills the needs of his people, then George VI was "a great king, and perhaps a very great king."

Greatness may have eluded King George, but decency and earnestness did not, and it was his good fortune to come into his own, and to find the best that was in him, through the accidents of time and chance.

ELIZABETH II

(1952–)

**"I REALLY CAN'T THINK OF ANY OCCASION WHEN I'VE
NOT FELT BETTER FOR DOING BUSINESS WITH HER.
SHE'S A STIFFENER OF BACKS. SHE'S REALISTIC.
SHE IS AS HONEST AS THE DAY IS LONG,
AND SHE'S HUMBLE. A VERY GOOD EGG."**

—LORD CHARTERIS

On July 9, 1982, very early in the morning, a man climbed through an unguarded window of Buckingham Palace and found his way into the queen's bedroom, where she was sleeping alone. It was not the first time he had entered the palace uninvited; on an earlier visit he had helped himself to a bottle of Riesling, frightened a housemaid and wandered along the corridors of the immense building without anyone challenging him until he found the throne room, where he sat on the royal throne for a while before finding his own way back outside.

Having located the queen's bedroom ("I passed the corgi food on the way," he said later, "and I knew then I'd find the queen soon"), the intruder, a disheveled, slightly drunk unemployed laborer named Michael Fagan, recently released from the psychiatric ward of Brixton Prison, went in and saw "a little bundle in the bed." Disturbed by the light from the raised curtains, the bundle awakened, sat up and stared at Fagan uncomprehendingly, then began to berate him.

"What are you doing here? Get out! Get out!" Queen Elizabeth picked up a phone beside the bed, called the police switchboard, then put on her dressing gown and slippers and repeated her orders.

But Fagan would not leave. According to the queen, he talked to her, saying "the usual sort of bilge that people talk to me on walkabout." He was frightening, wild-eyed and evidently unbalanced. He had smashed a glass ashtray, intending to slash his wrists, but had only cut his thumb. He bled all over the queen's blankets.

She called the switchboard again, and eventually, when help still did not arrive, she left the room, running as nimbly as a girl, Fagan thought.

When the police finally came, passing the queen, who was standing in an alcove, she was impatient with them.

"Oh, come on, get a bloody move on!"

Fagan was seized and escorted out of the palace, but not charged with any crime, since he had not stolen anything or hurt anyone and trespassing is not illegal in England.

The incident was vaguely farcical, but it could have been deadly. Instead of an out-of-work laborer curious about his monarch, whom he considered to be "a really nice woman," the intruder could just as well have been a terrorist or a sociopath, and the story could have had a tragic ending.

The queen's surprising vulnerability illuminates the changes that have transformed the monarchy over the nearly fifty years of her reign. In 1952, when Elizabeth II succeeded her father, the sovereign was regarded with awe and treated with a level of respect not unlike that accorded to the pope or the Dalai Lama. At the opening of the twenty-first century the members of the royal family, especially its younger members, have lost any claim to veneration or deference and are judged, ridiculed, trivialized, or, in the case of the late Princess of Wales, mourned, as crowned aristocrats worthy of little or no homage other than what they earn by their personal merits.

The sanctity of monarchy has all but evaporated under the pressure of a corrosive and vapid notoriety. The queen inhabits her vast, echoing palace in lonely splendor, her solitude occasionally interrupted by an unwelcome trespasser, as her subjects speculate about her family's future.

Even as a child Princess Elizabeth was not free from the distorting influence of an increasingly celebrity-conscious world. Born in 1926, the oldest child of Prince Albert, second son of George V, Elizabeth grew up at a time when the round-faced, curly-headed movie star Shirley Temple was the best-known child in Europe and America. The pretty little princess was coiffed and dressed like the actress, extensively photographed and presented to a public avid for details about the life of the royal family in a specially commissioned biography published when she was barely five years old.

At that time, of course, there was no expectation that Elizabeth would ever reign. Her uncle David, George V's first son, was heir to the throne and the family hoped that David would eventually marry and have children to continue the royal line. Along with her younger sister, Margaret Rose, Elizabeth was given the shallow education then thought appropriate for a highborn girl—a smattering of grammar, arithmetic, penmanship (the only subject her anti-intellectual grandfather King George considered to be essential), French and history, all taught by a clever but provincial governess, Marion Crawford ("Crawfie"), who herself had had a mediocre education.

The princesses' brief lessons, which were often interrupted, were squeezed in between long morning sessions of family playtime and elevenses; the afternoons were given over to dancing class, singing and drawing and music lessons and long walks.

Not only was Elizabeth's mind neglected and her learning short-changed but her experience of life was kept to a minimum. Kept away from other children, rarely allowed to go out of the palace except on carefully sanitized, infrequent excursions, Princess Elizabeth learned about the real world primarily by gazing at it through the palace windows. Often in the evenings, Crawfie remembered, the two little princesses would stand at the windows together, watching for the coming of the brewer's horses as the lights came on and people walked by on the sidewalks, intent on errands in a life the girls could only dream of.

Elizabeth had a passion for horses, and was given her first pony at the age of four. When not actually riding, she sat up in her bed holding the reins of imaginary horses. A long file of large toy horses stood outside the royal nursery and were groomed and fed daily. The country life of Balmoral and Glamis, the estate owned by the Bowes-Lyons, her mother's family, suited the princess admirably. With its numerous ghosts, romantic turreted castle and acres of forest and parkland, Glamis had a formative influence on Elizabeth, as did her beloved, rusticated and eccentric Scottish grandfather Lord Strathmore.

Attractive, prosaic and on the whole docile, obsessively neat and increasingly filled with a sense of obligation, Princess Elizabeth at ten years old was an unremarkable child. She was unbendingly scrupulous toward herself and others, with strength of will and a distinctive, at times flinty character, but she lacked particular gifts (apart from an exceptional rapport with horses and dogs) and possessed limited personal appeal. Accustomed to being overly protected by her fierce nursemaid Allah, waited on by a half-dozen personal servants, among them Margaret Macdonald ("Bobo") who slept in her room and was her constant companion, Elizabeth nonetheless emerged from childhood without affectation and surprisingly natural and innocent. In personality she was not unlike her great-great-grandmother Queen Victoria, who was raised in far less opulent and more psychologically uncomfortable circumstances.

In December of 1936, in the aftermath of Edward VIII's abdication, Elizabeth's diffident, withdrawn and anxious father became king as George VI. The ten-year-old princess wrote down the details of her parents' coronation morning.

"At five o'clock in the morning I was woken up by the band of the Royal Marines," she noted. "I leapt out of bed and so did Bobo. We put on dressing-gowns and shoes and Bobo made me put on an eiderdown as it was so cold and we crouched in the window looking on to a cold, misty morning.... Every now and then we were hopping in and out of bed looking at the bands and the soldiers."

Elizabeth was now heir presumptive. It was still possible for her mother to have a son, who would take precedence over the princess in the succession, but she did not and Elizabeth became accustomed to the idea that she would one day be queen. To prepare her for the future, she was taken to Eton and given special lessons in constitutional history by an expert, but this tutelage was too sketchy and insubstantial and came too late to fill in the deficiencies in her education; as she was later to say, she was largely unprepared for queenship.

Elizabeth was thirteen when World War II war broke out and it was decided that she and Margaret would be sent to Windsor rather than evacuated to Canada or to a rural village for protection from falling bombs. Over the next six years she spent much of her time behind the thick walls of the old castle, her days a monotonous round of lessons, contributions to the war effort, and, when no immediate danger threatened, pushing the elderly Victoria Mountbatten, a distant relative and granddaughter of Queen Victoria, through the gardens in her wheelchair. When she was fourteen Elizabeth had her first crush, on a young officer, but opportunities for flirtation were often truncated when the watchers on the castle rooftops spotted enemy planes approaching and sounded the warning bell which sent the princesses and others down into the dimly lit, beetle-infested castle dungeons until they heard the all clear.

At nineteen, in the last months of the war, Elizabeth announced that she intended to join the Auxiliary Transport Service and become a mechanic. By this time she had become an attractive young woman, poised and self-assured, much in love with her third cousin Philip Mountbatten. Her parents had misgivings about the handsome, rootless Philip, a Dane whose family had occupied the Greek throne briefly and precariously; Philip had neither money nor manners, was a reckless driver and was reputed to be a playboy like his disreputable father, an aging roué. But Elizabeth's strong will won out, and the couple became engaged. They were married on November 20, 1947, and their first child, Prince Charles, was born the following year.

The sudden death of George VI in February of 1952 brought Elizabeth to the throne, far sooner than she had expected. "My father died much too young," she said, "and so it was all a very sudden kind of taking-on and making the best job you can. Here you are, it's your fate."

Handed the job, she entered into it with poise and efficiency, submerging her grief and getting on with the many tasks presented to her in the early days and weeks of the new reign. When she met her first council, an observer thought, the queen looked very small as she spoke to them in her high-pitched, rather reedy voice. She played her part well, addressing the "hundreds of old men in black clothes with long faces." Unlike her father, she did not stumble over her words, and her air of authority, while far from overwhelming, was commendable. "The carriage of her head," thought one who saw her, "was unequalled, and there was about her that indescribable something which Queen Victoria had." She was twenty-five.

An unprecedented outburst of patriotic feeling and genuine loyalty and affection greeted the accession of Elizabeth II. *Time* magazine named her Woman of the Year for 1952, and tens of millions of people worldwide watched her coronation on television the following year. Journalists wrote enthusiastically of the dawning of a New Elizabethan Age, and waited for the epiphany.

But it never arrived. Instead, the queen's governments drifted, unsure how to confront the monumental challenges posed by the threat of nuclear confrontation with the communist bloc, the rapid crumbling of the Empire and the alarming shrinking of Britain's foreign trade. Instead of offering the vigor of youth and a modern spirit of engagement and optimism, Elizabeth seemed to many to become calcified, indurated, incurious. Her court was old-fashioned, enmired in antique ceremony, what the playwright John Osborne called "the protocol of ancient fatuity."

The queen appeared detached, regal, remote, correct. But flat, dull. Uninspired and uninspiring. Careless, or heedless, of the impact of her personal image, she allowed her elderly advisers to write her antiquated speeches, turned over her wardrobe to conservative designers, let the style-challenged Bobo choose her handbags and hats. The collective effect was of an upper-class icon, prematurely aged—indeed embalmed.

The change was rapid, and startling. Within a few years, the light-hearted, youthful princess had become an unsmiling, Olympian queen, chilly and aloof. The transformation was, in part, a result of Elizabeth's temperament. Her instinct, when confronted with complex issues and unpleasant interpersonal challenges, was to withdraw. Always dutiful, she had, in her effort to do what was expected of her, confused duty with obedience. Lacking independence—which she had never known—and lacking the boldness and daring to step outside tradition and carve out a new role and image appropriate to the radically different world in which she and her subjects lived, she did what her sclerotic staff told her to do, and adopted something of their stiffness and hauteur, and as a result the monarchy fell more and more behind the times.

But the change may have had another component. The queen's marriage had come under strain. Philip felt increasingly confined by the rigid protocols of the court and was outspokenly at odds with members of his wife's staff. He was heard to speak harshly and roughly to Elizabeth, stayed out late in risqué company and was said to lead a double life. There were rumors of liaisons with other women and an appearance of a marital rupture, if not outright estrangement. No proof of infidelity has ever come to public knowledge, but Philip certainly infuriated his wife again and again in the first decade of their marriage, and probably caused her much heartache as well—more than enough to account for the hardening of her personality.

As she reached her mid-thirties Elizabeth seemed to strike an equilibrium. She and Philip had two more children, and arrived at a compromise that allowed them to live amicable but largely separate lives. She continued to perform her responsibilities with admirable professionalism, got along well with her ministers, and through tireless journeying, cultivated the growing Commonwealth, a simulacrum of the former British Empire which has come to encompass nearly a quarter of the world's population.

As queen, Elizabeth's actual powers are very limited, and her clashes over prerogative have been infrequent and muted. She devotes herself to foreign tours, desk work, state visits and a full calendar of receptions, audiences, ceremonies and social events. On the wide issues of Britain's falling productivity, increasing economic decline, high unemployment and occasionally severe social problems, the throne has maintained a judicious silence, which has led to criticism.

"The queen is not a cozy person," one journalist has written. She is reputed to have a temper, which flares when anyone steps on one of the corgis' tails. She is frugal, turning off lights in unoccupied rooms and watching the expenses of the royal kitchens (she often cooks herself an omelette in her private suite). Nervous of cameras, somewhat embarrassed when talking to knowledgeable people—her own lack of education still a handicap, despite her decades of experience—and with a studied blandness of manner and speech when in public, in private the queen is said to be quite a different person.

She chatters—as those who have painted her portrait or come to the palace to tailor her clothes have discovered. She talks about her children, about celebrities, about the activities she is observing through the palace windows. With family and longtime friends she makes fun of people she has met, imitating their speech, criticizing their clothes, making others laugh with stories and anecdotes from her travels. At Balmoral, where she is at her least guarded, the queen becomes a different person, as a friend says, "rushing around in tatty clothes, laughing, joking, joining in, singing dirty songs."

She has a keen sense of humor, often directed at herself. "Hats make me look like a sheep," the queen once remarked. "Why should I want to look like a sheep?" On one occasion she was relaxing at a tea shop near Sandringham when a stranger came up to her.

"Excuse me," the woman said, "but you look awfully like the queen."

"How very reassuring," was the wry response.

In the last decades of the twentieth century the monarchy has come under increasing notoriety and has lost prestige. The queen's primary responsibility, in the view of many, is to be an appealing symbol of national unity, maintaining that appeal through the force of her own integrity and the admiration and affection she inspires for her faithful performance of her obligations.

But over the last two decades, the symbolic force and indeed the very raison d'etre of the monarchy have continued to erode, despite the queen's best intentions. The throne has become a symbol, not of moral force, but of moral vacuity. The queen herself still commands a measure of admiration (eroding, as of this writing, in the aftermath of fresh scandal in the fall of 2002), but her children do not—though her grandchildren are loved—and the monarchy has never before been held in as low esteem, not even during the heyday of the despised Prince Regent in the early nineteenth century.

Conservative Prime Minister Margaret Thatcher, by far the most dominant personality in Britain during the 1980s, appeared to provide the vigorous, determined leadership the United Kingdom needed in order to begin to rise out of its economic difficulties and recover some measure of initiative. The queen, by comparison, seemed, despite awkward public relations efforts such as the televised documentary *Royal Family*, to be largely ineffectual and remote.

During the Falklands War, an anxious time for the queen whose son Andrew was in danger as a helicopter pilot, the Prime Minister led the nation while Queen Elizabeth remained in the background, unnecessary and even irrelevant.

Elizabeth and Mrs. Thatcher did not get along; each found the other tiresome, and the Prime Minister, it was said, regarded her weekly visits to the palace with politely disguised scorn. As for the queen, who, like Mrs. Thatcher, was approaching sixty, the combined strains of the war, the increasingly invasive press, a campaign of IRA bombings and severe marital dissension within the family burdened her and aged her. By the early 1990s she was being called "the invisible monarch," "a victim of her own dullness." According to one poll, nearly half of her subjects thought she ought to abdicate in favor of Prince Charles.

The 1990s tested the queen's mettle to the utmost. In 1992 nine ancient rooms in Windsor Castle were destroyed by fire, just at a time when public opinion was turning against the royal family with renewed fervor. Dissolving royal marriages, embarrassing photographs and overly candid taped conversations became the stuff of everyday news; that the royals were dysfunctional was evident. "Like all the best families," the queen remarked, "we have our share of eccentricities, of impetuous and wayward youngsters and of family disagreements."

Out of the quagmire of trivialized lives and failed relationships Diana, Princess of Wales, emerged as a popular heroine, turning her immense worldwide notoriety to good effect in a variety of humanitarian and charitable endeavors. The perception of Diana was that, while admitting her flaws, she managed to find a purposeful, meaningful life—unlike her divorced husband Prince Charles and the rest of the royal family, who appeared to lead hollow and generally useless lives. When Diana died in an accident in 1997, the outpouring of grief was genuine and prolonged, and reached around the world.

At the celebrations for her Golden Jubilee in 2002, Britons showed great affection for Queen Elizabeth, accompanied by an upsurge in monarchical sentiment. But within months, renewed scandals threatened to drag the monarchy down again. And by the time Prince Charles and his longtime love and companion Camilla Parker Bowles wed, in April of 2005, public reaction was muted—an indication of widespread indifference.

Whatever the recent vicissitudes of the House of Windsor, the queen carries forward a tradition that has endured, with only brief interruptions, for over a thousand years, and the tradition will no doubt continue. Elizabeth goes on as she has for half a century, doing what is expected of her, making the best job she can, stalwart and dependable. She is more solitary than in the past. Her beloved mother and sister have died, as have others who were closest to her, among them her lifelong friend and confidante Bobo. Her husband is often away, and her relations with her children are cordial but not intimate.

Overall, the queen appears to be content, surrounded by her swarm of corgis, involved as ever with the horses of her racing stable, heartened by supportive letters from her subjects ("You see," she says, "they really do understand") and by the interest in her recently established website, visited 12,500,000 times in its first two months.

"I find that as the years pass my capacity for surprise has lessened," Elizabeth remarked in 1993. If her capacity for surprise has decreased, her capacity for survival clearly has not. She goes on, self-reliant, competent, guarded, more realistic and less detached than in the past, engaged with the challenges of the new century and with her admirably wide capacities undimmed.

INDEX

✦ ⋙✦⋘ ✦

A

Abdication Bill, 312

Aberystwyth, 110

Accession Declaration, 320

Acre, Battle of, 48, 49, 50

Adelaide of Saxe-Meiningen, 273, 276, 280

Adelaide (sister of William II), 16

Adeliza of Louvain, 24

Adolphus (son of George III), 255, 264

Agatha (daughter of William I), 4, 5

Agincourt, Battle of, 114–15, 154

Albert Edward (Bertie). *See* Edward VII

Albert of Austria, 103

Albert of Bavaria, 98

Albert of Saxe-Coburg, 281–84, 287, 288
    death, 284, 290

Alexander II, 58

Alexandra (wife of Edward VII), 291, 296

Alice (daughter of Louis VI), 45–46

Alice (daughter of Victoria), 286

Alphonso X of Castile, 68

Amelia (daughter of George III), 260, 266

Amiens, 132–33

Anarchy, the, 31, 33

Andrew (son of Elizabeth II), 330

Anglican church, 156, 164–65, 170, 214. *See also* Protestantism

Anjou, 24, 145

Anjou, counts of, 7, 21, 29

Anne, 228, 229–37
    Churchills and, 231–32, 236
    continental war and, 235
    personal characteristics, 229–30, 233–35

Anne (daughter of Warwick), 131

Anne of Bohemia, 95, 96, 101

Anne of Denmark, 188, 189

Anne (queen of Richard III), 140

Annebaut, Claude d', 163

H

Erickson, Carolly, 1943-
Royal panoply : brief lives

DATE DUE

GAYLORD		PRINTED IN U.S.A.

ABOUT THE AUTHOR

——◆◈◆——

A Ph.D. in medieval history from Columbia University led Carolly
Erickson to six years as a college professor, then to a career as a full-time
writer. Her many prize-winning biographies, including *The First
Elizabeth, Her Little Majesty,* and *Alexandra,* have reached a wide interna-
tional audience. *The Hidden Diary of Marie Antoinette* is her first novel.
Her second, *The Last Wife of Henry VIII,* will be published by St. Martin's
Press in fall 2006. Carolly Erickson lives in Hawaii.